D-Day Bombers: The Veterans' Story

D-DAY BOMBERS:
THE VETERANS' STORY

RAF Bomber Command and the
US Eighth Air Force Support to the
Normandy Invasion 1944

STEPHEN DARLOW

GRUB STREET · LONDON

Published by
Grub Street
4 Rainham Close
London
SW11 6SS

British Library Cataloguing in Publication Data
Darlow, Stephen
    D-Day bombers: the veterans' story: RAF Bomber Command
    and the US Eighth Air Force support to the Normandy
    invasion 1944
    1. World War, 1939-1945 – Personal narratives, British
    2. World War, 1939-1945 – Personal narratives, American
    3, World War, 1939-1945 – Aerial operations, British
    4. World War, 1939-1945 – Aerial operations, American
    5. World War, 1939-1945 – Campaigns – France – Normandy
    6. France – History – Bombardment 1944
    I. Title
    940.5'442

ISBN 1 904010 79 2

Typeset by Pearl Graphics, Hemel Hempstead

Printed and bound in Great Britain by
Biddles Ltd, King's Lynn

CONTENTS

ACKNOWLEDGEMENTS

There are many, many people who have made the research and writing of this book such a particular joy and I am most grateful to all of them. Without their help and encouragement this book would have remained a mere ambition. Of course special mention goes to all the veterans whose story appears in this book, in particular those men whose crews I have highlighted. I am indebted to them for their willingness to support my project and for giving permission to quote their stories and experiences around which I have constructed the book. (For the sake of space I have omitted ranks, but included decorations where I have been informed of them.)

US Eighth Air Force veterans
34th Bomb Group: George Ritchie DFC, Bob Gross, Oliver F. Bolduc, Rolland Whitehead, William Orton, Harold Province, Walter Sturdivan. *91st Bomb Group:* John Howland DFC (and 381st Bomb Group), James McPartlin DFC, Paul Chryst, Joe Harlick. *93rd Bomb Group:* Walter C. Fifer. *96th Bomb Group:* Bob Petty DFC, Warren Berg DFC, Sam H. Stone MD, Stanley Hand, Lew Warden, Neal B. Crawford, Frank Serio, Jack Croul. *388th Bomb Group:* Al Bibbens. *390th Bomb Group:* John Kearney, Daniel Coonan Jr, Ray Schleihs, Herbert Showers. *446th Bomb Group:* Stu Merwin. *339th Fighter Group:* James R. Starnes.

RAF Bomber Command veterans
7 Squadron: Ron Neills, J.H. Berry. *9 Squadron:* Fred Whitfield DFM. *50 Squadron:* Peter Antwis. *57/630 Squadron:* Allen Hudson. *61 Squadron:* Jim Johnson, Don Street DFC, Geoff Gilbert DFM. *75 Squadron:* George Robertson, Philip Deane, Gordon Ellis, Phil Matthew, Lin Drummond. *76 Squadron:* Bert Kirtland. *77 Squadron:* Tom Fox, Charles Hobgen, Arthur Inder, Horace Pearce, Geoffrey Haworth. *90 Squadron:* Dennis Field. *101 Squadron:* Edward Askew DFC. *115 Squadron:* Frank Leatherdale DFC. *156 Squadron:* Jack Watson DFM. *427 Squadron:* Stan Selfe, Ferdinand Slevar, Graham Cameron, Arthur Willis DVM. *428 Squadron:* Steve Yates. *463 Squadron:* Fred Fossett. *466 Squadron:* Verne Westley, Ken Handley. *582 Squadron:* Leslie Hood. *625 Squadron:* Bill Geeson.

Special mentions also go to Claude Helias for his excellent assistance in researching the French civilian experience and to June Ritchie for giving up so much time in correspondence. Geoff Ward's assistance with regard to the 96th Bomb Group has been invaluable, as has Joan Haine's help in telling her brother's story. In appreciation of their contribution to the photographs, I thank Howard Lees, the Mighty Eighth Air Force Heritage Museum (Michael Telzrow and Shasta Ireland), Bob Baxter, David Lyon, Michael Mockford, Sam McGowan, Frank (Tom) Atkinson, Todd Sager and Peter Garwood.

I am also particularly appreciative of the support given by John Davies, Louise King and Luke Norsworthy of Grub Street, and Amy Myers for her sound editorial suggestions.

In addition I would also like to extend my thanks to the following people and institutions: Jim Shortland, Jim Sheffield, Mark Antwis, Alan and Dorothy Masters, R. Barry Greenwood, Bob Farrell, Bill Davenport, Mary Haine, Eleanor Haine, Mrs G. Haine, Robert Haine, Rob Thornley, Steve Fraser, Steve Chalkley, Mick Yates, Jan Yates, Harry Shinkfield, Rusty Bloxom, Scott Fifer, The Library of Congress; Donita Pinkney and Frederick Bauman, Imperial War Museum; Alan Wakefield and Stephen Walton, Stotfold Library, Public Record Office, Battle of Britain Memorial Flight, Yorkshire Air Museum, Ian Reed, John Hunt, Greg Slevar, André Coilliot, Jan Smith. Stephen Ananian, Sean Welch, Kevin Welch, Eleanor Ehret, Mike Banta, Steve Smith, Lowell Getz, Suzanne Shepherd, Marie-Pierre Marcelot (Ville de Noisy-le-Sec, Documentation – archives), Richard Koval, Laurent Bailleul, Bill Chorley, Peter Johnson, Doreen Thorpe, Merryl Jenkins and Murlyn Hakon.

Finally I must thank Maggie, my wife, for putting up with all my flights of fantasy.

. . . This is no war of chieftains or of princes, of dynasties or national ambition; it is a war of peoples and of causes. There are vast numbers, not only in this island but in every land, who will render faithful service in this war, but whose names will never be known, whose deeds will never be recorded. This is a War of the Unknown Warriors; but let all strive without failing in faith or in duty, and the dark curse of Hitler will be lifted from our age . . .

Winston Churchill 14 July 1940

Dedicated to the wives and the mothers
who lost their husbands and sons

INTRODUCTION

It had been two full decades since American and Commonwealth air, sea and land forces had taken part in the greatest seaborne invasion in world history. Twenty years in which the scarred Normandy landscape had healed somewhat. Twenty years in which surviving combatants had tried to build new lives. It had been a time for veterans to reflect upon their experience. A time for bereaved families to come to terms with the loss of their loved ones.

For the mother of one of the British men lost in 1944 the postwar years had been hard, everything was in short supply in England, there was rationing, she had little money and in 1953 her husband had died. But now life had settled and with her daughter she was preparing to visit the grave of her son. The British Legion had made all the arrangements, and they travelled by boat from Newhaven to Dieppe and then by train to Caen to meet an escort. The next morning they made the short train journey to Bayeux and shortly after arrived by car at the British cemetery. Here they were met by an English gardener who directed them to the grave they were looking for. Both women stood facing the white headstone. On it was inscribed the RAF crest and motto 'Per Ardua Ad Astra'. Beneath this they read:

925316 FLIGHT SERGEANT
R. HAINE
AIR BOMBER
ROYAL AIR FORCE
6TH JUNE 1944 AGE 22.

Then beneath a Crucifix there was inscribed:

AT THE GOING DOWN
OF THE SUN
AND IN THE MORNING
WE WILL REMEMBER THEM

Interred in the French soil he had given his life to liberate, lay the body of a son and a brother. Every evening 'at the going down of the sun', and the next day 'in the morning', he had been remembered. The mother turned and spoke. 'Time does heal' she said. Tears were streaming down her face.

The above story tells of an attempt by one family to come to accept the loss of a loved one during World War II. Richard Haine was one of the many airmen lost by the Allies, during the campaign in support of the D-Day landings on the beaches of Normandy in 1944. Richard was killed on D-Day itself.

Loss through war spreads its grief widely, and each man gone leaves family and friends behind. But are the airmen remembered, save by their close family and as part of a general statistic of war casualties? In July 1944 Air Chief Marshal Sir Arthur Harris, Commander-in-Chief of RAF Bomber Command, wrote to Sir Charles Portal, the Chief of Air Staff, commenting on the lack of recognition he felt his airmen were getting as they battled supporting the D-Day campaign: 'I have no personal ambition that has not years ago been satisfied in full. But I for one cannot forbear a most emphatic protest against the grave injustice, which is being done to my crews. There are 10,500 aircrew in my operational squadrons. In three months we have lost over half that number. They have a right that their story should be adequately told, and it is a military necessity that it should be.'

The role of the Allied strategic heavy bomber forces in World War II is usually associated in the public mind today with the devastating raids on Hamburg and Dresden. These human tragedies must be remembered and examined. But other invaluable contributions to the hard-won peace, made by RAF Bomber Command and the US Eighth Air Force, should equally be remembered; the countering of the German V-weapon menace, minelaying operations, the dropping of agents and equipment to organise and arm the Resistance movements, the battle for and achievement of air superiority over western Europe in 1944, and, vitally, the success of the Normandy invasion. It appears all this has faded from public memory. It is my hope that this book will raise the profile of the heavy bomber contribution to the winning of the war in Europe, and in particular to D-Day and the violent struggle that followed it. Without it, I believe the invasion might well have faltered.

D-Day Bombers: The Veterans' Story concerns the US Eighth Air Force and RAF heavy bomber aircrew experience of supporting the build up to the Normandy landings, the day itself, and the aftermath. Also covered is the historical context of how the strategy and planning developed, a process which often led to bitter arguments between high ranking commanders. The book highlights eight crews, whose wartime careers covered a wide variety of aircraft type and operational experience. The story that unfolds is told largely in their own words. In my research I have met and corresponded with many air veterans, who have told me their story. It is quite clear that their experience is a defining, if not the defining, moment in their lives. They look back at a time of comradeship; the crew bond is ever present, particularly so with the RAF crews. It was a time when responsibility for personal actions was accepted and not avoided. And responsibility for being part of effecting greater change on a global scale was also accepted. They also look back with outspoken appreciation of true leadership. By the end of the war many of the young boys who appear in these pages had become men. Some did not make it, but their graves now tell the boys of today that the journey to manhood through war is not one completed by all who set out.

The book comes in two parts. The second part centres on D-Day itself and its aftermath. The first part concerns operations carried out during the planning period. D-Day was not a 24-hour event; it was the culmination of six months of detailed planning and operations, during which RAF Bomber Command and the US Eighth Air Force heavy bomber forces played a significant part, and made a considerable sacrifice, attacking strategic and tactical targets, preventing supplies reaching the enemy forces and winning air supremacy. Prior to this there had been two years of planning for the eventual invasion, and three years in which the heavy bomber crews involved in D-Day had trained and learned their skills the hard way. This book places the heavy bomber story within the context of the D-Day operation overall. It tells the story of the journey that brought the D-Day airmen together for their vital contribution to the Normandy campaign. And it tells the story of the decisions that were made in the corridors of power, and how these filtered down to the crewrooms of those that fought the battle.

PROLOGUE

On the evening of 14 November 1940, 17-year-old Dennis Field sat behind a desk, concentrating on his college homework in the front room of his home, a few miles from the centre of the Midlands city of Coventry, England. About 7 p.m. Dennis lifted his head as sirens began to wail. There was no initial panic. He had heard them before as German bombers had regularly visited the Midlands that summer, he recalls, 'mostly, there was little disruption if the raid was short, slight or sporadic and initially life was not greatly affected.'

But on this night as Dennis listened to the approaching German bombers, he began to realise that this was not going to be like most of the other raids. He and his mother decided to take cover in their neighbours' Anderson shelter. Dennis's father was still at work in the centre of the city.

The Luftwaffe, having failed to defeat the RAF in the Battle of Britain during the summer of 1940, had switched from daylight attacks to night bombing, concentrating on cities, industry and ports. On this night, thousands of feet above Coventry, the German aircrews, manning 13 Heinkel 111 bombers from Kampfgeschwader 100, prepared to release their load of incendiaries and high explosives. Their purpose was to act as pathfinders and start the fires, on to which the following force of nearly 500 bombers could home in and concentrate their attack.

At 7.20 p.m. KG100's incendiaries fell and the ground fires started. Six hundred tons of high explosive and thousands more incendiaries would follow.

Dennis Field: The bombs rained on us and many times we crouched down expecting the worst or at best hoping not to have a direct hit. Occasionally there were colossal bangs and blasts, which blew open the door. I wanted to go out to see what was happening and to help if I could but demurred to Mum's pleadings and restricted myself to occasional peers outside. The sky seemed aglow, with the brightest huge conflagration lighting the sky in the direction of the city centre. Nearby the smell of burning and of plaster and shattered buildings was powerful. I was surprised on several occasions to see our houses still standing.

The long cold fearful night seemed interminable and the effect on Mum must have been dreadful although superficially she bore up extremely well and with our neighbours we gleaned mutual support. The bright moon set a short while before the all-clear sounded around 6 a.m. and we privately offered thanks for our survival, but with much apprehension about what would unfold. We found the house, like most around, with windows out and roof damaged and clearly uninhabitable. As dawn broke groups of people appeared. Predictably they were stunned but there was, contrary to popular myth, no panic. Firemen, police and other services were evident with hosepipes criss-crossing roads, and as we walked further, we saw appliances from Birmingham and other outlying cities and towns. Then Dad arrived and we were mightily relieved . . . A huge weight was lifted by our common reassurance. Dad humorously claimed to have drunk the last pint at the Greyfriars Inn opposite to his shelter, pulling and despatching it just before the roof fell in on the burning building. He said the centre was shattered, the Cathedral ruined, and there was chaos all the way home. A pall of smoke hung over the stricken centre. I went for a short walkabout. Most roads locally had their ration of bombed buildings and craters. Shops on the corner of Cramper's Field were no more and sheets covered several bodies on the green opposite. Mrs Lampitt, from the wool shop, and several others had rushed towards a falling parachute thinking it was an airman; it was a land mine, which exploded on contact.

Over the next few days Dennis learnt more of the extreme devastation inflicted upon his city. Hundreds had been killed. Following the raid it was impossible for his family to stay in their home. His father moved in with his aunt and Dennis went to stay with a relative. His mother, who had a heart condition, went away for a while, but after a short time she returned and was admitted into the Coventry and Warwickshire hospital. Sadly her heart condition deteriorated and in February 1941 she passed away. And so it was that having lost his home and family life, Dennis decided to volunteer for the Royal Air Force. In three years time he would be one of thousands of young British, American and British Commonwealth airmen fighting an uncompromising air battle over Western Europe. His survival, as did theirs, depended on skill and good fortune and having survived, Dennis would play his part in one of the most significant military operations in World War II, the D-Day landings on the beaches of Normandy.

PART ONE

Flightpath to D-Day

CHAPTER 1

RAF BOMBER COMMAND'S NEW RECRUIT

Planning for D-Day, the Allied assaults on the Normandy beaches on 6 June 1944 gathered pace in December 1943, but the process had begun two years earlier. The responsibility for detailed and careful preparation applied not only to prime ministers, presidents and chiefs of staff, but also to the commanders of the fighting forces. RAF Bomber Command was no exception. Dennis Field's story is typical of the training of the heavy bomber crews.

In December 1941 Japanese aircraft had struck the American Navy at Pearl Harbor[1] and Hitler declared war on the USA. At that time German military might was dominating in the Western theatres of operation but Britain was holding out, just, though it clearly could not defeat Germany on its own. The British Commonwealth nations had rallied around but when American human and industrial resource was allied to British resolve, many believed, and many more hoped, that the seed of victory had been sown.

At the Anglo-American *Arcadia* conference in Washington, which began on 31 December 1941, the USA made its commitment to *Bolero*, the build-up of armed forces in Britain, to meet the priority of the defeat of Germany in the West. The major Allied offensive of 1942 saw the clash of German and Allied armies in North Africa, but the Americans believed an offensive across the English Channel would be the best way to initiate victory in the West, and had agreed only reluctantly to the invasion of North Africa. Then at the Casablanca conference in January 1943 the British again got their way, as *Husky*, the invasion of Sicily as a step towards that of Italy, became the next priority.

Whilst the land campaign raged, the Allies developed another way of hitting back at Hitler. At the Casablanca conference there had been agreement on direct action against Germany, with the issue of a directive (4 February 1943) to the British and American commanders of the Allied heavy bomber forces: 'Your primary object will be the progressive destruction and dislocation of the German military, industrial and economic system, and the undermining of the morale of the German people to a point where their capacity for armed resistance is fatally weakened.' The directive went on to prioritise German submarine construction, the German aircraft industry, transportation, oil and 'other targets in the enemy war industry'. In addition, the German capital Berlin was included to be 'attacked when conditions are suitable for the attainment of specially valuable results unfavourable to the morale of the enemy or favourable to that of Russia'.

For the next few months both Allied heavy bomber forces carried the war direct to the enemy: the British bombers, under the cover of night, went deep into Reich airspace, and the American forces in their daylight defensive formations steadily probed deeper. The Luftwaffe responded, exacting its toll, and it soon became apparent to the Allies that if they were to invade Fortress Europe successfully they would need control of the skies. In June 1943 the Casablanca directive was updated with the issue of the *Pointblank* amendment which attempted to change the emphasis; the achievement of air superiority in Western Europe became the priority by targeting the German aircraft industry along with attacking enemy airfields and directly engaging the Luftwaffe in the skies over Germany and the occupied territories. However, *Pointblank* also retained the objective of attacking the 'morale of the German people'. In the coming months, this indefinite wording gave RAF Bomber Command[2] the scope to maintain attacks on German cities, whilst the American heavy bomber forces focused on the defeat of the German air force.

The air offensive against Germany would require a considerable growth in the numbers of aircraft, aircrews and groundcrews with which to pound the enemy. *Pointblank* would draw on two main sources. The USA could train its men on home soil, then fly them across the Atlantic to join operational units in England. In contrast, the training of RAF aircrew required sending them away from the hostile and crowded skies over England to the peaceful skies over other British Commonwealth nations. Early in the war Commonwealth dominions reached agreement on providing a joint programme of air training. As such any new aircrew recruits could find themselves sent far from home in order to learn and hone their skills flying in a peaceful airspace. What follows is the story of one of them, but it is typical of the many.

When Dennis Field reached the age of 18 he volunteered for the Royal Air Force to train as a pilot, and in February 1942 he would start his flying career. Some of his friends, who had joined before Dennis, would, when on leave, enlighten him on some of their early training experiences.

> *Dennis Field:* The new recruits, dispersed in various seaside ITWs [Initial Training Wings], radiated health and well being when they arrived on leave in their new blue serge uniforms with a white flash in the forage cap signifying U/T aircrew. Jim Bird had been up for an aptitude test in a Tiger Moth and had enjoyed the gentler part but had not been too keen on the spinning exercise. This and other tales of early service life roused eager anticipation over guarded uncertainty. When I received my travel warrant to report to ACRC (Aircrew Recruiting Centre) in St John's Wood, London, my Pandora's box of travel, adventure and danger opened.

In May 1942 Dennis embarked for Canada (via the USA) aboard the SS *Thomas Hardy*. On arrival at New York harbour he was promptly entrained for Moncton, New Brunswick, the main transit base for the North American Empire Air Training Scheme. A further train journey followed to Calgary, Alberta, and then on to Bowden and the aerodrome. After a frustrating two weeks Dennis eventually became airborne: 'Sheer exhilaration overcame apprehension and the fleeting surprise of the strap hanging contortion of primary aerobatics.' As the training continued, however, the realisation that the training, whilst exciting, was nevertheless hazardous became apparent to him:

Circuits and bumps were augmented at a small auxiliary field called Netook, which frequently became crowded and the first fatality occurred when two aircraft collided. One chap bailed out but Pressland, who occupied a bed near mine, stayed in his plane and died in the crash. The blood-stained cockpit of the wreck brought back on a trailer was a grim reminder of ever-present hazards.

Eventually Dennis achieved the required number of training hours. Following an 'average' assessment and expressing a preference for single-engine aircraft, he was posted to SFTS (Service Flying Training School) at Swift Current, Saskatchewan, which then moved to share the airport at Calgary. Training continued with formation flying, instrument flying, and night flying, although a rugby injury, a dislocated elbow, held him up. In January 1943 Dennis received his pilot wings and the next month travelled to Moncton and then on to New York where he boarded the *Queen Mary*. In March Dennis arrived back in Britain. Further training followed, including being sent on an all pilot toughening-up course at Whitley Bay. Here Dennis was to receive some disappointing news. He had been detailed to continue training on multi-engined aircraft, four-engined bombers. Virtually all aspiring airmen strove for the glory associated with the fighter pilots.

> I felt totally deflated at the news. The very little I knew about them gave the impression that I should become a glorified bus driver, and I did not fancy the job of having to form a crew and losing a good measure of independence. The reason for the change was obvious as the bombing campaign was gathering strength and starting seriously to affect German war production and communications, but at heavy cost as rising losses showed. Communiqués such as 'Twenty of our aircraft are missing' became all too familiar so that three or four times a week meant that several hundred highly trained aircrew replacements were needed. Philosophically I reasoned that it was a case of being in the wrong place at the wrong time but that did not much improve morale. I was to learn how incorrect and misplaced my misgivings were and that the chance circumstance was one amongst many which I should have reason to bless for survival and a great deal of coincidental camaraderie and, albeit dangerous, reward.

On 1 June 1943 Dennis was posted to AFU (Advanced Flying Unit) South Cerney, Gloucestershire and the satellite airfield at Bibury, to fly Oxfords and undergo conversion to multi-engined aircraft. New friends were made and night-flying training was the focus with its inherent hazards. After 70 hours on Oxfords Dennis was posted to No. 82 OTU (Operational Training Unit) Ossington, near Newark, his introduction to RAF Bomber Command.

> . . . and with it a considerable change in attitude, aircraft and environment. The station was very much down to earth and under continuous pressure to provide an uninterrupted flow of crews to replace increasing losses. The 'permanent' flying (screened) staff were tour-expired and it showed. It was our first close contact with people who had completed operations,

surviving against unlikely odds. Gongs [medals] were common, almost part of the dress, and worn without flamboyance. Although we were keen to hear and learn all we could, in off-duty hours they stayed detached and there was little line-shooting in our presence. They had done it and we were about to. But we realised that within a few months we should all meet some ultimate of human experience.

Soon after our arrival, we were assembled for an introductory talk by the Wing-Co, a DSO, DFC type who had recently completed a second tour and wore his arm in a sling with a heavily bandaged hand. I suppose he was only about twenty-five but to me he seemed much older. The message was positive and matter-of-fact. We were told of our responsibilities, duties, security and programme and were left in no doubt of the seriousness of that training; we were now part of Bomber Command and would soon be going onto operations which in no way would be a joyride. We were told of basic rules, both flying and on the ground, DROs, SSOs, leave, crew working, flights and sections. The Wellington's handling and robustness were extolled, and the closeness of the props to the cockpit was mentioned. Injury resulting from carelessness would be considered as self-inflicted and be liable to court-martial and we were left in no doubt of our situation. Afterwards I learned that the CO's attitude was perhaps coloured by the fact that having come from a Lancaster squadron, he had been forgetful coming back to Wimpys [Wellingtons] and when waving the chocks away had lost several fingers of his left hand.

Training would soon continue following the all important crewing-up. Airmen from the various trades, the pilots, navigators, bomb aimers, wireless operators and air gunners were left in a hangar and basically told to sort themselves out.

Dennis Field: I was wandering about ineffectually and somewhat self-consciously in the general melee and hubbub wondering how to make the first contact when I was approached by a completed group of four fellow young sprog sergeants, gunner, wireless operator and two observers (with an 'O' brevet indicating qualification both as navigator and bomb-aimer) who asked me if I would make up their crew. It was not exactly what I had intended and I was rather taken aback by the suddenness and fait-accompli. We were likely, after all, within a short time to be confronted by dangerous and immediate situations demanding total interdependence and reliance. But believing in some intervention by Providence (fortified by later events) and noting that they seemed a bright bunch and with the distinct benefit of two observers, I quickly agreed following brief introductions.

Alan Turner, navigator, from Stockport, was a few weeks younger than me, but he looked even more youthful with neatly side-parted hair, slightly chubby cheeks and an almost cherubic look. As he only stood about five feet three inches in his socks, at least there was, I thought, not much for Jerry to aim at. But his application to his job was intense and perfectionist.

Gingery-haired Mancunian Arthur Borthwick, bomb aimer, and, as Alan, trained in South Africa, proved to be an extrovert and optimistic type, very keen on his job and willing to 'organise', which came in useful in extracting extra rations from the cookhouse WAAFs.

Hailing from Bradford, Gordon 'Yorky' Royston, rear gunner, was a thoroughbred Yorkshireman. He had dark crinkly hair, smog-induced slightly red-rimmed eyes, a fondness for black beer and chitterlings, a pleasant friendly character and a generous accent.

Eddie Durrans, wireless operator, from Batley, was thus not of such absolute pedigree as Yorky. He had a mischievous streak which often subsequently led to my being unsuspectingly subjected to mass attacks under his rallying call of 'Bloody hellfire' and finishing flattened under four representatives of the white and red roses. The excuse for such undisciplined behaviour was to ensure that I did not get too cocky on the ground after being 'chiefy' on duty and in the air, and in recompense for some ropey fledgling landings.

To complete our immediate crew (the flight engineer required for the four-engined aircraft would join us at Heavy Conversion Unit), Tony Faulconbridge, our future mid-upper gunner, joined us a few days later. Tony, tall and fair-haired, was from Hereford, and he and I were the Midland counterpart of the northern group. Quietly spoken but always readily involved, he was the youngest by a few months from Alan and myself. His brother had been lost on a mainforce raid the previous year.

Initial shyness and reticence soon melted away and we settled down, going almost everywhere together when not in our respective sections. We were all ex-grammar school or similar with not too different backgrounds, not that that would have made much difference anyway. But that we were welding into a unit spontaneously, building up mutual trust and respect and were keen to work hard and conscientiously, augured well. Teamwork was essential and it developed rapidly. There was plenty of banter but minimal moaning between us and, as skipper, I can remember only very rare harsh words or necessary remonstration. Nights in the mess or evening walks gave opportunity to talk shop and to find our own entertainment. Town jaunts usually lasted several hours, but our final semi-comatose condition on returning to the billet was as much due to exhaustion from walking, hitching lifts, finding pubs that were open and struggling to get to the bar, as it was to alcohol consumed. None of us was an abstainer, although our capacities varied somewhat. It was never any use trying to be pretentious, not that I wished to and, quite rightly, I became the chief butt for the leg-pulling and horseplay. But with anything connected with our work or flying there was application and discipline. In the air we remained on first name terms. Voices were instantly recognisable and I felt that the traditional 'navigator to skipper' or such only delayed the message. From curiosity some time later, I asked Eddie why they had picked on me. He replied that they were looking for a 'big bugger' when they suddenly realised that I was the only one left. It served me right for asking.

Training continued on twin-engined bombers with night flying and bombing, night cross-country and fighter affiliation, which included practising corkscrewing, an evasive action involving climbing, diving and turning in order to shake off unwanted company. Dennis's crew progressed steadily but the risks of operational training were always kept at the forefront of their mind.

> *Dennis Field:* One morning whilst queuing at the NAAFI wagon for a rock cake wad and mug of well-brewed char, we were idly watching a Wimpy taking off when the starboard engine spluttered just after lift-off and smoke began to pour from it. It struggled on at low level for a minute or so before disappearing below the treetops. We muttered a silent prayer before the sudden flash and column of black oily smoke told its tale. Later in the day I happened to go to flying control and bumped into a rescue squad sergeant who had gone straight to the scene. I stupidly asked him if there had been any survivors. He did not reply and I would not forget the sickened look he gave me. I made a mental reservation on the capability of our kites to cope on one engine take-off.

After passing out of OTU the crew was sent to 1651 HCU (Heavy Conversion Unit) Waterbeach (and later to Wratting Common) to gain experience of four-engined bombers, in this case the Short Stirling.

> *Dennis Field:* The Stirling was big and dwarfed the Wellington in much the same way as did the Oxford. In the cockpit at a height of nearly twenty-four feet, it was like sitting on the eaves of a detached house with a six-foot diameter wheel at each of the front corners. (My captive audience often accused me in colourful terms of carrying the analogy too far.) The tips of the airscrews could not be reached even with upstretched arms. The undercarriage was of majestic proportion and intricacy, the need for which arose from a revised design to obtain greater lift on a shorter wing span of less than a hundred feet so that it would fit inside the standard hangars of the period. The height exaggerated a tendency caused by the torque of the propellers, with or without crosswind, to swing to starboard during take-off and was the cause of many a crash. Additionally the Stirling, for its maximum loaded weight of 70,000 lb, was underpowered and had a practical ceiling of only 13,000-14,000 feet.

Flying the four-engined heavies required the need to pay considerable attention to fuel, engine and other mechanical management. As such a seventh member was added to the crew to take on this responsibility, and flight engineer Charlie Waller joined Dennis Field's crew.

> *Dennis Field:* Charlie Waller, a Londoner, was like many of his ilk, a remustered fitter. At over thirty and married he was by far the eldest amongst us, but quickly fitted in well and predictably was very knowledgeable. There was no call for him to volunteer for flying; he could most plausibly have remained with groundcrew.

After 30 hours of training the crew was cleared for operations, but given 10 days' leave whilst awaiting their posting. During this time Dennis met up with some old friends:

> I bumped into four uniformed ex-schoolmates who were also pilots. Tony Snell, a budding artist whose lino-cutting pictures often graced the school magazines, was now flying Spitfires. Bill Dodd, on Beaufighters, was a keen cricketer whose parents had rigged a practice net where I had spent energetic visits. His brother Stuart had been killed on an airfield during a bombing attack in 1941. Rodney Dryland, on Typhoons, was a cheerful extrovert. Brian Bastable, test flying, was a quieter character. Tony sported a DFC and Rodney and Brian were soon also to be similarly decorated. When I told then I was on Stirlings they laughed and insisted on buying the drinks when we adjourned to the Queen's Hotel. It was like a premature wake for me with much leg-pulling. As it turned out, I was the only one to survive. Within twelve months Tony and Bill went missing on operations and Rodney and Bill died later in accidents.

On Boxing Day 1943 news came through that Dennis's crew was posted to an RAF Bomber Command operational unit, 90 Squadron at Tuddenham, Suffolk. It was time to enter battle, a battle that would reach its zenith on D-Day.

CHAPTER 2

AMERICANS OVER BERLIN

Strategy for the success of the Normandy campaign placed certain
responsibilities on the American heavy bomber forces.
This would involve a change, not only in the nature of the missions, but
in the tactical conduct. In the lead up to D-Day, the number
of US Eighth Air Force airmen would grow and they would develop the
expertise to carry out their allotted task. John Howland was
one such American who played his part in these historic days.

John Howland, navigator US Eighth Air Force: Christmas away from
home is never pleasant, not even in Jolly Old England.

On 25 December 1943 American airman John Howland and his friend and fellow
aviator Jim Tyson took a walk into the town of Stone in Staffordshire, England.
One week earlier, just after midnight on 18 December 1943, Jim Tyson had lifted
his four-engined Boeing B-17 Flying Fortress heavy bomber from the runway at
Gander Lake, Newfoundland. From then on he had relied on his navigator John
Howland to direct them across the Atlantic Ocean. Approaching Ireland the
weather had deteriorated, as they had been forewarned at briefing. Clouds
enclosed the B-17.

John Howland: Jim decided to go down and take a look below. We
dropped to about 12,000 feet and hit some very bad icing conditions. One
minute the black perforated outer barrel of the machine gun sticking out
of the starboard navigator's window was merely a shadow in the dim light.
The next minute it looked like a huge white war club. Ominously, the air
speed indicator dropped to zero because the heater in the pitot tube had
failed. Jim applied power, climbing to try and find an altitude where icing
conditions weren't so severe. He flew by power settings from that point
on.

All John could do was plot their position by dead reckoning in order to meet his
ETA at Prestwick. When the time came Jim Tyson tried to radio Prestwick tower.

John Howland: Jim could make contact with both Nutts Corner and
Prestwick; but they wouldn't respond when he asked for a QDM
(magnetic heading) to their base. Finally, after trying fruitlessly for about
thirty minutes, he made another call to Burton (the code name for
Prestwick) saying:
    'Hello Burton. This is Harry How (our code name). Come in please.'
    The response was loud and clear in a cockney accent, 'Ello Airy Ow.
Where are you?'
    Jim replied, 'We don't know. What is the ceiling over your base?'

The cockney accent came back again saying, 'Ello Airy Ow. Where are you?'

Jim replied, 'We still don't know. What is the ceiling over your base?' Once more Prestwick came in with, 'Ello Airy Ow. Where are you?'

Finally, Jim replied, 'Burton, this is Harry How. We don't know where we are. We're sitting up here at 26,500 feet above a solid cloud layer in the vicinity of your field. We are low on oxygen, and running low on fuel. Our air speed indicator isn't working, and we are losing number four engine (low oil pressure). Unless you can give us some help in the next thirty minutes we are going to bail out and leave this SOB sitting up here.'

The response was immediate. 'Ello Airy Ow. *Don't do that!* Fly 180 degrees and give us a long count.'

Jim went through the ritual of counting slowly up to ten and back to one again. About one minute later the tower operator came back saying, 'Fly 270 degrees and give us another long count.'

Just a few moments later he was back on the air with, 'Come on down, Airy Ow, you are right over the base.'

At that moment the happiest navigator in the entire Eighth Air Force was sitting in the nose compartment of a B-17 numbered 237986.

At the beginning of 1944 John Howland was one of thousands of American airmen who were contributing to the Eighth Air Force's accession of strength in England. For many their motivation to join the air force was common.

Stu Merwin, radio operator 446th Bomb Group: The newspapers, radio, and movies of 1941 carried graphic images of the fighting in Europe. Edward R. Murrow was a newscaster who brought the Nazi conquests to us, on the radio, every night. As a 19-year-old, I along with millions of other 'kids' was galvanized into action by the Japanese attack on Pearl Harbor. Having watched movies of fighter aces, etc. we all wanted to be pilots. I joined the Army Air Corps on 17 March 1942, hoping to be a pilot cadet. So did thousands of others.

Rolland Whithead, pilot, 34th Bomb Group: The war in Europe, to me, seemed so distant and yet we were helping England in many ways but not getting involved until the Japanese hit Pearl Harbor. Boy, did we have an attitude adjustment.

Sam Stone, radio operator, 96th Bomb Group: My lifelong dream was to fly. I couldn't wait to get into the war. I am Jewish and my parents were both born and raised in Warsaw. My grandmother and many relatives were killed by Nazis. I was aware of what was happening and I was determined to kill as many Germans as I could.

John Howland had joined the Army Air Corps[3] because he simply just liked to fly. Whilst at college he had taken the opportunity, offered by the government, to take a course in pilot training, and began training on Piper Cubs at Colorado Springs.

John Howland: I passed the physical and mental tests and was about ready to solo when word was sent that I was to be dropped because my height was half an inch below the minimum requirement (5ft 4in). I was devastated. However, pre-med students at Colorado College told me a person was always about one inch taller upon arising in the morning. I used the right triangle from my engineering studies' kit and checked out this observation. They were right. I was told that my only chance for re-instatement was to pass the 5ft 4in height test. So, on a Sunday afternoon I went to bed and spent the evening and night stretched out flat. The next morning my friend Bill Clark, a six-foot-plus football player came by and slung my small frame over his shoulder like a 125 lb sack of grain. I laid down in the back seat of his car and when we reached the doctor's office, he carried me inside.

Doc Woodward was waiting for us and said, 'Howland, stand up and we'll measure you.' I replied, 'No, doc, just set that damned marker at 5ft 4in and we'll see if I can hit it.' The marker was set. I eased to my bare feet and could barely feel that marker scraping across the top of my head. I was then reinstated, finished the course, and was awarded a private pilot's license in January 1942.

At the end of his school year in May 1942, John took the decision to leave his studies and enlist with the Army Air Corps, but yet again he would run into problems.

John Howland: Further, without my friend Bill Clark and the other options I used, there was no way I could pass that height test. So, I decided to be a glider pilot. The height requirement was only 5ft. Early in July (42) I went to Mitchell Field, New York for testing and possible induction as a glider pilot. Glider pilot applicants were required to take the same mental and physical tests as Air Corps Cadet applicants for training as pilots, bombardiers or navigators. An applicant had to score 90 (out of 150) to be an air corps cadet or 70 to be a glider pilot. They must have had a bunch of dummies applying that day. I scored 128 and the nearest to me barely squeaked by with a 92. A fellow by the name of Lt O'Connor got hold of me and said, 'Have you ever thought of being a pilot as a cadet as opposed to a glider pilot?' I explained that lacking half an inch was the reason for my decision since I wasn't too interested in being a bombardier or a navigator. I presume Lt O'Connor was having trouble meeting his quota of cadets when he said, 'That's no problem at all. We can give you a waiver on that half inch.' That was all I needed to hear, and with eyes still out of focus from dilation drops, I signed on the dotted line to become an air corps cadet scheduled for pilot training. But that was the last I ever heard of that damned waiver.

Exactly one year following the Japanese attack on Pearl Harbor, John reported for Basic Training at San Antonio Aviation Cadet Center, Texas. Following initial physical and mental tests he was informed that he qualified for the positions of either pilot, bombardier, or navigator.

John Howland: Despite the fact that I had requested pilot training, had passed all mental and aptitude tests, and indeed, possessed a valid private pilot's license, the Army in all its wisdom decided the half inch I lacked to meet their minimum height requirement disqualified me for pilot training. So I opted for training as a celestial navigator.

Following initial training at Pre-Flight School at Ellington Field near Houston, Texas, John then went on to specialist navigational training at the Advanced Navigation School in Hondo, Texas. Six months' intensive training followed and some cadets dropped out, unable to keep up the expected grade standards. Following graduation on 5 August 1943 and a short leave, John reported at Ephrata, Washington, where he formed up in a B-17 bomber crew. The pilot of the new crew, Californian James L. Tyson, was its most senior member; he was 27 years old and married. The initial co-pilot appeared to have a problem with alcohol and was replaced by an Irishman from Boston, Massachusetts, Bill Doherty. Frank Palenik, from Phillips Wisconsin, was the bombardier. Along with John Howland these four men became second lieutenants. The engineer, top turret gunner position was filled by Richard C. Jensen from Cleveland, Ohio, the radio operator Henry N. White from St Louis, Missouri and the four gunners were Robert Miller, Charles Churchill, Edgar Berg and Arnold Farmer.

The fledgling crew was sent to Overseas Training Unit at Kearney, Nebraska, to hone its skills as a unit flying a B-17.

John Howland: I felt quite comfortable with my crew. As a pilot, Jim Tyson was steady as a rock; the kind of pilot who makes life easy for a navigator. If I set course of 245 degrees, I would watch the needle of my Flux Gate compass move around until it registered 245 deg. When Jim Tyson flew the plane, it was glued there. Whenever I observed course deviations, I would check to see whose feet were on the rudder pedals. Invariably, it was the co-pilot who was flying the plane. However no disrespect is intended for our fun-loving co-pilot. Bill Doherty just wasn't cut out to be a bomber pilot. He was a misplaced fighter pilot; a real life 'Hot Shot Charlie', the comic strip character made famous by cartoonist Milton Caniff in a strip called 'Terry and the Pirates'.

Frank Palenik, my companion in the nose compartment, proved to be a very competent, better than average, bombardier. He was not only an excellent bombardier; but a very good pilotage navigator as well. Unlike many bombardiers who read comic books or took naps on long flights, Frank always had a pilotage chart in his hands and fed position reports to me repeatedly whenever the weather was clear. This was a great help to me while I maintained our dead reckoning positions on the Mercator chart.

The two months spent in the Overseas Training Unit were quite rewarding. We learned to work together and respect the talent and contributions of other crew members.

On Thanksgiving Day, 1943 the crew began their journey to England, firstly to Syracuse, New York, then Presque Isle, Maine, on to Stephenville, Newfoundland and on 1 December to Gander, Newfoundland. Then the snow arrived, preventing any flights, and it was two weeks before the snow stopped and the runways were cleared. On 17 December 1943 however, John Howland,

Jim Tyson and their crew received the briefing for their final flight to England.

Upon arrival and following a brief stay at Prestwick, the crew moved on to the army distribution centre at Stone. Whilst there it learnt of the fate of some of the other crews who had also been detailed to make the flight across the Atlantic on 18 December. They had experienced similar problems, indeed three aircraft failed to arrive. Whilst at Stone the American airmen awaited their assignment to an operational base, and on Christmas Day, John and Jim had little else to do except take a walk, explore the area around Stone and unexpectedly meet some of the local people.

> *John Howland:* Not a word was said between us as we wandered aimlessly in the general direction of a church we could see in the distance. The silence was broken by the click of heels and scurrying feet as a middle-aged woman and a boy crossed the street and approached us. The woman spoke first saying, 'Won't you Yanks come home and have Christmas with our family?' Although somewhat startled by her generous and gracious offer, we were quick to accept.

The lady, Doris Redman, took the two men to her parents' home, which was full of people that day.

> *John Howland:* We wondered where to find the 'cold' and 'aloof' English people we had heard so much about. They certainly weren't part of this group. Conversation flowed freely. The tea and scones were delicious, and we were treated with a warmth and friendship we hadn't seen since leaving home.

On 28 December 1943 news came through of the crew's posting to an operational base, assigned to the 535th Squadron, one of four squadrons making up the 381st Bomb Group, based at Ridgewell in Essex. It was time to enter battle.

On New Year's day 1944, a new command was set up to direct the American heavy bomber forces in Europe, the United States Strategic Air Force (USSTAF)[4], encompassing the Eighth and Fifteenth Air Forces, under General Carl Spaatz. Carl 'Tooey' Spaatz, graduate of the US Military Academy at West Point, 1914, World War I veteran, and with a postwar career filling staff positions in the rapidly expanding Army Air Corps, will forever be remembered as a man who was at the forefront of American air power strategy in World War II.

In the summer of 1940 Spaatz had been sent as an observer to witness the Battle of Britain. The failure of the Luftwaffe to overcome the RAF had great influence on the American, developing his mindset that air superiority was a must as a prelude to any invasion operations. Since then Spaatz had been instrumental, once the Germany first strategy had been decided, in developing American air power in Europe. The Eighth Air Force moved to England early in 1942, to start contributing to the strategic air offensive against Germany, and Spaatz, promoted to major general, arrived shortly after; he took over command, with Brigadier General Ira Eaker as his deputy, and committed his bomber force to a precision daylight bombing offensive. This was a controversial decision considering both the Luftwaffe and the RAF had moved to night offensives as a result of unsustainable daylight losses. But Spaatz stuck to his guns. His bomber aircrews would wage war by day.

The Allied invasion of North Africa commenced towards the end of 1942 and Spaatz, promoted to three star rank, took command of all American air forces in Europe and the focus for American air power shifted to the Mediterranean and the desert. Eaker took over command of the Eighth Air Force in England. Then following the success of the North African campaign, and the invasions of Sicily and Italy, Spaatz's eyes turned once more to attacking Germany direct. In January 1944 he took up his position in England commanding the USSTAF, with plans to use, so he thought, the Eighth Air Force from England and the Fifteenth Air Force from Italy, in bombarding the German war machine.

In January 1944 the Eighth Air Force had a change of leader as General Ira Eaker was transferred to the Mediterranean theatre, not something Eaker took to kindly as he felt his bomber force was now starting to make a significant impact on the European war. Taking Eaker's place was James 'Jimmy' Doolittle who was promoted to lieutenant general, two months after arriving in England on 5 January 1944.

Doolittle had achieved notoriety when, on 18 April 1942, he had led a force of 16 B-25s, taking off from an aircraft carrier, on a raid bombing factories in the centre of Tokyo, then flying on to land in China. The 'Doolittle raid', as it came to be known, provided a much needed boost for the American nation. When Doolittle returned to the USA his President presented him with the Medal of Honor. Since then, Doolittle had been given command of the Twelfth Air Force as it took part in the North African and Mediterranean campaigns, and following this in November 1943, command of the newly formed strategic Fifteenth Air Force, which was set up to operate from bases in Italy. As 1943 drew to a close, however, another move was being planned for Doolittle.

In the Eighth Air Force, Doolittle inherited a bomber force of unprecedented strength. In the summer of 1942 the 'Mighty Eighth', as it has come to be known, had begun operating from English airfields, initially attacking targets in the occupied territories of western Europe. Throughout the following year and a half as the force grew in strength, it began to probe deeper into enemy airspace. In contrast to RAF Bomber Command, the Eighth sent its bombers into battle during daylight, believing in the fire-power of tight, defensive, well-armed bomber formations to counter aerial opposition. However, attacks on targets deep in Germany, as the Eighth strived to fulfil its commitment to the *Pointblank* objectives, particularly in September and October 1943, soon exposed weaknesses. The bomber formations were severely mauled. German fighter tactics evolved and exploited these weaknesses, notably engaging the bombers in frontal attacks, as the B-17 and B-24 had been designed to counter mainly rear attacks. In addition rockets fired from twin-engined German fighters were introduced to break bomber formations up, and thus hinder supportive fire.

It became clear to the American air commanders that to continue attacking Germany without increasing the range of fighter escorts was a sure way to lose the air war. When Doolittle took command of the Eighth at the beginning of 1944, however, long-range escorts, with drop tanks for extra fuel, were available and the German fighter threat over Germany could now be countered. Doolittle recorded in his autobiography that the 'steadily increased range of the escort fighters was an inheritance from which I benefited as commander of the 8th; their genesis began long before I took over. It was my job to use this increased capability to best advantage.' And one of Doolittle's first command decisions was to change the role of the fighter escorts, which up to that point had been to protect the bomber force. He ordered the Eighth Fighter Command to shift emphasis to the pursuit and destruction of enemy fighters. 'Your priority is to take the offensive,' he told Major General William Kepner of Eighth Fighter Command, who welcomed this new direction. Doolittle would later claim this as 'the most important and far-reaching military decision I made during the war. It was also the most controversial.'[5]

At the time of Jim Tyson and John Howland's arrival at Ridgewell the Eighth Air Force was set to embark upon what historians now recognise as a decisive air battle in World War II in western Europe. Jim, John and their crew would make their contribution to the battle and experience at first hand the uncompromising conflict for air superiority.

The 381st Bomb Group had been activated on New Year's day 1943, its aircrew initially honing their flying skills particularly formation flying, at Pyote, Texas; then they went on to Pueblo, Colorado to complete preparations for operational duty. On 2 May the 381st began transferring airmen, groundcrews, staff and equipment to England, arriving in June and conducting its first mission on 22 June to an airfield at Antwerp. The 381st entered battle at a cost: two aircraft failed to return and two more arrived back badly damaged carrying casualties. The next day there was further tragedy when, during preparations for a mission a bomb fell and exploded wiping out 24 lives. Over the next six months the 381st took up its responsibilities in executing the Eighth Air Force's commitments to *Pointblank* and the price was paid. On the Schweinfurt mission on 17 August 1943, 11 aircraft were lost.

On the day of arrival at the 381st Bomb Group's home at Ridgewell, Jim Tyson's crew received a welcome from a most surprising source. Broadcasting from Germany, the infamous Lord Haw Haw (William Joyce) welcomed the crew to England along with other crews who had also made the same transatlantic flight on 18 December 1943.

> *John Howland:* He assured us we would all soon be dead or shot down and captured as prisoners of war. The threats didn't bother us, but we were shocked at the breach of security. It wasn't until some time later we learned that our third lost plane [on 18 December 1943] made a serious navigation error. They failed to detect the strong tailwinds pushing them across the Atlantic and were hundreds of miles south of course. When they requested landing instructions over a German airport in Normandy, an alert English-speaking tower operator give the necessary information. They wound up as prisoners of war, and Lord Haw Haw and the Nazis gained access to the secret orders the men carried with them.

The first days at Ridgewell were spent settling in and undergoing further training on topics such as the British navigation equipment, dinghy drill and lectures on escape methods. Then early on the morning of 11 January 1944, John Howland

and Jim Tyson were awoken. The moment had come at last: they were to take part in an operational mission. Policy at the 381st Bomb Group was, on their first mission, to blood new pilots and navigators with experienced crews. Separated from his pilot, John was assigned to fly with a Lieutenant Jobe, who was flying his 25th mission and therefore completing his first tour of duty. The main target for the 1st Bomb Division heavies, including Lieutenant Jobe's, was a Focke-Wulf aircraft assembly plant at Oschersleben, approximately 75 miles south-west of Berlin, with a smaller force detailed for a Junkers plant at nearby Halberstadt. In addition 2nd and 3rd Bomb Division bomb groups were tasked to blast the aircraft industry around Brunswick. All this would require a deep penetration into Germany, and the groans at the unveiling of the planned route at briefing indicated the aircrew's displeasure.

Around 0800 hours the 381st's B-17s took off (33 airborne, of which two returned as unused spares) and at 0915 hours after forming up over the airfield within the 1st Combat Wing, the formation moved off. Lieutenant Jobe's aircraft took its place in the high composite group (which also included aircraft from the 91st Bomb Group), following the lead aircraft in the main lead group (91st Bomb Group aircraft), which in turn was followed by the low group (381st Bomb Group aircraft). This three-tiered 'Combat Box' (in this case totalling 62 bombers dispatched) of high, lead and low groups made up the typical defensive formation early in 1944. With each heavy bomber bristling with 0.50-inch calibre machine guns, any attacker challenging or entering the box would expose itself to a deadly crossfire. The tighter the formation the greater the concentration of supportive crossfire and the less chance enemy fighters or flak defences would have to target and pick off single aircraft. The compromise was manoeuvrability of the formation, particularly on the bomb run, and too tight a formation could expose more than one aircraft to a single enemy rocket or shell.

En route to the coastal town of Lowestoft further combat wings, detailed for Oschersleben, were met, the 41st and 94th, and the force proceeded across the North Sea toward the coast of Holland.

John Howland: Flak suits were donned as we crossed the coastline flying at 19,000 feet over a solid undercast. At 1052 hours we were over the north-east polder of the Zuider Zee when the pilot called me and asked for a mag [magnetic] heading home. I blurted out '245 degrees'. I wondered what was up as we broke away from the formation, went into a dive and started for home. Almost immediately we were ordered to test fire our machine guns. Shortly after we had done that, the tail gunner reported 'flak at 5:30'. I tried to see how close it was, but my vision was restricted. Things then quietened down. I went back to navigating and discovered that my 245-degree course was going to take us right over Amsterdam. To put it bluntly, it scared the stuffing out of me to realise we were heading for such a hot bed of flak. I grabbed the interphone switch and told the pilot to 'Fly 275 degrees, quick!'

We swung round to the new course and Lieutenant Jobe feathered the number 3 prop because oil pressure was dropping and oil temperature was rising. We were in a pretty steep dive at 16,000 feet with an indicated airspeed of 235 mph, doing our damndest to get away from enemy territory as quickly as possible. We were soon down close to the cloud cover. We would duck into them for protection in case enemy fighters jumped us. Tension on board the plane eased off considerably. The bombardier salvoed his forty-two 100 lb incendiary bombs over the North Sea.

Lieutenant Jobe had been forced to abort owing to the oil pressure and temperature problems, but managed to bring his B-17 safely back to Ridgewell. However not all the 381st's aircraft returned at the scheduled time, although it was known that some had landed at another airfield. John went to sleep, concerned about the welfare of his regular crewmates, and still unclear as to why they had aborted the mission when others hadn't. The next day he awoke relieved to find his colleagues all present. Throughout the day he was able to glean what had happened on the mission. Owing to expected bad weather a recall had been sent. Many heard it, some didn't, some chose to ignore it. Leading elements of the 2nd and 3rd BDs, near to the target, believed there was a possibility of visual bombing and carried on. Much of the 1st BD, with many later claiming not to have heard the recall, also pressed on.

James McPartlin, at the time a captain with the 1st Bomb Division's 91st Bomb Group, had also flown on the mission to Oschersleben on 11 January 1944, flying as a lead pilot with his squadron commanding officer, as part of the composite high box of the 1st Combat Wing. He would never forget this particular mission and gives a first hand account of the air battle between the 1st Bomb Division heavies and the Luftwaffe that day. As his formation neared the Dutch/German border they came across poor weather conditions; nevertheless the leader of their Combat Wing decided to press on.

> *James McPartlin:* We closed our formation and flew on instruments. A very scary situation for large formations loaded with ammo and bombs. My ship was named the Shamrock Special and with conditions like this I needed the luck of the Irish. Our weather did not last very long and we broke through the clouds to clear blue skies and beautiful sunshine.

It was then that German fighters, Me109s and FW190s pounced, falling on the American bombers from high cirrus clouds.

> *James McPartlin:* The attacks were on the lead and low Group. Two of our ship were hit badly and dropped out of formation with engines on fire, a third Fort exploded with no sign of chutes from the falling bird. My tail gunner, who always reported the activity in the rear formation, saw the two Forts that dropped out of formation. Both were shot down. Stragglers were almost always picked off. Little chance against a fighter.

As the formation approached the final run to the target there was a pause in the combat. But the bomber crews knew it wouldn't last as they watched their enemy prepare for the next engagement.

> *James McPartlin:* On both sides of our CW formation, enemy fighters were climbing up in long string formation to get in position for their frontal attack. I was surprised how long it took for them to pass us up to get in position. They were very close, but just far enough so our gunners could not reach them. It was a quiet time while we waited for the battle to

begin. The best guess from all the crew was that on each side of our formation there were at least 200 jerry fighters, both Me109s and FW190s. I did not see a twin engine in all that gaggle. The big question to all the crew was where the hell were our fighters?

Soon the German pilots began to turn their aircraft, preparing for the head-on attack. This, James McPartlin recalls, was:

> just slightly above our top box. This gave them position to fly through the entire depth of our formation and that is exactly what they did from both sides of the formation sometimes 6-8-10 abreast. The entire wing would light up with 20mm as they headed toward our formation. They flew through the formation and then did a half roll, giving our tail gunners a small chance for a kill. On many of the attacks you could see the face of the pilots as they flew between the B-17s in the formation, some colliding with the bombers. On one of the frontal attacks my top turret gunner destroyed an Me109. The pilot ejected and just missed hitting a Fort. My gunner made no effort to kill him, which would have been an easy target. During the continuous air battle we continued to the IP, about 3-4 minutes to the target.

It was then that the formation came into range of the German guns below. Jim McPartlin recalls the flak at Oschersleben as 'heavy and accurate', seeing 'one bomber blow up and several with smoke and engine fires'. Unsurprisingly, as a result of the aerial melee, the bombing at the target suffered. Owing to battle damage to the lead ship of the 91st BG, the bombsight was affected and the bombing fell short. But Jim McPartlin's composite formation placed its bombs accurately, inflicting severe damage on the target. Then the battered formations turned for home:

> *James McPartlin*: As we rallied off the target and began to regroup for the return trip, many of the Forts with extensive battle damage had great difficulty staying in formation. They knew the fighters would pick them off pronto. Some chose to abandon, or hit the deck and try to make it back to England. Some yes, some no. The trip home for us was uneventful. A little flak on the coast and a few fighters that were not aggressive enough for a fight. We had our share of flak and 20mm damage, but fortunately only the waist gunner had a superficial wound. We made it back to Bassingbourn in good weather and a smooth landing. The Shamrock Special Did Good.

John Howland would get his own first-hand account of this particular air battle from his normal pilot Jim Tyson, who was also in one of the aircraft that continued on to the enemy target.

> *John Howland's diary:* Jim tells of B-17s blowing up all over the place, fighters coming in one after the other, parachutes billowing and planes ramming. I am glad I wasn't there. I'm thankful Jim made it back OK. I really don't think Jim will have any trouble. He has lots of luck; and luck means a helluva lot around this place . . . Our squadron, the 535th, was the only Squadron in the 381st Bomb Group to get back without a loss. The 532nd lost three, the 534th lost one, and the 533rd lost six out of nine . . .

There's no way we can win this air war or survive our missions if the Brass is going to screw up like that very often.

It was Doolittle who ordered the recall, when he heard that the weather was closing in at the targets and the weather over the bases in England was also deteriorating. In fact of the 266 1st BD aircraft that continued on and attacked the target, 42 aircraft and crews failed to return. The 2nd and 3rd BD lost a total of 18 heavy bombers. Possibly the Brass, in some way, made amends as the 381st, along with other bomb groups, was awarded a Presidential Citation for battle honours, officially credited with shooting 28 enemy fighters from the sky. For Jim Tyson his first combat mission can certainly be described as a baptism of fire.

For the next ten days Jim Tyson's crew carried out training flights, with a short two-day trip to London in between, where the men witnessed some of the war damage suffered by the civilians in London.

> *John Howland's diary:* The Jerries sure pasted London. The bomb craters and buildings knocked out made me realize that Londoners have already seen a lot more war than most of our soldiers will ever see.

On return from London the crew took part in an unsuccessful air-sea rescue search, on 22 January, looking for any RAF aircrew who had been forced to ditch on the raid to Magdeburg the night before. On 24 January the crew was awoken, briefed and took off for an attack on Frankfurt. However when over the Channel the nose guns jammed whilst testing and Jim decided to abort. In fact a few minutes later the whole mission was called off. Doolittle again had stepped in when the weather over the targets was reported not as forecast, with poor conditions a possibility over English bases. However the bad weather failed to materialise over these bases and Doolittle received an unwelcome rebuke from Spaatz. Doolittle didn't want to risk the lives of his men unnecessarily. Spaatz questioned his subordinate's drive to forward the air offensive. The dispute would fade, prompted by a close call both men had, a few days later, when visiting bases in Spaatz's personal B-17. Good weather had been forecast but it deteriorated and following some perilous hedgehopping the B-17 was put down unceremoniously in a field. Doolittle would always maintain a distrust of long-range weather forecasts.[6]

On 26 January Jim Tyson's crew was again briefed for Frankfurt, but adverse weather intervened yet again and the mission was scrubbed. On 29 January Frankfurt was again detailed for attack, and this time Jim Tyson flew his crew to the target and back. Over the next month the crew took their part in carrying the bombing offensive to Germany; 30 January Brunswick (aborted), 3 February Wilhelmshaven, 4 February Frankfurt, 20 February Leipzig, 21 February Gütersloh, 22 February Oschersleben-Bunde, 24 February Schweinfurt, 25 February Augsburg and 2 March Frankfurt. (Jim Tyson had been ill in hospital on the last two missions, and the crew flew with a replacement pilot.)

Of particular note are the attacks in the third week of February. 'Big Week', as it was called, was a major attack on the German aircraft industry, by both the Eighth and Fifteenth Air Forces. It was a further attempt both to smash the German Air Force production plans and to draw the Luftwaffe into battle, not only with the heavy bomber formations, but with the escorting fighters as well, thus inflicting further heavy losses.

On these missions the crew ran the gauntlet of flak and witnessed the demise of some of their fellow airmen to both flak and fighters. There had been some close calls but to date the crew had been fortunate. The next four missions it took part in were to the heavily defended area around Berlin. Their first visit there on 3 March, with Jim back in the pilot seat, passed without major incident. The mission on 6 March was a different matter.

John Howland's diary: Up at 0345 and briefed again for Berlin. I didn't realise that I was setting out on the biggest adventure of my life at that time. The weather looked good. The fighter support we were briefed for was as good as we could get. Plenty of support on the way in and out. However there was only supposed to be one group of P-38s and one group of P-51s in the 300 mile area around the target. Col. Leber stressed that anyone who aborted would catch hell.

After crossing the Dutch coast the bomber formation was to fly virtually directly east to Berlin, carefully routed so as to avoid, as much as possible, flak defences. Just prior to Berlin a turn south-east would bring the formations to the Initial Points south of Berlin. Then a turn towards the targets, to fly into the wind. The 1st Bomb Division would front the attacking bomber force, with the 1st and 94th Combat Wings heading the way. The 3rd Bomb Division would follow with the 2nd Bomb Division in the rear. A planned 800 bombers and 8,000 bomber airmen stretched across 94 miles of sky, to be supported at various stages of the flight by small forces of escorting fighters, totalling nearly 800 Mustangs, Lightnings and Thunderbolts. Just before 11 a.m. on 6 March 1944, the 1st Combat Wing, at the head of the might of the Eighth Air Force, crossed the Dutch coast. In front of the American bombers lay heavily defended German air space. One of the greatest daylight air battles in the history of aerial combat was about to start and in its midst was Jim Tyson's crew. On crossing the enemy coast John Howland noted that their wing appeared to be off course and thus they ran into flak near Osnabrück. One plane was hit and had to abort.

John Howland's diary: We took some flak in the nose of our ship when a hunk of steel tore through the roof. It hit the armor plate in front of the pilot, bounced off, hit my helmet, and bounced again. Never did find the piece. It must have been about 3 inches long by the marks it made in the armor plate and on my helmet.

John began to get frustrated with what appeared to be poor navigation and when it appeared they were heading for further flak positions, despite knowing it was a violation of radio silence, he asked Jim to relay the information to the lead ship.

John Howland's diary: Jim complied, saying, 'My navigator has a pilotage fix placing us 15 miles west of Hanover. On our present heading we will pass directly over the town. Request return to flight plan course.' Response from the lead ship was immediate: 'Maintain radio silence over enemy territory! Over and out.'

However the lead ship altered course and passed Hanover. After passing

Brunswick and Magdeburg unwanted company appeared. German fighters closed in:

John Howland's diary: They hit the high group of our wing. We were flying [No.] 3 position, 2nd element of the low squadron, commonly called 'Purple Heart Corner'. I saw them start down from the left, but couldn't do a damned thing because I had no gun on that side of the ship. Their 20mm guns flashed and my first instinct was to duck behind the aluminium of the ship for protection. A few seconds later I realized it was rather foolish and came back to see what was going on. About that time, a Me410 whizzed by. He was so close I could distinguish features on the pilot such as oxygen mask and helmet. A fraction of a second later, there was an explosion with flying Plexiglass all through the nose compartment. I realised that we had been hit. However I couldn't seem to get my wits together to find out whether Frank or I were injured.

I then noticed that the window above my desk was completely gone and that both hands were bleeding, apparently from superficial wounds made by the flying Plexiglass. It was nothing serious so I turned my attention to Frank. I saw that there was a hole under Frank's left foot, and was worried whether he had been hurt seriously or not as he seemed to roll in his seat. Frank was okay. He was just looking for more fighters to shoot at with his chin turret twin fifties.

A few seconds before our ship was hit, a B-17 just above us and to our left was hit in the [No.] 4 engine. The plane had dropped down and was passing underneath us at the time we were hit by 20mm shells. My first reaction was that he had exploded. A short time after the attack, VE-N started smoking in the number 4 engine and had to drop out of formation. They didn't make it back to base.

Somewhere, out of my line of sight above us, another ship had been hit and the crew was bailing out. They were free falling, at our 26,000 ft altitude, trying to get safely through the formation and down to lower altitudes where they could survive. Through my broken window I saw one fellow falling end over end. He wasn't more than fifty feet off our left wing tip. However he cleared the formation, and disappeared from view.

While watching VE-N, (532nd Squadron marking) I saw a bunch of FW190s. They had queued up and peeled off to make a head-on attack on a wing that was flying to our right. One B-17 suddenly burst into a massive ball of flame that dropped like a rock. It hit another plane, knocking a wing off, and they both went down. There might have been three planes involved in the action, but I couldn't be sure. It was a horrible sight and I desperately searched the skies for parachutes. But there were none. All that we saw were four balls of fire as the gasoline tanks exploded.

Suddenly the interphone popped, and we heard the unmistakable Tennessee twang of our tailgunner, Arnold C. Farmer. The pitch of his voice told us he was excited. None of us could understand what he was saying. Jim Tyson gave him a brief lecture on intercom discipline, and he calmed down so that we could understand what he was talking about. We were pleased to learn that he had shot down a Me110 making an attack from the rear.

With intercom discipline obviously still fresh in his mind our headsets crackled just a few minutes later. The tailgunner was back again, this time with his normal, slow, Tennessee drawl.

'Tailgunner to pilot. Tailgunner to Pilot. Lieutenant Tyson, there are four Dee Oh two seventeen EEEs out back of us hyah, and they's a shooting rock . . . *Oh Lordy!* . . . Nevah mind, they missed us.'

The entire crew yelped with joy and roared with laughter, truly a release of pent-up emotion. The Dornier 217 bombers had each fired four rockets at the formation, but fuses were evidently incorrectly set for all missiles exploded about 500 yards in back of us. We then made a formation turn to the right heading for the IP. About that time some more Me410s attacked on our right. I blasted away with my 50 caliber. I don't think I hit anything.

The battered wing reached the target without further opposition of note. The lead ship then accidentally released half of its bombs, and with most of the other aircraft in the wing following its lead the target was missed. The wing then turned for and proceeded home encountering little opposition, which was being concentrated on other wings, although two aircraft were lost, succumbing to previously sustained battle damage. Our crew landed safely and after a lengthy interrogation during which the gunners made enemy aircraft claims, John Howland and Jim Tyson were ordered to see Colonel Leber.

John Howland's diary: 'Why did you break radio silence over enemy territory?' he asked.

'The lead navigator had his head up and locked,' I replied. 'Besides it was clear as a bell, and everyone in Germany could see us. We weren't giving away any secrets.'

Jim pointed out we had lost a ship, needlessly, over Osnabrück. 'It makes no difference', replied the Colonel. 'You are to maintain radio silence over enemy territory. Dismissed!'

Thoroughly chastised, and too tired to eat, wash up or give a damn, I made my way back to our room and went to bed.

The next day a mission was scheduled then scrubbed, but on 8 March the crew found itself once more over Berlin. In stark contrast to the previous mission they experienced little opposition, although other groups and wings did with 37 bombers not returning. The very next day the crew yet again took off for Berlin, with a strong accompanying fighter escort. Again, in terms of previous attacks on Berlin, very little opposition was met by the entire force, with flak near to the target the only major worry. However John again had his concerns over the lead ship's navigation and again he requested his pilot to ask the lead ship for a position. As before a curt reply was received: 'Maintain radio silence over enemy territory. Over and Out!'

On return to base a great sense of elation prevailed in the bomber crews mainly because of the low losses (only eight from the entire force). John attended the navigator's debriefing, where Major Delano asked some questions.

John Howland's diary: 'Where was the Group at 0945 and 1033 hours?'

asked the Major. There was no response. As the 'Unknown Soldier' of the 8th Air Force, it just wasn't my policy to speak up in such situations.

'Do you mean to tell me that no one knows where the Group was at 0945 hours?' continued Major Delano.

At that point I broke with personal policy and gave the Major latitude and longitude co-ordinates of our actual position at 0945 and 1033 hours.

Following the debriefing, Major Delano asked how I could be so certain of the Group's position. The other navigators used poor metro wind data and the solid undercast as an excuse for not having the data. I showed him my chart with the no wind plot. I then told how I had worked backward from the Bombs Away position over Berlin to find the actual wind and draw the DR plot. Nothing more was said.

Following interrogation and pilot and navigator's debriefing, Jim and I received an ominous message. Colonel Leber wanted to see us again.

'Why did you break radio silence over enemy territory again?' he asked.

'Colonel', I replied, 'we were flying in a ship without a Gee [electronic navigational aid[7]] Box, and we needed help from that Pathfinder ship to establish our position. My no wind plot showed us to be damned near in East Prussia. We were way overdue to the target area. I didn't want Jim to run out of gas before we got home.'

Colonel Leber's reply was brief and to the point. 'It makes no difference. You broke radio silence over enemy territory. *Don't do it again!* Dismissed!'

We had a 'Stand down' that night. After dinner I broke out a bottle of Canadian Club that I had stashed away in my footlocker. We celebrated surviving three Berlin missions in four days. But the ass-chewing we received for breaking radio silence was heavy on my mind. I reviewed my notes on procedures to be followed over enemy territory. I showed them to Jim. We passed the bottle and the notebook back and forth. Jim and I became more and more convinced that the Colonel was wrong.

It was about 1930 hours when a Jeep stopped in front of our shack and the driver told us: 'Colonel Leber wants to see Tyson and Howland.'

About that time, we wanted to see Colonel Leber. Jim Tyson stands a little over 6 feet, perhaps 3 or 4 inches taller than Colonel Leber does. As we walked into his office, Jim didn't hesitate. He walked up to him and said:

'Colonel, we had every right to ask for a position report on today's raid. It says so right in my navigator's instruction manual.'

'Just a moment', said the Colonel, 'Perhaps you are right. I didn't bring you down here to talk about that. I want to know if you would like to go to Pathfinder School and learn how to be a lead team'. Jim looked sceptical, and I smelled a rat. Our scepticism must have been apparent. He went on to say, 'It's all in this directive I just received. Here read it for yourselves.'

The directive requested Group Commanders to send two combat crews to Pathfinder School at the 305th Bomb Group, Chelveston. Group Commanders were also reminded that it was not an opportunity to get rid of unwanted crews, as their subsequent performance could reflect upon the record of the Group Commander who sent them.

John Howland's diary: Colonel Leber then said, 'Despite breaking radio silence, you fellows flew a good mission today, and on the 6th as well. I think you fill the bill.'

He then went on to extol the advantages of going to Pathfinder School. 'The study break away from combat duty will do you good. You will have an opportunity to lead and not make the mistakes you have observed in other lead teams. You will fly the best ships in the 8th Air Force, and there will be promotions.'

It all sounded pretty good. Jim and I looked at each other. We nodded in agreement. We would be on our way to Pathfinder School as soon as Colonel Leber could get approval and have our orders cut.

On 20 March 1944 John Howland and the crew arrived at the 305th Bomb Group at Chelveston, near Northampton. Early the next day John introduced himself to the group's staff.

John Howland's diary: This new set up is going to be quite a responsibility. I will be either the lead or deputy lead navigator for a Wing (54 ships). We will have a PFF Navigator (Mickey operator) in the radio room to help navigate when there is an undercast. Had a meeting of all PFF crew in the evening. Five crews were told to go to bed as they were scheduled to fly a lead mission tomorrow. We were among the five. Curtis E. LeMay formerly commanded this Group and has been promoted to command the 3rd Bombardment Division of the 8th Air Force. However he left behind a well-trained cadre of subordinates to carry on.

I asked 'We arrived yesterday. When does our training to become a lead team begin?' The Lt. Col. just shifted his cigar to the other side of his mouth and said, 'Lieutenant, as of right now you are a lead navigator. Get going!'

That was the shortest school and break in combat action I ever saw or heard of. I wonder about the rest of the crap that Col. Leber fed us concerning this job. It's beginning to look like we might have been conned.

For whatever reason the crew did not fly the next day but on 23 March they carried out their first flight on a B-17G that had been modified as a pathfinder ship containing Gee and H2X radar. John had the opportunity to look over the 'Mickey' ground radar set (referred to as the MKII radar, the person operating this airborne radar became known as the Mickey operator). The next day tragedy struck at Chelveston when one crew crashed on take-off, killing the entire crew and smashing into a barracks killing the seven men sleeping inside. Late on 25 March the crew was briefed to lead the 381st BG on a mission to Leipzig. It then flew to Ridgewell.

John Howland's diary: We went to bed in the MP site and they forgot about us. Briefing was at 0400. Someone finally remembered the PFF team was supposed to be there also. We were awakened at 0405. There was no time for breakfast.

Major Fitzgerald was to fly as co-pilot. We were to fly deputy lead for the group. The raid was to a factory near Leipzig. After rushing like hell to catch up with flight plans, chart courses etc., the mission was scrubbed just before taxi time. The PFF crews were told to go on back to Chelveston. The rest of the Group was told to get some rest since a short mission to occupied territory might be coming up in the afternoon. PFF planes and crews were 'too valuable to risk on milkrun raids'. I wonder why Col. Leber didn't mention that aspect of being a member of the Pathfinder Forces.

On 29 March Jim Tyson piloted his crew, with the addition of the CO of 533rd Squadron (381st Bomb Group) and the Mickey operator, on a mission to Brunswick. Frank Palenik had been replaced as bombardier on the mission, which was not popular with the crew, and the next day the crew were told that Frank would be leaving them permanently.

John Howland's diary: The entire crew is very upset at the prospect of losing our fine bombardier. Jim went down to see Col. Lawson, about the possibility of keeping him with us. But no soap. It seems General Williams put out the order. All 1st Division Groups will supply lead bombardiers, not the Pathfinder Force. We are beginning to see, and feel, the effects of all kinds of power struggles and political structures within the Pathfinder Force and the Eighth Air Force.

For the first three weeks of April 1944 John and the crew saw no action, mainly because of bad weather. However the Eighth Air Force maintained its offensive, particularly against the German aircraft industry and German secret weapon installations. On 24 and 26 April our crew carried out missions to an airport at Erding, near Munich, and Brunswick respectively. Upon reaching the coast on the return from Erding the crew had an unwelcome reception.

John Howland's diary: We had an undercast when we reached the coast and a few 'friendly' flak bursts were sent up through the clouds, evidently by a battery that couldn't read our IFF (Identification Friend or Foe) radio signals. One ball turret gunner didn't appreciate the reception and answered back with a few 'friendly' bursts pointed straight down.

About one week later, a notice was posted on the bulletin board advising all gunners, especially ball turret gunners, not to fire their guns over friendly territory. A farmer had complained about bullets making holes in the roof of his barn, and one bullet blew the bottom out of the milkmaid's favorite pail that was hanging on the wall'.

The next two weeks passed without operational duties for the crew. Their comrades in the Eighth still fought the fight in the air, maintaining the focus on depleting German air power and smashing enemy secret weapon installations. They would also initiate a series of attacks in support of the forthcoming invasion of France. However our crew, on their next mission, would be thrown back in at the deep end: it was to visit Berlin again.

CHAPTER 3

NIGHT BATTLES OVER GERMANY

Many of the airmen who flew with RAF Bomber Command in support of D-Day were still in their mid-teens when the war started in 1939. Since then they had joined the RAF, found their speciality, undergone training and formed with their crews. This process could last a couple of years. Some, like Ron Neills, Steve Masters and Ken Handley, would gain operational experience over Germany prior to making their contribution to the Normandy invasion.

When the Second World War started 16-year-old Englishman Ron Neills had only just left school and had begun work with British Rail. One day two of his colleagues approached him:

> . . . and tapped me on the shoulder saying 'we're going up to volunteer for the air force – coming?' As it was getting close to when my group was going to be called up I went. When I got home I told my mother what I had done. She did her nut, but there you are. I took the view that the water was too wet in the Navy. I didn't want a spear through my stomach in the Army. I thought well you've got a fair chance to jump out of a plane.

In the middle of 1941 Ron started his service life and began to learn his trade as a flight engineer. At that time the number of four-engined heavies in service with RAF Bomber Command was on the increase, replacing the two-engined bombers. The position of flight engineer was created to assist the pilot with the fuel and engine management of the aircraft.

> *Ron Neills:* They were a new breed for the bigger aircraft, who were an assistant to the pilot really. The course itself was 18 months when I went in. They did shorten it while we were going through on that system. So other people came in the air force after us, passed out as engineers and were shot down before we even got off the ground.

On completion of his 18-month-course Ron was transferred to a heavy conversion unit (HCU) at Waterbeach, Cambridgeshire. Here Ron met his crew, who had already formed as a unit at the operational training unit, prior to the HCU, flying twin-engined Wellington bombers. The complete fledgling crew began familiarising itself with the four-engined heavy bomber.

> *Ron Neills:* You always felt that being a new boy they knew more than you did, but when you work it out each one had his own job. We used to switch around when we used to go flying. I would go up in the mid-upper turret or something, or skipper might let me have a go in his chair, and we would bounce over the clouds.
>
> Alan Grant, the pilot, an Australian, was a lovely chap. Very quiet,

very efficient. Liked everything right and maintained a discipline in the crew. No funny talk on the intercom or anything like that. If you've got something to say, say it and don't hang about. Steve Masters was very meticulous. He was a good navigator, used to get us there on time. A navigator's got work to do all the time, with a little curtain over the front of where he sat and a little light behind it. On one occasion Steve came out to have a look, 'Good God' he said, shut the curtain and went back to his desk. Nat (Sydney Nathanson, wireless operator) was a funster. He was always laughing and had a good personality. He took to me and I took to him. Speed (Richard Martin) was the bomb aimer, called 'Speed' as being a Canadian he had that drawly speech. Tom Barrett, the mid-upper gunner, was a gay little lad, good for a gamble when we played cards. His wife was having a baby while we started flying together. Bill Newton, the rear gunner, was the other one in the crew that used to smoke and we had a thing before we went out. We always sat on the back of the tail and had a cigarette before we got in. The crew gelled. Once you were experienced, especially over Berlin, you closed in a bit and, whereas the Army and Navy mixed in large numbers, you more or less kept to your own crew. Something always happened to the other crew not yours – until it did.

Following satisfactory completion of the HCU course, the crew received their operational posting and in November 1943 reported to 622 Squadron at Mildenhall, Suffolk, to fly Stirlings. '*Bellamus noctu*' (we wage war by night), was the squadron's motto and it was not long before this applied to Alan Grant's crew. To familiarise new crews with operations they were often sent on supposedly 'quiet' trips, and in our crew's case this would be minelaying. Fortunately for the crew their first operation was quiet in terms of enemy opposition. However the perils of being part of a Bomber Command operation were not just of the enemy's making. Following the crew's briefing for minelaying off the Frisian Islands, and the boarding of their aircraft laden with six 1,500 lb mines, Alan Grant and his crew prepared for take-off.

Steve Masters: With my charts and instruments laid out on the navigation table I began to feel a bit more relaxed until with a good luck wish the groundcrew slammed the door shut. That was it. We were now committed as that door was not going to be opened again until we got back, unless of course we were in trouble and that didn't bear thinking about.

Brakes off, we taxied to the runway and as we lined up, well-wishers waved us goodbye and we were rolling. Gradually we gathered speed and with a slight lurch we were airborne, so now this really was it.

Nothing startling happened. German fighters didn't attack us, nor did we see searchlights or bursting shells. Not that we really expected to see anything as we were still over England but somehow the darkness around us seemed much more menacing than when we were on training flights. Eventually we crossed the coast and headed for the Dutch coast, our friendly England was left behind and we were on our own, but still no violent attacks. This wasn't quite the sort of activity to be expected but after all this was only a 'nursery trip'; maybe we would see more excitement on later trips.

Tension mounted a little as I announced that we were nearing the coast and were to prepare for the run-in. We descended to mining height and settled on to the required heading, then as we approached the starting point I called for mines to be released. The aircraft jolted as the first mine dropped, followed by the second, but no third or fourth either; in fact we had four hang-ups. This was an unpleasant experience, close to the enemy coast with 6,000 lb of sea mines strapped to the aircraft. We came to the end of the run and turned out to sea as briefed. We knew that we had to try again so I was told to reposition for a second run. The crew were now very alert for fighters as we reckoned that radar must have picked us up as we flew around the North Sea.

Alan Grant took his bomber through the second run but the mines again failed to release. Steve Masters gave his pilot a course for home.

Steve Masters: Approaching Mildenhall we informed the control tower of our situation and were quite calmly told we were clear to land. This was unbelievable as obviously they hadn't fully appreciated the situation so it was stressed that we had four sea mines still on board totalling 6,000 lb and we were just below our maximum landing weight, but back came the answer 'Clear to Land.'

We hoped they knew what they were doing and prepared to make our final approach. Naturally we discussed the likely reasons for the hang-ups and one suggestion was the possibility that the release mechanism was iced up. This being the case, what would happen if it thawed out? It was a disturbing thought that there was only a thin sheet of metal between ourselves and four chunks of explosive, any one of which was capable of sinking a ship. The skipper confirmed with the bomb aimer that the mines were set to 'Safe' and we felt a little better until he added, 'It doesn't make too much difference anyway as they are rather touchy things.'

Having digested that cheering piece of news we again tried to settle down only to be disturbed once more by the bomb aimer just as we were about a mile on the approach. In his slow, quiet, Canadian drawl, he said, 'This happened about two months ago not far from here and when the aircraft landed it blew up half the station.'

We got closer to the ground and the moment of truth was arriving: would the skipper be able to grease it on, we wondered? If so it would be the first time. It was not to be as when the throttles were closed we sank like a stone from about fifteen feet and hit the runway with a tremendous crash. This was followed by the sound of something breaking quite near to me. Were we still alive? We seemed to be, and we were still rolling, but what had been the sound of breaking? Was it something sinister happening in the bomb bay?

Quite by chance I looked down and there beside me was my smashed coffee flask; it had jumped clean out of the bulkhead pocket.

It was a rather shaken crew that climbed out of the aircraft in dispersal wondering that if this was a nursery trip what would the real thing be like?

On 30 November the crew completed another minelaying operation, again flying
a Stirling without incident. In December having said goodbye to the Stirling the
men began familiarising themselves with the workings of the Avro Lancaster. On
21 January 1944 they were detailed to take part in a raid to Magdeburg, their first
operation against a German target, and their first proper experience of hostile air
space.

After gaining height over England, Alan Grant's Lancaster became part of the
stream of 648 RAF bombers heading east, hidden in the dark. In such conditions
and such large numbers, formation flying was obviously out of the question.
Each bomber crew strove individually to follow the planned route and arrive at
the target at the time detailed. Much of the flight to and from the target was
characterised by its monotony, with crews working hard to maintain
concentration and vigilance. Every now and then crews would tense as enemy
ground defences, searchlights and flak, opened up, or they would see other
bombers suddenly catch fire, perhaps explode, or they would become aware of a
German nightfighter stalking them. On 21 January 1944, just after Alan Grant's
crew crossed the enemy coast, Steve Masters heard his crewmates tensely
commenting on their first sight of enemy opposition.

> *Steve Masters:* Being curious, I turned my chart lamp off then pulled aside
> the curtain to look out. I couldn't really understand what I was seeing at
> first but it was obvious that shells were bursting ahead of us and a few
> searchlights were to be seen. I had been accustomed to seeing such things
> before from ground level, and looking down on it was quite different. To
> add to my surprise I could see long lines of coloured lights running
> parallel to our track and I wondered what they were, but eventually
> decided that this must be a means by which ground defences were
> indicating our position to the nightfighters. Fascinated by these lights I
> kept watching them until I discovered that one particular line was getting
> shorter and shorter, what is more the lights were going out one by one
> with a little white flash.
>
> Suddenly the horrible truth dawned on me they were tracer shells, and
> what is more they were now being fired at us. For a little while longer I
> watched absolutely mesmerised to see the tiny red lights slowly climb
> towards us growing in size until with a sudden rush they hurtled upwards
> very close, but fortunately burst way above.

Steve returned to his navigator's table to guide his crew to the target. Once over
Magdeburg he felt the urge to see what a bombing attack on a city looked like:

> I once again stuck my head out from behind my curtains to see what was
> going on. I was expecting to see fires and searchlights but what I did see
> took me by surprise as there seemed to be lights everywhere. To me it
> looked like a peacetime version of Piccadilly Circus; there was a great big
> circle of lights hanging in the air surrounding the target and this was
> crossed by parallel lines of lights rather like roadways. In addition to this
> there were several other groups of lights dotted all over the sky. I had little
> idea of what it was all about, as they seemed to serve little purpose. The
> story told to me later which I had no reason to disbelieve was that once

the Germans had discovered where we were bombing they had instructed aircraft to drop flares to enable their own fighters to make a visual homing towards the attacking bombers. Our own fighters carried similar flares, which they dropped in different areas to help confuse the defending German fighters.

On the return route a navigational error almost brought the crew over the heavily defended city of Hamburg, with searchlights active and shells bursting. Steve soon realised that the variation setting control (taking into account differences between magnetic and true north) on his compass had not been adjusted and was still that of base. He quickly made the adjustment and Alan Grant took his crew on a quieter route, avoiding the perilous sky over Hamburg, and brought his crew home safely. Other crews had not fared so well. German nightfighters had penetrated the bomber stream and RAF Bomber Command lost 57 aircraft and 400 airmen. On 27 and 30 January Alan Grant took his crew to Berlin, and again our crew's good luck held out, although that of 66 other crews did not.

'It was what we remembered of the first world war soldiers, the poor bloody infantry, that I opted for the air force.' Recalls Ken Handley. He had always been good with his hands. He had spent eight months in 1941 helping in his local technical college, training girls to mend Tiger Moth wings. He was then called up and unsurprisingly his RAF training took advantage of his practical abilities. After applying for and being accepted for aircrew he began training as a flight engineer. In September 1943 Ken was posted to a heavy conversion unit at Marston Moor, Yorkshire, where he was to be crewed up ready for operations. Here he met and joined an otherwise all Australian crew, which had already flown and trained together, and established a crew bond. But now that they were converting to the four-engined heavies they needed help, something Ken could provide. 'Their attitudes were laid back, the whole lot,' he remembers. 'I was just one of those Pommies, but we blended in as a crew right from the start.'

Verne Westley was the navigator on the crew, and explains:

> We were an all Australian crew, except Ken, and therefore we had much in common although we came from differing walks of life: grazier (pilot), customs officer (myself as navigator), dairy farmer (bomb aimer), wheat/sheep farmers (wireless operator and mid-upper gunner), orchardist (rear gunner) and school teacher (engineer, Ken). We got on very well together both in the air, on the ground and on leave. Ken soon was an Australian and we enjoyed his company and efficiency.

> *Ken Handley:* Jack Scott was the pilot. He inspired a confidence right from the start. No bravado about him and he chatted with you as though he was just one of the crew rather than being in charge. Discipline when we were on a Bullseye [navigation exercise] or on a bombing raid was certainly there. You only spoke when required and then shut up and got on with your job. He was one you could take to and when you went out as a team he paid his full share in the kitty.

Verne Westley was the navigator. He was very laid back, having the same disposition about his job. Sometimes when on a trip we'd say, 'Where are we?' He would reply, 'I don't know where we are, we're just about there.' But he knew his job, there was no problem about knowing whether he had the right fixes or not.

Ron Tickell, the bomb aimer, woke up every morning with a hacking cough; he would smoke like the blazes. He was a chap who we felt could take over if the skipper was hurt and do his damndest.

Tom Drake-Brockman was the mid-upper gunner and we looked to him as the old man of the crew, but with experience brought from his former tours. We listened to him almost in awe, in a sense far more than to the skipper, but with the two of them you felt you had a good crew. Whereas Jack was on his first tour, Tom had experience and would tell you either when we were in the flight or beforehand what he thought we should do.

Ken Oaks, the rear gunner, was a round tubby chap, jovial, up for a drink, whisky just like mother's milk. He was out to enjoy himself socially. But in his turret in the sky he did his job properly, no extra words. How he could rotate that turret and fall out backwards when he had to, I don't know.

Max Pointen, the wireless operator, was the only one who didn't seem to blend fully with the crew. There was no question of him not doing his job but when we went out on the town as a crew he seemed to be the odd one who stood back a little bit.

Early in 1944 Ken's crew was posted to 466 Royal Australian Air Force Squadron at Leconfield, Yorkshire, but, unlike Alan Grant's crew, there was to be no easy entry into operations. It would be one of the hundreds of crews, used in the all-out effort to smash Germany direct. On 15 February 1944 the crew attended their first operational briefings, to attack Berlin. Fortune favoured them that night and despite once having to take evasive action and seeing fighter flares around the target and on the return flight, all returned safely. Other crews were not so fortunate, with 43 aircraft lost from the 891 that took part in the attack. Two 466 Squadron aircraft failed to return: one crew were all captured and there were no survivors from the other crew.

On 19 February Jack Scott and his crew were again detailed for operations, to conduct another deep penetration into Germany. On this night RAF Bomber Command sent 823 aircraft to Leipzig, of which 78 failed to return in what was to be RAF Bomber Command's heaviest loss of the war to date. Jack's crew met trouble on the outward journey over the Frisian Isles, receiving the attention of flak and searchlights which plucked the Halifax from the protective darkness. By throwing his Halifax through climbs and turns, Jack managed to break contact and return to the relative safety of the night. Both on the way to Leipzig and on the return Ken Handley saw numerous fighter flares going down, but once more fortune favoured the crew although one 466 Squadron crew did not return; all the men lost their lives. On the night of 24/25 February the crew took part in an attack on Schweinfurt and again encountered and witnessed considerable opposition.

Ken Handley's diary: Taking off we circled base and then set course at 4,000 ft 'down' England. Climbing out over the Channel we made 20,000 ft over France. Searchlights and cones were seen 50 to 100 miles away over the French coast. The rest of the trip was uneventful up to the target area. There the ground and sky markers could be plainly seen. No clouds obscured the target and it was shown up by cones of searchlights and fighter flares. The ground markers, giving off their orange colours, were spread over the target area. The town was blazing up like 'hell let loose' and fires could definitely be seen. Evasive action was taken running up to the target to keep clear of searchlights, one of which picked us up after bombing. Diving down we eluded it and almost 'cleaned up' a Lancaster below us. Flak was coming up but very little reached us for we bombed at 22,500 ft and climbed up to 24,000 ft out of the target area. One aircraft was coned by searchlights over Frankfurt and everything was thrown up at him including the 'kitchen sink'.

Jack Scott brought the crew back safely but RAF Bomber Command lost 33 aircraft from the 734 that took part in the operation. Jack had flown his Halifax and novice crew through three operations from which 154 aircraft had failed to return.

The crew made early returns from the next two operations, to Augsburg (25/26 February) and Stuttgart (1/2 March) owing to an unserviceable intercom and icing respectively. The following operation to Stuttgart was completed to the crew's satisfaction, despite considerable flak and searchlight opposition and having to avoid fighters a few times. 466 Squadron lost two aircraft on the Stuttgart raid. Pilot Officer Wills Halifax was intercepted by a nightfighter, but despite suffering burns, he kept the aircraft steady whilst his crew bailed out. All men survived, but all bar one were captured. Flight Sergeant Bond's Halifax was also badly damaged in a nightfighter attack forcing Bond to ditch his aircraft. One man was lost in the incident and never found. The rest of the crew were all rescued.

The next operation would take Jack's crew to Frankfurt and accompanying them in the bomber stream was Alan Grant's crew. Since the Magdeburg raid Alan's crew had been on operations to Berlin, and, as Ron Neills describes, were 'hot targets no doubt about it, but we got away with two'. However they would find the next operational flight on 18 March even hotter, though Jack Scott and his crew fared better.

At 6.45 p.m. that evening Jack lifted his Halifax from the Leconfield runway, climbed then flew to the south coast of England. After crossing the Channel they entered enemy air space.

Ken Handley's diary: Over the French coast Ken [Oaks, the rear gunner] saw the exhaust stubs of a fighter coming towards us and taking evasive action we lost him. We flew through a thin misty cloud all the way to the target area. Searchlights were seen miles away. The turning marker was not seen when we turned into the target. A glow was seen below the misty cloud and we bombed from 21,500 feet. Sky markers were seen. Flak was coming along light to moderate. Leaving the target area we landed in the middle of a 'shower' of searchlights and used plenty of evasive action to get clear of them. Tom saw a Ju88 over the target and Ken saw one or two other fighters. We left the target glowing good and proper. The misty cloud saved us from the searchlights. The rest of the trip was uneventful.

For other crews the trip was not so uneventful: three Halifaxes were lost by 466 Squadron, with only four out of 21 men surviving, all captured. Alan Grant's crew had met opposition on nearing the target.

Steve Masters: We had settled down on the bombing run, and I with pencil poised was waiting to record the time of bomb release, our speed and heading. Suddenly I heard Tom, the mid-upper gunner, scream, 'Look out Bill' then at the same instant as both turrets opened fire, there was a terrific explosion in the fuselage which left us stunned for an instant. 'Corkscrew port,' shouted Bill and down we went like a ton of bricks with me trying to prevent my navigation instruments from flying off the table in all directions. For a brief period confusion reigned. Everyone was trying to get his own particular message through: I was telling the wireless operator to go back and put the fire out, which was burning under the mid-upper turret; he was trying to tell everyone we were on fire, and the bomb aimer could be faintly heard trying to say something.

This was all too much for the skipper, who raising his voice, gave us the order to 'belt up' which we obeyed immediately and silence was restored. During this time we were still hurtling earthwards in the first stage of our fighter evasive tactics.

'Now,' said the skipper, 'what were you saying, bomb aimer?' and back came the reply in his normal slow and quiet Canadian drawl. 'I can pick up the target markers, go left, left, steady, ease out of your dive,' followed by 'bombs gone'. That was a relief at least, considering that we were on fire still.

'Right, wireless operator, what were you saying?'

'We are on fire in the vicinity of the mid-upper,' came the reply.

'Alright, go back and see if you can put it out,' was his order. During this exchange I was getting desperate as I knew my information was absolutely essential otherwise we would tangle with Mannheim [they had been warned about the Mannheim defences at briefing] but at last my turn came and I was able to get my message through.

While this was going on I could see that the fire was beginning to make the mid-upper uncomfortable as it was flaring up around his seat. After wriggling about a little while, I was not surprised to see him get out of his turret, fortunately unharmed. When comparative calm had descended on the crew, the skipper carried out his normal routine check asking each crew member to report in turn. We were very thankful to hear that all were present and uninjured except for Tom who had not answered. I explained this away by reporting that he was standing near his turret, but when I looked he was not to be seen. One of us was detailed to find out what had happened, but before we could move he reappeared looking rather dishevelled carrying a fire extinguisher. It later transpired that he had climbed out of his turret to put the fire out but during our violent aerobatics he had slipped in some oil and had finished up by the Elsan. Regaining his feet he had struggled forward again only to discover that the fire had been blown out by the stream of air coming through the shell hole to our side.

The crew now all accounted for, we should have felt happier, but Bill the rear gunner had reported that his turret was out of action and could only be rotated manually. This was not a good situation, so as soon as Tom was plugged into the intercom he was told of the trouble with the rear turret which meant he would have to be doubly vigilant. There was silence for a few minutes until Tom spoke up, 'Skipper, I hate to tell you this, but my turret is also out of action.' This was disastrous, we were defenceless.

After a few experiments it was discovered that one turret was capable of firing its guns but had to be manually manipulated, whereas the other turret could not fire. By careful co-operation between the gunners and a bit of luck, we might survive another attack.

I would have given anything to avoid the searchlight belt which we were now approaching but our orders were very strict: we had to cross it [informed at briefing that other tracks would be more dangerous]. It may have been that the fighters were patrolling outside the searchlight belt waiting for those who decided not to face it, but whatever the case, despite our fears, we didn't see another fighter all the way home.

After we landed we naturally examined the damage, which appeared to have been a 20 mm cannon shell in the fuselage and smaller calibre machine gun bullets in the tail unit. These had been fired from a Ju88. On closer inspection we discovered that the bomb bay floor had several shrapnel holes in it, so perhaps our 4,000 lb bomb had been burning when we dropped it. The biggest shock was waiting for the wireless operator whose attention was drawn to a large shrapnel hole caused by a piece which had gone out through the fuselage about nine inches behind his head. The turret failure and fire puzzled us until it was discovered that one hydraulic line to the mid-upper turret had been ruptured by the shell and on the other side of the fuselage the rear gunner's hydraulic line was pierced by a piece of shrapnel causing a hole less than one-eighth of an inch across.

If only that fighter had known our situation it might have ended differently, but then again we did not know his fate as he had come up against two very determined gunners who at one stage were firing at him from pointblank range.

In total RAF Bomber Command lost 22 aircraft on the raid. Many other crews had close calls, but skill and good fortune brought them home. On the morning following the raid, news of Alan Grant's crew's encounter with the enemy soon got around.

Steve Masters: Walking down to the crew room I happened to meet our skipper who was on his way to his own section. Having greeted me he gave me a very strange look and asked me what I had been up to and was I feeling alright. I told him I was fine except for feeling a little tired, but this was understandable as we had been on an operational sortie the night before.

'I have been getting some very strange comments,' he said, 'from people asking how seriously you have been hurt; others have asked which hospital you were in and several other odd questions.' I assured him I was just as puzzled as he.

'Very strange,' he continued, 'as these people seemed to know that we had been engaged in combat, but I assured them we had not been hit in any way and you certainly hadn't been injured.'

I again repeated that I didn't understand it as he was the first person I had spoken to that day apart from the other crew members.

'Then you had better get it sorted out,' he said. 'It is embarrassing to keep being asked. They have most likely got us mixed up with another crew, although it seems they think I am hiding something.'

I continued to the crew room still wondering where these stories had come from but as I entered the door there was a bit of commotion and I became the centre of attention. Then the questions came, 'Was I alright, was I badly hurt, how did I get out of hospital so soon?'

This was followed by a quick visual check to see if there were any signs of injury, but they could see none.

'What is this all about?' I enquired. 'My skipper has been questioned as well and he is just as mystified.' Still with an air of disbelief, I was led to the table where all the logs and charts from the previous night's sortie had been placed, then picking up a log and chart they asked if it was mine. I agreed it was which was hardly necessary as my name was on it and also it was signed by me. 'Then how do you account for this?' I was asked and turning to the appropriate place they pointed to the entry '0253 Attack by Ju88'. From that point on all the way down my log sheet right until the time I had signed off was a smear of blood.

It now all became very clear to me and was very easily explained. As the fighter made its attack we went into our usual diving turn, which was quite violent and although I had managed to grab most of my navigation equipment my pencil had dropped on to the floor. Reaching down to retrieve it, my little finger caught a piece of sharp wire and was slightly cut. At that moment I was extremely busy and had no time to stop the bleeding. From that time on I could not stop it whatever I did, I licked it, dabbed it, wrapped my handkerchief around it, but log keeping was then very difficult so I just had to let it bleed, hence the continuous smear of blood.

When I had described the simple facts, their sympathy turned to scorn. 'Was that all it was?' they asked. 'We imagined we had a hero in our midst qualifying for a gallantry medal; we feel let down.'

There was nothing much I could do to rectify the situation except go out and get myself injured, but as I didn't fancy that, I did the next best thing and slipped out quietly to join the rest of the crew having jam on toast at the local cafe.

On 22 March Alan Grant once more took his crew to Frankfurt, this time without major incident, and then they completed a relatively uneventful raid to Essen on 26 March. It would be one month before they next went into battle. Meanwhile Jack Scott's crew continued to see action over the Reich.

At Bomber Command stations all over England on 24 March 1944, 5,600 airmen attended briefings for that night's operations. Every one of these airmen would be ordered to visit the same target, Berlin. They were to crew 577 Lancasters, 216 Halifaxes and 18 Mosquitos and take 1,000 tons of high explosive to blast the German capital. In addition 1,500 tons of incendiaries were to be dropped to, as their Commander-in-Chief put it, 'burn out the black heart' of their enemy.

One of these crews was captained by Flight Lieutenant Picton, who lifted his 550 Squadron Lancaster off the North Killinghome runway at 6.30 p.m. into a dark but clear starlit sky. Throughout the winter of 1943/44 Picton and his crew had been in the frontline of Bomber Command attacks against Germany. They had had their close calls on these operations, surviving a combat with a Ju88 on a previous raid to Berlin and a mid-air collision on a raid to Stuttgart.

On this night RAF Bomber Command planners tried a number of ruses to keep German nightfighter controllers confused, attempting to minimise losses. Picton flew his Lancaster as part of the bomber stream that proceeded across the North Sea, over Denmark and the Baltic, before turning towards Berlin. It was hoped that an American raid on Schweinfurt, in southern Germany, earlier in the day would have kept much of the German air defenders in the south. Hopefully a training flight over France by 147 Bomber Command aircraft also persuaded the German controllers to keep their airmen in the south. However, unpredicted strong winds had dispersed the bomber stream, making it a larger target for the German 'Tame Boar' nightfighters.[8] On the route from the Baltic to Berlin RAF Bomber Command aircraft began falling prey to their Luftwaffe adversaries.

Since the raid to Frankfurt a week earlier, Jack Scott's crew had flown one further operation, which had been a relatively quiet trip minelaying near Kiel. On 24 March Jack's crew was detailed to contribute to the Berlin raid.

Ken Handley: Taking off in daylight, we climbed to 6,000 feet and setting course continued at 6,000 feet to 5 degrees east. From there we climbed to 20,000 feet over the enemy coast. Just north of Sylt we saw searchlights and flak coming up. Tom and Ken saw an aircraft hit the deck with a bang. A Lancaster came across our tail being 25 to 50 feet away. Ken hardly knew what to do. Searchlights were seen over Kiel and it was relatively quiet up to the target area. We did banking searches every now and again. Over the target fires could be seen plainly and ground markers were showing up well. A slight haze hung over the target area and searchlights predominated. Flak, tracer and rockets were being sent up at us. Three combats were seen. An aircraft was circling the target area and broadcasting a commentary. A Lancaster and Mosquito acted as MCs [Master of Ceremonies]: 'Hello everyone, hello everyone. The reds are going down now. Get into them,' and other comments. This eased the tenseness of the situation.

Out of the target we ran into a belt of searchlights and left track to scout them. There were hundreds of them and flak was being sent up into the cones. Evasive action was taken to get away from stray searchlights and also banking searches. We saw cones over the principal towns on the route and light flak. Putting the nose down over the coast of Holland we maintained 200 IAS [indicated air speed] to the English coast and made base at 6,000 feet and let down. Very tense over the target area and a slight reaction the following day.

Flight Lieutenant Picton had arrived over Berlin having avoided contact with the enemy. At 22.31 hours his bombs fell, from a height of 21,500 feet, then just after leaving the target area Picton's crew had company. The German nightfighter's cannon fire took out the mid-upper gunner and rear gunner, causing both men serious injury. Picton's wireless operator, Sergeant Williams, had been in the astrodome at the time and after warning his captain, he continued reporting the nightfighter's position, giving evasive instructions. They managed to lose contact with their foe at which point Sergeant Williams hurried down the fuselage to his rear gunner. Sergeant Porteous's oxygen tube was severed, and Williams gave his injured colleague his own as he helped him out of the turret. Once the situation was stabilised, Williams then radioed home requesting medical aid be available immediately they landed. Fortunately the return route was fairly direct and when Picton landed at 01.47 hours the injured airmen were rushed away for treatment and both survived.

Picton and his crew had managed to return, and those unscathed would go on to meet their enemy in combat again. Others had not been so fortunate. On leaving Berlin the German nightfighters penetrated the bomber stream in numbers and the carnage began. In total 72 bombers failed to return from the raid, the vast majority shot down on the return route.

CHAPTER 4

THE INESCAPABLE COMMITMENT

In this chapter we will look at the strategic considerations for the *Overlord* campaign and the pathway to the expected role that air power could play. This was no easy process. But of course, these decisions directly influenced the nature of the airmen's operational tours.

By the beginning of 1944 Germany's war machine had suffered serious setbacks. The Russians were pressing forward and punishing the German Army on the Eastern Front. The RAF was inflicting unprecedented bombing devastation on German cities and had embarked on the formidable task of the destruction of Berlin. The USAAF had joined the bombing campaign, penetrating deep into Germany to wreak further destruction and engage the Luftwaffe, with fighters as well as bombers. The Germans had been thrown out of North Africa, then Sicily but were vigorously defending Italy, whose forces had capitulated. Despite the defeats, Germany was showing no signs of collapse and the war appeared far from over.

On 17 August 1943 British Prime Minister Winston Churchill, American President Franklin D. Roosevelt, Canadian Prime Minister William Mackenzie King, and their advisers and Chiefs of Staff had met at the Quadrant Conference in Quebec to further plans for the opening of a second front against Germany. It was decided that Operation *Overlord*, the invasion of mainland Europe across the English Channel, would become the primary military campaign in Europe in 1944. Even though the Allies were to maintain the offensive in the Mediterranean, the cross-channel land invasion was seen as the means of securing the defeat of Germany in Western Europe. This of course required Allied armies to make a major assault across the sea at some point on the Atlantic coastline of Europe. The Germans realised it would come, of course, and Hitler had begun to throw resources into his 'Atlantic Wall', constructing beach defences and coastal gun emplacements and laying minefields. However, there were 3,000 miles of coastline to defend; the task of adequate fortification was formidable. Priorities would have to be made, which would expose weaknesses. The assignment for the Allied *Overlord* planners was to formulate a method for identifying weakness, then breach the Wall and break out beyond.

Plans for an invasion had started prior to Quadrant. Earlier in 1943 Lieutenant-General Frederick Morgan had been designated Chief of Staff to the, as yet unappointed, Supreme Allied Commander (COSSAC), and with his staff they were tasked to form an outline plan for the conduct of *Overlord*. It soon became clear that the best invasion sites were the beaches of the Pas de Calais and those of Normandy. Both areas were within range of air cover from England and sufficient force could be landed to establish a foothold and then break out. Eventually the Normandy beaches were chosen, mainly owing to the perceived German defensive strength in the Pas de Calais. Whilst COSSAC detailed the initial plans for the invasion, the chain of command needed to be addressed.

Wranglings over the command structure for *Overlord* were long and drawn out, American or British influence in key positions was keenly sought and political rivalries surfaced. Eventually American General Dwight Eisenhower was appointed Supreme Allied Commander, chosen for his experience gained in the Mediterranean campaigns, and the experienced airman Air Chief Marshal Sir Arthur Tedder took on responsibility as his deputy. General Sir Bernard Montgomery, on the back of his success in North Africa, received command of the land force, Admiral Sir Bertram Ramsay command at sea and Air Chief Marshal Sir Trafford Leigh-Mallory, formerly head of RAF Fighter Command, command of the Allied Expeditionary Air Force (AEAF).

Leigh-Mallory's initial appointment to lead the AEAF, gave him command of the US 9th (Tactical) Air Force, the RAF 2nd Tactical Air Force, and Air Marshal Sir Roderic Hill's Air Defence of Great Britain (previously known as Fighter Command). Leigh-Mallory was a fighter commander of some considerable experience; he was a controversial figure during the RAF's successful opposition to the Luftwaffe during the Battle of Britain in 1940, and had commanded the fighter forces on the Dieppe raid in 1942, in which the need for air superiority for any cross-Channel campaign became apparent. Indeed Leigh-Mallory believed that the battle for control of the skies would be fought above the Normandy beaches and he should be in charge of the overall strategy. As we shall see, this point of view was not shared by other Allied air force commanders. When planning his campaign for *Overlord* Leigh-Mallory was to venture into new territory by seeking the assistance of the strategic bomber forces. Unfortunately he fell short in the popularity stakes with the heavy bomber commanders, who saw him as having little understanding of the use of strategic bombers. Neither Sir Arthur Harris, Commander-in-Chief of RAF Bomber Command, nor General Carl Spaatz, commanding the United States Strategic Air Force, wanted to subordinate their commands to the influence of someone they considered a tactical commander, who would look to divert them from their responsibilities under *Pointblank*. Throughout the first few months of 1944 the role of the strategic bomber forces, and the command structure needed to fulfil their purposes, was hotly debated. Eisenhower, however, maintained his conviction that he should be given command of all the air forces during *Overlord*.

> . . . when a battle needs the last ounce of available force, the commander must not be in the position of depending upon request and negotiation to get it. It was vital that the entire sum of our assault power, including the two strategic Air Forces be available for use during the critical stages of the attack. I would accept no other solution, although I agreed that the two commanders of the heavy bombing forces would not be subordinated to my Tactical Air commander-in-chief but would receive orders directly from me.[9]

This, Eisenhower would delegate to Tedder, whom he viewed as 'not only an experienced air commander, but in addition enjoying the confidence of everybody in the air forces, both British and American'.[10] As Air Commander-in-Chief in the Mediterranean in 1943, Tedder had guided his air forces supporting the Army triumphs in North Africa and the invasions of Sicily and Italy. Once Eisenhower had been appointed Tedder had become the ideal candidate as his deputy, through whose offices he could attempt to bring the AEAF and the strategic bomber forces under one control. Tedder, when he arrived back in England to take up his new post, was tasked to form an overall *Overlord* air plan through discussion with Harris and Spaatz, with Leigh-Mallory under Tedder's supervision, working on a tactical air plan. Then, through the Chiefs of Staff, Eisenhower and Sir Charles Portal, the Chief of Air Staff, would seek sufficient heavy bomber resource to be allocated to support the land battle. But, as we shall see, Leigh-Mallory still sought, and indeed considered himself having, significant influence over RAF Bomber Command and the US Eighth Air Force, particularly during the tactical phase of the battle for Normandy, just prior to and after D-Day.

Essentially there were four phases to the invasion campaign. The preliminary phase was January to February 1944, during which much of the detailed planning took place. The main task of the strategic bombers, as experienced by our crews already, was to be the weakening of Germany's air force and war potential, all of which fell within the Casablanca directive, and later *Pointblank*. The preparatory phase, March to May, initially involved a continuation of *Pointblank* and attacks on rail targets through which enemy reinforcement would have to pass to reach the invasion battle area. Nearer to D-Day itself, and still within the preparatory phase, there would be a focus on tactical targets, notably those rail centres closer to the assault area, radar installations, airfields, naval targets and *Fortitude* targets. *Fortitude* was the codename for the deception plan for *Overlord*, whereby the Allies would attempt to mislead the enemy into believing the main thrust of the invasion would fall on the Pas de Calais coastline. The assault phase, D minus 2 to D plus 1, involved a complete air commitment to the support of the invading forces, attacking coastal batteries, beach defences, radio countermeasures and diversionary operations. The requirements placed on the heavy bombers during the follow-up phase from D plus 2 onwards was dependant on the progress of the land battle, but probably to focus on the German air force, rail, bridge and other targets of opportunity, such as enemy troop positions.

The first problem for the planners was to ensure sufficient Allied troops and armour landed on the selected section of the French coastline to break through the German defensive crust. Once this was achieved enough ground had to be overrun to secure airfield space and to set up and establish the supply lines from England across the Channel to the beaches and the front line. Whilst this was going on the German forces would be striving to throw the invading army back into the sea. The German soldier and his armour would be sent to engage his enemy via the road and rail networks in the invasion area. Both sides would be racing against time, the Allies to establish their armies and position, the Germans to amass enough opposing forces to counter effectively and destroy the Allied build-up. Hence for the Allies it was a major requirement to slow the German build-up in the chosen area, and air power, the British and American fighter and bomber forces, was seen as the means of achieving it. It was a major commitment, particularly for the American and British heavy bomber forces, and one that would not be entered into gladly by the two heavy bomber commanders, Sir Arthur Harris and General Spaatz. Harris's force would be the first to receive the call for direct action.

When Tedder first arrived back in England, after his appointment in late 1943, he ensured that Professor Solly Zuckerman, who had successfully planned the rail bombing in support of Mediterranean campaigns, be involved in the planning process for *Overlord*. On 31 December Zuckerman flew from North Africa to England and immediately set to work on the *Overlord* air plan. Zuckerman considered the initial AEAF plans flawed, of too tactical a nature, and he was requested to devise his own. On 10 January 1944 the AEAF Bombing Committee, chaired by Air Commodore E. J. Kingston-McCloughry, considered a first draft of a new plan, which, in general, was accepted, with Zuckerman and Kingston-McCloughry to work on some amendments. Throughout January Zuckerman, Kingston-McCloughry and AEAF planners worked in general harmony devising their contribution to the strategic plan in support of *Overlord*. Zuckerman would later write that: 'In my innocence, I did not realise that it was all too good to last. Those first three or four weeks in January were passed in a state of euphoria, working to all hours . . .'[11]. One particular product of their labours, henceforth called the Transportation Plan, called for a crippling of the rail system in north-west Europe and the destruction of the bridges linking road and rail routes to the proposed Normandy battle area. The 'euphoria' within the AEAF planning circles would be short-lived once the Allied heavy bomber commanders got wind of the sizeable commitment planned for their commands in the AEAF plans, particularly in the Transportation Plan.

RAF Bomber Command's Commander-in-Chief Air Chief Marshal Sir Arthur Travers Harris did not want to relieve the pressure he felt his force was exerting directly on Germany, by diverting his heavy bombers in support of an Army campaign. Within a few days of his arrival in England, Zuckerman, under prompting from Portal, had met and spent an evening with RAF Bomber Command's commander.

> I had never met him before and was much taken by his quiet sense of power and determination. No two of the many air marshals whom I already knew were alike, but he seemed more remote, more self-contained, than any I had met before. He changed into a mulberry-coloured velvet smoking jacket and disappeared into the kitchen to prepare Eggs Benedict with his own hands, so revealing to me that the culinary arts were one of the joys of his life. At the end of the meal he also surprised me by the ceremonial way he prepared what I took to be snuff. But after his wife left us, there was no question of my telling him anything about air operations in the Mediterranean. Nor did he put any questions to me. He began by expressing his bitter dismay that Ira Eaker was about to be transferred to the Mediterranean Theatre in place of Tooey Spaatz, who was returning to the United Kingdom to become commanding general of all the American Air Forces in Europe. This transfer he described as a disaster, and the sacrifice of a man whose heavy bombers had become

more and more effective over the course of the preceding year, and who understood about the vital importance of the strategic bombing of Germany, which he thought Spaatz appreciated not at all.[12]

Zuckerman was somewhat surprised that Harris had not quizzed him that night about bombing operations in the Mediterranean. That would come the next morning at breakfast.

He had only one question to put, he said, and he wanted a straight answer, 'yes or no – nothing more'. 'Could heavy bombers be used to bomb coastal defences?' I paused a second, and then said, 'yes'. It was clearly not the answer he wanted, and no further word was spoken.[13]

Early in January 1944 Harris, having discovered that his force was being considered for direct support to *Overlord*, had circulated a paper expressing his concerns. His stance was realistic, appreciating that his force would be called upon, describing the support of RAF Bomber Command as being an 'inescapable commitment', but he had his own opinions as to the best use of his strategic force.

Sir Arthur Harris's memo: It is thus clear that the best and indeed the only efficient support which Bomber Command can give to Overlord is the intensification of attacks on suitable industrial centres in Germany as and when opportunity offers. If we attempt to substitute for this process attacks on gun emplacements, beach defences, communications or dumps in occupied territory we shall commit the irremediable error of diverting our best weapons from the military function, for which it has been equipped and trained, to tasks which it cannot effectively carry out. Though this might give a specious appearance of 'supporting' the Army, in reality it would be the gravest disservice we could do them. It would lead directly to disaster.[14]

Since he took over as Commander-in-Chief in February 1942 'Bomber' Harris, as he became universally known, had turned the RAF's strategic bombing force around. Early in the war, apart from propaganda opportunities, RAF Bomber Command was making little impact on German military might. Yet by the winter of 1943/44 Harris commanded the most destructive bombing force ever engaged in the history of warfare. Indeed he had demonstrated on numerous occasions, such as the thousand bomber raids of 1942, the unrelenting bombing of the Ruhr, and the fire-storming of Hamburg, that the RAF's heavy bombers could inflict previously unimaginable devastation on the enemy. Harris contested that the bomber offensive could win the war outright provided further resources were made available, and provided the American bomber forces adopted a similar targeting policy. Harris also held the opinion that all this effort was not being recognised. He was not noted for his diplomatic skills, and his strong sense of purpose, combined with a resolute and often inflexible attitude, often caused friction outside RAF Bomber Command. When Tedder arrived in England in January 1944 he viewed Harris as 'being something of a dictator who had very much the reputation of not taking kindly to directions from outside his own command'. But Tedder also felt confident in assuring Eisenhower that 'if Harris were given specific orders to carry out specific jobs, he would do them loyally'[15]. And future events would back up Tedder's guarantee. Within his command Harris certainly had the respect of his subordinates, from group commanders right down to the aircrews and groundcrews.

However, Spaatz wanted to defeat the Luftwaffe and he was after a target system that would draw it into battle, which he believed he could win. But he did not believe that the battle for air supremacy would be fought over Normandy. Both he and Harris shared faith in the ability of their respective commands, but Spaatz would develop a belief that Harris's campaign of bombing Germany into submission was faltering. A week or so before D-Day Spaatz had informed Zuckerman of 'his view that Harris was "all washed-up", that the German nightfighters and ground defences had made night bombing too expensive, and that the chance to attack nodal points of the railway system of northern Europe had come just in time for [RAF] Bomber Command.'[16] However, both commanders were convinced that the proposed use of their bombers in support of *Overlord* was a misuse of their weaponry and they would fiercely defend their corners.

On 15 February, at a meeting at AEAF headquarters, Stanmore, the latest draft of the AEAF *Overlord* Air plan was presented to the senior air commanders. Confirmation was given that the Allied heavy bombers would be 'diverted' to support the invasion. Harris and Spaatz had difficulty controlling their anger. Leigh-Mallory opened the meeting by stressing the need for the disorganisation of the French and Belgian rail network. Spaatz weighed in first with his objections, the minutes of the meeting recording that:

> the Outline Bomber Plan appeared to disregard his present directive, which had only just been confirmed in a signal dated 13 February. He disagreed with the statement in the Plan that the decisive battle for air supremacy would not be joined before the launching of the Overlord assault; he thought it was essential that air supremacy must be won before that date. He felt that many of the suggested rail targets in western Germany would not contribute to that end since bombing attacks on them would not necessarily bring about air battles, as the Germans would fight to defend only Berlin and targets in the east of Germany. General Spaatz added that these railway targets would be engaged by the strategic bombers only when visual bombing was possible. General Spaatz then indicated that with the extension of operation Pointblank from an attack on a small number of specific aircraft factories to an attack on a variety of other German targets, the whole of his available effort in VIIIth Bomber Command would be absorbed.[17]

Not only was Spaatz concerned about the diversion from his attrition battle with the German air force, but both he and Harris were sceptical that their heavy bomber forces could achieve the required accuracy on such small targets without sufficient good weather. Following the meeting Harris would state in a memo to AEAF that the requirements made on his command 'cannot be fulfilled, and I am compelled to disavow any responsibility for the consequences which their non-fulfilment will entail'. At the conclusion of the 15 February meeting Spaatz turned to Leigh-Mallory asking when he was expecting to take control of the strategic bomber forces in implementing the *Overlord* Air Plan. When Leigh-Mallory replied '1 March' Spaatz responded, 'That's all I want to know; I've nothing further to say.' Zuckerman would later write that 'he left the meeting determined to do everything in his power to prevent his Strategic Air Forces coming under Leigh-Mallory.'[18] Tedder would write to Portal on 22 February stating that 'Spaatz has made it abundantly clear that he will not accept orders, or even co-ordination, from Leigh-Mallory.'[19] Unsurprisingly with such stubborn resistance apparent from Harris and Spaatz, the 15 February meeting concluded without any clear direction except for agreement that representatives of both RAF Bomber Command and the US Eighth Air Force would look to develop the planned use of the heavy bombers with Leigh-Mallory's staff. A further meeting on 25 February, which yet again involved considerable debate, again failed to bring about a definite decision on the use of the heavies. On the same day Harris fired off a minute in an attempt to bolster his position, complaining that the bombing offensive against Germany was not receiving the recognition it deserved.

> I understand that incontestable evidence derived from Most Secret sources exists to show that the continuance and probable intensification of the Offensive is regarded in the highest Nazi circles as something which, in the absence of unpredictable errors by the Allies, will certainly ensure a German defeat comparatively quickly by producing a collapse of morale as well as of production on the Home Front.

Harris then went on to challenge the observation that Germany was apparently showing outward apathy to the bombing. 'In sum, there is every ground for describing the reaction of the German people to bombing as one of despair, terror and panic, barely controlled even by the brutal systems of Nazi policing.'

Harris then called on the Joint Intelligence Committee (JIC) to investigate the level of German morale. On 4 March 1944 the JIC sub-committee produced a report suggesting that the bomber offensive was indeed adversely affecting German morale and industrial military production and causing the 'German High Command serious concern at a time when they appreciate that the opening of another major front is imminent.' However the report did go on to conclude that the direct support of *Overlord* had become the overriding priority.[20]

Despite Harris's open reservations about bomber support to *Overlord*, there are indications that he had resigned himself quite early on to his perceived diversion from the main purpose of bombing Germany direct. On 17 February 1944 he had requested more Mosquitos for his command, particularly his Pathfinders (8 Group), on the grounds that he would need them to conduct all the operations in support of *Overlord*.[21]

Although Eisenhower and Tedder both backed the Transportation Plan, at the start of March 1944 the heavy bomber forces remained under the control of the Combined Chiefs of Staff, who would have to agree to any change of priorities. It was decided that RAF Bomber Command should undergo an experiment. On 4 March 1944 Air Vice-Marshal W.A. Coryton (Assistant Chief of the Air Staff (Operations)), issued a directive to Harris concerning targets for attack by Bomber Command prior to *Overlord*:

> Sir, I am directed to inform you that a review has been made of targets for attack by Bomber Command during the present and forthcoming moonlight periods. The purpose of this review is to provide targets, the attack of which is most likely to be of assistance to 'Pointblank' and 'Overlord' either through the actual destruction of supplies and equipment of use to the enemy or by providing opportunity to obtain experience of the effects of night attack of airfields, communication centres and ammunition dumps, before operation 'Overlord'.

The directive went on to request attacks on Friedrichshafen, a major centre for German tank production, and industrial targets in the occupied countries. Then specific rail marshalling yards were named at Trappes, Aulnoye, Le Mans, Amiens/Longueau, Courtrai and Laon. These attacks were to be an experiment. The use of ground-marking techniques was specified, and the directive specifically stated that analysis of the raids would provide data to assist in the planning of *Overlord*. In addition it was noted that further rail targets would be subsequently identified as the *Overlord* plans developed.[22]

On the night of 6/7 March 1944 RAF Bomber Command opened up its direct support to *Overlord* as part of the preparatory phase; 261 Halifaxes and 6 Mosquitos were sent to unleash their destructive payloads on the railyards at Trappes. Harris's airmen were under scrutiny. Their commander did not believe, or did not want to be shown publicly believing, that they had the weaponry or ability to achieve the necessary degree of precision. His airmen would prove him wrong.

Just after 8.30 p.m. on the evening of 6 March 1944, Squadron Leader Stephens, piloting his RAF Bomber Command 109 Squadron Mosquito over German-occupied France, received his call sign, to begin his run-in to a target he was to identify and mark for the heavy bombers that would follow. His navigator switched on a transmitter thereby identifying their exact position to ground stations, called the Cat and Mouse, in England. Stephens then flew his twin-engined aircraft along the circumference of a circle, which had the Cat station at its centre. In his headphones he heard a steady tone if his path were true. A slight deviation closer to the Cat and the tone became dots, further from the Cat and he heard dashes. The Mouse station tracked the Mosquito along its path sending position signals. The navigator heard morse code As ten minutes from target, then at 8 minutes from the target he heard Bs, at 6 minutes Cs, and at 3 minutes Ds. As they closed in on the target, the navigator awaited the release signal, determined by the wind speed, aircraft speed, height and ballistic qualities of the payload. The signal finally came through, five dots followed by a 2^1/$_2$ second dash in his headphones.

At 2042 hours two caskets, each weighing 250 lb, fell from the bomb bay of Mosquito LR500 of 109 Squadron, which was flying at 26,000 feet. A few hundred feet above the ground the caskets burst open and the candles inside ignited, cascading to earth, and forming a bright red burning pool. The aim had been good; the first of these target indicators (TI) fell 70 yards from the aiming point, the second 140 yards.

Thousands of feet above the target, bomb aimers had been peering through the nose blister of their four-engined Halifax bombers, searching the darkness below for the red markers they had been told about at briefing. Once the markers burst into life the bomb runs could begin; each Halifax pilot lined up his aircraft, following his bomb aimer's instructions, such as 'left, left steady, steady' and then 'bomb's gone', and the explosives plummeted to the target.

Soon more TI burst below, dropped by another Mosquito. In the space of approximately 30 minutes 2,046 bombs totalling 699 tons fell on the railway marshalling yards at Trappes. Just after the attack on the western section of the railyards had finished, a 109 Squadron Mosquito lined up on the circumference of the circle, which this time passed over the eastern end of the Trappes railyards. At 2114 hours two TI fell from the Mosquito and the heavy bombers came in. In the next 20 minutes two further salvos of red TI marked the target and 1,582 bombs, weighing 555 tons, ripped up tracks, wrecked rolling stock and tore down engine sheds.

In the early hours of 7 March 1944 all the RAF Bomber Command aircraft returning from the raid to Trappes landed safely in England. They had experienced little opposition on their excursion into northern France. Only two engagements with enemy aircraft were reported and one of these was found to be friendly fire from another Halifax.

The very next day following the Trappes attack an RAF 541 Squadron Spitfire took off from Benson, arrived over the railyards, photographed the area and sped back to base in England. Two days later a further reconnaissance sortie returned with photographs of the railyards. The RAF Bomber Command analysts could be well pleased with the bomber crews' efforts. Extensive damage was apparent across the railyard and 190 hits were counted as directly on the tracks. Fifty bombs fell on rail lines carrying rolling stock, derailing and destroying many of the wagons. There was further damage to engines, engine sheds, electric lines and footbridges. The raid was a clear success but there had been one disturbing outcome. To the north-west of the target area bombs had fallen on French houses, killing and injuring civilians. In the context of RAF Bomber Command operations carried out in previous years, this raid could be deemed very accurate. Nevertheless the proximity of the target to residential areas meant there was always the risk of friendly civilian casualties. But as shall be seen, in terms of the desired outcome of the war, the Allies had to deem this risk not only necessary, but acceptable.

The next night RAF Bomber Command's experiment continued. The Le Mans railyards were targeted, and 304 aircraft were despatched. Bombing had to be conducted through cloud but post-raid analysis suggested a successful attack. The next experimental operation on French railyards took place on 13/14 March, also to Le Mans, and again a successful attack was conducted for the cost of just one Halifax from the force of 222 aircraft. Amiens was the next target detailed for attack and on the nights of 15/16 March and 16/17 March, 140 aircraft (3 lost) and 130 aircraft (no losses) respectively pounded the railyards causing considerable devastation. On 23/24 March an RAF Bomber Command heavy bomber force went to Laon. Over the target the master bomber, there to control the raid and ensure bombing did not spread outside of the target area, curtailed the bombing after 72 of the 143 aircraft despatched had released their bombs. Although the railyards were hit the bombing was somewhat scattered. Only two aircraft failed to return.

It is also worth noting that from these six experimental operations on the French railyards, of the 1,206 aircraft despatched only six had failed to return. In the same period three major operations to German targets had been conducted, by a total of 2,525 aircraft with 92 aircraft lost. This is a clear indication of the risks to bomber crews conducting operations to Germany, compared to operations to the French railyards. What of the overall results with respect to the experimental task set before RAF Bomber Command? Harris's men appeared up to the challenge. Through skill and application they had proved they could achieve the degree of accuracy necessary for the execution of the Transportation Plan.

Whilst the RAF Bomber Command airmen initiated the devastation of the French railyards, the Allied Air Commanders continued the debate about the best use of the strategic bombers in support of the Normandy Invasion. During March Spaatz presented and lobbied for support for an alternative to the Transportation Plan. By targeting German oil, falling within *Pointblank*, Spaatz believed that not only could his bombers greatly reduce enemy fuel production, but that targeting German oil would force the German Air Force to defend. He was still after a fight and he believed his bomber and fighter forces could withstand the attrition better than the Luftwaffe. Spaatz felt this was the one sure way to achieve daylight air superiority and his Oil Plan was certainly perceived as having merit, receiving serious and careful consideration. Not by Harris, however, who regarded the Oil Plan targets as being of the 'panacea targets . . . supposed by the economic experts to be such a vital bottleneck in the German war that when they were destroyed the enemy would have to pack up'.[23] He had no belief in attacking such target systems, again seeing it as a diversion from the main area attack policy.

Matters came to head at a meeting on 25 March. The day before Tedder had produced a paper expressing his views on the best use of the Allied Air Forces in support of *Overlord*:

> The choice, therefore, lies between the Oil Plan and the Transportation Plan. No one can question that the Oil Plan, in view of the proved ability of the U.S. Strategic Air Forces to carry out precision attacks deep in Germany, would ultimately have grave effects on the whole German war effort. It is difficult, however, to see evidence to support the view that it could be expected to take real effect in time for Overlord or the land operations following the assault. Moreover, it is not a plan in which [RAF] Bomber Command can take any really effective part, and it is one in

which AEAF would be unable to take any part at all. The Oil Plan, is in fact, not really an alternative to the Transportation Plan as regards [RAF] Bomber Command and the AEAF.

The Transportation Plan is the only plan offering a reasonable prospect of disorganising enemy movement and supply in the time available, and of preparing the ground for imposing the tactical delays which can be vital once land battle is joined. It is also consistent with Pointblank. Since attacks on Railway centres have repercussions far beyond the immediate targets, attacks on such centres within the Reich will certainly assist in creating the general dislocation required for Overlord. Moreover, since the Railway system is one common denominator of the whole war effort, it may well be that systematic attack on it will prove to be the final straw.

This plan also:-

a) Makes concentration possible: all the Air Forces, day and night, short range and long range, can in their various ways operate against the one system with one common object.

b) Provides excellent bombing targets: practically every bomb falling within the area of a railway centre pays its way; the proportion of ineffective hits for these targets is lower than for any other targets.

c) Allows for flexibility: by giving a wide selection of targets and allowing Commanders freedom to develop their attacks in accordance with the weather and other tactical and technical factors affecting their particular forces.[24]

Tedder's paper went on to recommend that *Pointblank* be replaced with a new *Pointblank/Overlord* directive, indicating that the German air force and certain rail centres in Germany and western Europe be the main objectives of the American and British strategic air forces. Tedder recommended that the directive, following agreement between Eisenhower and Portal, be issued by Eisenhower, who would direct the respective air forces. The implementation of the Transportation Plan was to be effected through the offices of Tedder, assisted by representatives of the key stake holders, notably including Harris, Spaatz and Leigh-Mallory.

At the meeting on 25 March the best use of the heavy bomber support to *Overlord* was again hotly debated. Eventually Harris would come down on the side of the Transportation Plan, seeing it as the lesser of two evils, believing the large number of precise 'panacea' targets within the Oil Plan was beyond his command's capability. Spaatz was not so easily persuaded. He felt that the Transportation Plan would fail to bring the German air force up for a fight. Spaatz was determined to defeat his enemy in the air and only by attacking what he considered vital targets would the Luftwaffe seek to oppose him in force. And once the German pilots were in the air, his American fighter pilots and heavy bomber gunners could destroy them and their machines. However, despite seeing value in the Oil Plan, which could be seriously considered at a later date, Eisenhower came down on the side of the Transportation Plan, and Chief of the Air Staff, Air Chief Marshal Sir Charles Portal, in concluding the meeting said that there appeared to be no suitable alternative.

The matter was passed to the British Combined Chiefs of Staff for a decision who passed control of the strategic bombers to Eisenhower, who in turn delegated authority for controlling the heavies on to Tedder. Effectively Tedder's 24 March recommendations were adopted. Despite further protestations from Harris and Spaatz, in the middle of April 1944 Eisenhower presented his first directive to the Allied heavy bomber commanders. Harris would be the more compliant of the two. Spaatz still sought an offensive against German oil.

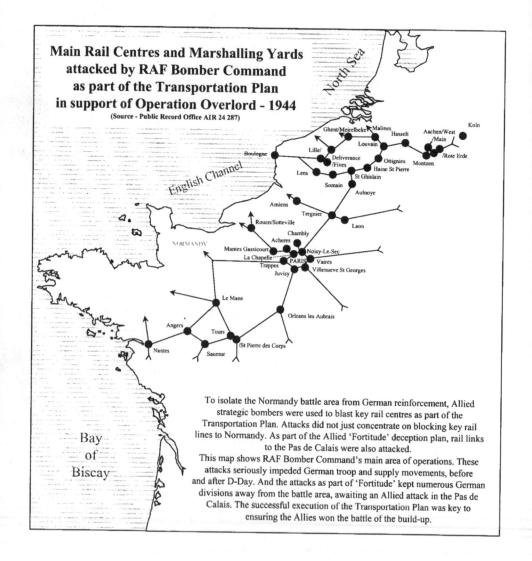

Main Rail Centres and Marshalling Yards attacked by RAF Bomber Command as part of the Transportation Plan in support of Operation Overlord - 1944

(Source - Public Record Office AIR 24 287)

To isolate the Normandy battle area from German reinforcement, Allied strategic bombers were used to blast key rail centres as part of the Transportation Plan. Attacks did not just concentrate on blocking key rail lines to Normandy. As part of the Allied 'Fortitude' deception plan, rail links to the Pas de Calais were also attacked.

This map shows RAF Bomber Command's main area of operations. These attacks seriously impeded German troop and supply movements, before and after D-Day. And the attacks as part of 'Fortitude' kept numerous German divisions away from the battle area, awaiting an Allied attack in the Pas de Calais. The successful execution of the Transportation Plan was key to ensuring the Allies won the battle of the build-up.

CHAPTER 5

ARMING THE RESISTANCE

Aerial bombardment was not the only means by which the Allied air forces could support Overlord. *Dennis Field's story continues and provides a personal insight into another aspect of the contribution made by the heavy bomber forces.*

As the year 1943 closed, RAF Bomber Command pilot Dennis Field and his crew arrived for operational duties with 90 Squadron, based at Tuddenham, Suffolk.

> *Dennis Field:* First impressions of our new base in the drizzle were not exactly exhilarating. Directed to the sergeants' mess we found it nearly empty but a cheerful log fire was blazing. Shortly afterwards the rest of the bods arrived and we had a beer and found a bite to eat. A friendly ground staff 'chiefy' directed me to a board in the foyer where our names were listed for a hut on No. 1 site. Having ascertained its general direction we trudged in the blackness with kit bags and cases past the WAAF site to a group of Nissen huts nestling beside a line of dripping trees and entered our new abode. Two-crew accommodation included the iron stove in the centre, and blankets and sheet were piled on the beds, which had a locker by each. The other crew nodded their welcome with the bomb aimer's comforting aside that we were the third crew in those beds in the last two months.

At this stage of the war the Stirling aircraft's limitations, mainly in terms of its operational ceiling against that of the Halifax and the Lancaster, had resulted in it being excluded from taking part in main RAF Bomber Command operations against German targets. Nevertheless other duties were found for it, notably attacks on German V1 (flying bomb) launch sites under construction in northern France, minelaying and SOE (Special Operation Executive) commitments. 90 Squadron was one of the 3 Group Stirling squadrons that had minelaying responsibilities and on 2 January 1944 operations were on. Dennis Field's crew was one of those detailed and following crew briefing, individual planning and collection of flying kit and transport to their aircraft's dispersal, the crew climbed aboard and checked over their four-engined bomber. With everything in order the crew disembarked and awaited the time to start the engines and prepare for take-off.

> *Dennis Field:* As take-off time approached we clambered back inside, closed the door and struggled with bulky equipment in the dark into our respective positions. Settled in, the engines were restarted, everyone checked as ready and the chocks signalled away. One of the groundcrew then guided us with torches carefully from the hard standing. I taxied the

heavily laden aircraft around the blue-lit perimeter track and on to the runway in use between the twin lines of white lights stretching and converging into the distance. Every loaded take-off in a Stirling amounted to an adventure in itself. Too rapid full throttle before adequate speed had built up for rudder control could readily develop swing but tardy full power lengthened the take-off run. There was never much runway to spare and usually it was a question of just about heaving her clear before the boundary.

Once airborne the crew settled for the flight ahead, and to apply themselves to their respective tasks.

Dennis Field: Each crew position was inevitably cramped and confined, but was left only in necessity and briefly during an operation. Gunners probably suffered most in the circumstances. Dressed in bulky clothing to withstand the cold, they filled the narrow turrets, restricting movement. They were isolated from other members of the crew and throughout the flight had to remain constantly vigilant staring usually into complete or near darkness. Much willpower was demanded to combat concentration-sapping fatigue. The wireless op., when not at his set, provided extra observation from the astrodome and dispensed an occasional drink of coffee. The second 'dicky' [second pilot] seat was taken up by either the bomb aimer or the flight engineer to assist the pilot and to help with forward observation and map-reading. In our case, Arthur sat there except when occupied in his bomb-aiming compartment. The flight engineer was preoccupied almost exclusively on an uncomfortable spa seat adjacent to the navigator, supervising engine dials, maintaining the fuel check and balancing tanks and petrol supply to each engine. The navigator had little time for pause, working almost continuously on his charts, calculating winds, turning points and times, course alterations and striving to obtain confirmatory fixes by Gee, pinpoint, W/T, astro or drift. Common to all was unrelenting application.

The crew's first operation proved uneventful, but their tour of operations had begun. At this stage of the war a tour of duty for main force RAF Bomber Command crews consisted of 30 operations. On the return to base Dennis called in to the flight office and 'chalked up 1' against his crew's name on the ops board. 'It was a start but thirty in ones seemed a long way off.' Two weeks later Dennis acted as second dickey with another crew attacking a V1 'ski'[25] site in the Abbeville area. This was followed up with two more attacks on ski sites in the Cherbourg peninsula with his original crew. There was one rather unpleasant incident experienced by a member of the crew whilst on one of these operations:

Dennis Field: I had my usual physical reaction when Alan said over the intercom the gut-tightening 'enemy coast coming up' and after a bit of a struggle in the confined cockpit seat, I managed to relieve myself contentedly into my can and Eddie took it carefully back to drop down a flare chute. Unfortunately, he let it go down the first of these and a volume of my nasty nature immediately blew back up the second before he could get out of the way. He received scant sympathy when he luridly related his woes over the intercom and when we'd stopped laughing rewarded him with predictable ostracism.

On 27 January Dennis and his original crew conducted a minelaying trip to Heligoland and on 28 January 90 Squadron aircraft and aircrews were again detailed for operations, minelaying in Kiel Bay. Although Dennis's crew was not one of those detailed, Gordon Royston was required to stand in as rear gunner on another crew, owing to their rear gunner being ill.

> *Dennis Field:* We pulled his leg about getting easy stooge trips in but we did not like being split up. We expected him to bustle in around dawn, so when he did not arrive I went to flying control to enquire, but nothing had been heard of them. Their target had been Kiel and other crews reported very difficult flying due to severe icing. Many things might have happened and it is possible that they became badly iced up and progressively lost flight control. Ditching in such circumstances would have been very difficult and even if successful, chances of survival would have been slim. We were shattered and it was difficult composing a letter to Yorky's parents and family trying to express our feelings and to soften their anguish. The wives of two members of the crew, who lived nearby, were expecting their first-born.
>
> As replacement, Jim Blackwell, a tall, fair-headed, very likable but quiet and phlegmatic, Aussie from Adelaide joined us. His previous crew had for some reason or other been broken up. Even the worst of landings evoked no protest but the rest made up for him.

The entire crew including Gordon Royston had indeed been lost and none of them were ever found.

Through February operations came and went for Dennis and his crew, but soon the crew began preparing for a new kind of operation.

The aerial bombing of railyards and bridges was not the only means of disrupting enemy communication networks in France. There was help available on the ground in the occupied territories, through the Resistance forces.

Officially established in the summer of 1940, the Special Operations Executive (SOE) was tasked to encourage and support Resistance networks in those countries under enemy oppression. SOE recruited trained and placed agents for the co-ordination of subversive action and supplied equipment to execute sabotage, enable communication and provide arms. The transport of agents into occupied countries and supply of equipment to the underground units required aerial support. Early in 1941 a call was made on the RAF, whose support was eventually reluctantly given. Sir Charles Portal, Chief of the Air Staff, had in one instance, not wanted his force to be associated with what he considered as unethical conduct.[26] Small units of aircraft initially assisted, but demand grew and on 25 August 1941, 138 Squadron was formed within RAF Bomber Command to conduct the special operations. In February 1942, 161

Squadron added to RAF Bomber Command's SOE contribution, and both squadrons settled at Tempsford airfield in Bedfordshire.

As the Allied invasion of western Europe approached SOE began to make a strong case for the support that the French and Belgian Resistance network could offer. They argued that subversive action would greatly assist with the build-up to the battle by the harassment of enemy troop movements. In January 1944 SOE began planning the increase of arms supply to the Maquis[27] groups operating in the south of France. In addition to normal SOE operations 186 extra sorties were requested for the arming of the Maquis during the February moon period (2nd to 16th). A total effort called for 282 successful sorties, comprising 60 from North Africa (specifically to supply the Maquis) and 222 from England (60 by the Tempsford Squadrons, 36 by a USAAF Squadron for normal work, 30 by the RAF's No. 38 Group and 96 by Stirling squadrons to supply the Maquis). If this could be achieved SOE claimed that in addition to normal special operations, arms for a further 16,000 men could be provided. Each sortie would involve the dropping of containers full of weaponry, the number of containers depending on the carrying capacity of the aircraft and the distance to the dropping zone. As an example, in February 1944, a load of 12 cylinders could be carried from England to a drop zone near Lyons, providing 4 Bren guns (with 1,000 rounds per gun), 18 rifles (150 rounds per gun), 70 Sten guns (300 rounds per gun), 145 lb of explosive, 10 pistols (50 rounds per gun), 80 Mills grenades and 24 Gammon grenades.[28]

During the February moon period, however, weather conditions proved unfavourable with only 10 out of the 60 sorties from North Africa completed. SOE planned to address the supply arrears to the Maquis in the March moon period; in particular a request was made to RAF Bomber Command and the USAAF to make more aircraft available, 33 Stirlings and 12 Liberators respectively. This could provide an extra 135 sorties from England to add to the planned repetition of the February effort from England of 126 sorties. An estimated arms supply to the Maquis, for approximately 20,000 men. SOE was seeking to ensure it could contribute to the build-up in Normandy. There would be more than just one front for the Germans to deal with in France when battle commenced; not only the head to head battlefront in Normandy, but also the less clearly defined interior front.

It also worth mentioning here, briefly, that in addition to *Overlord*, the Allies were planning an invasion on the south coast of France, to coincide with the Normandy assault. Codenamed *Anvil* (later changed to *Dragoon*) this was to act as a diversion, draw in German forces and prevent Hitler reinforcing the Normandy front. This operation would not place any direct bombardment demands upon RAF Bomber Command and the US Eighth Air Force. However it would need the support of the Maquis, which was to be armed through Allied heavy bomber supply drops.

In making the request for more Allied heavy bomber SOE sorties, however, there was a problem. Sir Arthur Harris, in particular, was extremely reluctant to divert any more of his bombers from what then was his all-out attack on Berlin, and the Chiefs of Staff were showing indifference towards SOE's cause. Indeed the *Overlord* planners at SHAEF were not convinced that the Resistance networks could cause sufficient disruption to warrant such an allocation of resources. In particular, with regard to the cutting of rail lines, AEAF Bombing Committee's Chairman Kingston-McCloughry noted on 10 February 1944 that 'it would be unwise to rely on their success to the extent of reducing planned air effort,' and he was backed by General Morgan, who in agreeing with Kingston-McCloughry noted that ' we must continue to do as we have in the past and treat any dividend we may get out of SOE as a windfall.'[29] Basically the *Overlord* planners were not prepared to gamble on the success of SOE operations. But SOE had one influential supporter on their side, Winston Churchill, and late in February 1944 he intervened, strengthening the case for an extra allocation of resource from RAF Bomber Command and the Eighth Air Force to be made for supply drops to the French. Churchill got his way.

RAF Bomber Command called upon 90 Squadron to meet its quota requested for SOE operations. The nature of the operations placed a requirement on some crews for further training.

> *Dennis Field:* Recent rumours of allocation to low flying work were fortified during the February full moon period when we were sent on a cross-country, flying at 500 feet, and I felt a bit wary about balloons and trigger happy defences but they had all been well briefed and we had free rein getting used to map reading and judging height over hills and valleys. Low level is always exciting and under such conditions this was especially exhilarating. Whatever our future duty, however this was the meagre sum total of our preparation for it, although more information of its nature filtered through in the coming weeks.

However throughout February operations for the crew consisted solely of minelaying duties. On one non-operational day flight the crew welcomed company and Dennis had the chance to test the technical prowess of his aircraft against that of one of his Allies.

> *Dennis Field:* One day we were formatted on by a Fortress. Exchanging waves from the cockpit, I mused that the Yanks, doing parallel work to us, were a friendly bunch without the reputed arrogance. When he showed off his kite by lowering the flaps I did the same and likewise when he put down his undercarriage, rather consciously noting how much longer ours took. Then he feathered an outboard engine, and not to be outdone I followed suit but had to use almost full power and a lot of rudder and aileron to keep her straight and level. After each gambit their skipper waved and laughed. But when he feathered another prop I gave the cocky bounder best, reciprocating his salute as he peeled off in a predictable traditional manner.

On 4 March 1944 Dennis and crew found themselves detailed to take off in their first special duties operation as part of 90 Squadron's requirement to supply the French Resistance network with arms and ammunition. This required a longer briefing than for previous operations, in an atmosphere of high security.

Dennis Field: In early afternoon Alan and I reported to the station intelligence offices where we met two army officers who gave us precise details of our 'drop'. The exact latitude and longitude were defined and we were issued with large-scale maps of the area and of the general route. The composition of, and means and height for dropping, our containers were told to us and also the recognition letter, which would be signalled from the ground and without which we were not to deliver. We were given time on target with reasonable latitude either way. The absolute importance of secrecy was impressed on us. All maps must be handed in on return and no reference made or record kept of the target position other than necessary for navigation. If we landed elsewhere than Tuddenham, no debriefing would be allowed except to report to base as to success or otherwise of the operation.

At dusk Dennis lifted his Stirling from the Tuddenham runway and in the moonlight gained height as he piloted his aircraft across England and the English Channel. Just after reaching the French coast, still at height to avoid flak defences, he then dropped the nose and flew down to just a few hundred feet above the ground. He then engaged 'George', the automatic pilot, and set about assisting his navigator Alan Turner and bomb aimer Arthur Borthwick with the navigation. After crossing the Loire, near Blois, course was set for Nevers and Alan reminded his skipper that they would be flying close to Bourges airfield.

Dennis Field: Almost immediately a bluish searchlight transfixed us, followed at once by hosepiping light flak as the defence opened up, with our gunners responding. The second or so it took to disengage George seemed like hours. Diving down to deck level I called Eddie to flick the IFF but he had already done so. The blue light wavered off but another caught and held. The luminous tracer arcing up started almost lazily before flashing by just outside the cockpit, every shell seemingly about to hit us between the eyes. Hugging the ground we were suddenly clear and the firing ceased.

The lesson had been learnt and Dennis would not be using 'George' on any similar operations again. The crew settled, re-established their position and proceeded on to the 'target'.

Dennis Field: On ETA I climbed a little and suddenly, crossing a small ridge, we saw ahead a field with a line of three lights and the correct letter was flashed up. Doing split-arsed turns to keep it in view and to line up on the short approach, I climbed to dropping height of about 4 – 500 feet and lowered flap to reduce speed. We did a couple of passes to despatch the containers from the bomb bay and then some packages by pushing them out of the entrance door. They all floated down on their chutes to the shadowy figures on the ground scurrying around to collect and remove them.

The return route was virtually a reciprocal course and as the Stirling approached the area around Bourges airfield, Alan Turner suggested a turn to bypass any trouble. Dennis responded but it was not soon enough and the aircraft came within range of some of the airfield's defences.

Dennis Field: We flew directly over one gun emplacement on the fringe of a wood and momentarily the tracer came up vertically. There was an explosion at the back and a kick on the controls as the nose shot up. We had been hit in the tail plane and the distortion caused extra elevation. I counteracted the climb by ramming the column forward and winding on full trim. As we climbed and the airspeed dropped I opened up the throttles, simultaneously turning away from the drome. It was a sickening feeling approaching a stall from which there could be no escape, but with Arthur and me bracing our legs behind the column to keep it fully forward the kite levelled out around 120 IAS and I forced it back down to the deck. We were clear of the airfield now and the firing stopped. A quick check around ascertained that no one had been hit and that damage was confined to the elevator. Jim laconically reported a rough-looking hole in it. When pylons loomed ahead, nothing happened as I eased back. At the last moment I saw Arthur still had his knees behind the column and I knocked them away just in time. (It was some time before we saw the funny side of it.)

Dennis kept the Stirling at low level, until feeling it was safe, he opened the throttles and climbed to 8,000 feet, all the time vigilant of any problems with the aircraft's trim. His skill brought his damaged aircraft over the French coast and then on to England, landing at Tuddenham without further incident.

Dennis Field: It had been a salutary first low level effort and we were relieved to get back in one piece, having in a very positive way learned a few lessons and do's and don'ts, gained a healthy respect for light flak, and endured a kind of 'knees-up' we were not keen on repeating.

In the March moon period, Dennis and his crew made one more contribution to the SOE operations. On 10 March he flew his Stirling across France to a drop point very close to that of their previous operation. Their route to and from the target generally followed that of the previous operation but modified so as give Bourges airfield a wide berth. A successful drop was made and Dennis returned his crew and aircraft safely.

Other 90 Squadron crews had not fared so well whilst conducting special duty operations during the March moon period. Three aircraft were lost, 7 men killed, 3 captured and 11 evaded.

With the March moon period over, SOE assessed its effort to supply the Maquis and the rest of France.[30] Below is a table detailing the scale of the supply drops, just for March 1944.

	Maquis	**Rest of France**	**Total**
Sorties Attempted	441	279	720
Sorties Successful	215	126	341
Total Tonnage	323	164	487
Rifles	4,650	247	4,897
LMG	960	114	1,074
SMG	13,480	8,376	21,856
Pistols	2,725	2,273	4,998
H.E. (tons)	17	29	46
Grenades	26,302	13,225	39,527
A/T Rif.	–	2	2
PIAT	2	40	42
PIAT bombs	40	800	840
Mortars	42	6	48
Mortar bombs	2,286	396	2,682
Incs.	632	–	632
S.A.A.	6,899,400	2,841,400	9,740,800
Food,boots,			
W/T etcs (tons)	34	29	63

The delivery to the Maquis would provide arms for 18,000 men. However a target figure of 26,000 had been set, the reason for the shortfall blamed on no increase in either the number of aircraft operating from North Africa or the number of USAAF Liberators available in England. Despite this it was estimated that over the February and March moon periods, enough munitions had been supplied to the whole of France, to arm approximately 42,000 men. Nevertheless SOE was keen to make up the shortfall and further demands would be placed on the RAF and USAAF special duty squadrons.

Following their two March moon period special duties operations, Dennis and his crew undertook a new operational experience on 15 March 1944, when 90 Squadron detailed aircrews to take part in one of RAF Bomber Command's experimental attacks on the railyards at Amiens. Here they would make their contribution to RAF Bomber Command's Transportation Plan experiment.

Dennis Field: It was a full squadron effort and the aircraft were marshalled on an adjacent runway to that in use for speedy and continuous take-offs. In our turn we lined up and straightened the tail-wheel. A bit over-anxious to get clear, I maybe opened the throttles too quickly and was perhaps affected by a gusty cross-wind but halfway down the runway with the tail nearly up we suddenly careered off at a tangent to port. It was too late to abort so I pulled the starboard throttles back momentarily, applied full rudder and we swung back on to the concrete. I rammed the throttles fully open again, correcting the swing and managed just to reach flying speed and somehow to lift her off and clear the nearby trees. Rather shaken, I climbed on to course with the rest of a largish gaggle. Shortly after crossing the French coast, it was obvious that the Germans were more than a bit antagonistic about our intentions and there was plenty of searchlight activity and flak towards the target. A Stirling nearby was caught by one light and, unable to dive clear, was coned as half a dozen others turned on him. The flak commenced and in spite of violent evasive action he was hit and set on fire, falling out of control. It was hard to stay straight and level as the lights flickered about rather than instinctively weave unless they came close.

It is likely that the aircraft seen falling was that of 149 Squadron Pilot Officer Munro. There were no survivors. 90 Squadron would also lose a crew that night, all killed, when the Stirling piloted by Flight Sergeant Spring collided with an OTU Wellington, whilst preparing to land.

The next night Dennis Field and crew were sent on ops again, this time a return trip to Amiens.

Dennis Field: Apparently our efforts had not been fully effective and so next night we returned to complete the job. After crossing the coast on the way back Arthur, as usual, went down to check for any hang-ups and reported that we had three but he thought he could release them. I opened the bomb doors about half way across and Arthur reported that they had gone. Immediately afterwards there were flashes from below and I dived to avoid anticipated flak, upsetting Alan's charts, equilibrium and verbal self-control. Then Arthur called up to say he had forgotten to defuse the bombs and they had gone off on impact. Next day, on the midday news, the announcer said, 'Last night enemy aircraft made isolated and inaccurate attacks on our shipping in the Channel. There were no casualties or damage.' I often wondered.

Dennis conducted two further operations minelaying in the Gironde estuary and at Kiel before his crew was again called on to arm the Resistance network in France.

For the April moon period the first priority for assisting the French Resistance had been to make arms drops north of the line Nantes-Orléans-Dijon-Strasbourg, an obvious move to strengthen the Resistance networks, which could directly engage the German reinforcement that would be sent to the Normandy invasion area. The remainder of France, including the Maquis, would be given second priority. Eventually of the 516 sorties attempted (only 133 to the Maquis area), 275 were deemed successful (60 with regard to the Maquis). SOE now estimated that taking into account February and March as well, arms had been provided for approximately 65,000 men over the whole of France.

On the night of Easter Sunday, Dennis Field's crew continued with their efforts to arm the French Resistance forces. The trip to the drop point was without incident, and the arms cargo released on 'target'.

Dennis Field: The return flight progressed equally well as we passed our crossing point on the Loire near to Blois, and I prepared to climb towards the coast. I avoided a train further up the line east of Le Mans as I built up speed and then, past the railway, pulled up the nose. Suddenly at about 2,000 feet, both Jim and Tony shouted, 'Weave', but as I rammed the aircraft down into a steep diving turn to port there were loud explosions just behind the cockpit as we were raked down the starboard side by light flak which poured up at us from the train. I kept her down and after a short time the firing, and our gunner's reply ceased.

Alan immediately came on saying that Charlie had been badly hit in his head, trunk and legs, collapsing over his table, and that Eddie, standing in the astrodome, had been severely wounded in the leg and also in the back. Jim and Tony reported safe and damage-free and I sent Arthur back to help and report. I asked Alan for a course but his charts were covered and ruined by Charlie's blood and other body fluids. A chunk of shrapnel missed Alan's head by inches and shattered his Gee set – had he been any taller he would have been decapitated.

I made a quick estimate and steered due north, and then opened to full power, built up speed and started the climb to height. A superficial check indicated that structurally the engineer's station as well as Alan's was a shambles; the shrapnel had entered through his side panel, destroying many of the instruments, and a piece of metal had also damaged the pitch lever bracket. Charlie was in a bad way and had been laid on the floor and given a morphine injection, but he still tried to help with advice on controls even though he must have known his chances were slim. Emergency dressings were applied to Eddie's wounds and he then returned to his station refusing morphia in case it might affect his reflexes, and continued to transmit and operate his set throughout the rest of the flight in spite of severe pain and shock. Whatever else had occurred I did not know, but the engines seemed OK although the fuel position and operation were uncertain because of the damage.

Whilst the wounded were being seen to and the adrenalin-fired gunners remained on full alert, Dennis lifted the Stirling. Within half an hour the Channel was reached and distress signals were sent. Approaching England it became clear to Dennis that he had to land as soon as possible and at the coast there was relief as a flarepath appeared on the edge of some cliffs. Dennis smartly requested permission to land, which was granted, and he prepared to put his aircraft down, conscious of the fact that the flarepath, facing to the sea, looked short, but the needs of his injured crewmates outweighed his concerns. Unknown to the crew at the time they were going to attempt to land a four-engined heavy bomber on the grass runway of a fighter airfield, Friston, near Beachy Head. Further problems arose when Dennis tried to lower the undercarriage. There was no response and Alan Turner had to crank it down by hand whilst the Stirling circled. Eventually Dennis could line his Stirling up and begin a landing.

Dennis Field: The green lights finally came on and I came in low touching down on the edge of the grass runway. About half way along, the stretch of lights ahead was rapidly running out and I rammed open the throttles. We were barely above stalling speed as we shot over the cliff edge and I was fortunate to sink fifty to a hundred feet and gain flying speed for a climb but was unable to retract the undercarriage. The second approach and touchdown at minimum speed were similar but this time there was insufficient room for overshoot. I made the instant decision to swing off applying full rudder and brake. The port wing dipped as the aircraft careered round and then the undercarriage collapsed. We thumped to a jarring halt, clods of torn earth flying up from the distorted propellers until I switched them off. No one had been further harmed by the violent arrival and there was no fire. Charlie lay still on the floor and was too injured to be moved inexpertly except in extremis. When I clambered out of the overhead hatch the others were helping Eddie from the rear escape. We carefully lifted him down, moved him clear and made him as comfortable as possible. By now, ambulance and fire engine should have arrived but there was no sign of them so I clambered back over the wing into the cockpit and called up on the R/T requesting in unequivocal terms that they pull their fingers out. They arrived shortly afterwards. The MO [medical officer] gave further first aid and the stretcher party carefully carried Charlie out through the rear door and into the ambulance to join Eddie for the short ride to Eastbourne hospital.

Dennis and the rest of the crew remained at the fighter station for the night. Early the next morning they went to the hospital.

Dennis Field: Our fears were realised when we were told that Charlie had died during the night in spite of massive blood transfusions. Eddie had undergone surgery to remove shrapnel from his leg and back. We were allowed to see him and he managed a joke about the large chunk of metal in a bottle by his bed, and which had lodged in his shinbone. Throughout their ordeal Eddie and Charlie had displayed extraordinary courage and fortitude. We left the hospital in sombre mood and went back to Friston to recover any important movables left in the aircraft.

The airmen caught the train to London, staying in a force's hostel for the night, and the next day, via tube, bus and train, returned to Tuddenham.

Dennis Field: It was perhaps typical of the times that five scruffy, hatless, unshaven aircrew carrying parachutes and helmets and one with his tunic covered in dried blood excited not a glance or comment let alone offer of a lift or assistance.[31]

Eddie Durrans's courage during the incident described would later be acknowledged with the awarding of the Conspicuous Gallantry Medal.

There were further 90 Squadron casualties that night. Flight Sergeant Gay RNZAF failed to return, and all his crew were captured. Both outer engines on Flight Sergeant Tower's Stirling failed whilst returning to base and the aircraft came down at Icklingham in Suffolk; the rear gunner lost his life in the incident. Towers survived but would later lose his life, along with one other member of the crew, when his partially abandoned aircraft crashed on return from a special duties operation on 28 April.

Following Charlie Waller's funeral, Dennis Field and his crew had been given leave, as there were no replacement crew members available. On return to Tuddenham, however, Dennis was called to the CO's office:

... where he and Squadron Leader Levien were waiting. I saluted before they lifted their heads from some papers they were looking at and was accused of not having done so – not a promising start. Asked whether I and the rest of the crew were ready to continue, I was very surprised at the suggestion that there might have been a choice, but replying in the affirmative as far as I was concerned, honestly but naively said that I had not asked them. That did not help much either, I suppose, and I left rather with my tail between my legs.

Johnny Evans, wireless operator, and 'Curly' Shelton, replacement for Charlie, joined us. Johnny hailed from Kettering, was new to the squadron and remained quiet and very efficient throughout his time with us. Curly, a Londoner, had in appearance, accent and humour many similarities with Bud Flanagan and was often the source of uproarious laughter. He had become spare when his skipper, reportedly, had become one of a very rare breed, and the only one I ever heard of personally, a deserter. Both of our new members were fully reliable and 'genned up' and quickly fitted in.

Following a minelaying operation to La Rochelle on 25 April they would then again be called upon to contribute to the supply of arms to the French Resistance. During the May moon period the focus of special duty supply drop operations to the north of France remained top priority. However the fact that there had been a considerable number of deliveries made in the area west of the Seine in the April moon period, gave cause for concern. The SOE operations had to be included as part of the overall deception plan. Other areas away from the forthcoming battle zone had also to be included. Orders were received to ensure a ratio of sorties conducted in northern France during the May moon period, between the area west of the Seine and east of the Seine (including Belgium and Holland) to be 1:3. In the event 446 sorties were deemed successful out of 858 conducted (148 out of 261 to the Maquis). SOE estimated that since the end of January 1944 arms for approximately 102,500 men had been supplied. Throughout France, Belgium and Holland, SOE agents and Resistance fighters were now awaiting the signal from England, informing them the invasion had begun and telling them to take up arms against their occupiers.

Dennis's crew carried out six special duty operations in the period. All the flights were of the order of seven hours and this proved a trying time for the crew, particularly when over a four-night period they conducted three operations. The squadron also suffered four losses. In addition to the loss of Flight Sergeant Towers's aircraft mentioned previously, three other aircraft from 90 Squadron failed to return, with 11 men killed, 5 captured and 5 evading capture.

CHAPTER 6

THE PRICE OF LIBERATION

In planning the bombing of the enemy in occupied territory, there was
one serious consideration for the Allied air commanders.
'Friendly' casualties would be unavoidable if the military requirement
placed upon the air forces was met. In this chapter personal
accounts of those on the front line, both in the air and on the ground,
provide examples of this tragic military necessity.

The night following RAF Bomber Command's last major raid on Berlin in the
war (24/25 March 1944), the RAF's heavies conducted the seventh operation of
the experimental pre-invasion Transportation Plan attacks. Aulnoye was targeted
by 192 aircraft, with no losses. The next night the experiment continued when
109 aircraft were sent to Courtrai. Again there were no losses, but scattered
bombing spread to civilian areas and resulted in casualties.

On 29/30 March 84 aircraft carried out an accurate attack on Vaires. Only one
Halifax was lost in the successful raid during which two ammunition trains blew
up with a reported 1,270 German troops killed.[32] With nine of the experimental
operations now completed and only seven aircraft lost from the 1,591
despatched, the evidence clearly indicated the lessening risks associated with
attacks on the French rail targets. On the night of 30/31 March 1944 came an
operation that provided another example of the substantial risk in attacking
targets in Germany, and which would go down in history as the highest losses
RAF Bomber Command would suffer in one night throughout the entire war.

Jack Scott and his crew had completed a raid against Essen on the night of
26/27 March, on which only 9 aircraft from the 705 despatched were lost. On 30
March they were detailed to take part in the attack on Nuremberg. Ken Handley
recorded his experience of the Nuremberg raid in his diary:

> We took off in the dark and climbed to 6,000 ft over base. Setting course
> we made 18,000 ft at the coast & 18,500 ft over France. Little flak and
> searchlights were seen. Near Aachen & along by Bonn fighter flares were
> dropped & as the sky was 'gin' clear we kept our eyes skinned for fighters.
> Jack gave the gunners banking searches all the way round. Rockets were
> seen & one appeared to have been projected at us from the ground. Ken
> [Oaks] called 'Go! Dive Jack' & when Jack levelled out a little yelled
> 'Keep the B.....d going'. We lost 2,000 ft over this descent making 250
> mph on the clock. Climbing again we dived away from an 'aircraft' which
> turned out to be a cloud. Over the target area we went through a haze &
> two scarecrows[33] were fired up from the ground. How impressive they are,
> but much too near to feel comfortable. A burst of a fiery fire like a petrol
> dump going up, with red & green dripping & cascading from it. Many
> false fires were set up by the ground forces but the target could be seen by

the red ground markers. We bombed at 19,000 ft 'because we couldn't get higher'. Away from the target area we kept up the searches & saw fighter flares near the French coast & flew right over a drome with the runway all lit up. We descended & made 6,000 ft over England. Landing at Lasham we refuelled & had a new pipeline put in the brake pressure system. Leaving around 6 p.m. we flew over Melton at 10,000 ft the time being 6.30 p.m. Landing at base around 7.15 p.m.

Awe-inspiring at times & most certainly frightening & tense. I've still got a 'hangover'.

The Nuremberg raid was a disaster for RAF Bomber Command: 95 aircraft and aircrews were lost, a staggering victory for the German nightfighter force, and one that rocked RAF Bomber Command. As such, it came as a welcome respite to the RAF's heavy bomber force that as April began its focus of attention would move to the conduct of the pre-invasion bombing, on which, to date, very few aircraft had been lost.

On 10 April 1944, 550 Squadron's Flight Lieutenant Picton and his crew, which had two replacement gunners, attended the operational briefing at North Killingholme. It had been two weeks since he had lost his original gunners, both seriously injured in a combat on the raid to Berlin. On this day Picton's crew was detailed to attack the railyards at Aulnoye. This would not involve a long trip across enemy defended air space. In fact RAF Bomber Command had now realised the lessening risk of attacks on targets in France. Air Vice-Marshal Don Bennett, in charge of RAF Bomber Command's Pathfinder Force, would later state that the *Overlord* support operations gave crews a 'relative holiday from the intense receptions to which they were accustomed in Germany'.[34] But there was a problem. If the rules concerning tours of duty remained the same as they were when RAF Bomber Command was committed to attacks in Germany, then aircrews could quite easily complete their tour in a few months. The high turnaround would place considerable demands on the aircrew training programme. As such it was decided that certain operations, mainly consisting of the pre-invasion targets in the occupied territories, would count as a third of an operation against a tour of duty. Many aircrew were not best pleased, but there was nothing they could do.

On the night of 10/11 April, RAF Bomber Command, in addition to the raid to Aulnoye, was sending forces to Tours, Tergnier, Laon and Ghent. The night before Jack Scott and his crew had taken part in a raid to Villeneuve St George, about which Ken Handley recorded in his diary 'a pleasant trip but only ⅓ of an op worse luck.' On 10 April they were detailed to bomb Tergnier.

As Picton taxied his Lancaster along the North Killingholme perimeter track, heading for Aulnoye, the force sent to Tergnier approached the target:

Ken Handley's diary: Taking off in daylight we climbed to 6,000 ft over base & set course down England at 6,000 ft. We climbed up to 7,500 ft to get above a cloud front & then let down to 6,000 ft again. Down south we climbed to 12,000 ft & continued at this height to the target area. No flak or searchlights were seen, but a few fighter flares were seen. The ground markers received a good 'pranging'. The return trip was uneventful except for searchlights towards the French coast.

A nice quiet trip & hardly any opposition.

Other crews did not have the same experience. Flight Lieutenant Barnes DFC had just taken his 10 Squadron Halifax through the last turning point prior to the target, when his mid-upper gunner suddenly saw a flash to the starboard side of the aircraft and below. Almost instantly cannon fire tore into the starboard wing, which burst into flames and part of the mid-upper gunner's turret was blown away. Barnes wasted little time in realising his aircraft had been fatally struck and he gave the order to bail out. The bomb aimer and navigator were the first out then, as the mid-upper gunner rushed to the exit, a large section of the starboard wing fell off and the Halifax went into a steep dive. He still managed to get out along with three other members of the crew. The rear gunner and pilot were the only fatalities from the crew of eight; the gunner was later found away from the wreckage with his parachute unopened.[35]

The 51 Squadron Halifax flown by Flight Sergeant Hall had just parted company with its bomb load over Tergnier, when a nightfighter attacked from head on; the enemy fire slammed into the aircraft and set the port wing alight. Hall thrust his aircraft into a dive to try to blow the fire out. His effort failed and he called his crew: 'We've had it. There is a fire in the port wing. bail out.' Flying Officer Kirkwood, the navigator, put on his parachute and rushed forward to the escape hatch. He had only just prised it open when the Halifax dived steeply and the hatch stuck. The aircraft then exploded and Kirkwood was blown clear, hit part of the aircraft and then tumbled through the night sky. Fortunately his parachute opened, and despite only being supported by the right hand strap of his harness he landed safely, suffering from only a slight burn to his face and a sprain of his right knee. The two gunners also survived; both were later captured. Kirkwood managed to evade. The rest of the crew were killed.[36]

In total 10 bombers failed to return from the Tergnier raid. However the German defences weren't having it all their own way. Horace Pearce, a pilot with 77 Squadron, recalled the following incident on the raid to Tergnier:

The route from the target included two turns to port to bring us on a parallel course to the incoming route passing south of Amiens and north of Dieppe. In the vicinity of Amiens at 11,000 feet on a heading of 278 degrees the rear gunner, Taffy Hancocks, reported three fighter flares dropped astern of us, and at the same time I saw navigation lights on the port bow 1,500 feet below us and climbing on a reciprocal course. I alerted the crew and told Roy Brooks, the mid-upper gunner, to keep a watch upward in case it was a decoy.

Gordon Edwards, the bomb aimer, who was in the nose position had the lights in view as they passed under our port wing out of my own field of vision. To make matters worse we were then subjected to some heavy flak, which meant I was forced to take some violent evasive action. Once back on course Taffy told me that what looked like an enemy twin-engined fighter was on our port beam some 700 feet below us with its navigation lights out but its nose light showing. He warned me it was coming in to attack and that I should prepare to corkscrew. There was a three-quarter full moon on our starboard quarter astern, giving good visibility above, but it was hazy below. Taffy was giving me a running commentary on the enemy aircraft's movements.

'Enemy range 400 yards and closing. Nose light out. Prepare to go.'

I could hear, over the intercom, the sudden clatter of machine-gun fire from the rear turret. At the same time the enemy fighter opened fire but failed to hit us. Seconds later, whilst I was waiting for an order from the rear gunner to start corkscrewing, firing from our aircraft ceased. I wondered whether Taffy had been hit and sent Fred Archbold, the flight engineer, aft to see whether all was well. It was then that Taffy came up with:

'Resume course. He won't bother us any more.'

I asked what was going on and whether I should corkscrew but was reassured by the rear gunner who said it would no longer be necessary to do so. Seemingly the enemy aircraft closed to 300 yards at which point Taffy had opened fire and at a range of 200 yards his fire caused the enemy aircraft to explode. He told me that as the enemy's fire was passing over the top of his turret and the aircraft's tail assembly directly in the line of fire, he had, therefore, held back from calling evasive action. This all made good sense and I was able to watch the flaming wreckage of the enemy aircraft fall to the ground.

Sergeant Taffy Hancocks, in recognition of his 'coolness and good marksmanship',[37] would later be awarded the DFM.

There was also considerable nightfighter opposition on the raid to Aulnoye, on which Flight Lieutenant Picton was flying. 101 Squadron pilot Flight Lieutenant Nimmo, on approaching the target, witnessed an aircraft fall in flames. Once over the target he had his own problems when on the bomb run six of the 1,000 lb bombs failed to release. Nimmo altered course, came in for a second bomb run, and this time the bombs fell. On approaching the Channel coast on the return flight, searchlights filled the air space through which they had been detailed to fly. Another Lancaster was coned, then two more Lancasters directly ahead were also coned and seen to go down. Nimmo and his crew managed to slip through but then luck ran out as the starboard wing burst into flames. With no explosion heard or felt the crew believed an unseen fighter had crept up. The flight engineer, Sergeant Alexander, reported flames burning on top of the wing and blobs of blazing petrol falling as if coming from the fuel tank. Nimmo at once ordered his crew to bail out. Alexander retrieved his pilot's chute, whilst the bomb aimer opened the escape hatch and jumped. He was followed by the navigator and Alexander who, suspended from his parachute, watched the Lancaster curve downwards as the fire spread along the wing before the aircraft finally exploded on impact with the ground. The wireless operator and two gunners were killed. Nimmo had managed to get out of the burning bomber and along with the other survivors succeeded in evading capture.[38]

In total eight aircraft were lost on the Aulnoye raid. One of those was the 550 Squadron Lancaster flown by Flight Lieutenant Picton. A nightfighter accounted for the aircraft and there were no survivors. Despite the fact that this crew had survived numerous operations over Germany, they lost their lives on what RAF Bomber Command perceived as 'easier' ops over France. As one RAF Bomber Command veteran recalled, 'If one bought it over France one was completely dead, not one-third.' Many RAF Bomber Command aircrew would also soon learn that the operations over occupied territory were far from easy.

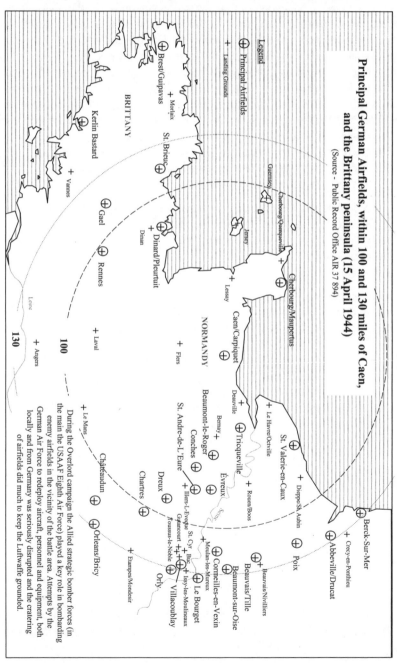

Principal German Airfields, within 100 and 130 miles of Caen, and the Brittany peninsula (15 April 1944)

(Source - Public Record Office AIR 37 894)

During the Overlord campaign the Allied strategic bomber forces (in the main the USAAF Eighth Air Force) played a key role in bombarding the main the USAAF Eighth Air Force) played a key role in bombarding enemy airfields in the vicinity of the battle area. Attempts by the German Air Force to redeploy aircraft, personnel and equipment, both locally and from Germany was seriously disrupted and the cratering of airfields did much to keep the Luftwaffe grounded.

On 15 April 1944 the final version of the *Overlord* Overall Air Plan was distributed. Allied air support was tasked to 'attain and maintain an air situation, which would assure freedom of action for our forces without effective interference by enemy air forces and to render air support to our land and naval forces in the achievement of this object'. The six primary responsibilities for the Allied air forces were essentially to attain and maintain air superiority over the battle zone, to ensure there was always sufficient reconnaissance of the German troop movements, to provide transport for airborne troops, to attack the enemy's naval forces when necessary, to directly support the landing and advance of the ground troops and to disrupt the German communication and supply lines.[39] The last three responsibilities would require support from the Allied heavy bomber forces.

On 17 April 1944 Eisenhower issued the directive outlining the role of the RAF and USAAF heavies in supporting *Overlord*. Initially the position of the American and British strategic bomber forces was made quite clear with respect to other forces: 'Our re-entry on the Continent constitutes the supreme operation for 1944; all possible support must, therefore, be afforded to the Allied Armies by our Air Forces to assist them in establishing themselves in the lodgement area.' Then the particular mission was stated:

a) To deplete the German air force and particularly the German fighter forces, and to destroy the facilities supporting them.

b) To destroy and disrupt the enemy's rail communications, particularly those affecting the enemy's movement towards the 'OVERLORD' lodgement area.

The Americans were given the targeting of the German air force as their primary objective, and the rail transportation system as secondary. The commitment in support of *Overlord* required of RAF Bomber Command was, quite frankly, vague, asking for operations complementary to the American operations, focusing on the German air force and enemy rail communications. The directive then addressed the potential political problems when bombing a country occupied by the enemy: 'The political aspects of this plan, as affecting the French, will be kept under continuous supervision, with especial reference to the casualties to the civilian populations involved.'[40]

With the majority of rail targets in urban built-up areas, any spread of bombing could fall on civilians. The AEAF planners saw this as a necessary consequence and unavoidable, but the potential scale of such friendly bombing had raised many an eyebrow amongst British politicians, notably that of Winston Churchill. The expected death toll from the attacks on rail targets prior to the issue of the directive had been relatively light. However on the night of 18/19 April 1944 RAF Bomber Command sent four large forces to attack rail marshalling yards in northern France, and the bombing spread to civilian areas, leading to tragedy. A total of 850 aircraft conducted the attacks on the rail targets, and in combination with other raids, Bomber Command set a new record for the war to date, with 1;125 sorties carried out. The attack on Juvisy involved 209 aircraft and John Pryor, a pilot with 5 Group's 617 Squadron, found his crew detailed for the raid. 617 Squadron fronted the attack, bombing from 8,000 feet, with the rest of the bomber force following.

John Pryor: A comforting and satisfying trip, this sort of target gave greater satisfaction than the main force raids we did on Berlin and other towns some months ago. It made us see things in a different light, conscious of how accurate we had to be; any target we missed meant we could be hitting the French people.

At briefing the need for accuracy was stressed. Wing Commander Leonard Cheshire, 617 Squadron's experienced commander, was to control the raid and attempt to ensure the bombing remained concentrated. Following briefing, John Pryor's crew prepared themselves for the raid.

John Pryor: The evening drew on, the cloud that existed during the day broke up, and a clear night was seen. We duly had our flying meal of eggs and bacon, then shipped on down to the flight together to collect our parachutes etc. We had done this so many times before, it became second nature to us. No one was ever in a hurry; there was always plenty of time unless something went wrong with a particular aircraft, and then the pace was faster, but fortunately this did not occur often.

No very great load – four 1,000 lb bombs and four 500 lb bombs, six 7 inch flares and a light petrol load. Although we had a slight wind we used the main runway to take off. There was a bit of a crosswind, but nothing very difficult.

It was a bright starlit night. We could see the Channel very clearly as we crossed. It was a shorter crossing than when we were on the main force, and then we flew the North Sea into Holland. Soon we were over the French coast. Our bombs were not armed as we flew over the coast (they would have been had it been the German coast). The short trip from the coast to Paris was soon over.

As we approached the target we could see the flares going down. We always carried flares in the aircraft and were asked to use them when necessary. I was asked our position; we were approaching the target in the correct position and on time, so I was asked to drop back-up flares for extra light and on this occasion we dropped three, one north of the yard, one over the middle and one to the south. We then turned back ready to make our bombing approach in about ten minutes. I flew quite a bit back so as to be on time, Lloyd watching the time to make sure we could get in and bomb, and away again before main force started to bomb 10,000 ft higher. As we were running in, the conditions were ideal.

Cheshire informed the 617 Squadron crews that the markers were well placed. The bombs were released and Cheshire congratulated the crews on the perceived accuracy. In case more flares were needed John Pryor was ordered to circle the target. He watched as the main force came in, with more TIs appearing dropped by Pathfinders. Unfortunately these began to drift.

John Pryor: We were bombing markers on the ground, the force were to bomb markers in the air. This was now necessary because of the dust and smoke, and the trouble that we had stirred up, started to look not too good.

The main force arrived. The first bombs that they dropped were only a little off, but the rest appeared to be as much as a mile to the north and west. The TIs dropped had obviously drifted in a crosswind and the force were bombing north of the yard, dropping their bombs in a built-up area. There was going to be trouble over this.

By now we were instructed to go home, and with a sinking feeling for the French people living in the built-up area who may have been hurt or even killed, we turned for home.

Through the dust and the smoke that we left we could see that the marshalling yard had been ripped to pieces. There were a lot more aircraft to come and they would do a bit more damage. Once the main force started bombing it appeared that all hell was let loose. It's very difficult to see when there are a lot of aircraft bombing. Not like our small group where twelve to twenty are involved and you have an interval between, not long, but long enough to see what's happening. We left the scene hoping it was a success . . . Having turned for base, 'Mac', our gunner, was giving us information on what was happening. There was still a stream of aircraft bombing. We believed that about 200 of the force aircraft were going to bomb after we left. We could hear Wing Commander Cheshire telling the force their bombs were going to the north. It didn't seem to have any effect on them.

That night, nineteen-year-old Marcelle Thiou was visiting her sister in Juvisy, to see her niece Danièle, born only 14 days earlier. Just before midnight they were awoken by the sound of sirens and the approaching heavy bombers:

We knew we were going to be on the receiving end as flares started to fall. My sister and brother-in-law immediately panicked and couldn't control themselves, unable to cope. I was ready, holding the baby in my arms. I wanted to run away, with my sister lying in a small trolley pushed by her husband. But their panic prevented anything. I threatened to leave with the baby but gave way and we went to what was supposed to be some kind of shelter, but was actually a sort of blast screen of earth and wooden boards facing the house, where the four of us huddled together. Some 30 minutes later the first bombs exploded. One bomb fell close to the shelter and blew the roof off. A second bomb followed and covered us with earth and the wooden boards. I had my knees drawn up and with the baby tight against me. Breathing was very difficult. We were buried alive. The baby managed a small cry, then the breathing stopped. My sister (I hadn't told her anything) didn't stop talking. 'Forgive me. Forgive me. I was wrong not to listen to you and get away.' I answered, 'Don't talk. Breathing's becoming very difficult. Save the air.' It didn't stop her talking of her four-year-old son, who fortunately was in a shelter in Orléanais with his grandparents. As for my brother-in-law I could hear him say, 'I'm not good. I'm going to have to say goodbye.' A short while afterwards my sister became incoherent and started to sing. After that I cannot recall.

We remained buried for three hours. With my knees tight against me I couldn't move. At dawn I heard voices in the street and I let out a small cry. Then I recognised the blows of shovels. A young man found me and tried to lift me out, which took a very long time as delayed action bombs were exploding everywhere. Finally I could feel the air, my head was about to burst, I was covered with mud and very thirsty. Someone passed me a bottle of water and then the little baby was lifted out. I told the rescuers that my brother and sister were still in there but I had to leave because the delayed action bombs were a continual danger. Later I recognised the body of my brother-in-law among dozens of bodies lined up on the ground one against the other. But it was my little niece that I found first of all, mouth open, deformed, eyes staring. As for me, I later found my body covered in bruises from the blows of the shovels.[41]

The stray bombing had spread to civilian housing, but there had also been considerable destruction to the railyards. Forty years after the event John Pryor went to visit Juvisy and met others who, like Marcelle Thiou, had experienced the bombing at first-hand.

John Pryor: With memories of that night they told us that utter chaos reigned, and there had been a considerable amount of casualties in the housing area to the side of the yard. The casualties were mostly caused by the delayed action bombs, hurting or killing the rescuers of the people who were already trapped under the debris. In hindsight if the delayed action bombs were used in the beginning when we could have seen the yard clearly they would have been put down in the right place, with the main force using the high explosive (immediate effect) bombs, but on reflection just as many people would have been killed.

We were invited up into one of the signal boxes to have a good look round the yard. We took some photographs and had a chat to one of the senior officers of the French railways. He told us it was long after D-Day before it was possible to get even one line through, and then every time a train went through they had to re-line it because about twenty to thirty feet of loose soil kept sinking, slipping and sliding on the track. It was a year or so before it was fairly well established to enable trains to go through without any problems. The French people told us that the main problem was removing the smashed and broken trucks and the stuff that was in them, because on the night of the raid there was so much traffic in the yard, everything was either smashed, broken or crushed leaving a tremendous amount of debris. People were imported to do this work. A large area of the yard was cleared so that debris could be piled up. They needed special equipment to pile it up and grade it off. The lines had to be taken up, it had to be an open space for the consolidation required to get it even possible for anything to go back over it. Took quite a long time. No trains moved through it for a month. The business of marshalling was totally impossible for something like three months, the trains had to go straight through. Some trains were diverted around Paris, but this became extremely difficult, everywhere was so congested.

I find it somewhat difficult to look back over the years, and relate what I remembered of that occasion to the reality of what I was looking at on the ground, forty years later. The feeling at that time I am sure, was our

raid was a great success. The feeling today when I know that between one
and two hundred people had been killed in the houses adjoining the yard,
well – it mattered. But of course it had to be done.[42]

That same night, 18/19 April 1944, the people of Noisy-le-Sec were also awoken,
yet again, by the noise of air raid sirens. Many felt complacent, because they had
heard them before and nothing had happened. On this night their indifference
was ill-founded. Thousands of feet above them, in the dark night sky, a force of
181 RAF bombers, each carrying a few tons of high explosive, was approaching
fast. The railyards were the bombers' target, which they would go on to
successfully smash, but on this night the attack spread beyond the target area and,
as had happened at Juvisy an hour before, the civilians of Noisy-le-Sec would
feel the full force of a friendly heavy bomber raid.

Mireille Ruquets lived with her parents, who ran the bakery in the boulevard
de la République. On this night both Mireille and her parents heard the sirens, but
they had been hearing them regularly many nights before and nothing had
happened. The bakehouse was at the bottom of the building. There had been a
continuous cellar going under adjacent buildings but a wall had been built,
creating a storage room for the flour. As the bombers closed in on Noisy-le-Sec,
Mireille's father went to have a look, standing in the doorway used for the
delivery of the flour. He looked up. The sky was lit by flares and he quickly
realised that on this night the sirens had good reason to be screaming.

Mireille Ruquets: The first bomb fell and my father was blasted to the
bottom of the staircase. There was a massive crash, the noise was terrible.
Very quickly help arrived, firemen and nurses, but we were unhurt.

The bomb had fallen on the pavement in front of the butchers, next door to the
bakery, blasting both buildings and the basements. When the sirens had sounded
the basements had quickly filled with people seeking shelter. They were now
trapped.

Mireille Ruquets: 'Do not be afraid my little Mimi,' said my mother, her
voice was trembling. 'It is nothing, it is nothing.' In the basement to the
side there was screaming. Quickly people started to smash at the dividing
wall with pickaxes. It was terrible, the crying and the moaning. There
were more than 70 victims, they were trapped and very few survived. The
butcher was killed, his daughter too. To release one victim they had to cut
off his leg. The horror of it all. I had a very good friend, and there is not
one evening when I do not think of poor Jacqueline, she was 22 years old.
She died, suffocated. Whole families disappeared. One man, I remember
it well, his daughter had just married. They all died.

One young man, belonging to the Paris fire service, was called in to Noisy-le-Sec
that night, to assist with rescuing victims. Along with three colleagues he was
sent to a building that had fallen, trapping three people beneath the rubble. The
firemen crawled into the devastation, trying to find the victims.

The delayed action bombs were exploding and the ground shook and we
had to run the risk that everything might collapse. Our task was to release

a man and two young girls. They had taken refuge in a cellar and the building above had fallen on them. The father was the most difficult to save; he was wedged under a lot of material. You tried to do your best without asking questions. He had to be released despite all the rubble. At one point the Captain in charge of our unit said, 'It would be better to try and work from the top.' One of my colleagues was actually in one of the holes we had dug. The Captain asked him to get out. He answered, 'No, no, do what you have to do but I'm not leaving.' He was stretched out over one of the small girls, to protect her.

We began around 2 a.m. and finished around 9 a.m. We got the father and one girl out alive. The other young girl died.

When I left I went up the street, covered from head to toe in dust. I heard someone say, 'He's not going to be short of work.' In the street on the ground, there was what appeared to be some kind of cloth material, but it became apparent that it was human flesh. I realised it was someone who had been blown apart by a bomb blast. Further along the street, in a garden, there was a crashed aircraft, with the pilot still in it.

What stays in my memory is what we achieved. I was happy that I could help victims and saved two lives. We didn't speak about it amongst ourselves. Each of the firemen from Paris had carried out his duty, wherever they were sent.

Over the next two days news of the RAF attacks went to print in the French press and the headlines berated the Allied attacks: *Les Nouveaux Temps (23 April)*: Dans le Décor Hallucinent des Ruines Paris et sa Banlieue pleurent Leurs Morts (Amidst extraordinary scenes of destruction, Paris and its suburbs mourn their dead.) And from *L'Œuvre (20 April)*: Le raid de mardi soir sur Paris et la banlieue a dépassé en horreur les massacres précédents. On compte dèjà, pour la Seine: 250 morts et 407 blessés. (Tuesday evening's raid on Paris and its suburbs supersedes in horror any preceding massacres. The current count for la Seine: 250 dead and 407 injured.)

The anti-Allied propaganda opportunity was seized, unsurprisingly considering newspapers were under German influence. The Allies were in fact keeping a close eye on the reporting of the bomber attacks. In a few months time the Allies hoped their land forces would be advancing through areas in which aerial bombardments had taken place and the potential political consequence of civilian casualties had not been overlooked.

On 29 March 1944 Sir Charles Portal had made Winston Churchill aware of the probable political problem with the execution of the Transportation Plan. With the targets located in built-up areas, close to civilian housing, it was inevitable that there would be friendly civilian casualties. Eisenhower was certainly aware of the obvious political effect of the proposed bombing and considered issuing warnings to all civilians living near targets to move. Portal made it clear to Churchill that the requirements of *Overlord* overrode any political concerns and the bombing attacks remained a high priority.

Churchill had his reservations. Early in April the War Cabinet and its Defence Committee had begun to consider the Transportation Plan with expected civilian casualty figures of 40,000 dead and 120,000 injured. Such carnage was deemed unacceptable and political pressure against the execution of the pre-invasion rail target attacks mounted.

Incident

Pilot Officer Charles Hobgen was the navigator in Squadron Leader Ken Bond's 77 Squadron Halifax crew, which was sent to attack the railyards at Laon on 22/23 April. As they flew over occupied territory the crew became aware of unwanted company, as they witnessed a bomber and German nightfighter exchange fire. Taking into account the proximity of enemy airfields, Charles Hobgen warned his pilot, who in turn informed the crew to remain vigilant. On approaching the target TI were seen to go down, directly ahead. The crew prepared for the bomb run:

Charles Hobgen: Flak was now beginning to become intense and above the pounding of our engines the occasional burst could be heard and, for that matter, seen. Shrapnel rattled on the fuselage in a quite disturbing way and I hoped none of it would hit any vital part of the aircraft or, for that matter, its crew.

Through the crackling static of the air waves I could now hear the voice of the master bomber. There was a slightly strained quality about it as though the speaker was experiencing some difficulty in directing the efforts of the bomber force beneath him.

'Come on, you Halifaxes, bomb the centre of the green markers, they've been well placed . . . Keep it coming . . . No edging back now. We don't want any fringe merchants . . . Bomb the greens . . . Well done . . . That's the stuff, but keep well up to the centre of the greens.'

John Grimer [the bomb aimer] started his bombing run.

'Bomb doors open please skipper . . . Bombs selected and fused . . . Hold it steady . . . Steady as you go . . . Right, right a little . . . right a shade more . . . steady . . . steady . . . steady.'

It was at this stage in any operation when we all held our breath, for it was essential, in the cause of accurate bombing, for the aircraft to be held steadily on the line of flight being called for by the bomb aimer and thus both it and its crew were placed in an unenviably vulnerable position. The one thought common to each of us was, for God's sake, John, get it right first time. Don't let's have to go round again as we did on a previous occasion.

The intensity of my own physical excitement was as though I had been dosed with a powerful stimulant, whilst at the same time the level of my fear reached an almost unbearable pitch. For those few minutes that seemed like hours, I felt a clammy sweat momentarily covering my whole body. There was nothing I could do to relieve the sensation, I had perforce to wait for a release from it. A release that lay in the lap of the gods and in the hands of the bomb aimer. Meantime my eyes remained glued to the thumb on John's right hand poised unwaveringly above the bomb release 'tit'. Suddenly it flashed downwards and I heard the welcoming words giving at least a semi-release from my tension.

'Bombs gone . . . jettison bar across . . . hold it steady for the flash.'

As the aircraft was released from the weight of the bombs it rose upwards but was otherwise held steady for a further thirty seconds to allow the photo flash to explode on the ground and for the camera to turn over to record the accuracy or otherwise of our bombing.

'Flash gone . . . Close bomb doors.'

Ken Bond, the pilot, sent his aircraft, and relieved crew, into a dive to clear the target area, and Charles Hobgen gave his skipper a course for home.

Charles Hobgen: On we ploughed into the night on the short leg out of the target area. Within minutes it would be necessary for me to pass a further change of course to the pilot to take us to Fécamp on the French coast and that much nearer to the comparative safety of the English Channel and home.

Suddenly the soporific drone of the engines was shattered as all hell was let loose within the aircraft. I was just about aware of a shouted warning: 'Fighter. Fighter. Corkscrew' from one or other of the gunners but it was cut short by several other happenings which, in retrospect, seemed to occur simultaneously.

There was the clatter of attacking gunfire that swept through the aircraft from the rear to the front and through the small window facing me as I sat at my desk I caught a glimpse of flames engulfing the port inner engine. Undoubtedly we were on fire with the aircraft already showing signs of falling out of control, suggesting Ken Bond might well have been wounded. As the attacking nightfighter raked the length of 'S' – Sugar, my desk disintegrated before my eyes as a hail of cannon shells sliced through it with explosive precision. Within micro-seconds my knees and feet were entangled in a pile of debris and I realised the intercom was no longer functioning.

Vaguely I became aware of Victor Clare peering down from the second pilot position where he stood outlined against the glare of the flames behind him. With one hand he gesticulated wildly in a way that could only mean the order to 'bail out' had been given . . . his gestures left me in no doubt we were to get out of the aircraft immediately. John Grimer was already on his feet and standing near me but Bob Johnson was still sitting in his seat looking dazed and uncomprehending. I leant towards him shouting: 'Bail out! Bail out!', at the same time pointing downwards. He raised the thumb of his right hand signifying he understood what I was about to do.

Having, with John Grimer's help, already pushed to one side the debris that had been my plotting desk I ripped off my helmet whilst at the same time I grabbed my parachute from its stowage position behind me. Using both hands, with a single movement I rammed the pack onto the two 'G' clips of the harness which, as a matter of standard practice, I was wearing and turned my attention to the escape hatch.

The navigator's seat in a Halifax was located atop the forward escape hatch. It therefore simply remained for me to fold my seat back against the starboard side of the aircraft and to seize the ring catch, securing the hatch in position. I gave the ring an almighty twist and pull whereupon, much to my surprise, because I had never operated the catch before, the whole of the door came away in my hand. For a brief second I gawped at it and then realising this was exactly what was supposed to happen I dropped the door through the gaping hole whence lay my way of escape.

Looking up, I noticed Bob Johnson dragging himself towards me. He was obviously in considerable pain. He had removed his helmet and I could see below his tousled fair hair that his face had taken on an ashen, almost deathlike appearance. Each of his flying boots was covered in blood as were the legs of his battledress trousers. Somehow he had managed to clip on his parachute. John Grimer, who was already standing at my side, helped me pull him to the hatch where, together, we helped him jump out. Not a word passed between us. Thereafter, in short order, I followed him. John Grimer, whose own severe wounds were not obvious to me at the time, and Vic Clare must have been hard on my heels.

As I hurtled into the night with my hands clasped protectively over the metal ring on the front of the parachute pack I counted a measured, One, Two, Three, then pulled the ring hard, at the same time uttering a hurried supplication to any deity within hearing distance that the wretched thing would deploy and gently lower me to mother earth.

There was a momentary pause before the canopy, with its attendant webbing and shrouds, swept upwards past my face and ballooned into its life saving position. As I floated downwards I was able to see 'S'-Sugar, by then engulfed in flames and in a shallow glide. Before I reached the ground I heard the crash and saw the flash of fire that lit up the sky, which, together, heralded her end. Momentarily my attention was diverted from what was happening to myself and all too suddenly, ill prepared as I was, I saw the ground rushing up towards me. For some reason or another I drew up my legs into what I can best describe as a sitting position thereby ensuring that when I did touch down I did so heavily and painfully on the base of my spine. The jarring shock from the jolt travelled up my back to my head and for a moment I thought I was about to lose consciousness. I have carried the residual pain with me from that day to this.

Despite managing to evade capture for the night, Charles Hobgen was caught the next day, when, accompanied by some French civilians, he went to the aid of Bob Johnson, who was badly injured. Both men were taken away by the Germans and were soon joined by John Grimer and Jock Mason (the mid-upper gunner). Johnson, Grimer and Mason all received treatment in German hospitals. Johnson and Mason, both badly wounded in the legs, had to have below the knee amputations. Of the rest of the crew, Victor Clare and rear gunner Bill Jacks managed to evade capture. Squadron Leader Bond suffered serious injury and despite being taken to a hospital, he died on arrival. His body now rests in the New Communal Cemetery at Clichy.

On 5 April 1944 the senior Allied *Overlord* commanders had been summoned to attend the late night War Cabinet's Defence Committee meeting. Portal decided to ask Zuckerman to attend, and he gave an insider's account of the meeting in his postwar memoirs. In addition to Churchill, senior politicans were also in attendance, together with Chiefs of Staff and Lord Cherwell (professor F. A. Lindemann), scientific adviser to Churchill. Zuckerman recorded feeling, 'just as excited as I would have been before the curtain went up at a theatre, although I was certainly not ready for the high drama that followed':

> It started quietly enough, and in good humour, with the P.M. reading from what looked like a narrow sheet of script, which it soon transpired was a brief written by the Prof [Lord Cherwell]. It began something like this. The meeting had been called to discuss the AEAF proposals for the use of the strategic bombers in the preparation for Overlord, and everyone was aware that Leigh-Mallory knew nothing about bombing or about the merits of the plan. The whole thing was 'the brain child of a biologist who happened to be passing through the Mediterranean'. These words were pleasurably imprinted into my brain. Portal then interrupted to say that that particular observation was grossly unfair, and that the biologist in question had done more than anyone else to analyse the effects of air operations. At this point the Prof moved his hand as though to pull the brief from the P.M. There were smiles on some faces as Churchill looked up, seemingly aware for the first time that the said biologist was in the room. He continued to read, and finished by asking Tedder whether the plan had his backing. Tedder replied that it had. 'You don't know a better plan?' asked the P.M. 'There is no better plan,' replied Tedder. 'I'll show you a better plan,' said the P.M., and I saw Tedder's knuckles whiten as he grasped the edge of the table. He knew better than I what the next few hours were going to bring.[43]

Two papers were considered at the meeting: Leigh-Mallory's AEAF paper requesting authorisation to attack rail centres; and a Joint Intelligence Committee one which highlighted the French casualty figures and the potential political consequences. Churchill expressed his grave concerns about the 'cold-blooded butchering' of French civilians. Nevertheless Portal and Tedder maintained their conviction that there was no alternative to the AEAF plan. Lord Cherwell weighed in challenging some of the basic principles of the plan and Zuckerman was given the opportunity to explain the scientific base for the calculations made devising the plan. Portal then informed the meeting that the methodology of calculating the JIC's casualty figures had been flawed. Churchill vented his anger at Zuckerman, who could only reply that he had not been party to the calculations. A rift between the politicians and the *Overlord* planners grew.

Incident

On the raid to the railyards at Montzen on the night of 27/28 April 1944 the 434 Squadron Halifax piloted by Flying Officer Maffre RCAF, was attacked by a German nightfighter and set on fire. The pilot and three of his crew lost their lives. Flying Officer Stacey RCAF was one of those who survived, coming down in a field near Gulpen in Holland. He was helped by the Resistance and taken to Liège where he remained until Americans liberated the area on 21 September. Whilst in hiding Stacey was informed of the fate of another aircrew, shot down on the same raid.

I was told that Belgians had found the wreckage of another Halifax, which had crashed at about the same time and in the vicinity as my own. There were several bodies in this aircraft, but due to their mangled condition and the arrival of the German troops almost immediately after the crash, it was not possible to make any identification nor was it possible to determine how many bodies were in the aircraft. An unopened chest parachute No.130 was found near the wreckage. About a quarter of a mile away an open parachute No.133 and a navigator's log folder were found. The folder had the name of F/O [Flying Officer] A.E. Young written on the cover. F/O Young was the navigator of another crew in my squadron which took part in the operation . . . German troops arrived shortly after the crash, mounted a guard around the wreckage and removed the bodies.[44]

This was the 434 Squadron Halifax crew of Warrant Officer Vigor RCAF and there were indeed no survivors resulting from the German nightfighter attack on their aircraft.

At yet another meeting at which the role of the strategic bombers in support of *Overlord* was discussed further heated debate ensued, with no consensus or firm decision reached except that the plan of attacks should be revised in order to reduce the risk of civilian casualties. At the conclusion of this meeting the supporters of the AEAF plan felt somewhat rebuffed. Zuckerman recalls Tedder's dismay:

On his way back to his house in Kingston-upon-Thames, Tedder dropped me off at my flat. He had clearly been shaken by the evening's proceedings, and particularly by the personal hostility, which Winston had directed at him as the night wore on. As I got out of the car, he said in his usual sardonic manner, 'I suppose that this might be the end, Zuck. I wonder how much it will cost to set up as a tomato grower?' I knew at the time that he was so committed that he would have asked to be relieved of his post as deputy Supreme Commander if the decision had gone against the plan.[45]

The target list was revised, this time with Zuckerman's assistance, and casualty estimates fell dramatically to 10,500 killed, 5,500 injured. Nevertheless throughout April and early May the Defence Committee remained reluctant to officially sanction the AEAF plan, and the meetings continually deferred its acceptance, with Winston Churchill leading the opposition. Early in April Churchill had written to Eisenhower expressing that 'Postwar France must be our friend. It is not alone a question of humanitarianism. It is also a question of high state policy.'[46] Following the Defence Committee meeting on 26 April and War Cabinet meeting the next day, Churchill again expressed his concerns to Eisenhower who maintained his support for the plan.

Against such unified commitment to the AEAF plan from Tedder, Portal, Eisenhower and Leigh-Mallory, at the 3 May Defence Committee meeting the plan was finally agreed, subject to the approval of the War Cabinet, with the proviso that casualties should not exceed 10,000. Zuckerman in his memoirs stated: 'as though, if the figure were exceeded, one could explain the cutting short of an operation as though its military value could be judged in terms of a fixed number of innocent lives sacrificed'.[47]

Still Churchill made one last effort to challenge the plan and on 7 May, via a cable, he took the issue up with Roosevelt, but the American President stood firmly behind the *Overlord* Commanders and despite his concerns he was not prepared to impose any restrictions on their plans. With this Churchill finally gave way and the scale of attacks on French and Belgian transportation targets escalated in the days leading up to and following the invasion. Despite the best efforts both human and technical, further incidents of civilian casualties arose. The exact figure for civilians killed or wounded as a result of the implementation of the Transportation Plan will never be known, but for those killed it was certainly thousands, probably of the order of ten to twelve. A heavy price for the return of *liberté*.

CHAPTER 7

SPAATZ'S OIL PLAN

In the run up to D-Day the Eighth Air Force would not only contribute
to the pre-invasion bombing plan. It would also assault
Germany itself, seeking to engage the Luftwaffe directly in battle.
Americans Warren Berg and Bob Petty would begin flying
missions with the Eighth Air Force in the spring of 1944, and join the
air battle. John Howland's story continues as he also find
himself over hostile German air space.

In the middle of the nineteenth century German immigrants began to establish new homes in a quiet corner of southern Minnesota. As many came from the province of Württemberg in Germany, with Ulm the principal city, the settlement became New Ulm. For the next half a century the friendly German invaders worked hard to turn their virgin territory into farmland and build up businesses to support the growth of agriculture. By 1919 the town had swelled to a population of approximately 6,000 and on 12 November that year there was another addition. Both sides of Warren Berg's family were of German extraction, and his father worked with his grandfather as an accountant in the Treasurer's office. His maternal grandfather had worked the land around New Ulm. In 1926 Warren's father took his wife and three sons to the nearby town of Mankato, where Warren grew up, graduated from his local college, in 1941, with a high school teaching degree, and then entered the University of Minnesota at Minneapolis for an advanced teaching degree. The Japanese attack on Pearl Harbor cut Warren's studies short.

> *Warren Berg:* I was 22-years-old at that time and had no dependants so I knew it would be only a short time before I would be called up for military service. Since I had long been interested in aviation I concluded I would prefer to enlist in the US Army Air Corps than to wait until I was drafted into the foot soldier army.

In January 1942 Warren took the necessary exams and was inducted into the Army Air Corps later that year:

> I was highly disappointed at the beginning, since I was classified as a navigator trainee rather than a pilot trainee. However, the Air Corps needed a 40% non-pilot officer crew complement for its various types of aircraft; thus for each five candidates accepted for training, two had to be non-pilot. This ratio provided a navigator, a bombardier, and two pilots for each bomber crew and one additional pilot to man fighter aircraft.

Warren's basic training began in California, and then he took a course in aerial gunnery at Las Vegas, Nevada. Navigation training followed at Mather Army Air

Base at Sacramento, California and in November 1943 Warren received his wings as an Air Corps Navigator. Warren was then posted for combat crew training on B-17s at Rapid City, South Dakota, where he became one of the ten men making up the crew of pilot Gary Miller. The tail gunner on the crew was 22-year-old Robert Petty, from Hot Springs, South Dakota.

Bob Petty: After combat training we, as a crew, went to Nebraska and were 'issued' a new B-17 to take to war. We flew to Florida, Trinidad, Belem, Brazil, Dakar, Tindouf, Algeria, Marrakech and to the UK. Our crew became locked together in a common goal almost immediately. We had two first pilots and one was a former boxer who challenged anybody to a fight who wanted to contest his status as boss pilot. We worked around this a bit and just about everybody was the object of an often not-too-funny trick. Mine was over the Atlantic from Belem to Dakar. Belem cooks had sent shoebox lunches with us. The engineer felt the urge to defecate and used a box but didn't know how to dispose of his boxed mess. I was asleep in the radio room. Someone suggested he throw it out the tail window. It was a small window and the box and contents splattered the tail area. That's a small area and I was the tail gunner. Most of the enlisted crew woke me up but the engineer was laughing so hard, he couldn't talk. I realized I was the brunt of the joke and I jumped on him to tell me what happened and all he could say was 'go look'. He did his best to clean it up, but I had to ride in place from Marrakech to the UK.

Early in February Gary Miller safely brought his crew to England and, as did John Howland and his crew, they spent a short time at Stone to familiarise themselves with the English way of life.

Warren Berg: This stay, including several sorties into the town of Stafford, gave us a good introduction to English weather, people, blackouts, roads, pubs, food, housing, and language peculiarities. Some of this we had been exposed to via wartime movie films, but nothing could match the opportunity to experience the real thing. The main reaction I had, shared by most of my companions, was a sincere respect and admiration for the British people for the manner in which they were coping with the severe effects of an all-out war effort. The known exploits of the British military forces, especially the RAF, were also cause for deep appreciation of the British fighting spirit.

Late in February 1944 Warren and his crew reported to the 96th Bomb Group at Snetterton Heath, Norfolk.

Warren Berg: We found a rather dreary, mid-winter environment, featuring stark-looking buildings with very basic amenities. This did not surprise us as we had seen similar facilities during our weeks of orientation. We simply concluded that wartime England just looked that way. We were quartered in hutments, with eight officers to a hut. Furnishings in the officers' huts were spartan with individual metal cots and a three biscuit mattress. Clothes racks and bedstands were provided along with a communal table. Bathroom facilities were provided in a separate building nearby. Each hut was equipped with one very small coal burning heating stove. Most Americans agreed that these were inadequate to heat the entire hut, but most adjusted to that discomfort except for an enterprising few who experimented with homemade stoves made out of empty fuel drums.

Food in the dining halls was adequate but lacking in variety. Australian mutton was often served and was quite generally disliked. Powdered eggs were a breakfast staple, except that flight crews were served fresh eggs on days they were scheduled to fly a combat mission. Movie films were shown in the base theater on a weekly schedule featuring many of the latest American productions. Monthly parties were held at both the Officers Club and Non-commissioned Officers Club and were very popular since local English girls were invited to join the festivities.

Following some practice missions, testing out combat formation tactics and familiarising themselves with the local geography, Gary Miller, his co-pilot Ken Leininger, Warren Berg and the rest of the crew took part in their first operational mission on 15 March 1944, to an aircraft factory at Brunswick in Germany. In the rear of Miller's B-17 was Bob Petty:

Bob Petty: My tail gunner's position was the coldest on the airplane. I had underwear, blue electric union suit, electric gloves, helmet and oxygen mask. My cheeks froze often but I scrubbed them with the fur on my mittens, so no permanent damage.

About my first mission . . . we were assigned to fly a very old ship named Helles Belles. In inspecting the ship on the ground, the pilot noticed two pieces of armor plating about 10 x 12 inches on the floor of the tail position. He said take them out – 'makes the ship tail heavy.' I said, 'Yes, sir,' and promptly forgot to do it. On the mission I heard a flak burst below and my left leg stung. I had the feeling of being wounded and wondered if I had lost a leg and why it didn't hurt worse. I looked down and I could see daylight that a two-inch piece of flak had made, hitting armor plating and then my boot and leg. No blood, no wound. Sure glad I kept those plates.

Flying in the rear of the 337 Squadron formation, Gary Miller and Ken Leininger were certainly tested as they sought to keep their B-17 from straying, drawing on their training but with the stakes now much higher. With skill and a little luck all aircraft of the 96th Bomb Group returned from the mission and Gary Miller's crew's confidence in his and his co-pilot's abilities grew.

Warren Berg's next four missions had him directing his pilot on further *Pointblank* sorties over German targets: Augsburg 16 and 17 March, Berlin on 22 March and Brunswick again on 23 March. Their next mission on 28 March took them to the airfield at Châteaudun, but then on 1 April it was back to Germany. They were detailed to attack Ludwigshafen, but heavy cloud over France forced the bombers to turn back. On 8 April the airfield at Achmer, Germany was targeted and then on 10 April Courcelles. On Gary's missions with the 96th to date, losses had been quite light but on their next mission the 96th Bomb Group would receive a severe mauling, as would the whole of the Eighth Air Force. It lost 64 bombers in an attack on the German aircraft industry, and the 96th BG suffered the highest bomb group losses of the mission, contributing 11 of its B-17s to the loss statistic.

On 13 and 18 April Gary Miller once more took his crew into action, visiting Augsburg and Berlin respectively, and again the 96th BG would pay a price, losing eight aircraft from the two missions. Gary and Warren's next four missions took them to Lippstadt on 19 April (no 96th BG losses), Friedrichshafen on 24 April (1 96th BG loss), Dijon airfield on 25 April (no 96th BG losses), and Juvincourt airfield on 9 May (no 96th BG losses). On these missions, involving Miller's crew, little opposition had been met, but on missions in the period involving other 96th BG crews they still encountered stiff opposition, notably on 8 May when ten 96th BG crews failed to return from an attack on Berlin. However, on Gary Miller's crew's next mission with the 96th BG they would be experiencing at first-hand an uncompromising air battle.

Despite the call on his command to contribute to the destruction of the communications network in the occupied territories starting in April 1944, 'Tooey' Spaatz still wanted to direct his heavy bombers on German oil targets, and he had some influential supporters. British MP Geoffrey Lloyd, Minister of Petroleum Warfare, had written to Churchill on 19 April outlining his views on the potential benefits of targeting the Reich's oil production:

> In the Ruhr there are nine synthetic plants producing 1,500,000 tons a year, which is a quarter of the total synthetic output. If our views are correct, daylight attack on these plants would force the Luftwaffe to give battle on a great scale and contribute to early Overlord operations by the further attrition of the German fighter force.[48]

However Lloyd also noted that the subsequent depletion in German oil production would not have an effect on the early stages of *Overlord*. A copy of Lloyd's letter is deposited amongst the files of Kingston-McCloughry held at the Imperial War Museum, London. Lloyd's support for using heavy bombers to attack German oil did not go down well with the advocates of the Transportation Plan. Kingston-McCloughry had added in pencil at the top of the letter a note to Zuckerman. 'Prof Z: Can't we shoot Mr Lloyd down in flames?'

When the senior air commanders next met to discuss *Overlord* bombing policy, with Churchill in attendance, the matter of attacking the enemy's synthetic fuel production was raised. Portal was of the opinion that once the Allied land forces had established themselves in Normandy, attention could and should shift to German oil. But there was also general consensus that attacks on the synthetic plants in the near future, would draw the German air force into a fight. Tedder looked to redress the balance and voiced his concerns that it was time the Americans began to fulfil their commitments to the Transportation Plan, but by the end of the meeting Spaatz had the concessions he was looking for. It had been agreed that one or two attacks could be made on synthetic oil. Spaatz's window of opportunity had opened, although poor weather would frustrate any immediate response.

Before Spaatz could open his oil campaign, he committed the Eighth Air Force to attacks on pre-invasion targets. On 9 and 11 May a total of 1,796 Eighth Air Force heavies, with fighter escort, were sent to France and Belgium, just short of 4,000 tons of bombs blasting airfields and railyards. Some opposition was met: 22 bombers were lost (1.2%) and 16 fighters. The bombers made no enemy aircraft claims; the fighters claimed 25 destroyed and 17 damaged.[49] This fell short of the enemy attrition rates Spaatz was seeking. He wanted larger and fiercer confrontations between his airmen and the enemy.

Incident

Jim Johnson was a rear gunner with RAF Bomber Command's 61 Squadron. Recalling a close call whilst on the raid to Lille on the night of 10/11 May 1944, he highlights yet another operational risk to bomber aircrews which was not of the enemy's making.

> It was very cloudy, we were flying about in low cloud and everyone switched on their navigation lights. Everyone was milling about so much and it was the only time I was really scared. It was only a matter of split seconds but this massive thing came in, a Lanc, and it took the tip off the port fin and rudder and smashed my turret. It bent all the guns and smashed all the remaining bits of perspex that were in the turret. The propeller could only have been a matter of a foot from me. I remember the pilot obviously saw what was happening and he lifted his wing, otherwise it would have been curtains for us. No one reported an accident so we can only assume that the Lanc went down. The rest of my crew didn't know anything about it. The mid-upper didn't even see it.[50]

On 12 May weather conditions finally proved favourable for the Eighth Air Force to begin their campaign against German oil, Doolittle's bomb groups opening up with a deep penetration over the Reich. Spaatz wanted an air battle and on this occasion the Luftwaffe would oblige.

All three Eighth Air Force Bomb Divisions would send their aircrews to Germany that day: six combat wings, of the 1st Bomb Division (BD), 326 aircraft dispatched, to oil refineries at Merseburg and Lützkendorf; four combat wings of the 2nd Bomb Division, 265 aircraft dispatched, to oil refineries at Zeitz and Böhlen; and five combat wings of the 3rd Bomb Division, 295 aircraft dispatched, including Gary Miller's 96th Bomb Group Fortress, to the oil refinery at Brüx and aircraft components plant at Zwickau. The force of 886 aircraft would be led by the 3rd BD, crossing the Belgian coast at approximately 1030 hours, followed by the 1st BD then the 2nd BD. The route for the bomber force took them south-west passing south of Brussels, then a turn to east-north-east, passing north of Frankfurt at which point the 3rd BD would head virtually due east, before splitting, the plan being for one CW to turn north to Zwickau, the other four CWs to continue on to Brüx. The 1st and 2nd BDs would continue east-north-east before turning north to attack their targets.

In addition to the vast bomber force dispatched by the Eighth Air Force, 735 P-38s, P-47s and P-51s from the Eighth's Fighter Command and 245 P-38s and P-51s from the Ninth's Fighter Command would support the heavy bombers. A detailed plan of fighter cover was devised ensuring close cover during the long flight in and out of German air space. This raid would give ample opportunity for Spaatz's men to inflict further losses on their enemy, ample opportunity for the

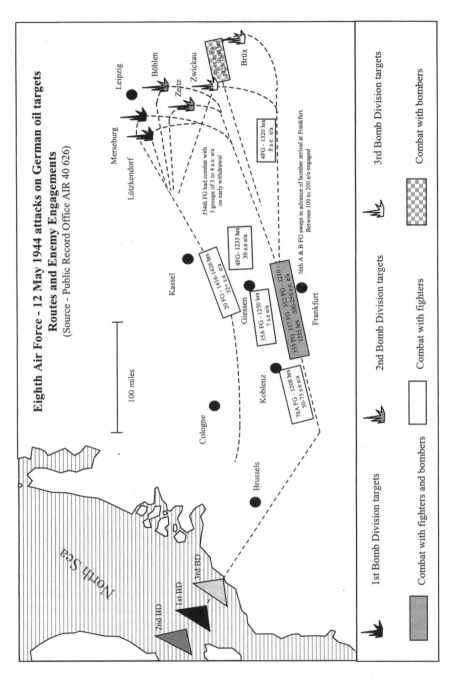

**Eighth Air Force - 12 May 1944 attacks on German oil targets
Routes and Enemy Engagements**
(Source – Public Record Office AIR 40 626)

German air force to show its will to counter the American bomber. And this they would do in strength against the 3rd BD. The fighter cover plan for the 3rd BD had four Fighter Groups (FG) escorting the division on the run-in to the target, whilst another FG swept possible enemy fighter approach routes. Over the target one FG was detailed to see off any enemy aerial opposition. As the 3rd BD heavies returned two FGs were detailed to provide cover.

As mentioned one of our featured crews was detailed to take part in the mission and each one of Gary Miller's crew would remember the experience for the rest of their lives.

> *Bob Petty:* I do remember with some clarity, after nearly 60 years has elapsed, so much so that I have marked May 12th of each year as a special day of homage to the many friends and brave airmen who ended up wounded, dead or POWs that day.

Below are the details of how the mission unfolded, with special focus on the 3rd Bomb Division and the 96th Bomb Group.[51]

Prior to 1030 hours

3rd Bomb Division: Assembles over England, crossing the North Sea and approaching the Belgian coast. The 96th BG puts 26 aircraft into the air: 12 in the 'A' group to fly lead in the 45th A Combat Wing and 14 in the B group to fly low. Taking off just after 0800 hours, the 96th's bombers assemble visually at 6,000 feet, climb to 14,000 feet, and the A group lead the way from over base at 0937 hours. They arrive over Ely at 0947 hours, March at 0951 hours, Kings Lynn at 0958 hours and Wymondham at 1010 hours. They cross the English coast at Clacton, Essex, one minute early.

3rd BD Fighter Support: 361st FG airborne and proceeding to rendezvous with 3rd BD heavies.

1st and 2nd Bomb Divisions: Assembling over England and proceeding across North Sea.

RAF Signals Intelligence: Commencing at 0818 hours a few scattered early plots are made of enemy movements. At 1020 a *Gruppe* of *Jagdgeschwader* 26 (possibly the third) is ordered to be at full readiness from 1045. It is noted that there is no actual radar reflection of a preliminary move but it is believed that *Jagdgeschwader* 26 moves to Rhineland bases in silence.

1030 to 1210 hours

3rd Bomb Division: Crosses the enemy coast, the 96th hitting landfall at 1056 hours, and proceeds south-east passing south of Brussels. Turns to east-north-east, heading for gap between Giessen and Frankfurt. Enemy aircraft seen ahead.

3rd BD Fighter Support: 361st FG rendezvous with 3rd BD heavies at 21,000 feet east of Coxyde and provides escort until force 65 miles south-east of Liège, breaking off at 1150 hours. No enemy opposition seen. At 1128 hours 353rd FG arrives south of Brussels. 353rd FG continues to provide escort and prepares to engage approaching enemy fighters.

The 56th FG sweeps the routes ahead of the bomber formations with some success, later claiming 19 kills and one probable, at a cost of 3 P-47s and pilots.

1st and 2nd Bomb Divisions: Cross Belgian coast and follow in wake of 3rd BD, with no opposition.

RAF Signals Intelligence: Hears the enemy reporting the American bomber force between Dunkirk and Ostend at 1102 hours, and hears of enemy aircraft taking off from Salzwedel (1125 hours), Sachan (1120 hours) and Burg (1125 hours), as the Luftwaffe prepares to meet its adversary.

1210 to 1235 hours

3rd Bomb Division: The air battle rages against enemy fighters. 22 plus enemy fighters open the attack, south-east of Coblenz, from head on. Their cannon fire and machine guns tear into the bombers. Some of the German pilots fly their fighters straight into B-17s. Then, north of Frankfurt, waves of 30 plus FW190s and Me109s, flying wing tip to wing tip, attack the bombers head on with cannon and machine guns, pass through the bomber formations and then reform for further attacks. At the same time Me109s, flying at 30,000 feet, bounce the bombers from above. Some American airmen lose their lives when their aircraft collide with attacking fighters. Many other Americans struggle to get out of their aircraft as the fatally damaged bombers fall out of formation.

96th Bomb Group Losses: 1st Lieutenant Simons's 339 Squadron B-17 falls out of control after being attacked by the enemy fighters. It is later assumed that the pilot and co-pilot were killed by the fighter attack. At approximately 2,000 feet the tail breaks off, enabling the tail gunner to clear the aircraft. He is the only survivor and is captured and taken to hospital with a broken left tibia.

The plexiglass and metallic section of the nose of 2nd Lieutenant Jerry Musser's 337 Squadron B-17 is blown off by 20 mm cannon fire, and the aircraft leaves formation, peeling off to the right under control. The navigator has been killed by the enemy fire along with the radio operator. Crews from other aircraft see a man hanging from the nose of Musser's plane. As the aircraft descends the tail gunner bails out, but the rest of the crew remain in the plane as a crash landing is attempted. This is achieved and those still alive leave the burning aircraft and are subsequently captured.

In 2nd Lieutenant Charles Filer's 338 Squadron bomber both his waist gunners are killed instantly by a 20mm cannon shell. Filer is seriously injured and fights to keep his crippled aircraft under control despite having three engines out, still carrying a full bomb load and most of the stabilizer shot away. His co-pilot is dead, slumped forward. The radio operator is first to leave the aircraft, bailing out on his own decision owing to his serious wounds and believing he could get aid on the ground. In the top turret the engineer, with facial wounds, fires away at his adversaries and despite prompting from the radio operator just before he bails, he refuses to leave his position. Just before the navigator bails out he recalls seeing the engineer putting on his chest chute. But the engineer loses his life in the incident along with the waist gunners, co-pilot and Filer, whose efforts did ensure the survival of five of his crew.

Fighter fire slams into 2nd Lieutenant Harold Tucker's 339 Squadron B-17 and ignites the fuel tanks. The nose of the aircraft is knocked off and the navigator and bombardier are killed. The aircraft goes into a spin but Tucker regains control. Nevertheless the situation is hopeless and the crew prepare to bail out. The co-pilot, suffering with burns, comes back into the radio room looking for and asking for an extra parachute; his original one has been burnt. Unable to find one he holds onto the radio operator as he bails out, in the hope that one parachute can hold the both of them. When the radio operator's parachute opens the co-pilot loses hold on his leg and falls to his death. The pilot and tail gunner also lose their lives, still in the aircraft when it hits the ground. Five men survive the incident, parachuting down on to a German fighter airfield where they are quickly captured.

The bombardier in the 337 Squadron B-17 of 2nd Lieutenant Herbert Moore, 2nd Lieutenant Edward McGlasson, sees the fire from his guns tear into an enemy fighter and the navigator reports the kill to his crewmates. Shortly after while trying to avoid an exploding bomber their aircraft swerves and collides with the 337 Squadron B-17 of 1st Lieutenant Arthur Hon. The nose section of Moore's aircraft is smashed away and the navigator and bombardier lose their lives. Despite the damage, control of the aircraft is maintained and after losing approximately 10,000 feet in height the tail gunner, two waist gunners, ball turret gunner and radio operator bail out, under orders, and are captured. Moore, his co-pilot and the engineer survive the crash landing. The crew of Hon's aircraft has not faired so well. In the initial impact Hon is killed when the props of the other B-17 rip through the pilot's compartment, which is then crushed. The aircraft breaks in two and the front end blows up, and the engineer, co-pilot, navigator and bombardier are also killed. The ball turret gunner loses his life, as his turret breaks away. The radio operator, along with the waist gunners, is able to escape the aircraft owing to the break and as he falls, parachute open, the tail gunner falls by, without a chute, to his death.

In 1st Lieutenant Robert Lewis's 338 Squadron B-17 the bombardier calls out over the interphone, 'Here they come again' as enemy fighters approach from dead ahead, 12 o'clock. Enemy fire tears into the bomber and the engineer reports shooting the tail assembly off one of the attackers. Nevertheless the Fortress is damaged and Lewis orders his crew to bail out. The tail gunner later reports that 'the crew I could see from my position were the waist gunners. They were getting ready to bail out, when the wing burned off from No. 4 engine on out; the plane rolled to the right and I fell out.' The aircraft then exploded. The ball turret gunner, having just climbed out of his turret, sees the waist gunners bail out and then he is blown through the side of the plane. The tail, waist and ball turret gunners all survive. The six other members of the crew lose their lives, either killed by enemy fire or in the explosion.

The 413 Squadron lead ship of Captain James Knupp with the command pilot aboard is struck by an FW190 between the number 3 and 4 engines. The wing is cut and the aircraft falls in a tight spiral. Only two men survive the incident, both captured.

Members of the crew of the 413 Squadron crew of 1st Lieutenant Thomas Moore, flying deputy lead, with Command Pilot 1st Lieutenant Richard Thomson on board, watch as the air battle rages; one claims, 'The Luftwaffe must all be here today.' They then see the collision of the two 337 Squadron B-17s. The engineer in the top turret calls to his pilot, 'Watch out these planes don't crash into us.' They are fortunate and Moore asks his crew, 'Am I clear of the falling planes?' They are, but then they are attacked and receive severe damage in the front, from 20mm cannon fire. From the radio operator's position, Technical Sergeant Raymond Hellstrom looks forward and can see a mass of twisted metal. He sees Thomson slumped over the instrument panel and Moore is slumped over him. One of his gunners lies on the floor near Hellstrom, his neck broken when he hit the roof of the aircraft owing to the convulsive motion of the B-17. Hellstrom would later report 'He was dying as I crawled by him. There was nothing I could do.' Hellstrom also later reports that the engineer 'was riddled with 20mm.' Hellstrom manages to get out and survives along with the right waist gunner, Mickey operator and co-pilot.

There is only one survivor from the crew of 2nd Lieutenant Jack Link's 339 Squadron B-17.

The left wing of 2nd Lieutenant Wilford Kinman's 337 Squadron B-17 is partially destroyed by a fighter attack from the rear. The pilot struggles to keep control. The navigator receives first aid owing to a wound and break to his left leg just below his knee. All men manage to escape the stricken bomber. The bombardier breaks his leg on landing and ends up in hospital with the navigator. They are later repatriated, but the rest of the crew will see the war out in captivity.

The tail gunner of 1st Lieutenant Robert Laurie's 339 Squadron B-17 hears in his headphones the pilot call, 'Fighter coming in head on boys'. Almost immediately there is a terrific crash, followed by an explosion, which blows the tail gunner out through the tail escape. He later records that he believes the crash was the impact of the enemy fighter. After falling some considerable distance the tail gunner, badly shaken, is still able to pull his parachute cord and he sees several other airmen from other crews suspended from their parachutes. A wing from his aircraft falls past him. The navigator also survives, having escaped through the nose hatch.

In addition to the losses two 96th BG aircraft have to jettison their bombs owing to combat damage.

The 96th's gunners also inflicted losses on their enemy, later claiming 11 destroyed, 4 probables and 16 damaged.

3rd BD Fighter Support: Initially pilots of the 353rd FG try desperately to support the five combat wings but they are seriously outnumbered, and can only account for a few enemy aircraft, although without loss to themselves. At 1212 hours the 357th FG arrive as the second wave of enemy fighters plough through the bomber formations. The 357th's pilots begin to notch up kills, later claiming 14 enemy fighters, but at a cost of two P-51s.

At 1214 hours the 4th FG, detailed for support over the target, is over Kassel heading east, when they hear of the battle north of Frankfurt. They turn south and as they approach the battle 30 enemy aircraft are seen at a very low altitude heading north-east of Giessen. The 4th FG's pilots take up the combat, shooting down a few of their enemy, without loss. After contact is broken they climb back to support the bombers.

1st and 2nd Bomb Divisions: Continue behind 3rd BD meeting minimal opposition.

RAF Signals Intelligence: Hears at 1210 hours that aircraft of *Jagddivisionen* 1, 2, 3 and 4 are attacking in the Frankfurt-Cologne area.

1235 to 1340 hours

3rd Bomb Division: The severely mauled formations turn due east and head for the targets, meeting no aerial opposition. Owing to the losses the number 4 aircraft of the 96th's A group takes over lead of their respective combat wing and the remnants of the 96th's B group join the A group. The 96th has not been the only bomb group to suffer. At the end of the day 14 bombers from the 45th CW's 452nd BG will be listed as missing in action.

One combat wing, the 4th, breaks north for Zwickau and is followed by the remnants of the 45th CW, including the 96th BG. Fifty-eight B-17s of the 4th CW drop their explosives, causing severe damage at the aircraft factory at Zwickau. The accompanying 96th BG aircraft attack a target of opportunity, the marshalling yards at Zwickau. The rest of the division, after continuing east for a short distance turn north towards Brüx and the bombs from 140 B-17s blast the oil refinery. 60 of the 3rd BD's heavy bombers attack other secondary and opportunity targets.

3rd BD Fighter Support: At 1240 hours the 353rd FG turns for home. The 357th and 4th FGs maintain the escort. No enemy fighters are encountered except for when, at 1320 hours, a section of the 4th FG breaks up a small formation of eight Me109s. Just prior to the target, sections of 4th FG have to turn for home owing to the fact that they had had to shed their extra fuel tanks earlier than expected when engaged in combat north of Frankfurt. The remaining sections see the bombers over the target then they too head for home.

1st and 2nd Bomb Divisions: Continue east-north-east, breaking from the route followed by the 3rd BD and start turns north towards targets. 510 heavies shed their loads on the primary targets (46 going for secondary and opportunity targets). Results at Lützkendorf are later assessed as fair, at Merseburg good, at Zeitz good to very good and at Böhlen very good.

1340 to 1500 hours

3rd Bomb Division: After turning west out of the target approximately 50 Me410s using rockets and closing with cannon fire engage the three CWs that had attacked Brüx, which now have no escort. This formation then heads west. After releasing their bombs on the Zwickau marshalling yards, the remnants of the 96th BG lose height and join the 4th CW echeloned low and left.

3rd BD Fighter Support: The 355th FG arrives late on the scene having passed the rear combat boxes of the 1st BD south of Brussels and escorted these to the turn north to its respective target. At 1340 it meets remnants of the 3rd BD, and then escorts this formation, uneventfully, until 1450 hours.

1st and 2nd Bomb Divisions: The formations turn west out of the targets and proceed on a broad front passing south of Kassel and Cologne, meeting no aerial opposition.

1500 onwards

All Bomb Divisions: On a broad front the formations head west, uneventfully, cross the Belgian coast and head for England. The 96th BG aircraft accompany the 4th CW as far as Clacton, at which point they turn away for their home base. The two 96th BG aircraft that had jettisoned their bombs owing to damage, land away from their base, at Manston, and those crew members injured receive treatment.

3rd BD Fighter Support: 55th FG rendezvous with two CWs of the 3rd BD at 1507 and provides escort to the vicinity of Ghent until 1615 hours. Engages some enemy fighters pursuing straggling bombers, claiming one kill. The 370th FG meets the bombers at 1550 hours and provides accompaniment as far as the English coast at Clacton at 1630 hours.

The 12 May 1944 mission takes its place in Eighth Air Force history as one of the fiercest aerial combats. The 96th BG's mission report would state that 'the aggressiveness of the e/a can't be overstated in today's operations and attest to the ability of their pilots.' In total the Eighth Air Force lost 43 B-17s and 3 B-24s, the vast majority to fighters. The 3rd BD met most of the opposition, losing 37 B-17s. The 96th BG contributed 12 of their aircraft to the statistic.

Warren Berg and Bob Petty recalled the attack by the waves of enemy aircraft as the bomber force passed between Coblenz and Frankfurt:

Warren Berg: They looked like a swarm of angry bees bearing down on us in attack mode. At a closure rate of more than 600 knots, the Me109s and FW190s were on to us almost instantly. All of our .50 caliber machine guns began to fire as soon as they came into range and continued as they swept through our formation, causing great damage and disruption. The Germans made three runs at our formations, all from the 12 o'clock position. On the last run, an FW190 made straight for our airplane. I was at the right nose machine gun and fired at him as soon as he came into range. I continued firing as he swept by but do not know if I was hitting his plane. I vividly recall seeing the pilot looking right at me before he disappeared under our right wing. I believe he had intended to ram us but Gary Miller expertly raised that wing just in time to let him slide by underneath.

The three German attacks were over in approximately 20 minutes but it seemed that there was non-stop action throughout that period. Machine guns rattling – gunners calling out attacking aircraft – reports of B-17s on fire – colliding – breaking up – crews bailing out in parachutes.

Bob Petty: I saw the plane directly behind me and lower, falling from above with only the wing tips outside the flames. The plane below swerved to not get hit and in doing so, his wing hit the plane beside him, folded back and cut open the other bomber. For seconds I could see the plane cut like an open peapod and see the guys inside. Then they all fell. Some did get out by parachute. One crew was our barracks mate and we had previously gone through training with them.

Neal B. Crawford was a ball turret gunner with the 96th Bomb Group and flew on the 12 May mission. He recorded what he saw in his diary:

This was really it! We got the hell kicked out of us today. I think they threw up just about everything that they had in the Luftwaffe. . . Airplanes (both German and American) and pieces of airplane filled the sky. They knocked down 6 B-17s from our group on the first pass. Two off our right broke in half by the ball turret. As I looked back behind me all I could see in the air was parachutes. One went the full 20 thousand feet without opening. All along the ground were fires where planes had it and burst into flames. Brother I was really in a cold sweat.

Navigator Jack Croul, of the 96th Bomb Group, also flew on the mission and recorded his experiences in his diary:

May 12, 1944 – We were hit by fighters about 30 miles west of Frankfurt.

Their first pass hit the group ahead and some followed thru to us, about 30 109s and FW190s. The next pass was at us and knocked down the group leader and his right wing man, both pathfinders. Knupp was lead and Moore who just left our squadron last week to join the pathfinder outfit, was [No.]2. I saw the right side of Moore's cockpit burst into flames and he pulled up under us; we had to pull up sharply to prevent his hitting us. Then he went down and someone said he chopped Link's tail off as he did so – Link has been with us since Dalhart; Rickaman was his navigator, Williams was Moore's navigator. Both swell boys. The fighters made 2 or 3 more passes at us; all head-on attacks, aiming to get our leaders. Thank God we weren't one today . . .

May 13 1944 – Slept until 0900. Went to hospital this afternoon for a few days rest. I'm still shaking from yesterday and those 3 group leads of the 3 days before have made me a nervous wreck.

May 14 1944 – Went to church at the post chapel. I've done a lot of praying today and yesterday. God was riding in our ship Friday.

In terms of damage to the 12 May mission targets the Eighth's airmen could be pleased with their efforts, as the 1,500 tons on the primary targets and 218 tons on opportunity targets caused considerable damage. But what was also pleasing to Spaatz was that the German air force had sought to oppose the attack in strength and suffered considerable loss. Spaatz knew his force could cope with its own loss. The Luftwaffe could not.

The Loss of a Brother

At midnight on 26 May 1944 a telegram arrived at the home in Portland, Oregon of 13-year-old Fred Paul. He took it to his mother, and, as Fred would later recall, the message brought a period of 'emotional destruction' to his family. Fred's brother, Technical Sergeant Harland Paul, was the top turret gunner/engineer on the 339th Squadron, 96th Bomb Group crew of 1st Lieutenant Robert Simons, which had been shot down on the 12 May 1944 mission to oil targets in Germany. Harland was missing in action.

Fred Paul: As a youngster I worshipped him with the big brother image so many young boys have. I always asked him, no matter where he went, 'When are you coming home Harland?' I had asked him that question in September 1942 when he left for boot camp, and again on 15 November 1943, which was the only time we saw him while in the air force. It was a 15-day leave prior to going overseas. His answer to me was 'When the war is over.' As I quietly wept the morning he left, I never for a moment thought God could be so cruel as to take such a fine young man only 21 years of age.

For the rest of the war Fred's life was filled with anxiety as to the fate of his brother. After the war, his family received a letter, as did all the next of kin of the crew, from the tail gunner on Fred's brother's aircraft, who had survived and been captured. He informed them that he believed there were no other survivors. This was later confirmed from captured official documents.

In the years after the war Fred maintained a desire to find out exactly what had happened to his brother that tragic day in 1944. It wasn't until June 1983, however, when Fred was asked to give a talk on the Second World War at his young son's school that Fred was galvanised into action. In preparing for the talk he discovered some military documents in his late mother's belongings, which proved the catalyst that would rekindle Fred's desire to discover the circumstances of his brother's death. Fred began a personal journey, visiting the graves of his brother and crew and finding the next of kin of the rest of the crew. He learned that the one survivor, the tail gunner, had died 21 years before, on the anniversary of the fateful 12 May mission, having never recovered from the physical and psychological trauma. Fred discovered the crash location in Germany and learned that there were still people living there who had vivid recollections of the day when an American bomber had come down near their community.

In May 1984 Fred made an emotional trip to the location of the crash, and visited the small cemetery where the nine killed airmen had first been buried (they were subsequently moved and ended up back in America). On 12 May 1984, exactly 40 years after the fateful event, at the crash site, he planted nine carnations. There were fragments of the bomber still embedded in a tree and the ground was still scarred. During his trip Fred met a veteran German soldier who had witnessed the whole incident from the air battle to the explosion of the aircraft a few thousand feet up, and the crash a few hundred metres from where he stood. He also met the farmer who had helped the badly shaken and traumatised tail gunner, who was suffering with a broken ankle, the only man able to escape from the plummeting bomber, and he met an old lady who had given the tail gunner water to drink. He learnt how some local people had taken the tail gunner in to prevent him falling into the hands of some fervent Nazis who would have killed the downed American, and that they eventually released him to more 'friendly' captors. Fred also met the priest who had overseen the burial of his brother and his colleagues. He heard that the day after the crash, a German Fieseler Storch aircraft had flown over and landed at the crash site, at which a crowd had gathered. A German officer climbed out, surveyed the wreckage, then saluted the dead American airmen. It was the Luftwaffe pilot who had claimed the kill the day before, but he too had been shot down by the top turret guns of the wrecked aircraft that lay in front of him. When asked by someone in the crowd, 'Why do you salute the enemy?' he had replied, 'For tomorrow it could be me lying there and I hope my adversary would do the same for me.'

When Fred returned to America he was able to assemble all the information he had accumulated and make it available to the next of kin of all the crew. It had been an extraordinary experience for him. He had established a bond with the German people whose community had been so touched by the whole episode that they would erect a memorial at the crash location. Forty years since his big brother had died fighting the war thousands of miles from home, Fred had pieced together what had happened that fateful day. Which perhaps went some way towards repairing Fred's 'emotional destruction.'

Ultra[52] decrypts gave Allied intelligence evidence of the success of the oil attacks and the concern within the German High Command. A signal intercept of 16

May informed them of the re-deployment of flak batteries to protect certain synthetic oil plants. A signal intercept of 21 May informed the Allies that the German armed forces were being warned of reductions in fuel allocations.[53]

According to Germany's Armaments Minister Albert Speer, the Allied offensive against oil opened one of the decisive campaigns of the war. In his postwar memoirs he states that he would 'never forget the date May 12.'

> On that day the technological war was decided. Until then we had managed to produce approximately as many weapons as the armed forces needed, in spite of their considerable losses. But with the attack of nine hundred and thirty-five daylight bombers of the American Eighth Air Force upon several fuel plants in central and eastern Germany, a new era in the air war began. It meant the end of German armaments production.[54]

Spaatz's convictions had been well founded, a weakness in the German war machine had been found. But pressure remained on the Eighth Air Force to commit fully to the Transportation Plan.

At the beginning of May, Jim Tyson, John Howland and their crew took up residence at Bassingbourn, where they were assigned to the 324th Squadron of the 91st Bomb Group. Their debut mission took them to Berlin and then it was almost two weeks before they next went to war. Once again the target was Berlin. Early on 19 May the crew landed at Ridgewell, home of their former bomb group.

> *John Howland's diary:* Our reception at breakfast is becoming a depressing ritual. When we walk through the door of the mess hall, there is an audible groan as the men recognize the PFF team members and realize, for the first time, that the scheduled mission will be a Deep Penetration. Old friends and acquaintances that we lived with and flew alongside just two months ago now shun us like we have the plague. There is no compassion in their voices and no consideration of the fact that under a Plan 'A' Deep Penetration or a Plan 'B' Milk Run to occupied territory, they get to go on the Milk Runs but we don't. I try to tell myself that it is nothing personal; but it is hard to get a lift when the greeting is, 'Here come those Poor F..... Flyboys. Why don't you PFF guys stay home in Bassingbourn?'

Jim Tyson's aircraft was to fly as lead ship for the 1st Combat Wing. Up until the start of the bomb run the flight was without major incident. Then things hotted up:

> *John Howland's diary:* Straight and level is bad news for bomber crews and it wasn't long before the flak started popping all around us. In addition to the oily, black, 88 mm bursts, we saw, and heard, some larger shell bursts. The big ones were probably 105 mm. We could hear these bursts even over the roar of the engines and with our helmets and earphones pressing against our ears. One burst must have gone off about fifty feet below us and just blasted the plane with shrapnel. There was a loud explosion. Something slammed against my left leg and a hole suddenly appeared in my wooden navigator's table. My left foot burned like Hades, and there was sawdust shimmering in the air. I wore a seat

pack parachute so that I could get out of a plane in a hurry if I had to. I thought we had bought it, and started to make tracks for the escape hatch. But I looked out of the windows and saw all four motors running and Jim's feet on the rudder pedals.

No alarm had been sounded. I decided we weren't hit too badly, and went back to my navigator's table. My foot was burning like fire, but I couldn't stop navigating to find out what was wrong. I watched the bombardier and saw him suddenly reach over and salvo the bombs. It developed that he had been having trouble with the clouds, and finally aimed for the center of the city. After bombs away, I wanted Jim to turn left, pick up a heading of 55 degrees, and get the hell out of there. I tried to call him on the interphone, but couldn't get through to him. In the excitement of it all, I didn't realize that my throat mike had become disconnected when I headed for the escape hatch.

I sat there and yelled, 'Fifty five degrees, Jim, for Christ's sake turn to 55 degrees.' But Jim never turned until I got my wits together and reconnected my throat mike.

There was a lot of smoke in the nose compartment, and we found that flak had knocked out the radio compass located on the wall just above my left shoulder. I grabbed a curved emergency knife with a cork handle. I cut through and pulled loose all of the wires going to the radio compass. The smoking stopped and I got back to navigating again.

It was good to get away from the Berlin flak; but I was still pretty badly shaken and not doing a good job navigating. The next turning point on the flight plan was just 6 minutes after the 'Bombs Away' turning point. I overshot it by four minutes, and by the time I got organized, I was 25 miles right of course and headed for Stettin.

John soon recovered the situation, getting his aircraft back on course for home, and when he was able to relax he checked on his left foot:

John Howland's diary: There was a hole, about the size of a half-dollar, in the floor by my left foot. I reached down and felt another hole in the side of my fur-lined outer boot, and thought for sure that my foot would be mangled. I poked my finger into the hole; but I could only feel the electric boot. There was no blood on my finger when I withdrew it. On closer inspection, I discovered that the heat was coming from a hot wire in my electric boot and the piece of flak had zipped by just nicking the side of my foot. The inner boot wasn't even torn. Imagination sure can play funny tricks on a person.

Once over the North Sea John assessed the damage to his aircraft:

John Howland's diary: A portable oxygen bottle that was lying right alongside my desk made the big explosion I heard over Berlin. I know these low-pressure bottles are not supposed to blow up, but this one ruptured like a balloon and slammed the aluminium partition into my leg. But most of the force blew the other way. I counted eight holes in the bottom of the plane, all within 3 feet of me. Marvin Fairbanks and I were lucky we didn't get hit with shrapnel. It was flak from this same burst that knocked out the radio compass.

I still don't know where the sawdust came from I saw shimmering in the air. Perhaps flak pulverized the wood when it made the hole in the tabletop. Perhaps it was dust from the bottom of the plane. Perhaps it was only my imagination.

After leaving the 381st BG over Ridgewell Jim Tyson finally landed his aircraft and tired crew back at Bassingbourn. Also flying in formation to Berlin was the crew of Gary Miller and Warren Berg, but fortune would favour the 96th BG that day, which lost no bombers, although the enemy defences prevented 28 American crews, from other groups, returning to England.

The very next day Jim Tyson's crew was briefed for another raid, either a trip to Ludwigshafen, Germany, or Villacoubley in France. It eventually turned out to be a mission to the French target so the PFF crew was not required. On 22 May the crew flew as deputy lead on a fairly uneventful mission to Kiel, as did Gary Miller and Warren Berg's crew. Warren next saw action with his crew in the attack on Berlin on 24 May but they would then not go back to war for another two weeks. On 27 May Jim Tyson piloted his aircraft as deputy lead on an attack on Ludwigshafen and on 28 May as lead ship on a raid to an oil refinery near Desau. After that neither crew returned to Germany for two weeks as the focus of attention switched, and the next time they flew operationally, they were contributing to the tactical phase of the Allied assault on the Normandy beaches.

Incident

Geoffrey Haworth was a pilot with 77 Squadron RAF Bomber Command and was shot down on the raid to Orleans on 22/23 May 1944. He recalls the turmoil of trying to control and then escape from a burning aircraft:

There was quite a lot of flak over France, but nothing very near and we reached the target, bombed and turned west for about 20 miles with no problems. We were almost due to turn north for home when suddenly there was a deafening noise and bullets and shells were exploding inside and outside the aircraft for 4 or 5 seconds. I started to 'weave' and called the crew to ask 'Where is it?' The rear gunner replied he couldn't see it. There was no reply from the mid-upper gunner. They were the only ones who could see behind. My flight engineer was behind me, in shouting range, despite the engine noise. I shouted to him to go and check the mid-upper gunner. Why was there no reply?

I continued weaving and trying to contact the others on the intercom but the only reply I got was from the rear gunner, reporting he could see no sign of a fighter. At some point the flight engineer re-appeared, making thumbs-down signs and pointing to the mid-upper gunner and the wireless operator. It was hard to judge time but after perhaps 2 minutes we got another long burst, the controls went floppy and the aircraft went into a steep dive. Until that point we were under control and I had hoped to fight off or evade any nightfighters. I shouted to the flight engineer to bail out and tell the navigator and bomber. He would pass them on his way to the front escape hatch.

My parachute was stored in the flight engineer's position and the drill laid down in the classroom was that he handed it to me. I do not remember that we had ever practised it but Reg [the flight engineer] remembered of his own accord and amid all the confusion spent a few valuable seconds in getting it. I do not know if this would have made any difference for him. He must have been killed later by the third burst. I was lucky he was still unhurt at the critical time and remembered the drill. I would never have found it in the dark. I had difficulty clipping it on, not enough hands with all the other activity going on. I continued to try and get control but it was no good. The rear gunner appeared alongside me and I shouted to him to bail out and tell the navigator and bomber. He too would pass them. He told me later that his turret had been put out of action. At some stage we got the third burst of fire.

Each crew position had an emergency signal light and I started to tap out 'P' the code for 'Parachute'; in case anyone didn't know. I had had no direct contact all through with the navigator, bomber, mid-upper gunner or wireless operator, but they should have got the message from the flight engineer and rear gunner, if they were able to act on it. I could see the light reflecting below so I knew it was working. By now the whole affair must have been going on for 8 or 10 minutes, though it was hard to judge. We were still diving and I knew we must be near the ground so I stopped signalling and made a dash. The escape hatch should have been jettisoned when the first man went out, but it was still there ajar. I lifted it and looked out, seeing ground features. It seemed as if we were too low to be able to jump and then count to five before pulling the ripcord, so I pulled it as I fell out. There was a bit of a tug as the parachute caught on the tailplane, then everything went quiet except for a gentle flapping sound. I looked up and saw a 'bite' out of the parachute. That was the last I knew for some hours. It must have been 90% effective or I would not have survived.

Geoffrey Haworth and his rear gunner and navigator managed to get out of the stricken aircraft, but the other four members of the crew lost their lives. The navigator was wounded and stayed in a French hospital. Tragically when he was being transferred in a German convoy a few weeks later, it was attacked by Allied aircraft and the wounds he suffered proved fatal. Geoffrey Haworth continues his story from the point after he blacked out:

I woke up in daylight. There were two larks singing overhead. I was sure that larks were English birds and that we must have got back. There was a farmstead about 100 yards away. It didn't look English. I managed to stand with difficulty, my ribs were fractured and although I didn't know it at the time my spine also, although not the spinal cord. I moved towards the farm, and three or four men came to meet me and took me to a bed in the barn. I had many visitors and handshakes and even kisses. I can't recall how long it was but I was told that because of the spinal injury they could not hide me. The SS arrived. They were very correct, and were front line troops, there to face any invasion. The standard dropped as I got farther behind the lines. We actually went to the scene of the crash and I asked them to turn the van I was in so I could see it but they refused, possibly out of sympathy.

I was taken to Orléans hospital. On the way I saw lots of friendly signs from the French in the streets, and one lady on the pavement put a sweet in my mouth. USAAF aircraft went over whilst I was there so I was taken to the cellars. It was very embarrassing but there was nothing but friendly signs from the staff and other patients. However, although my spine was visibly distorted I was nevertheless eventually sent to the local police gaol. Since I had probably helped to fill the hospital I felt I shouldn't grumble.

The next day Geoffrey Haworth was joined by his rear gunner and both men began their POW lives. Geoffrey Haworth, owing to his injury, was repatriated in January 1945.

At this point the last of the highlighted Eighth Air Force crews became operational towards the end of May 1944, in time for the Eighth Air Force's full commitment to the Allied invasion. New Yorker George Ritchie was drafted in October 1941 and following his initial training in artillery and automatic weapons he saw time as part of the 73rd Coast Artillery in the Panama Canal Zone. However George aspired to the Army Air Corps and in June of 1942 passed the exams, which meant a return to the States in November of that year. After failing pilot training George attended Bombardier School from where he graduated to the 34th Bomb Group (H) at Blythe, California.

Early in 1944 the 34th BG received the call to contribute to the Eighth Air Force's accession of strength in England.

George Ritchie: Lady Luck visited us one day in early 1944, when the Chief of the Air Corps, Hap Arnold, was on his way to a meeting in California and had engine trouble near our base in Blythe, CA. He landed for repairs and ordered our exec officer, Major Joseph Burton, to fly him to his meeting, then return him to pick up his plane. On the trip Major Burton sang the praises and efficiencies of the 34th BG and suggested that he order the 34th into the European Theater to prepare on the continent for D-Day.

Arnold obliged and in March and April 1944 aircrews and some of the groundcrews of the 34th flew in their B-24s via Brazil and Africa to their new home at Mendlesham in Suffolk, England. The rest of the 34th endured a stormy Atlantic arriving in a welcoming Liverpool. George soon settled in:

George Ritchie: Life at station was very similar to Blythe since all the officers and men were at both stations. One major difference was that we were in a war zone and had to follow all the rules. Blackout conditions were severe. Travel and liberty were restricted. Flight line, equipment and dispersal of aircraft were utilized and followed.

Pass and liberty was something else. I was used to a Spanish-speaking culture and a Central American Spanish population. Here, things were just like home and getting used to the weather, travel and people was easy. Then there were the girls, just like the girls back home. I still remember the dances in Norwich and London.

Walter Sturdivan was a radio operator with the 34th:

My impression of England was very favorable although it was a little different than my home in the state of Oklahoma, USA. I liked the cool weather, the green fields, the quaint little villages, the local pubs, and the friendliness of the natives. We could not have been treated any better by our own families. I liked the English. The children and the young people were a delight to be around. The adults showed their appreciation for our presence and what we were doing for the country.

On 23 May the 34th went into action with the Eighth Air Force for the first time, sending 36 aircraft to Etampes/Mondesir airfield: 24 of the Group's B-24s dropped 72 tons of explosive, and 10 aircraft received minor flak damage. The next day it was George Ritchie's turn to go into action; his aircraft was 1st Lieutenant John Terry's B-24, one of 36 sent by the 34th BG to take part in a major attack by 2nd and 3rd Bomb Division heavies on airfields.

George Ritchie's diary: . . . all lined up and starting run to target, when for some unknown reason we were turned off and did not bomb the 2nd target either. Brought bomb load back to base.

George later recalled, 'no one knew why the mission was aborted except the brass,' but 400 of the 490 bombers despatched did manage to attack the primary or secondary targets.

The Eighth Air Force had sent 1,214 heavies on 23 and 24 May, dropping 3,515 tons of bombs on airfields and rail targets in France; its fighter-bombers also made their contribution by attacking rail bridges. And the next few days the American airmen continued to put their lives on the line by bombing French and Belgian railyards and airfields. The 34th's airmen, including John Terry's crew, risked their lives, when they were sent to Metz on 27 May, but smoke and dust frustrated an attack on the primary targets and only 11 of the 36 aircraft despatched released their loads on the secondary target, a factory at Woippy. The next day, the 34th contributed 36 aircraft as Spaatz seized another opportunity to attack German oil. Within 24 hours the 34th's bombers, including John Terry's aircraft, would again be over Germany, involved in a major attack on German oil, along with aircraft factories. And here the 34th, attacking the oil plants at Politz, would add to the Eighth Air Force's loss statistics, as three bombers failed to return.

Incident

Despite the fact that the Luftwaffe was failing to offer serious opposition to Eighth Air Force bomber attacks in France and Belgium in May 1944, ground defences were still a danger. Al Bibbens flew with the 562nd Squadron of the 388th Bomb Group on his 23rd mission on 25 May 1944:

As I recall, we were to bomb the bridges in the center of Liège, Belgium. As we were the lead crew from the 562nd Squadron, we had Lt Colonel Chamberlain flying as command pilot with us. Though I was second radio, on this mission I was assigned to fly first radio, which I had done on previous missions. As we crossed the coast to France, I was told to send back to Division Headquarters, the first of several control points. After receiving all the info from the navigator, I was just about to start my transmission, when the plane shook from a 'close' hit from flak. It knocked a piece of the gun or gun mount from the overhead gun in the radio room, to the floor. As I turned to see what it was, I looked out the right porthole and saw the number four engine was on fire. I immediately switched the radio frequency to 'Command', which overrides all other circuits, and reported 'Number three's on fire' and reached for my chute. Bill Lazar, the regular radio operator, who was flying in my position in the right waist position, had already pulled the emergency door release and jumped. Gene Benson, the left-waist gunner, was standing in the open doorway and just ready to go; when he saw me coming, he went out. I was just ready to go when I noticed the ball turret hatch was not open. I paused a moment, thinking about going back to help Ed Leonard, but he burst out of the turret. I waved to him to hurry and I jumped.

Al was fortunate. He had managed to escape the stricken bomber, which, shortly after, blew up killing Lt Colonel Chamberlain, the top turret gunner and the engineer. Al was captured shortly after landing and saw out the war behind barbed wire.

The attacks at the end of May were the Eighth's last raids to German oil targets before the launch of the Allied invasion. On 30 May the Eighth would go after the aircraft industry in Germany, but from then on focus shifted completely to the support of D-Day.

Our crews had made their contributions to Spaatz's oil offensive, seriously disrupting German army and air force supplies. On the eve of D-Day itself the German code-breakers at Bletchley Park passed on a German signal cypher that clearly summed up the success of the oil attacks:

Following according to OKL [Luftwaffe High Command] on fifth. As result of renewed interference with production of aircraft fuel by Allied action, most essential requirements for training and carrying out production plans can scarcely be covered by quantities of aircraft fuel available/ Baker four allocations only possible to air officers for bombers, fighters and ground attack and director general of supply. No repeat No other quota holders can be considered in June. To assure defence of Reich repeat Reich and to prevent gradual collapse of readiness for defence of GAF [German air force] repeat GAF in east, it has been necessary to break into OKW [Armed Forces High Command] repeat OKW strategic reserve. Extending therefore existing regulations ordered that all units to arrange operations so as to manage at least until the beginning of July with present stocks or small allocations which may be possible. Date of arrival and quantities of July quota still undecided. Only very small quantities available for adjustments, provided Allied situation remains unchanged. In no repeat no circumstances can greater allocations be made. Attention again to existing orders for most extreme economy measures and strict supervision of consumption, especially for transport, personal and communications flights. Supply of goods where possible and duty journey in general (in Reich repeat Reich at least) to be by rail.[55]

Spaatz's determination to attack the main artery of the German armed forces, the oil supply, had brought success. His airmen had cut, deeply, and after the initial tactical support to the Normandy landings at the start of June they would return, this time with help from the RAF.

CHAPTER 8

TACTICAL BOMBING

In the few weeks leading up to D-Day the US Eighth Air Force and RAF Bomber Command placed greater emphasis on bombing tactical targets in support of the Normandy beach assault. In this chapter we introduce Stan Selfe and Richard Haine who begin their RAF Bomber Command operations during this tactical period, joining the rest of our featured airmen as the momentous day grew near.

In the early hours of 27 March 1944 Alan Grant, Ron Neills, Steve Masters and the rest of their 622 Squadron crew returned home from an attack on Essen. With eight operations now completed (six against German targets) the crew's experience and apparent operational ability received recognition. A certain Hamish Mahaddie was on the headquarters staff of RAF Bomber Command's 8 (PPF) Group, the Pathfinder Force, with responsibility for recruiting new 'Pathfinders'. This involved visiting squadrons and selecting crews who were deemed to have potential. On a visit to 622 Squadron he had identified two:

> *Ron Neills:* There were two crews, and one of us had to go to Pathfinders, but we were both about to go on a week's leave. We were pulled in and told, 'One crew has got to go to Pathfinders'. We didn't fancy that too much – a tour of operations in Pathfinders was 45 and in the ordinary run of things you'd finish at 30. But we tossed up with the other crew. We lost and we went. But I don't want to cheapen that because you're earmarked as a good crew and you've lasted a fairly long time. We were plucked out by Hamish Mahaddie and we took it as a privilege that he had spotted us and said we were an efficient crew.

Following selection, the crew conducted their Pathfinder training at Warboys, Cambridgeshire, and then news came through of a posting to 7 Squadron at Oakington, Cambridgeshire. Shortly after arriving Ron Neills discovered that he had been detailed to fly an operation with the commanding officer, Wing Commander Lockhart.

> *Ron Neills:* I had only been there a couple of days. I thought, well I don't fancy that and I went in and saw him saying 'I don't know anything about this bombsight.' (I had only just passed out on them.) He said, 'Well, you're no bloody good. Go and get me another engineer.' They all got the chop that night. It was taboo really for crew switching. You always thought there was a nasty bit on the end of it if you changed crews.

On 26 April news filtered through to the crew that they were to be sent on a training flight. Steve Masters asked his informer what route they would be flying and when they could expect to take off.

Steve Masters: The officer concerned looked at me in amazement. He brusquely informed me that he had no idea of the route and wouldn't tell me even if he did. I gathered from his conversation that we were to report to the briefing room in the afternoon when all would be revealed. I rather got the feeling that he considered me a lunatic and the sooner I left his company the better.

At the appointed time Alan Grant, Richard Martin and Steve Masters reported to briefing:

Steve Masters: Just as we were about to enter the door, a corporal policeman barred our way and requested our names. We thought this to be a rather strange procedure. While the pilot was giving the necessary information, I looked into the briefing room out of idle curiosity. This one quick look stopped me in my tracks.

'Just a minute,' I said, 'we have no right to be here, this is an operational briefing, and we are on a practice trip.' We turned to leave, only to be stopped once again by the corporal.

'Sorry but you can't leave now, you have to stay, as you are on my list as being one of the crews.' We knew this was a big mistake and we were quite determined to get it put right.

Alan Grant approached the briefing officer and tried to explain that they had actually been detailed for a training flight, not an operational flight. The briefing officer told him that the operational flight was the training flight. The initial part of briefing went ahead and then the rest of Alan Grant's crew came in for the main briefing.

Steve Masters: We watched our crew enter to see what their reaction would be. The look on their faces was a repeat of how we must have looked when we first walked in. Momentarily they hesitated when they saw the many crews assembled, that is until they spotted us at one of the tables.

'What is going on?' queried the rear gunner. 'This is an operational briefing, we shouldn't he here.'

'I am afraid we should,' said the pilot. 'It is a practice trip for us but on a major target.'

Their faces registered the same shocked disbelief we had experienced and sat down hardly believing it to be true. Recovering his composure, the gunner then asked the all important question:

'Which target are we on?'

'Essen,' came the reply. The relief was instantaneous.

'Essen,' they chorused. 'It could have been much worse, what a relief.'

Had anyone been listening they would have thought our crew a bunch of real lunatics. Being pleased at the thought of going to the Ruhr Valley could only really be appreciated by madmen. There was a very good reason for this attitude, known only to ourselves.

A month previously, the crew, whilst still at Mildenhall, had safely completed an operation to the same target. Despite their 'training flight' being in a hostile environment they completed a fairly uneventful flight, although on the approach to Essen, this time, the prospect of unloading their bomb load over the city looked most daunting.

Steve Masters: I had seen several major targets before, but this was the most frightening. The searchlights were massed either side of track to form solid walls of light which converged on the target. The space in between was a dark funnel into which we were flying. There was no apparent activity in the funnel, at least none that I could see, simply that dark threatening space. To believe there was nothing there would have been foolhardy, the nightfighters would most certainly be patrolling that area.

If there was deception in the dark space, there was certainly no pretence in the stopper at the end of the funnel. That was to me the real frightener. A solid wall of searchlights across the end of the funnel was backed up by hundreds of shells bursting at all heights in an apparently unpenetrable barrage.

My job now was quite simple; all I had to do was record the time of bomb release, the speed, the heading and the height. I would take over the navigation again once we arrived at the target. I regained my seat and stared at the instruments from which I was to make my recordings. I wondered was it worth it, as nobody would ever read them. I was almost convinced of that. We would never be able to get through that wall of bursting shells even if the nightfighters let us get that far.

I must admit that I felt alone; this was my problem, a very personal one. I thought it strange that in two or three minutes I might no longer exist. To stop my mind from thinking such thoughts I concentrated on the instruments, ready to record those things I was supposed to record. It was going to be a wasted effort, I knew that, but I had to do something while waiting.

The time seemed interminable as now the aircraft was under the control of the bomb aimer who had the target in sight. I had little to occupy my mind except the thought of what I had witnessed outside a few minutes earlier.

At last the bomb doors opened, minor adjustments were made to the heading, then we were on our final run in. This was what I had been waiting for as I knew that any minute we would be blasted from the sky – nothing happened and we flew on. I felt the jolt as the bomb aimer released the bombs, followed by the reassuring sound of the bomb doors closing again – still nothing happened. I couldn't understand why as I knew that all those guns had been firing at the bomb release point.

I made my recordings in the navigation log still waiting for the shock of the shells hitting us but still nothing. I could contain my anxiety no longer and went back to the astrodome to view the scene outside. When I looked forward where I expected to see activity, there was nothing but darkness, then I turned to look behind. It was with amazement that I saw the massed searchlights and bursting shells behind us; we were through, we had come through that concentration unscathed.

Alan Grant brought his crew back safely, their 'training' flight successfully completed. The crew's next duties involved bombing Montdidier airfield on the night of 3/4 May.

On the same night a RAF Bomber Command force of 362 aircraft was sent to Mailly-le-Camp. Identified as a German military facility, RAF Bomber Command had been called upon to blast the camp, at the time hosting various tank units including a battalion of the 21st Panzer Division. This the aircrews achieved but that night a price was paid. Delays in controlling the raid meant bombers had to wait over the target and German nightfighters seized their chance. Bill Geeson, a pilot with 625 Squadron, took part in the raid to Mailly-le-Camp:

> It was quite horrific. They told us, 'Oh it's easy, you know. You've only got to go to France.' But it was a bad one. There was low cloud and a bright moon, the very things that we didn't want. We saw aircraft being shot down and one in particular, which was rather unusual, was a bomber, which was seen to go in followed by a German nightfighter – both hit the ground. It was a night when everyone was tense and a bit stewed up.[56]

Charles Owen DSO and DFC was a pilot with 97 Squadron in the spring and summer of 1944 and also took part in the raid:

> Bright moonlit night, and Jerry fighters had a field day. Went in at 8,000 ft but circled outside target at 4,000 ft waiting for order to bomb. Saw several fighters, but were not attacked until on the bombing run at 5,000 ft. Luckily he was a rotten shot and we were able to carry on and drop our markers spot on. We were attacked again coming out of the target and he shot away our mid-upper turret and made a few holes elsewhere. The mid-upper gunner, miraculously, was only slightly wounded, but had to leave what was left of his turret. The fighter came in again, but the rear gunner drove him off and claimed him as damaged. I came home at 0 feet, crossing two German aerodromes below the level of the hangar roofs. One aerodrome turned a searchlight on us, but the rear gunner opened up on him and he doused pretty rapidly. Despite the heavy losses this was an extremely successful attack.[57]

The raid to Mailly-le-Camp takes its place in the annals of RAF Bomber Command as one of the fiercest air battles over France during World War II. In total 42 Lancasters were lost.

On 7 May Alan Grant and his crew went after the German air force again, successfully bombing the airfield at Nantes, and as in the 'training flight' met little opposition. On 10 May 7 Squadron sent its crews to Courtrai, and the crew again took part in a raid that met little opposition. Other RAF Bomber Command crews were not so fortunate, however. On the raid to Lille on the same night, 12 Lancasters were lost.

After the raid to Tergnier on 10/11 April Jack Scott's 466 Squadron crew took some leave. On their first day back they were detailed for operations. Whilst a tense Alan Grant and his crew flew through the fearful Essen defences on 26/27 April, Jack Scott took his crew on an uneventful trip to the railyards at Villeneuve St George. Indeed on the crew's next five operations to Aulnoye (28 April), Achères (30 April), Malines (1 May), Morsalines (9 May) and Colline-Beaumont (11 May), Ken Handley was able to describe them in his diary as 'quiet trips'.

The first four 'quiet trips' had counted as $^1/_3$ of an operation; however the crew was informed after the Colline-Beaumont raid that each operation would now be counted as a full operation, but that their tour had been extended from 30 to 40 operations. Taking into account some of the recent air battles over France, notably the Mailly-le-Camp raid, RAF Bomber Command's policy had altered somewhat in recognition of the fact that risks indeed remained high. As it was, and almost to emphasise the point, in contrast to their previous five operations Jack Scott's crew witnessed that the enemy still strove to offer opposition on their next operation on 12 May to Hasselt.

> *Ken Handley's diary:* We took off at 10 pm, climbed to 6,000 ft over base
> & set course at this height. Leaving the East coast we climbed from 2$^1/_2$
> degrees East & made 11,000 ft at the enemy coast. Light flak &
> searchlights were seen going over the Dutch coast. Towards zero hour
> things livened up with fighter flares, & combats could be seen taking
> place by the tracer between the aircraft. An aircraft was seen to go down,
> glowing beneath the clouds just like a flare. Our markers went down on
> time & photo flashes showed that our lads were there. Another attack was
> also taking place a few miles south west. The markers were getting a
> reasonable pranging. We bombed at 8,000 ft & left the target at 200+
> I.A.S. gradually descending to 5,000 ft. On the way we did violent evasive
> action corkscrewing & such like whenever an aircraft, believed enemy,
> were seen. Climbing again we made 10,500 ft near the enemy coast &
> once over it let down at 200 IAS. Rated Boost was needed to climb at 200
> IAS. Another aircraft was seen to crash into the earth 10,000 ft below &
> explode like a petrol dump. Combats were again seen by their tracers.
> Leaving the enemy coast a combat was going on over the sea. An
> explosion was seen in the sea & it looked like burning oil & petrol from
> an aircraft. Still descending we made 8,000ft at our coast again & let
> down over base from 6,000 ft. A more exciting time than previous targets.
> 2 missing from our Squadron.'

Seven RAF heavies were lost in total, two of the crews coming from 466 Squadron, with a total loss of life.

On 19 May both Jack Scott's and Alan Grant's crews would make their contributions to the Allied *Fortitude* deception plan. In order to fool the Germans as to the probable location of an invasion the pre-invasion bombing did not just limit itself to the Normandy area. The Pas de Calais received more than its fair share of explosive, as the Allies tried to bluff the Germans into keeping troops as far away as possible from the proposed battle area. On 19 May Alan Grant piloted his Lancaster, in the company of 38 other Lancasters and 5 Mosquitos on a short flight over the Channel, and dropped his explosives on a radar station on Cap Gris-Nez, in the Pas de Calais. Jack Scott and crew made their contribution a few miles down the coast on the railyards at Boulogne. On the way to the target, Ken Handley recalled seeing company:

> *Ken Handley's diary:* I could see from 30 to 50 aircraft setting course with
> us. They looked impressive with their navigation lights on. Just like a lot
> of luminous eyes in the sky. We climbed to 15,000 ft at the south coast &

went out over the channel. On leaving our shores we could see the illuminating flares going down over the target area. First a couple were dropped, then within the next 10 secs the place was 'lit up' like Piccadilly Circus. Closing in, fires had started & the ground markers could be plainly seen. Light flak was coming up but not uncomfortably close. Making a wide turn out & away from the target we descended at 220 IAS over the coast again. A large explosion was seen on leaving & the bomb bursts were well concentrated although the rear gunner saw one or two sticks fall short in the sea as the aiming point was only one mile inland.

A nice trip and a change to see something lit up these days.

To complete the month of May 1944, Alan Grant took his crew safely to Duisburg (21/22 May), Dortmund (22/23 May) and the railyards at Aachen (24/25May), which was an important rail link between Germany and France. 72 RAF heavy bombers and crew failed to return from these three raids. Jack Scott saw his crew safely through a successful attack on the military camp at Bourg Leopold (27/28 May).

Throughout May 1944 RAF Bomber Command's major commitment was in support of *Overlord*, blasting railyards, enemy military camps, airfields, ammunition dumps and coastal batteries in France and Belgium, with considerable success. As the month of June began, the effort continued. The next time our featured RAF Bomber Command crews would be called upon for operations, the Allied assault of the Normandy beaches was a matter of a few days away.

Since he was born in 1921, Richard Haine had spent his life on his father's farm, helping out where he could. But Dick, as he was known to his family, had developed a passion beyond a life of working the land. He wanted to fly and looked to the RAF for assistance. He needn't have joined up, as working on his father's farm in Datchet, next to the river Thames, would have exempted him. However ambition won the day and early in the war Dick joined the fray. Major disappointment followed, however, as his flying aspirations were crushed by a medical officer. Nevertheless Dick stayed in the RAF as groundcrew.

In the summer of 1941 Dick began work with newly formed 76 Squadron at RAF Middleton St George, County Durham. He wrote to his sister Joan, who was serving with the WRNS:

How are you, little sister? Surviving the blitz, I hope . . . I'm on four-engined bombers now on a new squadron, just formed & as we haven't many planes we don't get worked very hard. In fact today was the hardest I have worked. We were sitting outside the crew-room asleep in the sun when the CO walked up. He took a dim view & about 15 minutes after we were marched off & given picks & shovels & told to level a bit of ground. It was as hard as concrete . . . I don't think much of Darlington, in fact I don't think much of any northern town, & the women up here are terrible. I suppose there are some decent ones but I haven't seen them. Must close now, the corporal's terrier is chewing his way into my bed. All the best, Dick.

Whilst serving his time as groundcrew Dick still maintained his ambition to fly.

In December 1941 Dick again wrote to Joan: 'At the moment your young brother who is serving his King and country in the RAF is fire-watching, a very peaceful occupation (I hope).' Dick also informed his sister that he had gone back to school in an attempt to improve his education and keep his flying aspirations alive. He asked Joan what she was doing for Christmas and whether or not she could be free, so they could celebrate together in their home town. 'I should think things will hum around Datchet, wouldn't you? Have a shot at it anyhow and a good time will be had by all, especially if you supply an additional Wren, pleasing to the eye and of medium intelligence.'

Early in 1942 Dick again wrote to Joan. 'I am led to believe that I owe you a double congratulation. One on attaining the ripe old age of 22 summers and the second your promotion. The whole of the Thames Valley is ringing with it and even round Middleton St George the news was received with joyous chants. We would have celebrated the occasion as fitting only unfortunately we are all temporarily embarrassed financially.' Joan had by then, in an extraordinary coincidence, met another man by the name of Richard Haine. Dick's letter continued: 'How is the second R. Haine, has he got much money? Is he a rich relative 'cos I feel in need of one just now?' Dick also informed his sister of some good news concerning his flying dream:

Here of course life is much the same, the only difference is I have taken up fencing and am at the moment receiving lessons in foil. I have also been chasing about getting forms signed and yesterday I had a medical, which I passed FIT for pilot. Today I had to interview the CO who was a very decent bloke, this being the first time I have met him personally. He seemed to think I was the right type and signed my form with pleasure. I gave him quite a long lecture on how a milking machine works, incidentally. This afternoon, it being our half day, we went down to the gym and endeavoured to cut ourselves to pieces with foils. By the way, don't tell mother about me going as a pilot as it may still fall through 'cos I've still got a selection board and another medical.

Dick passed and embarked upon his aircrew training as part of the Empire Training Scheme. On 28 January 1943 Dick wrote to Joan from 48 Air School, East London, South Africa. Following an unpleasant train journey from Southern Rhodesia, the young energetic airman began enjoying his new environs.

Eventually after nearly 4 days on the train we arrived here in East London, which is on the east coast and a very nice little place. There is some marvellous swimming to be had here practically all the year round. There are also beautiful sands with beautiful damsels all sun-tanned and jolly good swimmers. You need to be pretty good too as there are terrific breakers and the current can be very strong. Nearly everyone goes surf-riding but I haven't attempted it yet, want to have some practice first without a board.

The people here are very hospitable and friendly and the girls much easier on the eye than up north. We went to a party last night and met a few of them and we are going on a picnic with them out to one of the coves on Sunday, which should be a pretty good show.

Amidst South Africa's delights Dick completed his initial training. But there was disappointment. Dick could get a plane into the air and fly it. His problem was getting back down again. Eventually he was given an ultimatum, either he could train as a bomb aimer or go back to groundcrew. Dick, unsurprisingly chose the former: he wanted to fly. Soon Dick was posted back to a gloomy England and before resuming his training he took the chance to return to his home village and meet up with some old friends.

> *Letter to Joan Haine:* Tony and I painted Datchet and district a pretty lurid colour during my short stay, in fact the other customers in the Stag told me it was about time I left as there was a danger of them running short. The Stag hasn't changed a bit, has it? They still manage to push 'em back at a rate bordering on the alarming.

However the revelries soon ended as Dick moved on to RAF Halfpenny Green, near Stourbridge in Worcestershire.

> *Letter to Joan Haine:* This place is one of the most lousy holes in creation and the CO, well words fail me there, he and I are not the best of pals ... within just over a week of arriving he had given me a Reprimand and one day's pay stopped and a fortnight's privileges stopped, which was a bit steep for 8 hours overdue.
>
> It is right out in the country miles from anywhere and no means of getting in to a town; the only saving grace is we are here for only two weeks more. There is a very slim hope of a few days' leave, but hope springs eternal, you know.
>
> We are working very hard here, getting bags of hours in; we have not much time to brood on our sorry lot.

In the spring of 1944 Dick was posted to No. 16 OTU (Silverstone) and then on to 1645 HCU to familiarise himself with Lancasters and a crew: pilot Australian Roland Ward, navigator Kenneth Smith, flight engineer Denis Mangan, wireless operator George Livingstone, mid-upper gunner Stanley Reading and rear gunner Australian Malcolm Burgess. On 20 May 1944 Dick arrived with his crew at 5 Group's 50 Squadron, RAF Skellingthorpe, Lincolnshire – just in time to begin their operational duties on tactical targets in support of D-Day.

Since he was four years old, Stan Selfe's Christmas and birthday present had had an aviation theme. Stan left Welling Central school early in 1939, when he was 14, and after an engineering apprenticeship with Elliot Brothers he went to work at the Royal Ordnance factory, Woolwich. When the Air Training Corps set up a squadron at Stan's old school he took the opportunity to develop his passion. 'There was a fight to be the first one to enrol. I managed to get in second.'

At the beginning of 1943 Stan's ambition drove him to enrol for RAF aircrew, aiming to be a pilot. Stan took all the necessary examinations and then found himself in front of a panel of officers, who were to judge his suitability as a pilot.

> *Stan Selfe:* They were asking me to recognise various model aircraft hanging from the ceiling and then they looked at my documents. One said, 'I'm afraid you can't be a pilot, your left eye is unbalancing.' I said

'Pardon?' I wanted to fly. I got the reply, 'You can be an air gunner.' Even though I was only 18 I thumped the desk and said, 'I've got a bad eye. How can I be an air gunner.' They chatted amongst themselves and told me to go outside for 5 minutes. When I came back in they said, 'Well, if you don't want to be an air gunner you won't be any good.' So I said, 'What about a flight engineer?' They coughed and spluttered, 'Where did you hear this?'

Stan had recently met an old schoolfriend, who was a flight engineer but at that time the creation of the new position, specifically for the four-engined heavy bombers, was supposed to be kept secret. Stan informed the panel that he had heard about the position from 'an old school pal'.

Stan Selfe: They sent me outside again. When I went back in they said, 'Right, here you are. Take this and if you pass the trade test you can take the training as a flight engineer.' I went across for the test and at the counter a chap pushed a vernier gauge to me and a micrometer to mark some pieces up. Before I did that I tested the micrometer to make sure it was zero zero first. The sergeant behind the counter said, 'Where did you work?' I said, 'Elliot Brothers.' He responded, 'Well I'm blowed. I'm not asking you any more. You would know it. That's where I used to work.' He stamped the documents, I took them back to the panel and they said I'd qualified.

When Stan was 18 he received his call-up papers and had to report to Lords cricket ground. From here he was sent to complete initial training in Torquay and after six weeks of 'square bashing, rifle drill, bayonet charging, assault courses, swimming, navigation, morse code, dinghy practice, mathematics, aircraft recognition etc,' Stan was sent to St Athan, near Cardiff, one of the largest engineer training schools in the RAF. Over the next few months Stan successfully completed generic practical and theoretical training. Then he went on to type training, focusing on the RAF's four-engined heavies.

Stan Selfe: At the passing out nobody knew who had passed and who had failed. They made four chaps fall out like markers 1, 2, 3, and 4. Then they would call out a name and a number, to which that person would fall out. Once everyone had been dealt with they said, 'Right all you 4s are being remustered for other training. All you 3s put back six months. All you 2s back two weeks. All you 1s have passed, congratulations.' I was a number one. We took our caps, threw them in the air, took the white bit out of the front, and all went down to the local pub.

Soon the newly qualified flight engineers received news of their postings. A few were posted to serve with the Royal Canadian Air Force and Stan Selfe was one of the them:

Stan Selfe: I objected as I had joined the RAF to fly with the RAF. Others had got RAF places. Anyway I had to as I was ordered. There was 14 days' end of training leave and then I had to report to 1659 Heavy Conversion Unit (HCU) at Topcliffe. They had the oldest Halifaxes you could ever think of. In fact they cost quite a few lives. They'd say that if you could get through the HCU training, ops were nothing.

Following some initial ground training, Stan was introduced to a French Canadian crew, who had been together at OTU, flying twin-engined Wellingtons, on which a flight engineer was not necessary.

Stan Selfe: We were up doing circuit and bump training with one of the flying instructors. We were at about 12,000 feet and I was instructed to stop all four engines, one after another. Now, they cool down quickly. I stopped them all and then started to get a bit agitated as the temperatures were falling, which would make it difficult to start them up again. I said to the flying instructor, 'Better start up soon, sir, the coolant's getting low.' He replied, 'No, that's alright.' I had to go by what he said but they were getting into a dangerous cooling position. I asked him again saying, 'I should restart' and he said, 'Go on then.' Well the first one wouldn't start. All of a sudden I'm getting in my earphones a lot of French, all this jabbering, all the crew. I managed to start up the others, with the instructor, and then I managed to get the first one going. I clipped on my parachute, switched my mike on and said, 'Speak English or I jump. I'm getting out.' I didn't want to fly with that crew anymore and when we landed I went straight to the chief flying instructor and said, 'I refuse to fly with that crew, find me another one.'

Stan's request was accepted. A few weeks later some new trainees arrived and whilst Stan was doing some work assisting the flight engineer instructor, the instructor said to him, 'I've got a pilot for you. Come out here and see what you think of him.' Stan was then introduced to Canadian Bill Brown. Stan and Bill immediately got on well, Stan comforted by the fact that he was English-speaking. They then went on to meet the rest of the crew.

Stan Selfe: They appeared a funny old crowd, all laughing and joking and I took a liking to them. The skipper was William Brown, a very nice, cool-headed leader of men. No panic. He used to lower his seat over enemy territory, so he didn't get put off by searchlights or flak and leave it up to the gunner and my eyes to see where the flak or danger points were.

The navigator was Graham 'Cliff' Cameron from Ontario. He was a very educated man, and had been a university student at Boston. He was a metallurgist and used to go prospecting back in Canada for uranium. He gave us a lot of good precise navigated trips.

Art Willis was the bomb aimer and assistant navigator. He was born in Canada but moved to Boston. However before the United States joined the war Art crossed the border into Canada to join up. He was the only one in the crew who was married. We didn't know or we would never have flown with him. We were superstitious about anyone who was married or had girlfriends. People like that used to go for the chop. Anyway he kept it a big secret. He was a very good bomb aimer and a cool chap to fly with.

Hugh Mackenzie from Vancouver was my room-mate and the wireless operator. His parents were originally Scottish and had emigrated to Canada. He was very good at his jobs, one of which was to listen out for air to air, or air to ground radio nightfighter controls over enemy territory. Behind our engines we had microphones and he would pick up the wavelength and as they were talking he would turn on to transmit and slam his key down, deafening whoever was on the air. Quite often he used to put it back to us so we could all hear the replies that came after: 'Verdammen Engländer'.

Ferdinand Slevar from Ontario was very keen, had a good eye as a mid-upper gunner and was cool. He was too tall, over 6 foot, to go in the rear turret. George Percy was the rear gunner. He played ice hockey for the Toronto Maple Leafs back in Canada. We used to say he was '5 by 5', 5 foot tall by 5 foot wide. He was a very likable, jokable chap, very cool, calm and a good shot.

We were a jolly crew really, the way we used to joke about.

The newly formed crew settled down to familiarising themselves with the handling of a four-engine bomber, developing the teamwork necessary to be a successful crew. On one training operation the shooting ability of the gunners was made apparent to the rest of the crew.

Stan Selfe: We used to go up and down the North Sea training and used to do target practice on a drogue. This was pulled by fighter pilots who had been bad boys and was about 20 foot or so from their tail. One particular evening we had somewhere to go after the practice. The skipper called over to the target aircraft and said, 'We've got something on in the mess tonight. Do you mind if we do it quick?' The reply was, 'Yes, that will be alright.' So our gunners shot the tow rope and away went the drogue. He didn't have any others so we went back to base.

Near the end of the crew's training the crew was given a stern reminder of the perils of flying and that despite all the training, luck was now a prominent feature in their lives.

Stan Selfe: We were taking off in a Mark II Halifax on our first solo as a crew, to pass out. As we were going up the runway the flight engineer's position was to sit next to the pilot. It was a dual control aircraft. I snapped up the co-pilot's seat, which worked by pushing a press button to lock it. As we were going up the runway we were gathering speed. I was following the skipper with the throttles and just before I could get far enough to lock and we were halfway up the runway, my seat catch went wrong and the seat slid back. I let go of the throttles and I nearly grabbed the control column, which would have been fatal. I managed to grab something to stop me going right back, released the seat and took over from where I'd abruptly left off, following the throttles through the gate and lock. I continued to assist with the rest of the take-off which was successful. We went round a couple of times, came into land and the instructor said we were OK as a crew and we were finished. There was another crew also waiting to go on their first solo and I reported the defect on the seat. I said to the flight engineer, 'When you go on your trip don't for heaven's sake, use that seat. It slid back and I nearly grabbed the control column.' He said, 'Yeah OK.'

It was evening time and we were going off towards the mess for our evening meal. We were walking in the same take-off direction as the runway and we heard engines revving up. We turned round to watch the second crew take the kite off. They got to a certain point and she just rose straight up on her tail, stalled and came back down, exploding into a ball of fire, with the ammunition going off, killing all the crew. The mid-upper gunner appeared to wave as the aircraft descended back on her tail. The instructor flew up after us in a jeep and said, 'Come on, come back, you are going up again'. We said 'no' but he said, 'come on you are going and if you don't go up you might never go up again.' He took us back to another aircraft, we did our checks and had to take off and fly over the crashed aircraft, which really turned our stomachs.

The Halifax that crashed was that of Flying Officer J. L. McKinnon RCAF. There were no survivors from the crew. The statistic of 8,195 RAF Bomber Command men killed during the war in non-operational accidents in the air and on the ground bears testament to the risks associated with training for operational duty.

As the month of May drew to a close Stan Selfe's crew was posted to an operational squadron, 6 Group's Canadian 427 Squadron, just in time to make their contribution to the assault on the Normandy beaches.

At St Paul's School, Hammersmith, London, on 15 May 1944, the senior Allied leaders and commanders gathered for a presentation of the *Overlord* plan. Eisenhower opened the proceedings, to be followed by his three commanders-in-chief. The main seaborne assault area, codenamed *Neptune*, was based on five landing beaches on the Normandy coast. From west to east, these were codenamed *Utah, Omaha, Gold, Juno* and *Sword. Fortitude* was the codename for diversionary operations threatening invasion on the Pas de Calais and Somme area coastlines.

Montgomery had control of 21st Army Group made up of the British Second Army (Lieutenant-General Sir Miles C. Dempsey) attacking on the left and the US First Army (Lieutenant-General Omar N. Bradley) attacking on the right. The Order of Battle was as follows:

The British Second Army comprised the British I and XXX Corps. The I Corps would assault *Sword* beach on the Allied extreme left (bounded to the east by the river Orne) and *Juno* beach. Leading the way on to *Juno* was the 3rd Canadian Infantry Division and the 2nd Canadian Armoured Brigade followed by the Commandos of the 4th Special Service Brigade. Leading the way onto *Sword* would be the 3rd British Infantry Division and 27th Armoured Brigade followed by the 1st Special Service Brigade, the 51st Highland Division and the 4th Armoured Brigade. The British XXX Corps would assault *Gold* with the British 50th Northumbrian Division and 8th Armoured Brigade first into the attack, followed by the 49th Infantry Division and the 7th Armoured Division.

The US First Army comprised the US V Corps and VII Corps. The V Corps had responsibility for *Omaha*, led by the 1st and 29th Infantry Divisions, with the 2nd Infantry Division to follow. On the other side of the Vire estuary the US VII Corps would assault *Utah*, led by the 4th Infantry Division and followed by the 9th, 79th and 90th Divisions. In addition to the seaborne troops, the US 101st and 82nd Airborne Divisions would be dropped inland of *Utah* beach to secure the Allied right flank and the British 6th Airborne Division dropped to the east of the river Orne to secure the Allied left flank. Small Ranger and Commando units would also take part in the beach assaults.

In effect this comprised a nine-division initial assault, six divisions through the beaches, three securing the flanks. Allied naval forces would support the assault protecting the troops from any German naval response and bombarding enemy coastal positions. Once the beachheads were secured the battle of the build-up would commence. The British and Canadian forces on the Allied left would push inland to secure airfields and protect the US flank and then pivot on Caen to counter German reinforcement from the east. The US forces aimed to sweep up the Cotentin peninsula, capture the port of Cherbourg and then advance south towards St Lô, and on to Avranches and then to clear Brittany and its ports of any German defenders.

At the 15 May presentation Montgomery outlined the keys to success. The Allies would have the initiative and would rely on the violence of the assault, the terrific supporting fire from the navies and air forces, operational simplicity and a 'robust mentality'.

> We must blast our way ashore and get a good lodgement before the enemy can bring sufficient reserves up to turn us out. Armoured columns must penetrate deep inland, and quickly on D-Day; this will upset the plans and tend to hold him off while we build up strength. We must gain space rapidly, and peg out claims well inland. And while we are engaged in doing this the air must hold the ring, and must hinder and make very difficult the movement of enemy reserves by train or road.[58]

The role of the strategic heavy bomber forces has already been outlined, to date working predominantly on a strategic level, in preparation to 'hold the ring'. As *Overlord* moved towards the tactical phase and the day of the assault, D-Day, the British and American Air Chiefs began to meet regularly, to ensure effective co-ordination with their colleagues both on the ground and in the air. On 23 May the first Allied Air Commanders (AAC) Conference took place.[59] Present were Leigh-Mallory and Tedder, Spaatz and Doolittle to represent the interests of the American heavy bombers, and Air Vice-Marshal Robert Oxland and Air Marshal Sir Robert Saundby to represent RAF Bomber Command. The other air forces were represented as were the Army and Navy. The meeting, as with all subsequent AAC meetings, opened with a weather report and a general appraisal of the German military situation. Then the priorities for the air forces were discussed. With regard to targeting priorities at the 23 May meeting the following was agreed:

RAF Bomber Command	
	1) Rail Centres
	2) Coastal Batteries
	3) Airfields (particularly those in the Brest peninsula, see map p. 77)
	4) *Crossbow* (German secret weapon) rocket and flying bomb sites

US Eighth Air Force	1) Railway centres 2) Airfields 3) Rocket sites in the following order – Watten, Siracourt, Mimoyecques
AEAF	1) Railways 2) Airfields 3) Coastal Batteries 4) Radar targets

For the next few days Harris's and Doolittle's men fulfilled the AAC meeting's priorities. A RAF Bomber Command force, including the crew of Alan Grant, hit the important rail link between Germany and France at Aachen on the night of 24/25 May. In addition, that night RAF heavy bomber crews also blasted four coastal batteries. On 23, 24 and 25 May the Eighth Air Force launched substantial attacks against enemy railyards and airfields.

On 26 May the second AAC conference took place, and this time RAF Bomber Command's commander-in-chief Sir Arthur Harris was in attendance. There was general optimism at the meeting concerning the results of the attack on the transportation targets although further heavy bomber resources would still be needed. As the tactical phase of the battle approached consideration was given to the direct support of the assaulting forces. Zuckerman gave an appreciation of the attacks on the coastal gun positions. To date, a total of 8,700 tons of high explosive had been dropped on targets in both the *Neptune* and *Fortitude* areas, of which RAF Bomber Command was responsible for 3,700 tons and the AEAF 5,000 tons. Of the 51 targets in the *Neptune* area 18 were partially damaged. Of the 101 in the *Fortitude* area 26 were damaged. Zuckerman went on to point out that in light of these results it would need approximately 97 sorties and 420 tons of bombs to hit one gun and 2,500 bombs to be aimed for one of them to fall within 5 yards of the target. Zuckerman's analysis would lead directly to RAF Bomber Command being allocated just 10 gun batteries to attack a few hours before the beach assaults. At the meeting Leigh-Mallory ordered that no further attacks should be conducted on batteries under construction, which would not be completed before the invasion began. However despite the huge number of bombs that would be required on attacks on coastal batteries, they still remained a priority.

Doolittle gave the meeting an update on the practice bombing his force had been undertaking involving the use of the ground radar H2X. On the morning of D-Day his airmen would be blasting the German beach defences, literally minutes before the seaborne troops came ashore. Obviously, ensuring accuracy was key to suppressing the enemy defences and avoiding the tragic consequences of bombing friendly troops. From the practice bombing results, Doolittle claimed that the Eighth could achieve accuracy within a half to one mile, providing there were recognisable land features, such as a coastline or river. Leigh-Mallory said that the Army was prepared to accept some risk and would accept five minutes prior to the first landings as the time for cessation of the bombardment. This meant that the invasion troops, approaching the beaches in their landing craft, would be within 500 yards (or 900 yards at low tide) when the bombardment ceased. Tedder expressed some concern over the fact that the weather conditions might allow a sea assault but not be suitable for visual bombing. Doolittle stepped in, stating that provided his aircrews could get airborne and provided the Army were prepared to accept an accuracy of $1/2$ mile then he was prepared to commit his force to any task allotted to them.

In the meantime however heavy bomber resources were directed to more immediate priorities, allocated thus:

RAF Bomber Command	1) Rail centres in the following order i) Nantes ii) Saumur iii) Angers 2) Coastal Batteries 3) Airfields
US Eighth Air Force	1) Rail targets 2) Bridges 3) Airfields

In addition attacks against *Crossbow* targets were to be maintained at 10% until D-Day and should then be suspended. Again the heavy bomber commanders complied, and Harris fully committed his force to the designated priorities. Doolittle sent large forces to his allocated targets, but also took the opportunity to attack oil and aircraft industry targets in Germany on 28 May.

The third and fourth meetings of the Allied Air Commanders (29 and 31 May respectively) called for further attacks by all air forces on road and rail targets, airfields, coastal batteries and radar targets. Of note is the inclusion of *Crossbow* targets in the Eighth Air Force list of priorities, notably the large sites at Watten and Siracourt.

At the fourth meeting it was reported that of the 82 rail centres on the original Transportation Plan, 44 were now category A damaged and 13 category B. It was also noted that Saumur and Le Bourget were still to be attacked. Saumur would soon receive the attention of the RAF's heavies but Tedder questioned the inclusion of Le Bourget owing to the potentially high civilian casualties, which had been estimated at 2,000. A shift in the aiming point had brought the estimate down to 500. Tedder reasoned that there would be less criticism if the target was attacked after the assault and therefore requested Le Bourget be taken off RAF Bomber Command's list. Eisenhower backed Tedder; the minutes of the meeting recorded Eisenhower saying, 'The Prime Minister, who had stood by them like a brick when the railway bombing plan was under criticism, would be in a different position if there were many civilian casualties at this stage.' As such RAF Bomber Command, instead of attacking Le Bourget, took on three radio jamming stations instead.

As before the Eighth Air Force allocated considerable resources to attacking invasion targets between 29 and 31 May, with minimal losses from the forces sent. However Doolittle still took the opportunity to send large forces after German oil and aircraft industry targets, something that was starting to cause concern within AEAF circles. Harris met with greater favour within the AEAF as his force again committed fully to attacking invasion targets.

On the Eighth's missions to Germany, the American force suffered losses, and 34 bombers were 'missing in action' on the 29 May mission. As Spaatz had forecast, the Luftwaffe was focusing on the defence of German air space and by doing so would also be losing aircraft and skilled pilots. But could the German air force cope with the losses and would they have enough capability to oppose effectively the forthcoming Allied invasion from the air? Would Spaatz's belief in battling the Luftwaffe over Germany prove to be the key to achieving air superiority?

A week after their arrival at 50 Squadron, Dick Haine and his crew flew a Lancaster to Nantes, as part of a force of 104 aircraft, and acting upon the priorities laid out at the AAC conference meeting the day before. After having to wait until the red markers were clearly seen at the target, Dick released the bomb load at 0153 hours from 10,000 feet. Such was the accuracy of the initial bombing only half the force bombed; the rest, under instruction, were told to retain their bombs. The next day the crew was back in action, successfully placing its bombs on the coastal battery at St Martin-de-Varreville, which overlooked *Utah* beach.

On 31 May aircrews at 6 Group squadrons were called upon to respond to the priorities set out at the AAC conference as they prepared for an attack on the coastal wireless transmitting station at Au Fèvre. 427 Squadron's Bill Brown and his crew were one of the group's 129 aircrews detailed; it was their first operation. And as had happened to numerous crews before them, indiscipline set in early in the flight.

Stan Selfe: We were all chattering away, which upset the navigator and he kept doglegging, which made us late over the target. All the others had dropped their loads and gone.

Fortunately the lone bomber met no opposition. Had this occurred over a German target their chances of survival would have been very small. The raid was a success, and four of the six masts were destroyed. Bill Brown and his crew had learnt their lesson.

Ferd Slevar: After we landed we inquired at interrogation, 'Where were the other bombers?' The reply was that they all returned and that we were 20 minutes late on target. We thought of a mini lecture we'd had in the course of our training. Briefly it was that we had one minute either side of ETA to drop our bombs. After that our chances of returning began to diminish rapidly. The navigator immediately blamed himself for the error and said that he wished to withdraw from the crew. Well, now the six members of our crew put their shoulders together and with one voice, told the navigator that we had full confidence in his ability. Finally the navigator relented and said he would take another crack navigating on the next operation. Needless to say he did a superlative job.

Pointless talk on operations was distracting and dangerous and during future operations strict intercom discipline was observed. The crew had completed their first operational sortie, although six of them challenged whether or not their rear gunner could claim the operation, teasing him that actually he was the only one of the crew that, whilst bombing the coastal target, had not crossed the enemy coast.

On the same night Roland Ward took Dick Haine and the rest of his crew to bomb the rail junction at Saumur, accompanied by 85 other aircraft from 5 Group. The controller of the raid deemed the initial bombing so successful, he called off the rest of the attack. Dick Haine was one of those ordered to retain his 13,000 lb bomb load.

Our RAF Bomber Command aircrews, along with thousands of other RAF heavy bomber airmen, groundcrews and station personnel, were now fully committed to the tactical phase of the *Overlord* bombing campaign. It was a period of time many would vividly remember for the rest of their lives.

On 26 May Doolittle had informed the AAC conference that his aircrews were beginning training in preparation for the bombing of enemy coastal defences. One of those crews came from the 91st Bomb Group and on 29 May Jim Tyson's crew flew a practice mission to Skegness on the Lincolnshire coast, near the Wash, honing their instrument bombing technique, which involved close co-operation between navigator, Mickey operator and bombardier. On 31 May the crew again went on a practice bombing flight in the vicinity of the Wash and John Howland directed his pilot as he placed their aircraft on a Gee line running approximately at right angles to the beach. When the target came into sight and range of the Norden bombsight, the bombardier took over. The Mickey operator, using his H2X radar, measured the range or distance to the target, regularly updating the bombardier who input all the information into the Norden bombsight. If the clouds should clear, revealing the target the bombardier would take over visually. Although they didn't know it at the time, these practice missions were preparing the crew for their direct involvement in the Normandy landings.

Whilst Jim Tyson's crew prepared for direct intervention in the D-Day beach assault, the Eighth Air Force, along with RAF Bomber Command, continued to target railyards and airfields. At the AAC Conference on 31 May future target allocations were made for the heavy bomber forces, with particular attention given to deceiving the Germans by attacking targets in the *Fortitude* area.

Thursday 1 June	100% effort
Friday 2 June	100% effort (40% *Fortitude* targets and 60% other targets)
Saturday 3 June	50% effort (30% *Fortitude* targets and 20% other targets)
Sunday 4 June	50% effort

Both RAF Bomber Command and the Eighth Air Force in the next few days would fully commit to the invasion priorities. Both forces would go after coastal defences and rail targets, the Americans would also bomb airfields and the RAF would hit German coastal radar and signals stations.

The main series of targets in the *Fortitude* area consisted of coastal positions and

Top left: RAF 90 Squadron pilot Dennis Field. *(Dennis Field)*

Top right: Front row, from left to right: John Evans, 'Curly' Shelton, Arthur Borthwick. Back row, from left to right: Dennis Field, Alan Turner, Jim Blackwell, Tony Faulconbridge. *(Dennis Field)*

Left: Dennis Field's mid-upper gunner, Tony Faulconbridge. *(Dennis Field)*

Below: 'J' JIG LK516, Dennis Field's 90 Squadron Stirling, Tuddenham, April 1944. *(Dennis Field)*

Inset: Pilot Officer Ken Handley, RAF 466 Squadron flight engineer, August 1944. *(Ken Handley)*

Above: Ken Handley's crew at Leconfield, June 1944. From left to right: flight engineer Ken Handley, rear gunner Ken Oaks, bomb aimer Ron Tickell, mid-upper gunner Tom Drake-Brockman, pilot Jack Scott, navigator Verne Westley, wireless operator Max Pointon. *(Ken Handley)*

Right: RAF 427 Squadron pilot Bill Brown in the cockpit of his Halifax 'Hoiboit de Hoimit' and his crew, from left to right: Art Willis, Graham Cameron, Hugh Mackenzie, George Percy, Ferd Slevar, Stan Selfe. *(Stan Selfe)*

Top: Front row, from left to right: Ferd Slevar, George Percy. Back row, from left to right: Art Willis, Hugh Mackenzie, Graham Cameron, Bill Brown, Stan Selfe. *(Stan Selfe)*

Middle left: Stan Selfe. *(Stan Selfe)*

Middle centre: Stan Selfe and Hugh Mackenzie, with armourer, on a trolley of bombs destined for a V1 site. *(Stan Selfe)*

Middle right: Richard 'Dick' Haine, bomb aimer, RAF 50 Squadron. *(Joan Haine)*

Left: Ferdinand Slevar. *(Stan Selfe)*

Right: The RAF 7 Squadron crew of Pilot Officer Alan Grant. From left to right: Ron Neills, Steve Masters, Alan Grant, Sydney Nathanson, Tom Barrett, Richard Martin, Bill Newton. *(Ron Neills)*

Middle left: John Howland, Pathfinder navigator, USAAF 381st & 91st Bomb Groups. *(John Howland)*

Middle centre: The flight crew of 'Sunkist Special'. Front row, from left to right: navigator John Howland, pilot James L. Tyson, co-pilot William Doherty. Back row, from left to right: engineer Richard Jensen, tail gunner Arnold Farmer, right waist gunner Robert Miller, left waist gunner/ radio operator Harry White. *(John Howland)*

Middle right: James Tyson, Pathfinder pilot, USAAF 381st & 91st Bomb Groups. *(John Howland)*

Left: The crew of USAAF 96th Bomb Group's 'The Reluctant Dragon'. Front row, from left to right: navigator Warren Berg, original co-pilot Kenneth Leininger, pilot Gary Miller, second co-pilot Walter Hoyer, bombardier James Gardner. Back row, from left to right: radio operator/gunner Roy Strid, engineer/ waist gunner Austin Abbott, engineer/ top-turret gunner Lawrence Menard, waist gunner Arvil McKeown, ball-turret gunner Warren Christmas, tail gunner Robert Petty. *(Warren Berg)*

Top left: An artist at the 96th Bomb Group painted the bomber emblem on the back of Bob Petty's jacket. Taken whilst Bob was on leave in London. *(Bob Petty)*

Top right: 1st Lieutenant Warren Berg, 96th Bomb Group. *(Warren Berg)*

Middle left: The Special Maintenance Crew of Jim Tyson's aircraft 'Sunkist Special'. Note the radar dome in place of the ball turret. *(John Howland)*

Middle right: John Spierling, H2X radar operator, 91st Bomb Group. *(John Howland)*

Right: Bombardier George Ritchie, 34th Bomb Group. *(George Ritchie)*

Top: Crews of the 95th Bomb Group en route to a target across the channel. Reaching altitude, vapour trails stream behind the B-17s. *(Bob Petty)*

Middle left: The Eighth Air Force sent its bomber crews to war flying in formation, believing in supportive crossfire. This shows 48 B-17s in stacked formation. *(Joe Harlick)*

Middle right: John Howland receives his DFC, June 1944. *(John Howland)*

Bottom: Carl 'Tooey' Spaatz (seated, second from left) and Jimmy Doolittle (seated, third from left) in discussion with Eighth Air Force aircrews. *(Courtesy of The Mighty Eighth Air Force Heritage Museum)*

Top: Senior Allied air commanders. From left to right: Lieutenant General James H. Doolittle (commanding the Eighth Air Force during the *Overlord* campaign), Lieutenant General Lewis H. Brereton (US 9th Air Force), Lieutenant General Carl 'Tooey' Spaatz (commanding the US Strategic Air Force in Europe), Lieutenant General Ira Eaker (who commanded the Eighth Air Force prior to 1944) and Air Chief Marshal Sir Arthur Harris (RAF Bomber Command's C-in-C). *(Courtesy of The Mighty Eighth Air Force Heritage Museum)*

Bottom left: Air Chief Marshal Sir Trafford Leigh-Mallory, C-in-C of the Allied Expeditionary Air Force. *(RAF Museum Hendon)*

Bottom right: Air Chief Marshal Sir Arthur Tedder, Deputy Supreme Commander. *(RAF Museum Hendon)*

Above: General Dwight D. Eisenhower, Supreme Allied Commander Allied Expeditionary Force (second from left) with Air Chief Marshal Sir Trafford Leigh-Mallory, C-in-C of the Allied Expeditionary Air Force (third from left). *(RAF Museum Hendon)*

The principal heavy bombers used in support of Operation *Overlord*.

Middle left: The Halifax. *(Frank 'Tom' Atkinson)*

Middle right: The Stirling. *(Todd Sager)*

Bottom left: The Lancaster. *(Peter Johnson)*

Bottom right: The B-17 Flying Fortress. *(Paul Chryst)*

Opposite page, top: The B-24 Liberator. *(National Archives)*

Middle and bottom: Damage to bridges over the river Seine. (*Courtesy of the Medmenham Collection*)

Top left: The Saumur road bridge. *(Courtesy of the Medmenham Collection)*

Top right: Damage from 12,000lb bombs dropped by 617 Squadron, blocking the Saumur rail tunnel. *(Courtesy of the Medmenham Collection)*

Middle: On 11 January 1944 the Eighth Air Force sent a large force to attack the German aircraft industry. Many of them turned back due to poor weather, except for one wing of the 3rd Division and the 1st Division. With hardly any fighter escort the Eighth's bombers had little to protect them from the awaiting German fighters. 60 bombers would be listed as missing in action that day. This photo shows the target at Oschersleben during bombing.

Bottom: 11 January 1944, a B-17 being pursued by an Me109.

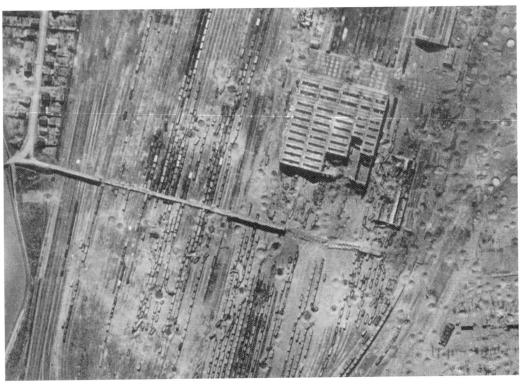

Top: Damage to the Trappes railyards following the first Bomber Command attack, on the night of 6/7 March 1944, as part of the pre-invasion bombing of rail facilities. *(Courtesy of the Medmenham Collection)*

Bottom: Severe damage to the railyards at Tergnier resulting from the attack on the night of 10/11 April 1944. *(Courtesy of the Medmenham Collection)*

Above and right: On the night of 18/19 April 1944 an RAF Bomber Command attack caused serious damage to the railyards at Noisy-le-Sec. However, some bombing spread to urban areas, destroying housing and resulting in civilian casualties. *(Courtesy of the Mairie de Noisy-le-Sec)*

Below: Lens railyards. This scene was similar to many at railyards across France and Belgium as the Allies sought to block the German movement of reinforcements and supplies. *(Courtesy of the Medmenham Collection)*

Left: On 12 May 1944, the Eighth Air Force attacked German oil production in force. Here the installations at Brüx burn fiercely following the attack. *(Courtesy of the Medmenham Collection)*

Middle: Here an Me410 shows its underside as it passes a B-17 from the force heading for home just after bombing Brüx on 12 May 1944. *(Courtesy of the Medmenham Collection)*

Bottom: Photo of 96th Bomb Group's 2nd Lt Herbert Moore's B-17, which he managed to crash-land following a collision with another 96th BG aircraft, which took out his nose section, in the melee of the 12 May 1944 air battle. *(Geoff Ward)*

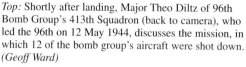

Top: Shortly after landing, Major Theo Diltz of 96th Bomb Group's 413th Squadron (back to camera), who led the 96th on 12 May 1944, discusses the mission, in which 12 of the bomb group's aircraft were shot down. *(Geoff Ward)*

Middle left: Bombing photograph (from a 75 Squadron crew) of the attack on the coastal batteries at Boulogne, Pas de Calais, on the night of 24/25 May 1944. *(David Lyon)*

Middle right: Aerial photograph of the German gun emplacements at Mont Fleury, prior to D-Day. Ten such positions were attacked by Bomber Command on the eve of the invasion, with limited success. *(Courtesy of the Medmenham Collection)*

Bottom: The Bomber Command attack on Pointe du Hoc in progress on the night of 5/6 June 1944. This shows the view from the bomb aimer's position as target indicators fell accurately on the gun emplacement defending *Utah* and *Omaha* beaches. *(Courtesy of the Medmenham Collection)*

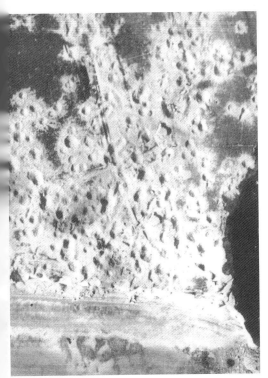

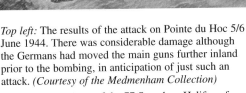

Top left: The results of the attack on Pointe du Hoc 5/6 June 1944. There was considerable damage although the Germans had moved the main guns further inland prior to the bombing, in anticipation of just such an attack. *(Courtesy of the Medmenham Collection)*

Top right: Wreckage of the 77 Squadron Halifax of mid-upper gunner Arthur Inder. On 5 June 1944, Arthur and his crew were detailed to bomb gun positions on the Normandy coast, but owing to engine failure the aircraft crashed on take-off. The crew, with various injuries, all managed to get away from the bomber before the bomb load went off. *(Arthur Inder)*

Middle right: Much of the Eighth Air Force's first mission on the morning of D-Day was hindered and frustrated by poor weather conditions. Here the cloud cover over the Normandy beaches is clearly visible from the bomb bay of a B-17. *(Joe Harlick)*

Bottom left: Aerial photograph showing the bomb craters owing to the D-Day Eighth Air Force bombing, at La Rive, *Juno* beach. *(Courtesy of the Medmenham Collection)*

Bottom right: View from a 75 Squadron bomber of the bombing attack on enemy positions at Villers-Bocage on 30 June 1944. *(David Lyon)*

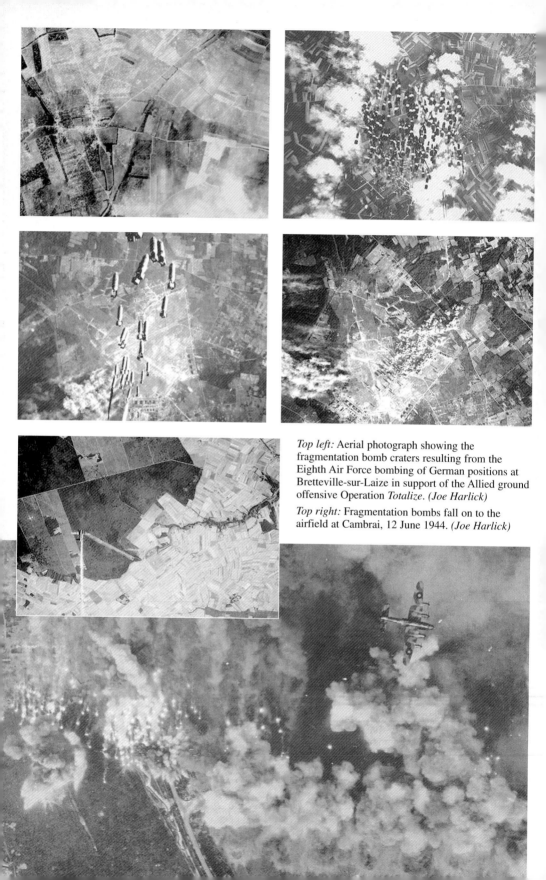

Top left: Aerial photograph showing the fragmentation bomb craters resulting from the Eighth Air Force bombing of German positions at Bretteville-sur-Laize in support of the Allied ground offensive Operation *Totalize*. *(Joe Harlick)*

Top right: Fragmentation bombs fall on to the airfield at Cambrai, 12 June 1944. *(Joe Harlick)*

Opposite page, middle left and middle right:
15 June 1944. Bombs falling and exploding in an Eighth Air Force attack on Bordeaux airfield.

Opposite page, inset: A 91st Bomb Group B-17 going down during the attack on Toulouse airfield on 25 June 1944.

Opposite page, bottom and this page, top: RAF bombers over Calais and Le Havre. The attacks made a significant contribution to the capitulation of the defending German forces, although the French inhabitants suffered as a result.
(Courtesy of the Medmenham Collection)

Left: B-17s over dock installations, Lorient.
(Joe Harlick)

Top: Modern photograph of the gun position at Longues-sur-Mer. *(Steve Fraser/Steve Chalkley)*

Middle left: Bombing photograph from Jack Scott's 466 Squadron Halifax, during the attack on German positions in support of Operation *Charnwood* on 7 July 1944. *(Ken Handley)*

Middle right: Eighth Air Force bombers form over England and head towards Germany. *(Bob Petty)*

Bottom: View from the cockpit of a RAF Bomber Command attack in progress on the fuel storage dump at Forêt de Mormal on 9 August 1944. *(Howard Lees)*

Top: V1 modified/simplified site. This aerial photograph clearly shows the difficulty in locating and bombing V1 launch sites. Just to the right of A is the square building where the V1 was prepared before launch. Just below B is the launch ramp hidden in the trees. The Allies' attempt to knock out the launch sites through bombing met with limited success. It wasn't until they began targeting V1 storage sites that the bombing had a serious effect on launch rates. *(Courtesy of the Medmenham Collection)*

Middle: Modern photograph of a V1 on the launch ramp at the preserved site at Val Ygot, Forêt d'Eawy, France. *(Steve Darlow)*

Bottom: A damaged V1 launch ramp at Roquetoire, Hameau de Blanc Pignon, Pas de Calais. *(Mr Wimez, Collection Laurent Bailleul)*

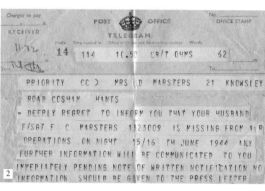

Top left: Richard Haine's grave at the Commonwealth War Grave Cemetery, Bayeux. *(Joan Haine)*

Top right: The graves of Alan Grant, Tom Barrett and Bill Newton. *(Ron Neills)*

Middle left: The final resting place, at the American cemetery, Madingley, England of pilot 2nd Lieutenant Herman M. Doell. He lost his life, along with the rest of his crew, on the morning of 6 June 1944, when, on the return from Normandy, the 34th Bomb Group B-24 in which he was flying crashed near Corfe Castle in Dorset. Four other members of the crew are buried at Madingley. The remains of the other four were returned to the US. *(Steve Darlow)*

Middle right 1: 'Deeply regret to inform you' – the telegram telling Ron Neills's family that he had failed to return from operations on the night of 15/16 June 1944. *(Ron Neills)*

Middle right 2: The telegram addressed to Steve Masters's wife (surname incorrectly spelt) informing her that he had failed to return from operations on the night of 15/16 June 1944. *(Alan Masters)*

Above: Resting place at Brookwood Military Cemetery of Sergeant Charles Waller, flight engineer to Dennis Field's crew, 90 Squadron, killed on the supply drop to the French Resistance on the night of 10/11 April 1944. *(Steve Darlow)*

on 2 June 1944 Jim Tyson's crew, although ignorant of the fact, played their part in the *Fortitude* deception plan, briefed to attack gun batteries in the Pas de Calais. It was time to put their training into practice.

John Howland's diary: At first we thought the invasion was on, but the Colonel assured us it wasn't. We were all a little disappointed. Our bombing was to be done visually if possible, and by Mickey radar and Gee if it was undercast.

Flew to Ridgewell and got to bed about 2330 hours; but tossed and turned as usual for a couple of hours before getting off to sleep. The base had a ground alert during the night, but I just woke up long enough to find out what the hell was going on, and went back to sleep again.

The orderly awakened us at 0530 hours for our regular briefing. Ridgewell was to put up two Groups of 18 planes each. We were to lead the 'A' Group, and Clark and Obler the 'B' Group. Ours was the first Group from the 1st Bombardment Division scheduled over the target area, but the 3rd Division preceded us by 10 minutes. Bomb load for the Group was 500 lb demolition. As usual, we carried 10 demolition and 2 smoke bombs while the rest of the ships in the formation carried 12 demos each.

After climbing to 22,000 feet and forming up, Jim Tyson's formation headed for the south coast of England.

John Howland's diary: We left Beachy Head on time and on course and flew east along the coast to Dungeness, which was the IP.

Our bomb bay doors were opened, damned near over England. I picked up 4.12 on the Gee line and rode it in till 'Bombs Away'. They didn't shoot a single piece of flak at us, although we passed within range of something like 120 guns. I can't figure out why they didn't shoot.

We were on time at the IP and 15 seconds late at the target, so I was pretty proud of the job. Some fellow named McLean flew with me in the nose, but he kept out of my way, and didn't do anything but keep a record of the mission. I find this is a good way to keep these 'co-navigators' out of my hair.

Gee signals came in strong throughout the mission so I had no trouble keeping the Group on course and we came home on Gee. It really was a milk run, and my first mission to France. Sure was happy to get an easy one in for a change. However, I hope we hit the coast, and the target through the thick layer of clouds. If we did, it might mean a few more easy ones to the coast for us. Jim and I were both happy with the way the mission went because there was hardly a hitch anywhere.

On the night of 2/3 June the Eighth Air Force prepared to conduct further raids against gun batteries in the Pas de Calais area and again it would call on the 91st Bomb Group to lead its bombers in:

John Howland's diary: About 0130 hours an orderly came into our room and advised us that [Clem] Obler was flying. For a change I got to stay home. Clem cussed a little, and I urged him to 'Go and win the war for me, Clem'. I promptly rolled over and went back to sleep.

An hour later the same orderly returned and said, 'Lt Howland, Get up! Lt Obler crashed on take-off and you have to fly his mission.'

In an emotional outburst brought out by gut-tearing apprehension I yelled at the orderly, 'What happened? What happened? Tell me what happened?'

The excited orderly replied, 'A bomb truck and trailer stalled in the center of the runway while they were taking off. They barely got the plane in the air before they hit it. The right landing gear was wiped out, and they lost No.3 engine; but they did manage to stay airborne. They have a full load of gas on board, but no bombs. Right now they are flying around to use up their gasoline before they come in for a crash landing.'

Greatly relieved to hear that Carl Clark [Clem Obler was his navigator] was able to get the plane into the air, I reached for my clothes and started dressing. I was still worried about Clem who, like me, always rides in the nose of the ship at take-off. However, by the time we reached the flight line, Clark had radioed back that all on board were safe so I was able to take off and fly Clem's mission with my mind at ease.

The mission unfolded in a very similar fashion to that of the previous day, bombing conducted through cloud using Gee and the Mickey radar, with no opposition.

John Howland's diary: After the return to Bassingbourn, we found that Carl Clark had made a perfect one-wheel landing and all on board were safe. After interrogation, I tried to return to my quarters. But I couldn't. It seems the navigators in the sleeping bay locked the door when Captain Westwood tried to move in some new crews. All involved were restricted. I was too tired to put up with crap like that, so I slept for a while on the floor of the Mess Hall.

Clem is safe and wearing his 45 Cal automatic in an armpit holster. He went looking for the 'Dumb SOB' who abandoned his truck in the middle of the runway; but he didn't have much success finding him. As Clem put it, 'One guy told me the SOB was on pass. Another told me he was transferred, and still another told me he was in hospital. I don't believe any of them.'

In addition to the Eighth's contribution to *Fortitude*, the RAF gave its assistance. Alan Grant and his crew bombed coastal batteries at Calais on the night of 3/4 June and Dick Haine dropped his bombs along with 95 other Lancasters on the German signals station at Ferme-d'Urville, near the invasion coast. With no cloud to hamper proceedings, three 8 Group Mosquitos had accurately placed their markers and the station was demolished.

At the Fifth AAC Conference on 3 June Leigh-Mallory declared the strategic phase of the railway plan over. An intelligence outline of the German ground force situation estimated that on D-Day 9 enemy divisions (some incomplete) would be in Normandy, of which 3 would be in a position to oppose the incoming Allied troops, with 3 more early into combat. Within 48 hours this would increase to 13, of which 5 would be Panzer divisions. After a week, this would be 24 divisions (9 Panzer) and after 17 days 30 divisions (10 Panzer). Leigh-Mallory informed the meeting that one of the major tasks for the Allied air forces in the first stages of the battle involved the direct harassment and prevention of the German ability to reinforce and build up opposition in the vicinity of the beachhead. When the Normandy front opened and the enemy responded, rushing units to the battle area, the Allied air forces had to block their path, cause them to divert, pound the soldiers and their armament. This would involve bombing the towns and villages at important communications junctions, and Leigh-Mallory proposed warning the French civilians by dropping leaflets and making radio broadcasts.

His suggestions did not meet with the approval he was looking for. Tedder weighed in first, questioning the value of blasting towns as a means of interrupting communications. The minutes of the meeting record that 'he had tried it in Sicily and only in one instance had it been effective.' Tedder went on to say that he hoped the Army was not expecting better results than it would actually get. In response to Leigh-Mallory's statement that the objectives in Caen were road and rail crossings, with bridges wherever possible, being the aiming points, Spaatz then took the view that the fighter-bombers would be best employed on such missions. He was backed by the tactical air force commanders, Brereton (US 9th Air Force) and Coningham (2nd Tactical Air Force). Spaatz suggested an alternative task for his bombers, unsurprisingly wanting to go after the Luftwaffe, and specifically German airfields.

Once more Leigh-Mallory had to respond to a challenge to his plans, as he put his faith in fighter cover keeping the German air force at a safe distance. Then Tedder again went after the AEAF commander asking whether 'air superiority could be maintained by purely defensive methods without offensive operations against occupied airfields'. Spaatz bolstered the Deputy Supreme Commander's query, stating that Leigh-Mallory was 'using a doubtful means of delaying enemy movement on the ground while giving up a positive means of protecting our Armies from air attack'. Leigh-Mallory had had enough. He insisted that the delay of enemy reinforcements was the prime concern and only the air forces could do this. The minutes of the meeting record that Leigh-Mallory had:

> made quite clear to General Montgomery that immunity could not be guaranteed and casualties would have to be accepted. The two risks – of attack from the air and of splitting our Armies [believed to be the chief aim of German strategy in countering the invasion] – must be balanced against one another and he was in no doubt as to which was the greater. The responsibility was his and he was prepared to accept it. He was not, however, prepared to accept responsibility as Air Commander-in-Chief if the air plan were changed.[60]

Basically Leigh-Mallory was putting his position on the line. Just a few days before the launch of the invasion the AEAF commander was threatening resignation. Leigh-Mallory felt slighted, in particular by Tedder's criticism. On 5 June Leigh-Mallory wrote to Tedder:

> I am sure you will agree that complete frankness and understanding between us is essential and I therefore write to let you know that I considered your criticism at the Allied Air Commanders conference on Saturday of the Plan, which had already been laid on and generally agreed, was embarrassing and must inevitably make the handling of a difficult team even more difficult.

My task controlling commanders of another nationality can never be easy, and will become impossible if I am to be subjected to somewhat carping criticism in front of them. I am always prepared to listen to criticism and to accept advice, but I should much prefer that they were offered when we were alone, or before the Supreme Commander, rather than in front of my own staff, and more especially, before Americans, who have already shown themselves to be antagonistic to the Plan.[61]

However by the end of the AAC meeting on 3 June the matter seemed to have been resolved. Leigh-Mallory's plan would stand. From this moment, and during the first day of the invasion, the bomber forces would focus on beach defences, bombard and block rail and road networks and maintain the diversion by bombing positions in the Pas de Calais, ensuring that the German command withheld certain forces in anticipation of a second Allied landing.

As the planned day for the invasion, 5 June, approached, concerns grew over the turn for the worse in the weather. On 4 June a storm over the planned shipping routes to Normandy put paid to opening the invasion the next morning. Eisenhower ordered a 24-hour postponement. Late on the 4th Eisenhower was informed that there would be a slight improvement in conditions on 6 June. He consulted his commanders, but Leigh-Mallory and Tedder had reservations on the support that could be given from the air. The accuracy of the planned heavy bomber operations would be seriously hindered by cloud cover. Nevertheless Montgomery wanted to go and Eisenhower's hand was forced somewhat, since there were only three days in early June, the 5th to the 7th, in which conditions would be suitable: moonlight for the airborne troop drops and low tides for the landings and destruction of German underwater beach defences. Early on 5 June 1944 the Allied land, sea and air forces in England were told that the invasion was now on for the morning of 6 June.

The 24-hour delay in launching the invasion gave the air forces another chance to bombard coastal defences before the troops hit the beaches. On 4 June, Jim Tyson's crew conducted yet another mission to the Pas de Calais, one of the 509 Eighth Air Force bombers attacking coastal targets. That night Bill Brown's crew contributed to the attack on coastal batteries, one of 259 RAF bombers despatched to the Pas de Calais and Normandy. On 5 June 626 Eighth Air Force heavy bombers rained 1,896 tons of explosives on enemy coastal positions near Le Havre, Caen, Boulogne and Cherbourg. Jim's crew was one of those despatched, to fly as wing lead for the 398th Bomb Group at Nuthampstead. The mission was again to blast gun batteries, but this time on the Normandy coast north of Caen. It should have been a fairly simple mission.

John Howland's diary: As usual I arrived at the plane just prior to engine time and crawled through the hatch into my flying office in the nose of our B-17. My co-navigator from the 398th BG had preceded me, and already had a sparkling new chart stretched out across the navigator's table. Not a single line had been drawn on it. In addition, right in the middle of everything sat a Fairchild A-10 Octant. I was dumbfounded.

'Who are you?' I asked.

'I am Lt. . . .', the young man replied. 'I am the lead navigator on this mission.'

I looked at the blank chart and that A-10 Octant and said, 'Tell me something, lieutenant, how many lead mission have you flown?'

'This is my first lead mission', was the reply.

That A-10 Octant drew my eyes like a magnet and I went on to ask, 'Tell me something else. How many missions have you flown?'
'Oh, this is my first mission', was the reply.

I was not at all gentle when I told him to, 'Get that crap off my table, especially that stupid A-10 Octant.' I then handed a pilotage chart with the assembly area drawn in and told him, 'Your job on this mission is to feed me position reports in latitude and longitude when I ask for them. Furthermore, the positions are to be accurate, and you are to stay the hell out of my way.'

With things under control in the nose of the ship, we took off and made our assembly, but not without problems. Jim was having his difficulties with his co-pilot, who was a major from Nuthampstead and the Acting Wing Commander. During assembly he insisted upon making minor changes in the flight plan, which was very upsetting to me. I presume the major had about as much combat experience as my co-navigator, and it showed in his performance.

In the target area north of the Normandy beaches, we picked up a westerly heading parallel to the beaches. We made a dry run out of range of the shoreline flak guns at our flight-plan bombing altitude of 15,000 feet. There was a cloudbank off to the south; but we could see the beaches and the target area. Nevertheless, the Acting Wing Commander decided to climb over our flight-plan bombing altitude to get above the cloudbank. On the basis of the flight plan and temperature, I hadn't bothered to wear my electric 'baby blue' flying suit. We climbed and climbed to get above a cloudbank that wasn't covering the target area and I was about to freeze my butt off for, as usual, the heater in the nose wasn't working.

Finally, when we reached 28,000 feet, I asked Jim to go ahead and make the bomb run before the cloudbank moved in and obscured the target. The bomb run was made; but we had a malfunction in the bomb racks. Only one smoke bomb and one 500 lb demo dropped out of the racks. However the rest of the formation dropped on us. Matty, the bombardier, then headed for a secondary target just west of the primary, and was able to toggle out about half the remaining load despite a frozen salvo handle. Once again we had no anti-aircraft fire over the target area.

It really wasn't a good mission. I had trouble getting Jim to fly the flight-plan. However I didn't have the Acting Wing Commander sitting next to me. Obviously the AWC didn't have the experience and was poorly qualified for the responsibility entrusted to him. Acting Wing Commanders are supposed to know what they are doing. Ours didn't.

Jim Tyson took his crew back to Bassingbourn. Meanwhile orders were already being prepared for their next mission. Within 24 hours, they, along with thousands of RAF Bomber Command and Eighth Air Force heavy bomber aircrew, would pave the way for the greatest seaborne land invasion in world history.

CHAPTER 9

A NIGHT BATTLE OVER FRANCE

The Transportation Plan called on RAF Bomber Command to bomb rail centres in northern France. These trips were of shorter duration than those previously experienced by aircrews, who were used to penetrating German air space. Nevertheless, on numerous operations over France the German nightfighter force provided considerable opposition. In this chapter one such air battle is detailed.

At the start of June 1944, the Eighth Air Force heavy bombers roamed across northern France during daylight hours meeting very little opposition, with their fighter escorts countering any threat from the diminishing strength of the German daylight fighter force. However, at night the sky was not so safe for the RAF crews. The German nightfighter defences remained formidable and if marshalled effectively could wreak havoc amongst bomber streams. On the night of 31 May/1 June, 219 aircraft attacked the railyards at Trappes, lying just to the west-south-west of Paris, which provided a key rail link between the French capital and Normandy. Despite a reported successful attack, the railyards, owing to their key strategic location, were deemed worthy of further attention, and on 2/3 June RAF Bomber Command sent 128 aircraft to the railyards from which one eighth did not return. In this chapter we shall focus on the raid to Trappes on the night of 2/3 June, which gives a clear example of the ferocity that could still exist in the night air battles over France in the summer of 1944.

In total RAF Bomber Command would conduct 15 operations on that night. In addition to the force sent to Trappes, attacks were made on five coastal defence positions in the Pas de Calais area (as part of the *Fortitude* deception plan) and on the radar jamming station at Berneval near Dieppe. A Mosquito force was sent to Leverkusen, and minor Mosquito attacks conducted on Laval and Lison. Fifty-three aircraft were sent on minelaying duties, 11 aircraft on leaflet drops, 12 aircraft in a bomber-support role, 6 aircraft acting as Intruders and 49 aircraft conducting special operations. It looked a relatively simple operation for the Trappes force in terms of expected opposition, but of the 900 men who attended the operational briefing, 115 would not be returning and 78 of these men would die. Below is a summary of how the night's events unfolded.[62]

To 0030 hours
Trappes Force: The bomber force crosses the English coast at Pevensey Bay, proceeds across the Channel, crossing the French coast over St Valéry-en-Caux. *Other Forces:* Between 0010 and 0020 hours, 71 RAF bombers attack the coastal battery at Neufchâtel, Pas de Calais.

At 0026 hours an attack by 47 RAF bombers starts on the coastal battery at Calais.

German Reaction: As early as 2345 hours the German nightfighter controller in northern France starts to marshal his forces. From midnight nightfighters from NJG4 gather in the Paris-Trappes-Evreux area.

Engagements: Both gunners in a 192 Squadron Halifax open fire on a single-engined aircraft, seeing strikes on their foe's nose and wing. An explosion on the ground follows shortly after.

0031 to 0045 hours

Trappes Force: The bomber force proceeds on a south-west course to the south of Rouen then turns almost due east to arrive over Trappes. The Pathfinders start dropping their markers.

Other Forces: The attack by 47 RAF bombers on the gun battery at Calais ends at 0040 hours.

A 166 Squadron Lancaster is shot down over the target and there are no survivors.

German Reaction: The German controller keeps his main force of nightfighters in the Paris-Trappes-Evreux area.

Engagements: A Ju88 opens fire on a 77 Squadron Halifax; the mid-upper gunner returned fire to no effect.

A 214 Squadron Fortress is fired upon by what appears to be a single-tailed four-engined aircraft, resulting in damage to the leading edge of the tailplane and in the waist position, with one bullet going right through and out the other side.

0046 to 0100 hours

Trappes Force: The bombers attack the railyards, then fly almost due south out of the target. Numerous contacts are made with nightfighters and British radio signal interceptors start to hear 'Sieg Heils', the German nightfighter's victory call.

Other Forces: At 0054 hours 23 Mosquitos open an attack on Leverkusen.

German Reaction: The German controller plots the RAF bombers as they approach Trappes. The German nightfighters are now in the bomber stream and the air battle rages.

Trappes Force Losses: Only three men survive as a nightfighter shoots down a 466 Squadron Halifax, which plummets from the night sky and burns on the ground.

With both port engines on fire, a 76 Squadron Halifax spirals to earth and explodes on contact. Only one man survives.

After bombing the target, and whilst on the return flight, the flight engineer on a 158 Squadron Halifax hears a bang and his aircraft rocks. He sees flames blazing under the flap just inboard of the port inner engine. He tells his pilot and then sees flames from the corresponding point under the starboard wing, which he again reports to his pilot. He then sees an Me210 dead astern and tells his rear gunner but gets no reply. The bomber starts to lose height steadily, and the pilot works hard to keep control. The fire in the starboard wing starts to spread from the wing to the fuselage just behind the flight engineer's position. He tries the extinguisher to no avail, his intercom being disconnected in the process, and the fire engulfs the whole fuselage. The fire starts to spread forward and the flight engineer retrieves his parachute. He also retrieves his pilot's parachute and places it on the co-pilot's seat. He moves forward and bails out. The flight engineer and only one other member of the crew survive the incident. Later three bodies are found in the aircraft wreckage and another body 50 yards away. The mid-upper gunner is found 5 kilometres away from the aircraft; his parachute is open but the cause of death appears to be machine-gun bullet injuries to his face.

Engagements: From 500 yards an Me210 is shot at from a 405 Squadron Lancaster. The nightfighter catches fire, dives and is lost to view.

The rear gunner of a 192 Squadron Halifax, sees tracer from an Me109 as it attacks another aircraft. He opens fire then contact is lost.

A Ju88 opens fire on a 405 Squadron Lancaster, which returns fire. The German nightfighter bursts into flames, breaks up and falls to earth.

A twin-engined German nightfighter opens fire on a 78 Squadron Halifax. The gunners return fire and their foe explodes.

A rear gunner in a 35 Squadron Lancaster sees air to air tracer from a single-engined aircraft aimed at another bomber. The gunner opens fire then contact is lost.

A single-engined German nightfighter approaches a 158 Squadron Halifax from behind. Twice the German pilot fires his guns. The Halifax rear gunner lets off 600 rounds in the combat and witnesses his enemy burst into flames and fall to earth.

An attack from an Me210 damages a 166 Squadron Halifax and wounds the flight engineer. The return fire is seen to hit the nightfighter, then contact is broken.

A 640 Squadron Halifax is fired upon by an unidentified enemy aircraft then contact is lost.

A 640 Squadron Halifax gunner sees what he believes is a hostile twin-engined aircraft and opens fire. Contact is broken off with no reply.

Both gunners in a 10 Squadron Halifax open fire on an Me109. Their enemy is lost to sight without returning any fire.

0101 to 0115 hours

Trappes Force: The bomber force turns west, flying to the north of Chartres and starts to turn almost due north towards Rouen.

Other Forces: Between 0100 and 0110 hours 50 RAF bombers attack the coastal gun battery at Haringzelles. Opposition is negligible.

German Reaction: The German nightfighters pursue their enemy, the Trappes force, and the air battle continues.

Trappes Force Losses: There are no survivors when a 640 Squadron Halifax crashes to the ground; only two men survive when another 640 Squadron Halifax is shot down by a nightfighter and it falls to earth in flames.

A nightfighter shoots a 10 Squadron Halifax out of the night sky. The bomber crashes to earth and only one man survives.

A 76 Squadron Halifax falls prey to a nightfighter, which shoots it out of the sky to burst into flames on the ground with a total loss of life. Shortly after, a second 76 Squadron Halifax falls to earth, again with no survivors.

A nightfighter takes out a 158 Squadron Halifax and only one man escapes and survives as the heavy bomber plummets and smashes into the ground.

A nightfighter attack results in the subsequent explosion of a 405 Squadron Lancaster, which falls to burn on the ground, with only two men surviving.

An unseen fighter fires, from below, a short burst at a 158 Squadron Halifax, resulting in no damage or injury to the crew. The rear gunner asks for a banking search and his pilot obliges but nothing is seen. Just after the pilot has returned to an even keel the Halifax is hit by a long burst, which rakes the whole underside of the bomber from the flight engineer's position to the rear turret. The centre of the fuselage bursts into flames, controls have been shot away, the rear turret perspex is shattered on the port side, the gunner's door is shot away and the intercom becomes useless. The enemy remains unseen. The pilot calls out that the aircraft is out of control and stalling, and gives the order to bail out. All men survive and only the pilot is captured.

In the 15 minutes since leaving the target area the mid-upper gunner in a 10 Squadron Halifax reports seeing six aircraft go down in flames. The rear gunner then sees an aircraft on the starboard quarter below. He asks the mid-upper gunner if he can see it, but he is not able to do so. The rear gunner gives 'Corkscrew starboard – go' and the pilot immediately responds and after three corkscrews the rear gunner reports, 'I think we have lost him. Resume course.' Just as the pilot levels out, the fighter attacks scoring hits with tracer in the port outer engine. A few moments later a second burst strikes the Halifax in the starboard outer engine. With both outer engines on fire and flames streaming back, the pilot and flight engineer attempt, unsuccessfully, to feather the damaged engines. The mid-upper gunner scans the night sky but is unable to see his enemy. After approximately a minute, two more bursts follow in quick succession from a fighter; the first tears up the port inner engine, the second rakes the rear part of the fuselage. The pilot gives the order to bail out. The mid-upper gunner climbs out of his turret, opens the rear exit door and sees his foe, an Me110 flying on a parallel course, 150 feet below. The German nightfighter overtakes the Lancaster and is lost to sight. Just after the mid-upper gunner jumps from his stricken aircraft there is a loud explosion and he then watches the aircraft plunge to earth hitting the ground with a bright flash. The mid-upper gunner and four others survive the incident. The pilot and one other member of the crew are killed.

The mid-upper gunner on a 158 Squadron Halifax sees an enemy fighter flash past on a reciprocal course. He tells his rear gunner, who asks the pilot to corkscrew, which he does for two minutes. The rear gunner tells his skipper to resume course. At 0115 hours a long burst of cannon fire slams into the Halifax, from vertically below, raking the aircraft along the underside of the fuselage. Cannon shell takes out the intercom and lighting system. The rear turret is lit up by tracer and the nose of the aircraft is smashed. The inside of the bomber becomes a mass of flames. The wireless operator and flight engineer try to use the fire extinguisher, but the situation appears beyond saving. The navigator opens the front hatch and the flames then appear to subside. The wireless operator again goes back with the extinguisher, but by then the pilot is shouting, 'Bail out.' An attempt is made to contact the rear gunner using call-lights, without success. The navigator, bomb aimer and wireless operator bail out. The flight engineer gives his skipper his parachute and both follow. The mid-upper gunner leaves by the rear exit, through the fire and exploding ammunition. On the way down the navigator has to swing violently and pull on his parachute cords to avoid tracer fired from a fighter at another Halifax. The Halifax falls in flames, breaks in two, hits the ground and explodes. The rear gunner is the only fatality from the crew.

Roughly 15 miles from the target the rear gunner on a 640 Squadron Halifax sights an Me210 on his starboard quarter. He barks, 'Diving turn to starboard – go!' and the pilot automatically complies. Whilst in the dive a second Me210 previously unseen, fires a burst from the port quarter. The mid-upper gunner responds, firing continuously as his enemy passes overhead. The nightfighter fire hits the Halifax in the fuselage starting near the pilot's position. The flight engineer receives a wound to his face. The pilot is hit in the left side of his body, his controls are wrecked and he slumps forward. The rear gunner calls out, 'Keep on weaving skipper', but his pilot replies, 'I can't. Put on parachutes. Jump!' The navigator and wireless operator, after a struggle, remove the forward escape hatch. The navigator and bomb aimer bail out. The wireless operator returns to his pilot, shakes him, but he appears to be unconscious and gives no reply. The wireless operator returns to the escape hatch and as he passes through, the Halifax bursts into flames and goes out of control. He watches, suspended from his parachute, as the Halifax falls and explodes 100 feet above the ground. Only three members of the crew survive. The pilot, flight engineer and both gunners lose their lives.

Engagements: A Ju88 is hit by fire from a 640 Squadron Halifax, and returns fire. The combat ends with neither being able to claim damage to their foe.

An unidentified single-engine aircraft approaches a 10 Squadron Halifax. Its hostile intentions become apparent when it lets off rockets and then tracer. The Halifax's rear gunner responds with his machine guns, his fire striking his enemy and setting it alight. He then watches as his enemy spirals down, slamming into the ground where it explodes.

The rear gunner of a 35 Squadron Lancaster sights a single-engined aircraft and lets off two long bursts of machine-gun fire. At the same time his target fires and then breaks away. Contact is lost.

The fire from an Me110 strikes the port wing of a 78 Squadron Halifax. The heavy bomber's gunners return fire with no hits. The Me110 positions itself behind the Halifax, but seven bursts from the machine guns of the bomber's mid-upper gunner put paid to the nightfighter; its port wing catches fire and it plunges to earth.

Fishpond (an onboard radar) warns the crew of a 10 Squadron Halifax that an aircraft with seemingly hostile intention is approaching. The gunners soon pick out an FW190 and at 1,000 yards open fire. Their enemy disappears.

An Me109 opens fire on a 76 Squadron Halifax, and the bomber's gunners reply sending the single-engined nightfighter into a spin. It smashes into the ground and explodes.

The gunners in a 76 Squadron Halifax return fire after an Me109 attacks. The German aircraft bursts into flames and slams into the ground.

Visual Monica (an onboard radar) warns a 640 Squadron Halifax crew of an aircraft approaching. Shortly after a twin-engined aircraft opens fire on the heavy bomber. Before any fire can be returned contact is lost.

The port waist gunner in a 214 Squadron Fortress sees an FW190 bear down on his aircraft in a curved pursuit from port and below. He opens fire at 400 yards and his pilot throws the aircraft into a corkscrew. The German nightfighter hurtles over his adversary and contact is lost.

0116 to 0130 hours

Trappes Force: The bomber force proceeds north towards Rouen, then turns north-west.

Other Forces: Between 0118 and 0132 hours 104 RAF bombers attack the coastal radar station at Berneval, unopposed.

German Reaction: The German nightfighters continue to pursue and engage the Trappes force.

Trappes Force Losses: There is a total loss of life as a 466 Squadron Halifax crashes to the ground.

A 158 Squadron Halifax is hit in the nose. The mid-upper gunner is knocked from his turret, loses his flying boots, his intercom is disconnected, and he is hit in the leg by shrapnel. As he regains his feet his flight engineer pushes past carrying his parachute. Assuming the order to bail out has been given the mid-upper gunner grabs his parachute. The aircraft is in a steep dive and the mid-upper gunner struggles to reach the rear exit. The door is opened but not fixed back. He fixes it and then jumps. Only the flight engineer and mid-upper gunner survive and the Germans later retrieve five bodies from in and near the Halifax wreckage.

The cannon fire from a Ju88 rips a large hole in the centre section of a 158 Squadron Halifax and sets it alight. Confusion follows and three of the crew exit the aircraft. However the pilot, using all his skill, manages to bring his aircraft under control and eventually takes the rest of the crew and the damaged Halifax back to England. Of the three men who left the aircraft, two survive and one man is lost without trace.

Engagements: The mid-upper gunner in a 76 Squadron Halifax opens fire on a Ju88, which breaks away.

A Ju88 stalks a 78 Squadron Halifax. The nightfighter opens fire, the Halifax's gunners reply, seeing their bullets strike their enemy. The attack is broken off.

A single-engined nightfighter shoots at a 76 Squadron Halifax, whose gunners reply. Contact is lost.

A 35 Squadron Lancaster is attacked by an Me109. The heavy bomber pilots throws his aircraft into a corkscrew, whilst his rear gunner gives a short burst from his machine guns. Contact is lost.

A single-engined aircraft approaches a 158 Squadron Halifax, but breaks off the attack following fire from the rear gunner.

A single-engined nightfighter and 76 Squadron Halifax exchange fire then lose contact.

Both gunners in a 158 Squadron Halifax let lose their machine guns on a single-engined aircraft then contact is lost.

The rear gunner of a 192 Squadron Halifax fires off three short bursts at a twin-engined aircraft, then contact is lost.

A flaming FW190 is seen flying on a parallel course by crew members of a 10 Squadron Halifax. As the FW190 changes course to come in and attack, machine guns from the Halifax open up. Both heavy bomber gunners watch their enemy fall to the ground in flames.

0131 hours onwards

Trappes Force: Proceeds north-west over the Seine, crosses the French coast near St Valéry-en-Caux, and carries on over the Channel.

Other Forces: The coastal batteries at Wimereux (0136 to 0143 hours) and Wissant (0206 to 0215 hours) are attacked by 17 and 30 RAF bombers respectively. These RAF aircrews are fortunate. The German nightfighters have been busy elsewhere.

German Reaction: The German nightfighters break off the pursuit against the Trappes force.

Engagements: A 10 Squadron Halifax is on the receiving end of three short bursts of fire from an unidentified aircraft. The heavy bomber's pilot throws the aircraft into a corkscrew and contact is lost.

Jack Scott's crew took part in the Trappes raid and Ken Handley recorded in his diary:

> A little flak was seen just beyond the target. The illuminating flares went down followed by the red & white ground markers. We made our bombing run & heard the 'master of ceremonies' say 'bomb the white TI' so bomb them we did. Leaving the target we saw several combats behind us & over the target. A fighter was seen approaching on our port side about 300 yards away. He went straight past. A large explosion was seen about half way from Trappes to the French coast. Either a 'scarecrow' but I believe it was an aircraft. Other targets could be seen getting a good pranging, bang on the TIs near the coast.
>
> Our 21st op, still going strong.

Jack had managed to pilot his aircraft through an uncompromising air battle, and Ken's use of the term 'scarecrow' is of particular interest. Bomber crews had been told that the Germans were firing up large shells that would resemble an aircraft exploding, as an attack on the morale of the bomber aircrews. However the evidence for the use of such a device is scant and Ken had guessed correctly. It had been an exploding bomber.

The losses on the Trappes raid were not the only casualties for Bomber Command that night. Three aircraft on SOE operations failed to return, including a Stirling from Dennis Field's 90 Squadron. Fortunately the entire crew survived to fight another day, although five men were subsequently captured.

PART TWO

D-Day and the
Battle for Normandy

CHAPTER 10

'IT'S ON BOYS. D-DAY!'

The Germans knew the Allies were going to launch an invasion but the basic problem was where and when. In June 1944 59 divisions were available to defend the coastlines of Holland, Belgium and France, approximately 3,000 miles. Eight divisions were in Holland and Belgium, and just over half were either static coastal defence divisions or were training divisions. There were 27 field divisions, 10 of which were armoured (panzer) divisions. The German dilemma was where to position these units? Where could they best be deployed to counter the Allied offensive?

German Positions, as identified by Allied Intelligence, OB West (von Rundstedt) - 6 June 1944 (source - Public Record Office CAB 44/242)

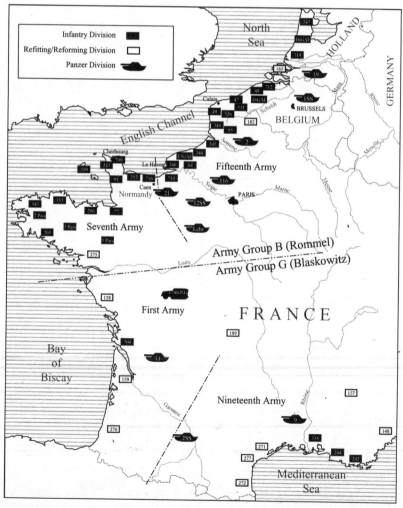

Dealing with this problem was the main responsibility of Commander-in-Chief of the West Field Marshal Gerd von Rundstedt, who had control of Army Group G, Army Group B and Panzer Group West. Army Group G was positioned south of the river Loire, outside the invasion area. The Normandy battlefield would fall within the sector of France covered by Field Marshal Erwin Rommel's Army Group B, which consisted of the Fifteenth and Seventh Armies along with panzer divisions of Panzer Group West. However a complicated command structure would seriously hamper deployment of divisions, notably the armoured units, when the Allies landed.

The first problem for the defending commanders was the quality of the coastal defence units. In a postwar interrogation von Rundstedt made clear his concerns.

As for the Atlantic wall itself, according to Rundstedt, it had to be seen to be believed. It had no depth and little surface, and was an unmitigated fake. At best it might have proved an obstacle for twenty-four hours but one day's intensive assault by a strong determined force was all that was needed to break any part of this line. Once through the wall the rest of these fortifications and fortresses with their eyes to the sea, were of no use at all. Rundstedt, in any event, placed little faith in a rigid defence, favouring a war of movement, and constantly attempted to form some kind of effective reserve in the interior of France.

But bad as the defences themselves were, the men to man them were worse still. The twenty to twenty-five infantry divisions which were put to occupy the Atlantic wall had no mobility, were equipped with a hodgepodge of foreign artillery and were filled with personnel from older age groups and low physical categories. Mixed in amongst these relics were thousands of Russians (Ost troops) who constituted a menace and nuisance to operations in France. Only the armoured and parachute divisions contained young men, but there were too few of these to form an adequate fighting force. Once the various divisions were stretched along the huge coastal front, there was hardly anything left in the interior.[63]

Rommel, also aware of the fragility of the coastal defence, favoured using the panzer divisions to defeat the Allied troop landings and throw them back into the sea.

Von Rundstedt's postwar interrogation: Field Marshal Rommel argued that the bulk of the mobile reserves must be as close to the threatened coastal areas as possible, so that they could immediately affect the battle before the Allies had gained a serious foothold. Up to a point Rundstedt agreed with this principle, but since he did not know where the main invasion effort would be, he did not want to spread his armour too thin along the ground, where most of it would be useless once the assault began. General Geyr von Schweppenburg, commander of the Armoured troops in the West, was of the opinion that all operational reserves should be concentrated in the area of Paris from whence they could be sent to any menaced sector.[64]

The issue of where to place the panzer divisions was referred to Hitler and a compromise was reached. Rommel's Army Group B would have three panzer divisions as a mobile reserve. Hitler through the offices of OKW (Oberkommando der Wehrmacht – Supreme Command of the Armed Forces) would then have command of four other panzer divisions. As such, neither von Rundstedt nor Rommel had adequate tactical control of the forces available in the battle area. The fact that they had to refer some of their command decisions would result in delay, and time was something they could ill afford as the Allies sought to build up sufficient forces on the beachheads with which to break out.

On 5 June 1944, six German divisions defended the Normandy coast, three in the Cherbourg peninsula, two between the rivers Vire and Orne and one between the rivers Orne and Seine. The nearest armoured unit was 21st Panzer Division, near Caen. Rommel's other two armoured divisions lay east of the Seine. However two of the panzer divisions under OKW control lay to the south-west of the forthcoming battle area.

For the first few days of the invasion the key for the Allies was the breaking of the German coastal defence, and the establishment of the beachhead resulting from sufficient advance inland before the panzers could counter-attack. Along the Normandy coast the Germans had placed a number of large gun emplacements, all threatening the sea approaches to the beaches. A direct hit from any of these on a landing craft would undoubtedly sink it. The Navy, in particular, were keen to have these guns silenced.

It became a responsibility of the Allied heavy bombers to soften up the beach defenders and to take out the coastal guns and RAF Bomber Command was detailed to attack ten gun emplacements on the night of 5/6 June. The Eighth Air Force was required to bomb enemy troop positions on the coastline, just prior to the beach landings, requiring precision timing and great accuracy bearing in mind the approaching assault troops.

However in addition to these commitments, other special operations were planned for the night of 5/6 June, with the purpose of causing as much confusion for the Germans as possible. The longer the exact landing location could be hidden the better. Certain specially trained RAF heavy bomber squadrons and their respective crews were called on. One of these was the crew of Dennis Field from 90 Squadron.

Towards the end of May, at Tuddenham, it became apparent to newly commissioned Dennis Field that the invasion was approaching, evidenced by the activity at the squadron with security tightening and bomb stocks growing. The June moon period fell at the beginning of the month and 90 Squadron was again called on to conduct special duties. So after a minelaying trip to Gravelines on 27 May Dennis and his crew found themselves detailed again to arm the Resistance networks in France. On the night of 1 June Dennis flew his Stirling on their 27th operation, to a drop zone in western France near Angoulême. Unable to find any reception, the operation had to be aborted, but the next night they returned, this time completing the drop successfully.

Then on 5 June 1944, 90 Squadron detailed aircraft to be part of a particularly momentous operation. Under the codename *Titanic*, Halifaxes and Stirlings of the special duties squadrons would simulate airborne troop landings in areas away from the forthcoming invasion location, attempting to confuse the German defenders and draw their forces away from the beaches.

Dennis Field: The briefing was carried out in even closer security than usual and great emphasis was paid to adhering closely to the heights and timings of the flight plans. Met. forecast intermittent heavy cloud throughout. In conjunction with 149 Squadron we were to carry out a deception operation dropping dummy parachutists and pyrotechnics in the St. Lô area of the Cherbourg peninsula, and as the first kite ('J') of 'B' flight we should lead. Additionally as we crossed the Channel we would drop bundles of special paper *(Window)* to reflect on enemy radar as further cover and deception. The quantity half filled the centre section of the fuselage and two crew, Curly and an additional eighth member, were needed to drop it every timed few seconds. We took off in wet conditions and climbed through overcast to level off at our prescribed height and follow an accurate course with regular Gee fixes. There was much aerial activity with aircraft navigation lights in plentiful evidence above and below moving along and across our path. Navigation lights were as usual switched off at the coast and 'windowing' through the flare chutes commenced. Halfway across Curly's microphone crackled on and he asked if he could borrow my wristwatch as he had inadvertently thrown his issued one out with a bundle of window. I reluctantly lent him mine with the promise that if he lost that I would personally throw him out after it. (Whether or not he craftily 'won' a service watch or not I do not know, but I still have and use mine.) We crossed the enemy coast on the western side of the Cherbourg peninsula at one minute past midnight and proceeded by DR [dead reckoning] to our destination where we dropped our load into darkness to simulate a clandestine troop drop. We returned by virtually a reciprocal route, having met only small amounts of desultory flak and took good care to keep to our designated path back to base, touching down after four and three-quarter hours.[65]

Dennis's dummy parachutists landed in an area under the control of the German 352nd Division. This division was part of LXXXIV Corps, Seventh Army and shortly after 1 a.m. the corps commander General Erich Marcks, as a result of reported paratroop landings, alerted his corps. At 4 a.m. 352nd Division despatched a regiment, on bicycles, to engage a believed Allied paratroop landing, only to find they were just dummies. News of the discovery of dummy parachutists quickly travelled and the Allies soon became aware that their deception plan was being well publicised. A German signal intercept processed at Bletchley Park uncovered that 'Sea defence commandant Normandy aware at two three five five hours fifth that quote some of parachutists reported were straw dummies unquote.'[66] The discovery of the dummy paratroop drops also reinforced some German commanders' opinions that the activity in Normandy was just a diversion and nothing more.[67]

As well as the simulated airborne landings two further diversion operations were conducted, *Glimmer* and *Taxable*, whereby the heavy bombers simulated convoys approaching the French coast away from the actual invasion area. *Glimmer* was executed by aircraft of 218 Squadron simulating a convoy approaching the coast near Boulogne. *Taxable* was to simulate a convoy approaching the coast between Dieppe and Cap d'Antifer. Small Royal Navy craft would tow balloons, which would show as large ships on that part of the German radar which still existed, and Lancasters of 617 Squadron, under the leadership of Wing Commander Leonard Cheshire, would fly spiralling circuits across the Channel, slowly approaching the French coast. *Window* would be dropped by the aircraft to suggest to German radar there was a fleet of ships approaching at eight knots. The operation had required considerable planning and training for the 617 Squadron airmen. With the Lancasters cruising at 160 knots, the timing of the *Window* drops was of paramount importance.

> *Leonard Cheshire VC:* I think our great worry was whether we would make a mistake, because we had been told that if one mistake was made the German radar would notice it; they would then realise that we were doing a spoof, they would then recognise the urgency of getting all their armour across to the Normandy beachhead, and we were really not trained for this kind of flying.
>
> At briefing we were unexpectedly given a bird's eye view of the whole of the D-Day operation. It startled us because it made you realise we were just one tiny cog in a vast operation, but at the same time you were one of those cogs that could not afford to go wrong; if you made a mistake then perhaps everything would suffer, you had that feeling that so many people were taking the brunt of the invasion landing on the beachheads, and were depending on us for something we weren't quite sure we could really do.[68]

The execution of both *Glimmer* and *Taxable* was a success, but what of the outcomes? In the *Glimmer* area the German defences opened up on the approaching 'convoy', E-boats were launched and sent to the area and German fighter aircraft were also sent to where ABC operations (airborne radio countermeasures) were being conducted, between the *Taxable* and *Glimmer* zones, as this was believed to be air cover for the 'convoy'. It appeared that *Taxable* had little success in fooling the Germans into making any response, and it is quite possible that they had, in fact, little knowledge of the approaching 'convoy' owing to the success of the Allied radar jamming and the bombing destruction of the radar installations that would have 'seen' the 'convoy'.

In addition to the above deception operations, 24 aircraft from 101 Squadron were detailed to hinder German nightfighter control. The 101 Squadron crews consisted of eight airmen, the additional German-speaking airman operating ABC (*Airborne Cigar*), attempting to jam German nightfighter communications. In addition the 101 Squadron crews would drop *Window* which would interfere with German radar. Edward Askew, a pilot with RAF Bomber Command's 101 Squadron, took part in the operation:

> I do remember the excitement felt on 3 June when the whole of 101 Squadron station personnel were confined to camp. Usually before an operation we would hear of the bomb and fuel loading and speculated on the likely target. The news for 5 June was full tanks and no bombs; the

favoured speculation was a trip to Russia. When we assembled for
briefing and the concealed route was uncovered – it was from base to
Calais and then Paris. We had to reach Calais at a set time and continue
the circuit Paris to Calais for six hours dropping *Window* to interfere with
German fighter control. When we got to the aircraft to take off we could
hardly get in because they were stacked full of *Window*, which was to be
thrown out at 22,000 feet. So that was our D-Day mission. To provide a
bit of excitement, once we saw twin-engine aircraft identified as a
Mosquito or Me210. But our D-Day experience must have been the most
boring on record. It was not until our return that we heard our first news
of the landings on the radio.

RAF Bomber Command targets (night 5/6 June 1944)
and USAAF 8th Air Force targets (first mission 6 June 1944)

While the RAF's special duty squadrons carried out their various diversionary
ruses, at air stations all over England other RAF Bomber Command and US
Eighth Air Force crews prepared to support the main assault directly, blast gun
emplacements, smash the defences on the assault beaches and shatter the bodies
and nerve of the German coastal troops.

On the evening of 5 June 1944, RAF Bomber Command stations throughout
England were a hive of activity as aircraft were checked over, bombed and
fuelled up, and aircrew went through their pre-operational procedure.
Throughout the evening and night 8,000 RAF Bomber Command aircrew
attended briefings with the vast majority oblivious to the fact that in the next few
hours they would be paving the way for the long awaited invasion.

The main targets that night were ten enemy coastal gun batteries, which defended the Normandy beaches. In addition to the various diversionary ruses RAF Bomber Command aircraft would also conduct 1,211 sorties, a record for the war to date.

Arthur Inder was a mid-upper gunner with 77 Squadron and attended the briefing at RAF Full Sutton on 5 June 1944:

> We were not officially informed it was D-Day but the emphasis on not to jettison any bombs in the Channel at any cost made one think. Even so this significance did not completely register because it was normal practice for us, in case we hit some of our Navy boys, or others. At our aircraft, pre-op checks done and whilst then waiting outside, some high-rankers and civilian people shook our hands. This we thought queer, especially as one of them said, 'You are going to make history tonight, boys.' I personally did not imagine it to be D-Day but did feel a bit perplexed.

> *Horace Pearce DFC, pilot, 77 Squadron:* Just seconds before start up time a staff car containing 'Top Brass' came to each dispersal to tell us that the destruction of the target was vitally essential to the incoming D-Day troops. We had already been told at briefing that routes, turning points and heights had to be rigidly adhered to.

At 2215 hours on 5 June 1944 Bill Brown lifted his 427 Squadron Halifax III from the runway at RAF Leeming. As far as his crew were concerned there was nothing extraordinary about this particular operation. After joining the bomber stream, Bill Brown piloted his explosive-laden bomber down England, crossing the south coast over Hastings and as they left friendly shores behind, the crew were unaware that beneath them 6,000 Allied ships carrying 185,000 men and 20,000 vehicles were heading in the same direction. They were unaware that with them in the night skies, hundreds of other Allied aircraft followed a similar course, all part of the airborne assault, either carrying paratroopers or towing gliders full of Allied soldiers, who were waiting pensively for the moment when they would land on French soil and secure the flanks of the invasion area, assault certain gun batteries, secure bridges, and mark landing zones for further troops to be dropped by parachute or glider.

As Bill Brown's Halifax approached the French coast, and the gun battery at Sallenelles (defending *Sword* beach), Art Willis peered through the nose blister, searching for the target markers they had been told about at briefing. It became apparent that visual identification of the target or direct sighting of the markers would be impossible, as there was complete cloud cover. Nevertheless beneath them on the clouds was the glow of the red markers. At 0039 hours from 11,000 feet sixteen 500 lb general purpose bombs fell from Bill Brown's Halifax. In total 88 aircraft would release 389 tons of explosive.

Bill Brown then turned his aircraft due west, out of the target area: with the main part of the operation completed, his task was now to ensure his crew were returned safely back to England. Flying almost parallel to the Normandy coast they approached the west coast of the Cherbourg peninsula. Stan Selfe recalls the return trip: 'Cliff, the navigator, said to the skipper "crossing enemy coast now", and he asked Art, the bomb aimer, to give another fix, to work out an ETA for the

English coast.' As they flew back across the Channel towards England a rather confusing picture appeared on the H2S radar screen. It appeared that they had reached the English coast much sooner than expected. Stan Selfe continues:

> I was looking out of the cabin window and I suddenly saw all these ships, dozens of them. They were landing barges and behind them were the battleships. I nudged the skipper and spoke to him, not on the intercom so that the rest couldn't hear in case I was wrong, and I pointed down. He switched his microphone on and said, 'It's on, boys. D-Day!'

The confusing picture on their H2S screen was a reflection of the invasion fleet; many ships had departed the English coast at the same time and were now proceeding across the Channel apparently in the shape of the coastline. As such it had seemed to the confused crew that they had reached the English coast in less than five minutes.

As Bill Brown's Halifax proceeded across the Cherbourg peninsula, Jack Scott and his crew sat poised in their 466 Squadron Halifax at RAF Driffield. When their time came, drill took over.

> *Ken Handley:* We lined up at the end of the runway. A number of the ground staff gave us the 'thumbs-up', and we began to move. Flaps at 1/3 down, engines revved up almost to the gate, being held back by the brakes. The whole aircraft shuddered as the build-up of vibrations increased prior to getting airborne. The 'green' was given by the aldis lamp. Brakes were released, the throttles pushed through the 'gate' for take-off power and full boost. Gathering momentum, the tail wheel began to lift and at approx 110 mph the aircraft was airborne. 60,000 lb including bomb load now in the air. So very slowly we gained altitude. With an 11,000 lb bomb load it appeared doubly slow. Jack Scott asked for flaps and undercarriage 'up'. Ron Tickell carried out the action, confirming over the intercom. The aircraft now had a smoother feel with the undercarriage up and the streamlined cowlings in place. Gaining altitude and circling to port we slowly reach an altitude of 2,000 feet.
>
> As we took off, Jack Scott said, 'Here we go.' From that moment on our crew was committed to the task ahead. Any inner doubt was swept away, the crew as a single team would act with a single thought in mind, to accomplish the mission successfully. I do not know how the rest of the crew was reacting to the skipper's 'Here we go' but for me it was not a prayer but a cold-blooded, 'Its either you or me tonight.'

At RAF Full Sutton the Halifaxes of 4 Group's 77 Squadron also prepared to take off on the raid to Maisy, on the mouth of the Vire river in Normandy. Arthur Inder was the mid-upper gunner on Pilot Officer Baldwin's Halifax III:

> We were the first aircraft off and everything appeared quite normal; away we went on a green signal from tower, at 0100 hours. The run-up was quite normal and we soon became airborne. I waited until the sound of the propeller pitches were altered to 2750; that was my signal to move out of the rest position and move into my mid-upper turret position.

Unfortunately for me however I moved a split second too soon. I had stood up and moved away in readiness. In doing so I had pulled out my intercom. Apparently at that moment our skipper had called a warning to the crew, which I did not hear, that the starboard engines had gone. We had lost all power on that side. I believe that with terrific foresight he throttled back on his port engines from maximum thrust to equalise, and in doing so prevented a corkscrew effect, which would have killed us all. In my estimation we could not have survived.

I was standing and did not have a chance of evasive action. At that moment the world struck me on the head and tore me apart.

Despite Pilot Officer Baldwin's attempts he could not prevent the Halifax hitting the ground. The Halifax broke up, the fuselage was propped up and burning fiercely, the wings, engines and forward section similarly burning, all with the bombs still aboard. The central crew section was part of the fuselage near the break, and those who were able made a rapid exit. Realising some of their comrades were still in the aircraft they turned back towards the inferno. Until that point none of the bombs had gone off. Arthur Inder was one of those needing help:

I was pulled and pushed out of the aircraft, to fall and hit the ground. This fall helped in a way to bring me to a semi-conscious state. I was vomiting with shock. I was slung over a partly open gate and just hung there whilst the others tried to get to Pilot Officer Lettington, the bomb aimer, who was trapped and badly injured. I was aware of massive flames and sounds then I unfortunately went with the gate as it opened and fell forwards and staggered to the ground. I had tried to stand but failed, only to collapse into a ditch. But this was the wrong way; it was towards the flames and the explosions of ammo and fuel and the bomb blasts. I passed out again, then recovered, but was protected to a point in the ditch. It was exactly like being in a dream. I could not see very well but instinctively knew I had to get away.

I managed to crawl out after a lot of effort and just kept on dragging myself away from the heat and ammo blasts. I could only see out of part of one eye. The dream imagery kept drawing my thoughts to a welding of all things. But I kept on going. My worst fear by now was how many bombs had to go? I managed to get to a fence but it was barbed wire. I tried to clamber over but got caught up hanging head down. I remember the feeling that a stuck pig would have felt. I started to try thinking in a clearer way and I realised I could release my harness with a twist and blow centrally. I then fell out to the ground and just kept going until I reached a ditch behind a hedge and I was completely spent, exhausted and generally browned off, and still in profound shock.

It was then I believe a couple more bombs decided to go. I was glad then that I had made the effort to get away. The blast was so severe the trees on the bank surrounding just flattened out with a swish. And the explosion – I can still hear it.

Our Motor Transport people had been searching and found me and got me thankfully back to the medical department. It took the medical orderly some time to take off my helmet, because apparently I stopped him, thinking my head was coming with it. Shock. However at York military hospital I was soon put to grateful sleep and operated on.

Arthur Inder suffered head, face and leg injuries. Amazingly the rest of the crew also survived, all suffering to some extent from burns, cuts and shock. The worst was to Pilot Officer Lettington who suffered very bad face injuries, losing one eye and teeth, and his face had to be reconstructed by surgery.

Other 77 Squadron crews awaiting their turn to take off, witnessed the incident. Horace Pearce DFC, a pilot with 77 Squadron remembers: 'The rest of us were kept waiting for a possible change of runway – we thought – but no, in the event we were sent off on the same runway to fly over the burning aircraft with fears that its bomb load might explode at any minute.' Fortunately for the other crews, none was flying over the crash site when the bombs did go off.

Meanwhile at RAF Driffield, the aircraft were now airborne without major incident. As instructed at briefing Jack Scott kept his 466 Squadron Halifax circling, gaining altitude over base until they reached 6,000 feet. Then course was set south, and the Halifax climbed further reaching 11,500 feet as it crossed the south coast of England near Bridport. Just after 0300 hours they approached the French coast, and Ron Tickell began scanning the ground below, searching for the Pathfinder markers which were to mark the German gun battery at Maisy, which threatened the sea approaches to *Utah* and *Omaha* beaches. Everything appeared to be going to plan and despite considerable cloud cover Ron Tickell could see the red and green markers go down. Running up on the target he released the bomb load on the markers at zero + 30 seconds and, as Ken Handley later recorded in his diary, 'pranged them good and proper'. The cloud cover did prove a problem with regard to aiming the bombs but also provided the crew with a sense of safety by blotting out the moonlight which, they feared, could have illuminated the Halifax sufficiently to attract any prowling German nightfighters. In fact opposition was negligible, and only one lot of light flak seen. After the 'bombs gone' and the wait whilst the Halifax was kept straight and level for the bombing photograph, Jack Scott turned the RAF heavy bomber out of the target area, piloted his crew safely back to England and after a flight of 4 hours 20 mins they landed at Driffield.

As Jack's 466 Squadron crew approached the Normandy beaches Alan Grant's 7 Squadron Lancaster left the Oakington runway at 0249 hours, detailed to attack the gun battery at Longues, which defended *Gold* beach.

Steve Masters: The target was to be bombed early on the morning of the 6th. This seemed a strange time to bomb, especially as we were told that the last bombing time was to be fifteen minutes before daylight. One other peculiar feature was the warning that we might see large numbers of ships, but we were to avoid flying directly over them. Speculation ran high as to what this might mean, because there were rumours circulating that an invasion of Europe was imminent.

As hundreds of other aircraft had done already that night, Alan Grant piloted his Lancaster across the south coast of England, and Steve using his Gee set and the H2S, monitored the flight path closely. After crossing the Normandy coast north of Caen, Alan swung his Lancaster westward, flying a quarter of a mile inland, parallel to the coastline. At 0415 hours the Lancaster approached the cloud-covered target.

> *Steve Masters:* Ron Neills, who was as alert as any of us, was lying in the bomb aimer's position ready to take over visually should the radar fail. When given the order, he opened the bomb doors while Alan concentrated on maintaining steady flight. Everything seemed very peaceful, too peaceful in fact.
> 'Is everything all right, is anything happening below?' enquired Alan.
> 'Only one gun firing,' answered Ron.
> We continued, as I watched the radar signals intently. 'The gun has now stopped firing' commented Ron, 'and I can see the target marker.'

The first red marker was seen to go down but soon became intermittently obscured by the cloud cover. Steve took over and the bomb load was released blindly using Gee and H2S.

> *Steve Masters:* 'Bombs away,' I called with relief when we felt the thud as the bombs left the bomb bay.
> 'Bomb doors closed,' called Ron and we knew that we had achieved our mission. All we had to do now was get home safely. Ron informed us that he was quite satisfied we were on target, as when I had called for bomb release, he saw the target marker in the bombsight.

Again, as with the previous attacks that night, the bomber force met very little opposition near the target area. However one aircraft would not return from the attack on Longues. Squadron Leader Raybould DSO DFM of 582 Squadron was killed along with his entire crew; all were lost without trace.

> *Steve Masters:* Turning north we headed for home thankful to be doing so. After a little while Dick Martin who was watching the H2S pointed to a blip on the screen, indicating that we were approaching a ship. We altered course to avoid it, then another appeared, followed by another. After three or four such alterations, Alan told me not to bother; he could see so many ships now it was daylight, that we couldn't possibly avoid them all.
> I thought that as I was not so busy I would look out to see how many other bombers there were with us. There was none. I hunted all round the sky but still I could spot no other aircraft. I admit I was concerned, but consoled myself that we were probably one of the last to bomb and the others were ahead of us.
> As it got lighter we felt more and more vulnerable as here we were over the Channel on our own, ill equipped to meet fighters in daylight. As a night bomber we felt more security in the dark as under those conditions we could cope, but daylight was quite different.
> 'Fighter starboard quarter,' called Bill our rear gunner. We tensed, how far away was it? We all wondered, no one daring to speak while Bill had

control.

I knew it had all been too easy, no opposition going into or over the target and up to this time we had been enjoying a peaceful journey home.

'Standby to corkscrew starboard' ordered Bill.

'Stay as you are,' yelled Tom. 'We have another on our port quarter.'

This was serious, one we might have been able to deal with, but now, if we had turned to attack one, the other fighter would be presented with a very easy target.

'Two more coming up fast,' said Bill.

'I can see several more,' reported Tom. 'In fact there are twelve altogether.' I who had wished to see other aircraft, hadn't reckoned on this outcome, and felt quite sick at heart.

'It looks as though we have had it' Alan remarked in a level tone of voice, 'but see how many you can get before they get us.'

I wondered what the next few minutes was going to be like, supposing we lasted even that long. To face such odds seemed a cruel fate. To say I wasn't scared would have been very far from the truth, but I also felt resigned to what we were about to have meted out on us.

'Closing range rapidly,' called the gunners. 'Ready to fire.'

'Don't shoot,' screamed Bill. 'They are Americans, they will blow us out of the sky if you do.'

There was a stunned silence in our aircraft. Were we to survive after all? We waited and waited. Would they open fire?

'Seems they are satisfied,' called Bill. 'They are leaving us.'

The rest of the flight went without incident and Alan Grant landed his Lancaster at 0614 hours. The crew, still unaware of what they had been taking part in, went to briefing.

Ron Neills: We had seen an extra lot of shipping in the Channel, which did ring bells, but we didn't know that there was going to be an invasion and we reported the fact that there was a hell of a lot of activity in the Channel.

Following the debriefing the crew dispersed.

Steve Masters: As I walked across the fields to the house in which I was staying with my wife, I pondered on the peace of the summer morning and how different it might have been.

Crawling into bed at about 8 o'clock that morning I fell sound asleep but not for long. I was sure I had only been asleep a few minutes when Dorothy brought me a cup of tea, the clock said half past twelve.

'It has started,' said Dorothy.

'What has?' I enquired none too graciously.

'The invasion of Europe,' I was told.

'Has it?' I grunted and tried to go back to sleep. No more sleep for me as invasion or not I still had to report for duty, so reluctantly I climbed out of bed.

Shortly after the attack on Longues had finished the nearby gun battery at Mont Fleury, defending *Gold* beach, received the attention of the RAF's heavies. On the approach to the target the 76 Squadron Halifax of Pilot Officer Walker was shot down with no survivors from the crew of seven. Over the target the bomb aimers, as their colleagues had done on many of the other targets that night, released their destructive loads to fall through cloud. Squadron Leader Watson DFC, on his second tour of operations and on his 51st sortie, piloted his 578 Squadron Halifax through a good bombing run on the attack on Mont Fleury. In the Halifax's astrodome his flight engineer Flight Sergeant Middleton watched as another Halifax, just above his aircraft on the port side, released its high explosive bombs. There followed, almost immediately, a blinding flash just off their port wing, which Middleton would later describe as yellow and lingering with green fingers of flaming material. Fragments of hot metal peppered Watson's Halifax, puncturing the fuselage, piercing the aircraft's perspex nose and gashing Sergeant Goode, the mid-upper gunner.

Watson quickly assessed the situation, informing his crew that his controls were still functioning. Middleton checked his fuel gauges, relieved to see there was no apparent loss of fuel, but the situation worsened as he watched a small 'blowlamp-like fire' breaking out on the port wing. He cut and feathered the port outer engine and the flames reduced. The situation again deteriorated when sparks began to fly from the trailing edge of the port wing and a large fire grew between the engines, central to the main plane. The port inner engine was feathered but there was no effect on the growing fire.

Watson's experience and skill enabled him to keep the Halifax flying on just the two starboard engines, but then an explosion on the port wing shook the Halifax. He called up his crew, informing them that he would be unable to fly the aircraft on two engines any longer, and he instructed them to bail out. His navigator went first, exiting via the forward escape hatch, assisted by a shove from the bomb aimer when he stuck in the narrow opening. The bomb aimer then stuck, owing to the dinghy pack on his seat and parachute on his chest, and had to be pushed out by the wireless operator who quickly followed. Meanwhile Middleton had collected his own and his pilot's gear and with the Halifax lurching to starboard, twice tried to put the parachute on Watson's chest, without success. Watson ordered Middleton to bail out. He would never see his pilot again.

As soon as Middleton cleared the aircraft he pulled his ripcord and before he had time to pull his mae west cord he hit the sea. Middleton, the bomb aimer and the wireless operator all survived and were later picked up by a US Navy Tank Landing Craft. The navigator, despite bailing out, rear gunner, mid-upper gunner and pilot were all lost. It is unlikely that Watson, with his aircraft at such low level, had time to escape the burning Halifax. He had risked everything to buy time for his crew, and it cost him his life.

Lieutenant General Omar N. Bradley, commanding the First US Army, and on board the *Augusta* witnessed the demise of one RAF Bomber Command aircraft:

It was 3.35 a.m. when the clanking bell outside my cabin called the crew to battle stations . . . The moon hung misted in an overcast sky and the wind still lashed the Channel . . . A faraway roar echoed across the Channel and off our starboard bow orange fires ignited the sky as . . . RAF bombers swarmed over the French coast line from the Seine to Cherbourg. An enemy AA battery stabbed blindly through the night. A shower of spark splintered the darkness and a ribbon of fire peeled out of the sky as a stricken bomber plunged towards the *Augusta*. It levelled off, banked around our stern, and exploded into the Channel.[69]

It is likely that this was the Halifax piloted by Squadron Leader Watson DFC.

In the post-raid analysis the squadron commander of 582 Squadron recounted that he had also seen a flash and 'green fingers' just like that mentioned by Flight Sergeant Middleton above, and that it had resembled an aircraft exploding. This could possibly have been the 76 Squadron Halifax of Pilot Officer Walker, although its crash location suggests it fell on the approach to the target. Owing to the fact that the raid was after dawn, no photo flashes were being carried by the main force, although the Pathfinder aircraft did. There is also a possibility that the aircraft exploding could have been the 582 Squadron aircraft lost on the attack to Longues.

At about the same time as Alan Grant and crew had taken off on their 'uneventful flight', Roland Ward hauled his 50 Squadron Lancaster into the air from the RAF Skellingthorpe runway, on what would be a far from uneventful operation. Crossing the English coast over Bridport, at 11,000 feet, the Lancaster tore towards the German gun emplacement at Pointe du Hoc (St Pierre du Mont), which defended *Omaha* and *Utah* beaches. However on approaching the target the cloud cover forced Roland to decrease height to 9,000 feet. In the nose of the Lancaster Dick Haine peered through his bombsight, lining up on the target markers placed by Mosquitos. At 0450 hours Dick released his bomb load on the centre of visible green markers, reporting 'bombs gone' to his pilot and crew. While Roland kept the aircraft on the straight and level, awaiting the strike photograph, Ken Smith gave his pilot the new course out of the target area.

Charles Owen, a pilot with 97 Squadron, also took part in the attack on the coastal battery at Pointe du Hoc and recorded in his diary:

> We thought the briefing sounded a little odd for this trip and sure enough when we broke over the French coast the Channel was full of ships. The army had pulled its finger out at last and D-Day was on. We bombed at 05.00 just as it was getting light, and had a grandstand view of the Americans running in on the beach. First class prang on the battery, but saw Jimmy Carter shot down by a Ju88 over the target. Marvellous sight coming back as the sun came up. We on the way back and the Americans on the way out. Landed back in time for breakfast, but very disappointed that there was nothing on the 8 o'clock news.[70]

Defences were certainly active against the force attacking Pointe du Hoc. Owen had witnessed the demise of Wing Commander E. J. Carter DFC's Lancaster with no survivors from the crew of eight. In addition the 97 Squadron Lancaster of Lieutenant F. V. Jespersen RNAF was downed, all seven of the crew losing their lives.

We left Roland Ward's crew just after they had bombed the target. In the mid-upper turret Stanley Reading had listened over the intercom as his crewmates went through the well practised bombing procedure. What came next though was something they had never practised before. Suddenly the great heavy bomber shook as a flak shell struck the Lancaster in the bomb bay causing a violent explosion. Within seconds Roland realised his aircraft had suffered a fatal blow and he called over the intercom, 'We've been hit kids, get out.' Stan Reading reported back to his pilot that he was leaving his turret and he climbed down into an inferno. The gun ammunition was exploding and flames engulfed the inside of the Lancaster's fuselage. He tried to look ahead to his forward colleagues but the intensity of the fire forced him to turn away. Stan had little choice but to grab his parachute and fight his way through the fire as it spread down the fuselage, while the heat inflicted serious burns on the desperate airman. He managed to get to the rear exit, open it and put on his parachute fixing it just by the right buckle, the left hanging loose, something he had known about but neglected to repair. He jumped out and in a few seconds pulled the rip cord.

The chaos of the inside of the burning aircraft was replaced by the darkness of the night and the roar from the engines of other bombers. As Stan, suffering with serious burns, neared the ground he just managed to clear some trees before landing in a ditch, sustaining further injury by spraining his ankle. On his descent he had lost sight of the falling Lancaster and was not able to witness it plummeting into the ground and exploding. Within those few moments six men with whom Stan had spent the last few months eating, sleeping, fighting, drinking and laughing, died.

The next day a telegram arrived at the home of Dick Haine's mother. Her worst fears were realised and any hopes that her son may have survived were soon dashed when news came through that Dick had been killed. It would be twenty years before she had the chance, with her daughter, to visit his grave. The bodies of Denis Mangan, Kenneth Smith and George Livingstone were never found, and their names were later commemorated on the Runnymede memorial. The bodies of Roland Ward, Dick Haine and Malcolm Burgess were recovered, and the three men were later interred in Bayeux Cemetery.

The last gun battery to be targeted by RAF Bomber Command was at Ouistreham, on the mouth of the river Orne, and defending *Sword* beach. Zero hour was 0505 hours. Initial post-raid analysis generally suggested successful attacks but, as forecast by Leigh-Mallory and Tedder, the cloud cover had hampered operations. Damage to the gun emplacements fell below expectation, but as German POWs would later testify, the bombardment had a significant demoralising effect on the defenders. As the RAF Bomber Command airmen flew back to, and landed in, England, the Eighth Air Force heavies were thundering across the Channel, intent upon wreaking their havoc upon the German beach defences.

CHAPTER 11

'THIS IS IT!'

John Howland: During the evening of 5 June, at about 2000 hours, we were alerted by the 324th Squadron Commander, Lt Colonel Robert Weitzenfeld. We were informed in the classic manner, 'This is it!' We knew 'it' meant invasion, but we didn't know where 'it' was to take place.

Warren Berg: Our first inkling that D-Day might be imminent was the order from Group headquarters in early May 1944 that all personnel who had been issued sidearms were to wear them while on base so as to repel possible German parachute attacks. This order was issued on the assumption that German Intelligence groups knew enough about Allied invasion preparations to attempt suicide attacks to cripple that operation. A general order restricting all personnel to the base was issued in early June and this of course heightened our anticipation of imminent D-Day action.

Then on 5 June, at approximately 10 p.m. British double summer time with the sun still shining brightly, all combat crews were ordered to report immediately to the Group mission briefing room. There we learned that the invasion would take place early the next morning. Take-off was scheduled for 2 a.m. and thus few of us got significant sleep with all the excitement surrounding us.

On Eighth Air Force bases all over the east of England on the evening of 5 June 1944, personnel and groundcrews applied themselves to the task of readying their aircraft and aircrews. Security measures were strict, and most would not know what they were preparing for. While Warren Berg tried to get some rest, Jim Tyson was already airborne, flying the short distance to Ridgewell.

John Howland: We took off from Bassingbourn with about 17 other PFF crews flying to various bomb groups in the 1st Bombardment Division. Three of us, Clark, Tyson and one other PFF team, which served as a spare, headed for the 381st Bomb Group at Ridgewell. We didn't get any sleep, and received our final briefing at 0130 hours. Security was extremely tight. Only pilots, navigators and bombardiers were allowed in the briefing room. All persons briefed were pledged to secrecy until the planes were in the air and the mission was underway. Only then could location of the target be released to the crew.

At Mendlesham, home of the 34th Bomb Group, some crews had the privilege of finding out about their mission, prior to their Bomb Group colleagues.

George Ritchie: The evening of 5 June, I was told to turn in early for an early mission call. This was not so unusual, since in double daylight summer time, the sun was up till around midnight. Actually we turned in early every pre-mission evening, but sleeping was another matter. Before

157

the sun actually set my navigator and I were called up to report for briefing. It was only 11 p.m. We dressed and reported to lead crew briefing. We were hours early (earlier than usual). They told us that this was D-Day and the drone of airplanes already filled the sky. They were the Airborne preparing to go over for the initial paratrooper and glider attacks, programmed to land in France before daylight. We briefed before the regular crews and were ordered to say nothing until the commanding officer formally announced it at the general briefing. D-Day sent a thrill through the base. This was what we were waiting for, and now we would have our men under us needing and getting direct assistance from us. A great feeling now exuded from every airman and support personnel. Everyone was highly confident of success and watched the news very closely.

Edwin R. Ehret was a radio operator with the 91st Bomb Group and provides a good account of aircrew preparation on the day of the invasion:

On the morning of 6 June, 1944 I was aroused by the voice of Sergeant Klien, CQ, shouting, 'Breakfast At 0100; briefing at 0200' followed by 'You've 'ad it today ol' boy', meaning I could expect most anything. I quickly dressed, freshened up with a dash of cold water and thence out into the cool June air to combat mess for the usual powdered scrambled eggs. They had cheese mixed with them today, which almost camouflaged the awful distaste we had for the ETO food. The meal was topped off with wheatflakes and powered milk, very tart canned grapefruit juice and very, very strong black coffee.

Out into the extra cool June night air again for the mile trek to the briefing hut. This sudden trend of early events started to bring our reasoning powers more in focus. GI rumors as to the impending mission had been flying fast and furious in the mess hall. Fred Cascone, tail gunner on my old crew, and I talked over three possible conclusions as we walked along. Taking the time of briefing into consideration, the number of ships our squadron was flying and the bomb load for each ship (38 – 100 lb. Frag.) we boiled our flight plan down to Big 'B' (Berlin), our first shuttle raid to Russia or – *Invasion!*

We entered the briefing hut, sat down alongside other combat men on flimsy wooden benches and waited tensely for briefing officers to draw the curtains covering the huge map on the wall. The map has red yarn strung around pins to indicate the mission for the day from our base to enemy territory and return.

Something big was in the wind! The base photographer was busy with flash bulbs and camera taking shots of us waiting for briefing.

Here's the briefing officer . . . tense silence, then he speaks: *'This is it, men! This is invasion day!'*

Then he launched into the details of our flight plan. Altitude, weather, rendezvous, zero hour, friendly activity and target, photos of which were flashed on the screen, etc., etc. '11,000 Allied aircraft will be over this morning. Keep on the alert to avoid collisions.' 'There should be little if any flak or enemy fighters. The enemy's heavy 155 mm coast gun emplacements will be too busy answering the Navy's challenge to fire at you.' (We hope). '4,000 ships will be in the Channel down below you so don't test-fire your guns; you might hurt your own men or hit one of those 11,000 planes filling the sky about you. Remember your POW instructions and special invasion instructions in case you go down. Chaplain Regan is in the back if you wish to see him when you go out. Any questions?' 'Will we use chaff?' 'Only when your pilot receives orders and informs you over interphone.' 'Any more questions?' 'What's the ETR?' 'About 0900!' 'Okay, men, stations at 0250. That's all.'

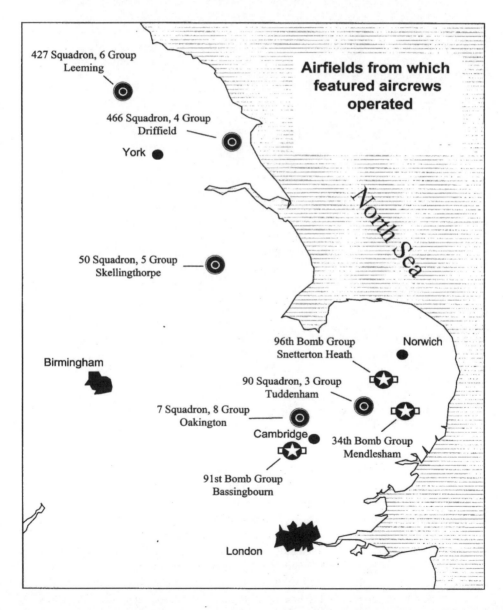

Airfields from which featured aircrews operated

427 Squadron, 6 Group
Leeming

466 Squadron, 4 Group
Driffield

York

North Sea

50 Squadron, 5 Group
Skellingthorpe

96th Bomb Group
Snetterton Heath

Norwich

90 Squadron, 3 Group
Tuddenham

Birmingham

7 Squadron, 8 Group
Oakington

Cambridge

34th Bomb Group
Mendlesham

91st Bomb Group
Bassingbourn

London

Witness to Events

On 5 June 1944, just after returning from a mission to bomb Cap Gris-Nez on the Pas de Calais coast, Stanley I. Hand, Air Executive Officer of the 96th Bomb Group, was informed that the group commander had been reassigned and he would be the acting group commander until a replacement would arrive. His diary recorded his involvement in the momentous D-Day landings.

Stanley Hand's diary: Monday, 5 June 1944. Group went out one time today. I led the 45th Combat Wing on a tactical target in France – that made good old [No.] 24 for me. We had a very interesting day in that Colonel Travis called us in to tell us D-Day is tomorrow. I ate dinner in my office and worked like hell. We sent out 36 aircraft and crews were briefed at 22.00 tonight. You can't imagine the largeness of this operation. I had tears in my eyes when I heard it and if I felt that way I wonder how the British will feel. We worked like hell from 4.30 p.m. until way past midnight getting the 36 aircraft ready to go. I'll write further tomorrow.

Tuesday 6 June 1944. D-Day landings made at 07.25 a.m. The group of 36 aircraft took off at 02.10 to bomb the coast of France between 07.15 a.m. and 07.35 a.m. At that time the invasion will be 400 yards off the coast. As soon as that formation took off we briefed 6 more crews who will take off at 06.10 for the same area. The total number of aircraft that will be over that part of France today will be between 15,000 and 16,000. The fighter support on our first raid is 1,600. I have been up 22 hours and am now off to bed for a couple of hours.

Oh thank God all aircraft returned safely on first two raids. The third group took off again at 5.10 p.m. to bomb the invasion coast. I went on that raid leading the 45th Combat Wing. I saw a wonderful sight of invasion boats landing on French soil. We bombed successfully. On way home I saw at least 100 troop carrier aircraft with a glider at the end of each one. We also saw another large convoy that was going to the Cherbourg area. I didn't get to land until 11.45 tonight in darkness and very low ceilings. You can't imagine my feelings landing 36 aircraft under these conditions. Oh God is so good to keep bringing me home safely. We're stood down for tomorrow. Some crews flew 18 hours out of 24. How I stayed awake today I'll never know. Colonel Travis is gone and I am now 96th Group CO for at least 10 days anyway. Oh golly. If God will give me strength.

During the night of 5/6 June 1944, the Eighth Air Force heavy bomber crews had learnt that this day their task was to bomb the beach defences between the Orne and the Vire, covering *Gold*, *Juno*, *Sword* and *Omaha*. *Utah* beach would be the responsibility of the US Ninth Air Force. The bombs, all of 1,000 lb or less, and most with instantaneous fuses, were planned to fall on the defenders immediately prior to the Allied assault forces landing on the beaches, sending the Germans for shelter, shattering their morale and causing chaos on the communication lines for any reserve forces. It was realised that the bombs would do little damage to the concrete emplacements on the beaches, but that was not the intention. The Allies wanted the Germans to be under cover whilst the landings began. The aircrews were also told unless they could be certain that they were going to hit their target, they were not to bomb. Friendly bombing could lead to catastrophe.

In the early hours of 6 June thousands of American airmen made their way to their fuelled and bombed-up four-engined aircraft. It had been a busy night for the base personnel and groundcrews. Following the specific radio operators' briefing, Edwin Ehret of the 91st Bomb Group picked up his flying kit, and went to his aircraft to prepare for take-off. Just after 4 a.m. he heard aircraft overhead.

> *Edwin Ehret:* RAF planes are just coming back from their nightflight. Their green and red wing lights dot the black sky over our field. I wonder how they made out? All night they have been thundering across the Channel, being the first to start the gigantic invasion machinery to roll like the headwaters of a devastating flood. Now and then the soft full moon filters through thinning clouds; tiny stars blink down – the weather looks promising.
>
> Our engines are being revved up now with a deafening roar. How's the oil pressure? RPM? How many pounds mercury indicated on the panel gauge? 'Co-pilot to Waist Gunner! Check flaps!' 'Flaps down okay.' 'Flaps up okay!' The ship ahead of us guns forward and disappears from view. Others just ahead of it are already circling the field and starting to climb to altitude. 0450 o'clock, a surge of speed and power as four mighty Wright Cyclones lift 63,000 lb. Plus 3,800 lb of bombs toward the heavens. We're airborne! A silent prayer to the Powers Above to give us all courage and guide our ship safely.

In the event the Eighth Air Force put all its bomb groups into the air on the morning of 6 June. Marshalling such a vast force and ensuring the Eighth's armada hit the beaches at the right time was a fairly complex procedure. The 2nd Bomb Division heavies began their flight heading north-west to assemble over the north of England; they then turned south and, taking the right flank of the bomber fleet, crossed the English coast between Selsey Bill and Littlehampton, to head for *Omaha* beach. The 1st Bomb Division's bomb groups after assembling near their bases, headed south as the centre of the bomber force, crossing the English coast between Worthing and Brighton, flying on towards the beaches at *Gold* and the right side of *Juno*. The 3rd Bomb Division's heavies, after assembly near their bases, took the left flank of the bomber force, crossing the English coast between Newhaven and Beachy Head, heading towards *Sword* beach and the left side of *Juno*.

Private Thoughts

Sam Stone was a member of the crew 'Sweet 17 Gee', a bomber crew in the 337th Bomb Squadron, 96th Bomb Group.

> D-Day started, for me, at about 2:00 a.m. We were awakened to prepare for a bombing mission.
> Since we were never told the target until briefing, it seemed like any

other morning before a mission. After breakfast we headed for the briefing room. Upon arrival we found a major at the door holding a clipboard and checking off the names of all who entered the briefing room. This had never occurred before so we knew something unusual was up. After we were all seated, an officer strode up to the platform behind which was a covered map of the target area. This was the mission map showing the target, the route taken to and from the target as well as the location of flak concentrations and checkpoints where we could expect to rendezvous with our fighter cover. That was standard procedure. However, on this day, when the cover was removed from the map we saw a red ribbon going into the Normandy area and another coming out on a different heading. Another officer climbed onto the platform in front of the map. His first words were, 'Anyone who divulges any of the information given at this briefing will be shot.' We were then given the details, as they pertained to us, of the D-Day mission. All fighters, fighter-bombers and medium bombers would have white stripes painted around the wings and fuselage. All aircraft must fly the designated routes in and out of the target area. Those that did not would be shot down.

As the radio-operator for our crew, it was my assignment to pick up the radio codes we were to use that day. Our next stop was the equipment room where we kept our parachute harnesses and parachutes. From there to the armament shack for our .50 caliber machine guns. This was all loaded on a truck, which took us to the aircraft.

On arrival at the aircraft we stowed our gear. I installed my machine gun in the top position of the radio compartment and then tuned my radios to the frequencies being used that day. After finishing these tasks I decided to get out of the plane and have a smoke. I walked a short distance away from the plane, sat down and lit up. I noticed the airplane guard walking back and forth so I offered him a cigarette. He declined the offer. At that time each airplane was guarded by a soldier patrolling back and forth. There was fear of sabotage or German paratroopers dropping on our airfields to destroy the bombers.

The guard and I began to talk. He said how weary he was of his job and that it seemed he would be doing this forever. There seemed to be no end in sight. He felt that if the invasion would occur soon he would feel his efforts were not in vain. I felt this explosive urge to tell him that today was D-Day but, remembering the officer's words, managed to control this impulse. I decided I better leave before I 'spilled the beans.' I climbed back into the aircraft, went to the radio room and sat down. A few minutes later I thought I heard someone crying softly behind me in the waist. I got up and went back to see what was happening. In the waist I found our engineer and top turret gunner sitting on the floor quietly sobbing. This was totally out of character for the short, hard-drinking, self-centered individual I had come to know. I thought he was crying because he felt we might not make it back so I said, 'It's OK, Jimmy, we will be fine. You know we always make it back.' His reply stunned me. 'I'm not crying for us. I'm crying for all the poor bastards that are going to die today.' I was so overwhelmed by this unexpected response I turned and walked back to the radio room overcome by my own emotions.

As the might of the Eighth Air Force thundered across the English Channel, the aircrews looked out expectantly at the weather conditions. Could the bombing be done visually or would they have to bomb blind using the H2X? Could they be certain they could achieve the desired accuracy?

Taking their place in the central 1st Bomb Division was Jim Tyson's and John Howland's crew leading a formation of the 381st Bomb Group. The Group contributed two formations of 18 aircraft each, and Jim Tyson led the first. Their task was to bomb enemy positions on *Gold* beach. In addition to attacks on beach defences the Eighth Air Force would also send heavy bomber formations to inland targets that morning, and the second 381st Bomb Group formation would make its contribution by attacking an airfield near St Lô.

John Howland: The bomb load for our group on June 6th was twenty 100 lb HE demolition bombs in all eighteen planes. The load seemed almost puny by comparison with the 2,000 lb, 1,000 lb and 500 lb bombs we had dropped on Pas de Calais on 2, 3 and 4 June and Normandy gun emplacements on 5 June. Our principal target on 6 June, D-Day, was a gun battery on the beach north of Bayeux. However, our formation consisted of a shallow Vee of Vees with six planes in each Vee. Pilots normally allowed about fifty feet between wing tips. The distance from outside wing tip to outside wing tip of the 18-ship group formation was over 1,300 ft. There was little likelihood that our total of 360 diminutive 100 lb bombs scattered along a one-quarter mile stretch of beach would wipe out a gun battery. However, we were told the 100 lb bombs were supposed to make foxholes for the troops.

The weather looked bad, and we were given strict orders to make certain our bombs didn't fall short. Our assigned target area was the *Gold* beach and we were flying in support of British and Canadian troops.

The assembly went off smoothly. Our three months of practice and training in formation assembly paid off. We left Beachy Head on time, and headed south and west across the English Channel to pick up a Gee line that would guide us in to the target. Mickey operator John Spierling said his radarscope was full of reflections from hundreds of boats in the Channel. Until he said that, I didn't believe it was the real thing. I thought it was just a big practice mission.

Edwin Ehret recalled his experience of being part of the 1st Bomb Division's attack on the beaches.

Edwin Ehret: Fortresses fill the sky ahead. . behind . . below . . to the sides . . they're everywhere. Underneath the clouds one will probably find hundreds of fighters and medium bombers shuttling across, having the same destination as ours. Too bad the heavy cloud coverage below will be hiding the greatest of spectacles the Allies have intensely waited for these many months.

We are well out in the Channel now. Ten more minutes to the IP. The groups ahead have already dropped smoke flares. Now we can see them clearly – dripping from the sky for miles along the invasion coast of

France. An odd sight these target smoke signals, hanging in the blue in lazy grotesque forms. Like twisting serpents crawling through the heavy cloud lying below us.

Bombardier over interphone: 'Bomb-bay doors opening.' Radio operator to bombardier: 'Roger! Bomb-bay doors are open.' We're not far from landfall now. A thin cloud-break below reveals hundreds of Navy boats and landing craft streaming in the direction of the continent.

As Jim Tyson's aircraft neared the beaches, John Howland kept his:

. . . eyes glued to the blips of the Gee Box keeping us on course. John Spierling gave range and ground speed data to the bombardier who cranked the information into his Norden bombsight. Charlie Eager, our bombardier from the 381st BG, looked for a break in the clouds so he could take over visually. But it never came. Nevertheless, our training paid off. We had confidence the Gee Box course line was reasonably accurate, and our practice bombing sessions had proved the Mickey operator and bombardier could hit the beachline with good accuracy. We did what we were trained to do, and did it to the best of our ability with full confidence in our equipment and procedures.

Bombs were dropped at 0704. Zero hour for landings on the British-Canadian sector Gold Beach below us was 0725 hours. At 'Bombs Away' I left the scope of my Gee Box and came up for air and to look out my window. But all I could see was a solid undercast, and one solitary puff of black smoke in the sky. The collision and accidental explosion of two 100 lb bombs evidently made this mark as they tumbled earthward and collided in mid air. There was no enemy flak over the beaches or after bombs away. Evidently the Germans were saving or using their ammunition on other targets.

Edwin Ehret: The lead ship in our squadron has released a target smoke signal. Bombs away! Impressive isn't the word for it as hundreds of Forts go over their respective targets each dropping its load of destruction from its yawning bomb bay. Down the bombs tumble through the soft clouds, like ears of corn falling out of a bushel basket. Thousands and thousands of them speeding on their downward journey to hit the target and *Destroy!* And here we ride, like kings reigning above all, helping to set the stage for the greatest and most horrible show the world has ever witnessed. Right here we have a million-dollar seat high in the blue above the screaming and pounding of our bombs.

I wonder if any of the 'big-wigs' back home would like a seat to this great show going on in the air, in the water and on the land thousands of feet below us. There's only one price and it might come high. It could be your own skin.

Another silent prayer for the boys down there. They'll be pushing open the very jaws of hell. We're upstairs – no noise – no muss – just click as the bomb-bay racks release their hold on their missiles then a lurch or lift of the ship as almost two tons of bombs drop away.

Upon leaving the target Jim Tyson took his formation across the Cherbourg peninsula, over the Channel Islands and back to base.

John Howland: It was a very easy raid. There was no need for the extra boxes of ammunition we had stashed throughout the plane. We didn't see a single enemy fighter. There was no flak over the target or along the route. Breaking with PFF standard operating procedures, we didn't return to Bassingbourn, but landed at Ridgewell about 1030 hours and were debriefed. The aircraft were again loaded with bombs and serviced to fly another mission. The lead crews of Jim Tyson and Carl Clark were confined to the operations building. Rumors were rampant including one that, 'in the event the invasion went badly, B-17s would be used at low altitudes to drop fragmentation bombs and strafe.' The rumors really didn't bother us. However, the lack of sleep for more than thirty hours was wearing us down. We made pallets of flak vests and sheepskin-lined flight suits. Using partially inflated Mae West lifevests for pillows, we went to sleep on the floor of the equipment room. Lt Colonel George Shackley awakened us at 1600 hours. The afternoon mission had been scrubbed and we were instructed to return to Bassingbourn.

On his return John Howland heard from his colleague Clem Obler about the 381st's attack on the airfield near St Lô. Clem and his pilot Carl Clark had led the group.

A German truck or weapons carrier came roaring across the tarmac at high speed. I could see the faces of two men clearly as they looked up at us. They came to a screeching halt at the hangar and one man jumped out to open a door. He jumped back into the truck and they drove inside. Just then, our bombs struck the hangar and blew it to pieces. The air war becomes quite personal at lower altitudes.

The 3rd Bomb Division's 96th Bomb Group's initial contribution to the invasion was to attack the beach defences near St Aubin-sur-Mer on *Juno* beach to the north of Caen, opposing the British and Canadian landings.

Warren Berg: Our briefing on 5 June 1944 was explicitly referenced to the need for accurate bombing on 6 June. With many thousands of Allied troops approaching the coast in landing craft it was imperative that we not drop short and hit them and we must not drop late and destroy the Allied paratroopers who had dropped behind the German defences during the night. Fortunately, the coastline gave us a very good radar image and we were able to place our bombs on target at the appointed time.

Similarly the 34th Bomb Group was detailed to bomb coastal defences opposing the British and Canadian forces. But the 34th's airmen, including George Ritchie's crew, were frustrated over the target by complete cloud cover and unsure of hitting their target they followed orders and no bombs were released. And here circumstances compounded to cause tragedy. Unable to jettison bomb loads over the sea, because of the traffic in the Channel, the 34th's aircrews sought to return with their bomb loads. Fuel began to run short. On board one aircraft, 'Misery Agent', the situation became desperate and the pilot, Herman Doell, decided to attempt a ditch in Poole Harbour on the south coast. But time ran out and the bomber plunged into a copse, the bombs exploded and there was a total loss of life.

Bob Gross was the navigator with the crew, but had not taken part in the mission owing to an order that navigators were surplus to requirements, and Bob 'was a little disgusted that the crew were going to be one mission ahead of me'. Late on the morning of 6 June, Bob along with other personnel at Mendlesham, awaited the return of the 34th's bombers. When Bob's crew failed to return, he thought it possible that they might have landed at another airfield, but news eventually came through of the tragedy. A few days later he was driven to Brookwood Military Cemetery to attend the funeral, but on arrival Bob saw 'the ditches being dug by bulldozers and the hundreds of body bags lying on the ground'. Bob looked at his driver and said, 'Let's go.'

Although many of the Eighth Air Force's bombers had to bring their bombs back (the highest percentage was from the 3rd Bomb Division), 3,205 tons of explosive were dropped on enemy positions in Normandy that morning. But, as the air commanders had feared, results of the bombing varied considerably owing to the weather conditions. As the Eighth's bombers returned to their bases in England the Navy continued with the bombardment of beach positions. But the day was far from over for the American heavy bomber airmen. Many would be returning to Normandy, detailed to attack enemy communications around the beachhead: 782 aircraft were eventually despatched, and 508 effective.

Groundcrews worked feverishly at Mendlesham on 6 June. The 34th Bomb Group's bombers would eventually carry out 119 sorties on three missions that day. However the second mission of the day, as had the first, proved fruitless, as complete cloud cover prevented an attack on enemy communications at Lisieux. On the third mission, again to Lisieux, the 34th bombed. John Terry and George Ritchie flew their B-24 as part of the 7th Bomb Squadron's contribution.

Unscheduled Flight

On D-Day Major James H. McPartlin, with the 91st Bomb Group, took part in a most unusual mission. He wasn't expecting to fly that day. As a squadron commander he only flew when his squadron led. On 6 June 1944 this was not the case:

> After the briefing, I went to my operations office to help with the details of seeing that the squadron crews were taken care of. I personally was feeling a bit sad that I would not be going on the mission.
>
> I was one of the original 91st Bomb Group pilots and had waited a long time for this moment. The entire 91st Bomb Group got airborne on time without incident. I settled down with a cup of coffee and was shooting the breeze with a Sergeant Birdie, our operations NCO. Within 30 minutes the phone rang. Sergeant Birdie answered and said, 'Major, General Gross wants to talk to you.' B/Gen. William Gross

was commander of the First Combat Wing. I was not accustomed to talking with the General but got on the line immediately. He said, 'Mac, do you have a bird flyable that is not on the mission today?' I said, 'Yes sir, we have an old G model ('Old Faithful') that we use for transition and practice missions. It has no bombs or guns or ammunition.' The General replied, 'That's OK. Can you get a skeleton crew together? I want to catch up with our combat wing formation and observe the bombing and the landings.' 'Yes, sir,' I said. 'I'll check on a crew and call you back ASAP.' Frantic phone calls recruited a skeleton crew.

James McPartlin met the General at their aircraft. They took off and, as they crossed the English Channel, caught up with their combat wing.

We flew alongside the formation until we saw the bomb-bay doors open and soon it was bombs away. There was a fair amount of flak but not a sign of an enemy fighter, nor did we see any of our aircraft go down. A milk run compared to missions flown over Germany prior to D-Day. At this point I expected we would do a 180 turn and return to our base in Bassingbourn, England. *Not so!* General Gross said, 'Let's go down and observe the landings.' I asked the navigator to give me a heading to the landing area on Normandy and he said, *'What?'* No way was he prepared for this request but said, 'OK, give me a minute or two.' I pulled off the power and started a descent. Soon I had a new heading, with periodic corrections. Down we went through solid overcast in an area that we were forbidden to be in! This was a perfect scenario for a mid-air collision.

We finally broke out of the overcast at about 700-800 feet above the water in light rain and low clouds but visibility was surprisingly good. What a sight to behold! Ships everywhere. I asked the General, 'What now?' He said, 'Make a right turn.' This would give him a full view of the beach area. During the course of the turn, I began to see black puffs of flak and hear the familiar sounds like rain on a tin roof. The battleship guns on my left were flashing and it was my guess that our Navy was shooting at us! I said to General Gross, 'We don't belong here' and immediately without waiting for his reply rammed the throttles and RPM full forward and began a climb back into the overcast while asking the navigator for a heading back to England. We broke out of the overcast at about 18,000 feet and continued directly to Bassingbourn without further incident.

On landing, we discovered minor flak damage. I felt we were very lucky to escape with only minor damage and no injuries. General Gross thanked the crew and was gone. I heard later via the grapevine that Major General Williams, our division CO, gave General Gross a verbal reprimand for ordering us to go on an unauthorized mission *with no bombs, no guns, no ammunition and no credit for a mission.*

It had been a long day for the men of the Eighth Air Force, who had done everything in their power to assist the beach assault. For some fatigue got the better of them. John Kearney was a pilot with 390th Bomb Group:

It just so happens that my first mission for the 390th was on D-Day. After four weeks of practice missions I was posted to fly on the third 390th mission of D-Day. To gain experience, I was to fly as co-pilot for a veteran pilot who had already flown a mission on that day. I was quite excited to think of entering combat and wondering what it was like. After take-off in late afternoon, we began to see the huge numbers of ships and boats – unbelievable! No enemy opposition, either by fighters or flak. After dropping our bombs we began our return to England in the gathering darkness. The pilot, stating he was tired, again gave me the controls and in a few minutes he was asleep! As we approached our base, it was now fully dark and I had not had the opportunity to land in England in the dark with the British landing procedure and different lighting. It was an interesting event, with the pilot still asleep.

The Eighth's heavy bomber crew had met little if any opposition from the German air force, the Luftwaffe managing no more than 100 sorties during the day of the invasion. In addition to the 34th BG loss mentioned above, the Eighth Air Force only lost another four heavy bombers. Over the Channel Islands the right wing of a B-24 of the 493rd BG, struck the tail of another bomber from the same group. Aircrews in other bombers in the formation watched as both aircraft fell through the undercast, and a few parachutes were seen.[71] Another bomber of the 490th BG crashed on the English coast at Chesil beach, Dorset, with seven airmen rescued. The only loss to enemy action was a 487th BG B-24. On return to base other aircrews were able to report seeing this bomber with four dead engines. The bomber fell into the sea, and the entire crew were missing. The cause of the loss was put down to a probable gas leak.[72] Despite these losses the Eighth was reaping the reward of *Pointblank* and the attrition battles over Germany in the run-up to *Overlord*. The Allies held air superiority.

CHAPTER 12

INTRUDER

At 11 a.m. on the morning of 6 June, there was general optimism at the sixth AAC conference. Naval operations were reported as going to plan, with opposition from the coastal batteries reported as slight 'though Pointe du Hoc, Gatteville and Ouistreham were still firing'. The airborne operations were deemed an unexpected success, and the seaborne troops were on the beaches although no contact had yet been made between the British and American forces. It was also noted that there appeared to be significant enemy troop movements inland in the Châteaudun and Évreux areas. There was a general air of satisfaction about the bombing operations. Tactical surprise for the landing was claimed owing to the pre-invasion bombing of radar installations, with enemy radar activity at 5% of its normal level. Leigh-Mallory also paid tribute to the groundcrews, noting the high percentage of Allied aircraft serviceability.

Now that the battle was well and truly into the tactical phase, it was necessary for a quick response to any call to action. Commanders, aircrew, groundcrew, equipment officers, cooks, every person involved in the complex working of RAF Bomber Command and the Eighth Air Force, feverishly worked to turn their aircrews and aircraft around as quickly as possible.

RAF Bomber Command sent 1,065 aircraft, on the afternoon and evening of 6 June, to bomb various rail and road centres inland of the beaches. Three of our RAF crews, on landing from the previous night's bombing of the coastal batteries, found themselves detailed to make their contribution. On the return from their first D-Day raid Bill Brown and his crew were immediately briefed for Condé-sur-Noireau. Navigator Graham 'Cliff' Cameron recalls returning from the attacks on the coastal gun:

> *Graham Cameron:* On this second flight to Normandy the most vivid and longest lasting memory comes to mind. As navigator my station in the aircraft was curtained off, giving me no opportunity to observe what was taking place around us. On this occasion, Bill excitedly called me to 'come and take a look at this'. We had a panoramic view of history in the making. The thought crossed my mind, 'I'm glad I am not down there'. Months later, after the war, I had occasion to make a friend of a Canadian soldier who 'was down there'. He tells me that they looked up at us and thought, 'I'm glad I am not up there.'

Later in the day Jack Scott's crew had to penetrate further inland to Châteaudun. Over the moonlit target the weather cleared but with no TI down Jack flew his Halifax beyond the target. Then the TI came down. Jack took the perilous decision to stay in the target area, orbit and bomb going against the rest of the bomber stream. Fortunately there was no collision, the bombs fell and on the way home the crew was able to watch the pyrotechnic display as the battle on the ground raged. Dennis Field would also be airborne that night, his thirtieth operation, successfully carrying out a supply drop in Normandy.

After 24 hours of battle, early indications of progress on the Allied beaches were promising. Beachheads at *Utah*, *Gold*, *Juno* and *Sword* had been fought for and won and troops were pushing inland. At *Omaha* beach the Americans faced the stiffest opposition but had nevertheless established a foothold. The heavy bomber forces had made their contribution, although not with the success hoped for. The weather, the cloud cover, had caused problems. Many of the gun emplacements targeted by RAF Bomber Command were damaged but few were taken out. Indeed at a few the Germans had removed the main guns further inland, in anticipation of a bombardment. The bombing of the beach defences by the Eighth Air Force had not been as accurate as hoped for, particularly at *Omaha*, but in the prevailing weather conditions little more could be expected. There was less damage to beach defences than planned, but as interrogation of enemy POWs would later show, the bombardments had a significant demoralising effect on the troops manning the defences. One war correspondent recorded from one of the offshore ships that:

> . . . the air power that we have seen most forcibly was the final attack by the American 8th Air Force. Immediately before H-hour they dropped a vast weight of bombs on the beaches. The beaches shook and seemed to rise into the air, and ships well out at sea quivered and shook.[73]

The thoughts of the Allied commanders now turned away from the coast: how would their German counterparts respond? What would they do with their reserves? In particular how would the enemy panzer divisions be deployed? What would the Luftwaffe do? Their involvement on the first day had been minimal. Surely the Allies' freedom of the skies over the battle would be resisted. Allied reconnaissance aircraft watched closely for any enemy movements, reports from agents in France were processed quickly and Allied Intelligence carefully monitored German signals traffic.

The summary of the military situation at the seventh AAC conference at 11 a.m. on 7 June noted heavy loading of enemy troops in the Rouen area, 'probably for a movement of 1st SS Panzer Corps and 179 Panzer Training Division'. Owing mainly to the bombing of the Seine bridges these enemy reinforcements would have to go via Paris before joining the battle. It was also noted that the Luftwaffe had begun to move aircraft from Germany to airfields from which they too could join the battle. An intelligence briefing at the meeting stated that ten Ju88s had been moved from Bordeaux to Kerlin-Bastard in Brittany, and German long-range bombers were also being deployed within range of the battle zone. The heavy bomber forces received the call to block the enemy deployments: the Eighth Air Force was to attack airfields at Tours, Angers, Nantes and Kerlin-Bastard and RAF Bomber Command to bomb rail target at Versailles, Massy/Palaiseau, Juvisy, Achères, and also Étampes and Orléans to block an apparent gap between the Seine and the Loire.

The Mighty Eighth sent its aircraft and airmen on two missions on 7 June. In the morning 473 aircraft were despatched to attack communication targets behind the enemy front lines. In the afternoon, in response to the priorities identified at that morning's AAC meeting, 575 aircraft were sent to blast the four airfields identified as destinations for Luftwaffe reinforcements.

Late that afternoon Jim Tyson flew his B-17 to Ridgewell, where the 381st Bomb Group's aircraft were lined up waiting. Preparations for the mission had been rushed and Jim's crew had had little time to prepare. John Howland, realising they actually had no flight plan, made his predicament known to a colonel who had joined the crew as acting wing commander (AWC). Details were soon supplied and Jim led the 381st off on its mission to the Kerlin-Bastard airfield, near Lorient. On approaching the Brest peninsula, John informed his captain of the presence of a flak battery, and suggested a course change. The AWC responded that there was no need to worry, since all the flak batteries had been overrun by American ground troops. John's faith in the AWC diminished somewhat as he informed him that they were over the Brest peninsula and not the Cherbourg peninsula. The course change was made.

On the first run over Kerlin-Bastard, clouds obscured the target and no bombs were released (the use of H2X was not allowed on the mission). Jim led the group out over the Bay of Biscay and John requested that the turn, back to the target, be delayed, fearful of coming within range of a 4-gun flak battery. The AWC overruled the request and ordered the course change immediately.

John Howland: We made the 180-deg turn right into the 4-gun flak battery that was spotted on my flak chart. They pounded away at us during the entire four minutes of the 180-deg turn. They finally hit one ship, and knocked it out of formation. I was furious . . . for the needless loss of one B-17 and ten men. It was the first and only plane out of a formation led by me lost to flak outside of the target area.

The clouds cleared for the second run on the target, bombs fell and a successful concentration of hits was reported. As the formation headed home, the low group became separated and John Howland's frustration with the AWC grew as, on his orders, a number of 360-degree turns were executed.

John Howland: He was 'playing' Air-Sea Rescue giving the location of the B-17 that was ditching. It wasted time. The low Group never showed up. They were long gone for home, and we couldn't do a damned thing for that B-17 that was ditching below us. I had to add 8 minutes to my Ridgewell ETA every time we made a 360-deg turn, and was deeply concerned about our Air-Sea Rescue with a formation of combat bombers, needlessly risking the lives of combat men and equipment. Further, our arrival back at base after dark placed us in serious danger of being hit by German intruders. The Germans often used the Ju88 fighter-bomber to knock down vulnerable bombers as they circled in their traffic pattern after dark.

Ditching

The B-17 John Howland saw falling on the 8 June 1944 mission to Lorient, was captained by 2nd Lt John A. Martyniak. Fragments from the flak burst tore into and damaged his bomber's engines, and Martyniak had to try full boost to keep in formation, to no avail as the Fortress lost speed and began to fall behind. When two engines lost all power and another began to falter, Martyniak, realising his aircraft was mortally wounded, radioed for fighter support. Falling at 500 feet a minute the crew were ordered to jettison all equipment, except the ball turret, in a hope that Martyniak could pilot his stricken bomber to the English coast. Soon it became apparent that reaching England was not possible and a watery end loomed. Contact was made with Air-Sea Rescue, and Martyniak reported the steady loss in height while his crew huddled into the radio room, bracing themselves for the ditching. The tail of the B-17 hit the sea first, its belly then sliding along the surface. Fortunately only a few of the crew received slight injury. Water began to fill the radio room and the men exited rapidly through the hatch above them.

Within two minutes the Fortress sank, enough time for the crew to release and inflate their dinghies. A few minutes later two Spitfires appeared, no doubt relaxing tension amongst the downed airmen, to be joined 10 minutes later by several more, which maintained contact defending the Americans from any possible enemy attack. Within an hour an RAF Wellington arrived, circled and from 300 feet released a motor launch. John Martyniak recalled:

> The launch floated down supported by the parachute. When it hit the water there were sharp explosions and the chutes were blown clear of the boat. It was beautifully carried out.

The Americans boarded the launch and secured their dinghies, just in case, but then when starting the motor the propeller caught in the dinghy lines and the motor cut out. Fortunately there was a second motor. After travelling a mile, they met a rescue ship and climbed aboard, and the motor launch was secured to the ship's stern. Then the ship's propeller caught in a line and the motor cut out, but again, fortunately, there was more than one. Arriving at the Air-Sea Rescue station on the southern coast the American aircrew were given dry clothing, hot food and their injuries received attention. The following day they flew back to base, arriving in their borrowed RAF clothing and, as the 381st BG diary recorded, 'grinning and unharmed except for minor cuts and bruises', telling a story 'giving high praise to the efficiency and skill of the Air-Sea Rescue Service'.

The rest of the flight back to England was uneventful, although by the time the formation approached Ridgewell it was getting dark. Jim led his formation in a standard traffic pattern, peeling off from the 381st's aircraft on approach to land. As far as Jim's crew were concerned everything went as it was supposed to, but the AWC didn't agree and called it the 'sorriest piece of navigation' he had ever seen. John tried to enlighten his senior to the fact that everything had gone as planned, to no avail. Jim flew his crew back to Bassingbourn, where the weather had closed in.

John Howland: We landed in some real soup. We were lucky to get the formation back to Ridgewell before it socked in. I was still furious over the needless loss of a B-17. At interrogation I had two stiff belts of bourbon to calm me down.

John's fear of landing during twilight hours when enemy intruders might be present, was well founded. Indeed there was a German Intruder over England that night seeking out returning bombers whose aircrew had dropped their guard. The 34th Bomb Group had made its contribution to the priorities outlined that morning at the Allied air commanders' meeting, by sending 26 B-24s to the airfield at Tours. The 34th's airmen had difficulties meeting the mission's objective, with only 13 aircraft bombing a secondary target. As the returning pilots assembled their bombers in the traffic pattern near Mendlesham, a German Intruder pounced. George Ritchie witnessed the aerial melee that followed and recorded his experience in his diary the next day:

Things are really happening now. It is 'whole hog' for Jerry now, or none. He played one of his 'trump cards' on our ace last might. What a mess!! The boys were returning from a mission and were circling the field when Jerry struck. It was just after dark and the alarm was given, 'All personnel take cover!' I was in the sack asleep, and before I completely awoke, I was outside, fully dressed watching Jerry shoot down one of our returning boys. He had followed them home and opened up right in the traffic pattern. It was an awful sight; the boys in perfect formation with their running lights on, being shot down over their home base. Eastman got it first. He didn't have a chance . . . headed straight for the ground, burning. He crashed on the field and exploded. Flames and smoke poured forth and lit up the whole area.

Jerry came back and strafed the barracks area of the 391st Squadron. We stood in the open field like fools and watched. The fires on the field grew – a call came in for all hands to report to the line to save equipment. I piled on a jeep with about 20 other men. We arrived to see the personal equipment building going up in flames. What a fire! We had the task of unloading equipment from non-burning parts of the building. Smoke and flames were everywhere. The fire department had their hands full. We attempted to get most of the non-burnt equipment out. On the other side of the building, there was a burning B-24. Across the field another ship was burning. Only one got out. Lt Mead, a boy I went to school with, lay dead, guess the others burnt with the ship.

As we worked, Jerry came back again. This time he was after another plane with the bombardier named Humphreys. At 1,400 feet he started burning – 20 mm shells cut them from tail to bomb bay. Two gunners, ball and tail, were killed on the first pass. After the second pass fires started in the hydraulic system and the electrical system went out. They had to leave her. Humphreys, the bombardier, bailed out along with the co-pilot. No word as yet on the navigator, pilot or rest of the crew. We watched the ship head down and it came at us. We scattered. It hit short in a farmer's field just off the runway. What an explosion! It lit the sky for minutes.

We went back to our work. There were chutes to be recovered and the boys broke out the windows and passed them outside. The Chief (Lt G. Holmes) was inside doing a good job of directing the recovery. The burning B-24 on the other side of the building was still burning, cooking the ammo, but smoke and water were the main hardships we encountered. Afterward, stories were all over. Jerry paratroopers were reported and everyone was on edge. However, we went to bed hoping we would be called to fly. We wanted to give them a return call and pay a debt.

From the four B-24s that fell victim to the Intruder attack 12 men lost their lives, 8 others received wounds and one man was listed as MIA (Missing in Action).

While the 34th Bomb Group personnel attempted to restore some kind of order at Mendlesham, RAF Bomber Command station personnel prepared their crews and airmen for their contribution to the priorities allocated that morning. The rail centres at Achères, Juvisy, Massy-Palaiseau and Versailles would receive the attention of 337 RAF heavies. At 10.30 p.m. Jack Scott's crew embarked upon the attack on Juvisy, planning to contribute to the devastation of the railyards with their 9,000 lb bomb load. As the crew neared the target Jack brought the Halifax beneath the cloud, at 6,000 feet, and Ron Tickell began scanning ahead for any sign of the target markers. On the run-up, the master bomber signalled to all crews to 'cease bombing' but shortly after directed the bombers on to specific markers. Ron obliged.

As Jack turned out of the target area he was warned of the presence of an enemy fighter, and before it could close on the Halifax, he quickly threw the aircraft into a dive and found the relative safety of cloud. He kept his Halifax in the cloud cover all the way to the French coast, where the cloud cleared. A flak ship then made its presence known to the crew and, as Ken Handley recalled, 'sent up a stream of lovely coloured tracer just off our port beam.' Four hours thirty minutes after taking off, Jack Scott safely landed his Halifax back at base. His crew had experienced some opposition on the raid, but their luck had held out.

For 28 other bomber crews that night, their luck ran out, as all four bomber forces met considerable opposition. The raids required deeper penetrations over France than had been the case in recent attacks and the German nightfighters seized their opportunity. One crew failed to return from 466 Squadron (Jack Scott's squadron), all losing their lives on what was their first operational flight.

The attacks on the railyards were not the only contribution RAF Bomber Command made in support of the land battle that night. There was another more direct attack detailed for the RAF's aircrews, made at the request of the US First Army.[74] At 7 Squadron, Alan Grant and crew were detailed to be part of the attack on a road junction at Forêt de Cerisy, a few miles behind the German front-line, between St Lô and Bayeux. It was believed enemy fuel dumps were located there and German armoured units were forming up for a counter-attack, which would threaten the expansion and linking of the *Omaha* and *Gold* beachheads. Our crew's contribution to the raid didn't start too well when Steve Masters found he had mislaid his parachute. As a result the crew was 15 minutes late on take-off and on approaching the target area, Alan Grant with Steve's assistance, aware that they were still lagging behind the main force, cut a corner from the planned route. As they neared the target Alan asked his navigator where the target was supposed to be.

> *Steve Masters:* 'Surely you can see it? I told him.
> 'No I can't,' he replied.
> 'No flares at all?' I insisted.
> 'Yes certainly there are flares, but they are in two groups about five miles apart.'
> I thought about this for a minute then suggested that we continue until the estimated time for the target had elapsed and in this way we could identify it.
> 'That's no good,' came the reply. 'We will be between the two of them at that time.'
> I was of little help as I could not see the targets from my position, and my timing had been so imprecise I could easily have a five-mile error, just about the distance between the two sets of target markers.

By then the Master Bomber could be heard, 'Don't bomb the green flares they are a dummy target, bomb the reds.' It appeared a number of other crews were also confused. Alan decided they would release their bomb load on the first set of markers, and on return to base suggested that they had in fact bombed the wrong target.

> *Steve Masters:* Back at base at last, I thankfully climbed into the truck, which was to take me back to the crewroom. There was to be no comfort in the truck for me. 'What a fiasco,' stated one pilot as he climbed into the truck, 'Somebody was bombing the wrong target.' I tried to hide in the shadows but it was no good as the same pilot turned to me and asked: 'Which target did you bomb, Steve, the greens or the reds?' I admitted that we had bombed the reds, which met with a shout of derision from all on board. The comments were little consolation to me, as I was assured I would be court martialled, grounded, disgraced and many other dreadful things. As each crew boarded the truck they were all informed that Steve had bombed the wrong target. This of course inspired fresh comments, which I had to endure. It was a very long trip back to the crewroom.

The next day Steve was again regularly reminded of his error. Later in the day all navigators and bomb aimers were ordered to report to the briefing room to be addressed by a squadron leader navigator from 8 Group HQ.

> *Steve Masters:* I knew what it was all about, even if the others were mystified. I was going to be publicly roasted.

Once all were settled the squadron leader gave those present a severe lecture, focusing on sloppy timing.

> *Steve Masters:* The more he spoke, the more discomfited I felt, especially as the other navigators now realised that he was talking about my effort of the night before, even if it was indirectly. The real purpose of the lecture was to explain why there had been such confusion over the bombing of

the ammunition dump: poor timing on the part of some navigators. I knew what was coming and dreaded it. Addressing me directly, he asked me to stand.

'Will you all please turn and look at him,' he said.

There had been no need for that statement, they were waiting for it and all eyes stared at me. No sympathy there, the axe was about to fall.

'Last night,' said the squadron leader, 'one hundred and fifty aircraft attacked the ammunition dump and only three of them bombed the correct target. This man was the only one from this unit who was right.' There was a stunned silence.

I realised there was more to come and wished that I could hide.

'Tell them,' said the squadron leader, satisfied at the impact he had made, 'tell them the accuracy of your time on target.' The attention was once again on me; they knew as well as I did what the error had been, so waited to hear what excuse I might come up with.

'I was two and a half minutes late, sir,' I told him.

He was shocked speechless, the point of his lecture ruined. Not so my colleagues, they enjoyed it to the full and fell about laughing all over the place. If a bolt of lightning had descended and struck either the squadron leader or myself I would have been grateful. My prayers unanswered I just stood there and suffered.

I believe that in that instant I had made an enemy of one of my own countrymen.

Incident

Attacks on relatively small targets, compared to those against German cities, by hundreds of heavy bombers concentrating in the air space over the target, resulted in aircrews enduring more than just the perils associated with enemy nightfighters and flak. Bombers funnelling into a target ran risks not of the enemy's making. Tom Fox was a flight engineer with 77 Squadron and took part in RAF Bomber Command's attack on Alençon on 8/9 June 1944:

We were heading for the target on our bombing run when an aircraft just a few yards above us opened his bomb doors; he was also on his bombing run. Our mid-upper gunner shouted to the skipper (through intercom), 'Dive, dive, dive' and immediately the aircraft took a steep diving turn to port and we had to go round again. It was a very lonely journey on the run-up to the target for the second time, but we dropped our bomb load where it mattered with no more interruptions. We all knew that we must have lost a lot of our bombers in that way; it was a fact realized by all operational aircrews on Bomber Command and in the majority of cases it was unavoidable with droves of aircraft flying over the target at the same time. Fortunately for us the flak was rather light that night.

We turned and made a bee line for home a few minutes after the rest of the stream. It always seemed important to the powers that be for us to carry as much weight in bombs as possible and never mind the petrol. We never had much petrol to spare on any trip and this one was no exception. Getting close to the French coast we got our usual ETA from the navigator (estimated time of arrival) and after checking and calculating our petrol reserves, I realised that we would be rather tight for petrol to get home. I informed the skipper of our situation and he duly sent out a 'Darkie' call for permission to land at the Carnaby emergency landing strip near Bridlington and as we got nearer, there was quite a commotion as lots of aircraft were in the same trouble. We circled the airstrip for quite some time until we were given permission to land, and eventually we touched the tarmac with some relief all safe and sound. Aircraft were landing three abreast (the airstrip being 300 yards wide) and in the space of twenty minutes, 75 aircraft had landed. My recollections bring back to mind that on this occasion, two aircraft had ditched in Bridlington Bay with both crews being rescued by Air-Sea Rescue crews.

CHAPTER 13

ENIGMA

The German armoured formations immediately able to counter the Allied beach assaults were 21 Panzer Division (under Rommel), Panzer Lehr Division and 12 SS Panzer Division, but here the complicated command chain seriously delayed deployment when time was essential. To release Panzer Lehr and 12 SS Panzer, von Rundstedt had to request permission from OKW. This request was placed just after midnight on 6 June, but he didn't receive a reply until 1600 hours. It wasn't until 7 June that leading elements of 12 SS Panzer saw action, and the division did not reach full strength until the next day.

In von Rundstedt's postwar interrogation he explained the difficulties of bringing up sufficient reinforcement to counter the Allied expansion from the Normandy beaches.

> As Allied troops poured into the bridgehead, the need for an aggressive, full scale counter-attack, became evident. But to date the only formations that had been able to reach Normandy were armoured divisions, and they were now acting as infantry in an attempt to contain the swelling bridgehead. Infantry divisions struggling to arrive at the scene of operations were constantly hampered and delayed by Allied air attacks, and most of these formations had to mount bicycles or march on their flat feet for hundreds of kilometres, due to the complete destruction of the railways. Many of these troops took well over a week before they put in an appearance, and hardly a division arrived complete, but rather straggled in by bits and pieces.[75]

In the south of France, following their call to arms, Resistance units began blowing rail lines, blocking roads and harassing and attacking German garrisons. Army Group G was swamped with signals from German units holding towns in the south, informing of what they classed as 'terrorist' attacks, and then played directly into the hands of Allied strategy, by ordering its forces to counter and suppress the uprisings. As historian Max Hastings noted, 'Perhaps the greatest contribution that Resistance made to D-Day was now to goad the Germans into deploying against the *maquis* forces out of all proportion to the real threat that they represented.'[76] In October 1944 Lord Selborne, British Minister of Economic Warfare, would report to Winston Churchill that 'evidence from many quarters, including the unsolicited testimonials of high ranking German POWs has testified to the great part played by Resistance in the debacle of German arms in the West.'

When the invasion began, various Resistance and *maquisard* units, supported by SOE agents and using arms parachuted in by men such as Dennis Field, sought to delay their enemy and gain revenge for the years of occupation and oppression. Not that the attacks on the German columns and defended towns were very well co-ordinated, as political differences and rivalries between the groups interfered. Nevertheless, in terms of the impact of their actions some success could be claimed.

Early on 8 June the 2nd SS Panzer Division, 'Das Reich', began a deployment north from around Montauban in the south, and its infantry and armour began their infamous march to the Normandy battlefront. The division, frequently assailed by guerilla action, took time suppressing the 'terrorists'. There were open battles with the armed Frenchmen, but there were also the terrible reprisals. On 10 June one unit of this division destroyed the village of Oradour-sur-Glane: 642 of the villagers, men, women and children, were killed, either shot in their homes, on the streets, or herded into the church and burned. But delayed the Das Reich was and as it neared the battlefront its frustration was further compounded by the Allied bombing attacks on the rail lines and fighter-bomber attacks on any daylight movements. On 15 June its leading units reached the rear of the battlefront and over the next two weeks, the rest of the division 'rather straggled in by bits and pieces'.

In the early stages of the Normandy battle von Rundstedt wanted to pull the armoured divisions out, replacing them with infantry divisions, and then mount a counter-attack. Desperate for more infantry he asked if the infantry divisions in the south of France could be released; he was frustrated however, as the move was deemed politically impossible. His other source would be the 15th Army divisions north of the Seine but here the *Fortitude* deception plan bore fruit, as von Rundstedt, believing another Allied army group was assembled in SE England awaiting embarkation, decided not to seek a weakening of his northern defences. It took two weeks before von Rundstedt accepted that a second Allied landing was no longer a risk, and requested that 15th Army troops be moved to Normandy. Permission was not granted, however. OKW still believed operations were likely in the Pas de Calais and did not abandon this idea until early in August. The fact that he had to get permission to move virtually every division, caused enormous frustration for the veteran commander, a fact that he reported to his interrogators after the war.

> I could have stood on my head but I would still not have been able to budge a division if Hitler disagreed with my judgement. As Commander-in-Chief West my only authority was to change the guard in front of my gate.[77]

Despite the ongoing reinforcement problems there were Panzer divisions at the disposal of the defenders and plans were formulated for an armoured counter-attack to prevent the linking of the American and British beachheads near Bayeux. General Leo Freiherr Geyr von Schweppenburg, commanding Panzer Group West, was extremely anxious to initiate the attack by 10 June at the latest, but SS General Sepp Dietrich, commanding I SS Panzer Corps, felt his respective forces would not be ready to attack so soon. Nevertheless by 9 June 21 Panzer and 12 SS Panzer tank units were assembled and ready. However Allied air power now intervened. The location of the headquarters of Panzer Group West was known to the Allies. Early on 10 June, a German signals intercept enabled Ultra to pass on the exact location of von Schweppenburg's command centre, south-west of Caen, near la Caine.[78] That evening AEAF aircraft blasted and destroyed von Schweppenburg's headquarters, killing many officers, including his Chief of Staff. With von Schweppenburg unable to organise the planned Panzer counter-offensive, Dietrich, who had already expressed his reluctance to make any serious moves with the Panzers, assumed command. The staff of Panzer Group West were pulled out to reform and the armoured counter-offensive was called off.

At the Allied Air Commanders' Conferences on 8,9,10 and 11 June the focus of attention for RAF Bomber Command mainly remained on attacking rail centres and for the Eighth Air Force enemy airfields and bridges over the Loire. In addition on 8 June Tedder made two further targeting suggestions. Firstly he felt attacks on *Fortitude* targets would still bring dividends, by holding enemy forces in the Pas de Calais area. Secondly, and no doubt supported by evidence from Ultra, German supplies were diminishing alarmingly, and he felt it was time to go after oil again. Action would be taken but not for a few days as tactical targets in or near the invasion area received the attention of the Allied air might.

Bill Brown and Jack Scott's crews gave their input, attacking Versailles railyards (10/11 June) and Laval airfield (9/10 June) respectively. Ken Handley recorded in his diary:

> *Friday 9/10 June – Laval airfield:* Nearing the target, still in cloud, we flew on & at one minute to our bombing time we saw a yellow glow coming up through the clouds. Opening the bomb doors we flew on & luckily for us the cloud turned into a slight haze for about 15 secs over the target. Tick [Ron Tickell] picked the markers out & down went the bombs. This airfield should be a sorry mess if the markers were down in the correct place.

Indeed the attack was successful. The III Gruppe Schlactgeschwader 4 (ground attack unit) had just been deployed to Laval airfield and recorded in its diary that the runway had been cut in several places. The unit was released from operations over the next two days as work was carried out on the runway.[79]

On 10/11 June Bill Brown's crew successfully completed their operation to Versailles, which was one of four railyards hit by RAF Bomber Command that night. Bill Brown's luck held out as a considerable German defensive response accounted for 18 RAF heavies. On their next operation the strength of opposition became more apparent.

Nightfighter

On the night of 10/11 June Bill Geeson was piloting a 625 Squadron Lancaster on the raid to the railyards at Achères, approximately 12 miles to the north-west of Paris and just south of the Seine. He recalls his engagement with an enemy nightfighter:

> It was another bad do. We lost three aircraft from the squadron that night and the entire crew of both the other aircraft were killed. We lost our rear gunner and two other crew members were injured.

It was one of those uncomfortable nights, everything seemed strange and unusual. It was very dark owing to high cloud, there was no visible horizon and we were practically flying on instruments. We went in at very low altitude, presumably to concentrate again on the accuracy of the bombing. We approached the target at about 2,000 feet, had the bomb doors open and were lining up on the target. Evidently one of their nightfighters managed to get just underneath us. We were hit by the first burst from him, there was no tracer used that time. We had Fishpond (a radar detection device) but this failed to detect the fighter. We assume that was when the rear gunner was hit as we heard nothing at all from him. Working with the mid-upper gunner I managed to start a corkscrew manoeuvre. We weren't very far into this manoeuvre when the whole of the starboard wing caught fire. A mass of flame followed far behind the aircraft and the glare was dazzling.

I managed to stand the plane on its port wing, at almost 90 degrees bank, even though the bombs were still on board. I pulled back hard on the stick and rammed the throttles full open. Thank goodness the Lanc could take it, and another burst of fire, probably cannon, including tracer, followed us around like a hosepipe, but did not connect. Naturally the Lanc practically stalled, but as I pushed the stick forward again we seemed to have lost elevator control and I was only able to roll level again using ailerons and the artificial horizon. The fighter pilot evidently concluded that we had had it, as he did not fire another burst, probably not so much out of consideration but if he had closed in we would have been shooting back, from the mid-upper turret at any rate. He knew there was no need to fire further; we were on our way down.

It was utter confusion everywhere as we really were so close to the ground. There was no time. It would have been pointless to operate the graviner or anything to fight the fire because the whole wing was going and my consideration was to get everyone out before the wing came off, which I was fully expecting. In fact it didn't, the aircraft just went into a shallow dive. I don't think the bombs were even fused, there was no question of it doing a lot of damage.

We got out of the front of the aircraft alright and the mid-upper gunner got out. We were never able to find out exactly what happened to the rear gunner except that he was killed. By the time I got out I had barely got time for the chute to open before I hit some trees. The trouble was that we were very low. Two members of the crew, the navigator and the mid-upper became suspended in the trees, released their parachutes, fell and suffered various back injuries. The wireless operator was suffering from severe shock when he was picked up by the French and couldn't say exactly how he got out. The bomb aimer got either shrapnel or a bullet through the calf of his leg. However he managed to get away successfully and was never taken prisoner. The mid-upper and navigator both ended up in hospital; the navigator eventually got back to England and went back on flying again. The mid-upper was seriously lame. He did make a pretty much complete recovery but did walk with a stick. I was extremely lucky because my parachute hung in the trees for a matter of a second and then the branches gave way and I didn't have any option whether to release or not. Fortunately I landed on a soft bushy bank and was unhurt.

The rear gunner, Sergeant Dunn, was the only fatality from the crew. The rest of them evaded capture except for the flight engineer, Sergeant Dawson, who ended up at Bankau POW camp.

At RAF Leeming on the morning of 12 June, 427 Squadron airmen went through the usual rituals: the aircrews caught up on any of the latest gen, and groundcrews attended to their beloved aircraft. Conversation over dinner consisted mainly of 'shop'. Then there was news that a briefing for operations was scheduled for that night and the speculation started. What was the target? A close eye would be kept on the bomb loads and the fuel allocated to aircraft. A small quantity of fuel and hence large bomb load suggested a short trip to the target – France? A high quantity of fuel and small bomb load suggested a long trip – Germany? On 12 June it was to be low fuel, large bomb load. France and support to the invasion was likely and many airmen, whilst unlikely to show it, felt some relief. However, that night 21 of 427 Squadron's aircrew would not be returning from the raid.

Early that evening expectant airmen filed into the ops room. The time for speculation was over. In front of them was a large map. On it was lengths of tape. The 427 Squadron airmen, including Bill Brown's crew, followed the tape from their Yorkshire station down England, across the Channel into hostile air space and to the target for the night. The railyards at Arras. But why Arras? What intelligence had persuaded the senior air commanders to choose this particular target? In this case Ultra, the interception and analysis of enemy signals traffic, played its part.

Late on the evening of 9 June a German signals operator, attached to Army Group B had been tasked to signal a message requesting that supply data for XLVII Panzer Corps, located north of the Seine, be made available to the ordnance officer and chief quartermaster of the Seventh Army. Before sending the signal he had to encrypt the message. He sat down before his keyboard, laid out in the normal pattern of a German typewriter. But this was no ordinary typewriter. Above the keys was a 'lampboard' of 26 letters in the same layout as the keyboard, each of which could be illuminated. Above the lampboard three small windows revealed individual letters on three rotating wheels, each wheel having 26 letters; the signals operator, having chosen the three wheels from a box of five, then placed them in the machine in a specified order.

The right wheel had a turnover position at one point in its revolution that would turn the middle wheel. The middle wheel had a similar arrangement with respect to turning the left wheel. As the operator depressed a key two things happened. The right rotating wheel moved on one place, with the possibility of the middle and left wheel doing the same, and an electric current flowed from a point under the key to a 'plugboard', again laid out in the normal keyboard lettering. Some of the sockets in this plugboard were connected by a short lead to another socket, others were not. The electric current either flowed through the lead, to re-map the letter, or not as the case may be. Via either route it then passed to an entry wheel to the right of the three rotating wheels, then through terminals on the entry wheel, through terminals on the rotating wheels to a reversing wheel. Then back through the rotating wheels to the entry wheel and to the plugboard where it might, again, pass through a lead or not. All this constituted further re-maps of the letter. From here the electric current finally went to the lampboard where it illuminated a letter. All of this was of course virtually instantaneous, but the initial letter keyed by the operator had been re-mapped, basically swapped, numerous times through a machine that could be set up in a considerable number of different ways. The Germans had great confidence in their encoding device called Enigma. A device the Allies were well aware of since 1936 thanks to a Polish interception.

On 9 June the German signals operator, having set up his machine, began keying in the message that was to be encrypted. Working with the operator was another clerk who wrote down the letter illuminated on the lampboard. Once the encryption was complete the resultant sequence of letters was transmitted, by morse code, to his intended recipient, who then keyed the list of letters into his Enigma machine, set up with the same daily specification. The message was decyphered and the job complete. However on this night, as had been happening on every night since early in the war, others were listening.

In England at Y Stations (listening stations), simultaneously with the German receiver, the morse code transmission of an apparently random string of letters was heard and written down. This was soon passed to Station X and the codebreakers at Bletchley Park, where it arrived at the 'Control' in Hut 6.

Meanwhile Hut 6's 'Watch' had been seeking the Enigma machine settings for the day, the 'key'. Initially they had sought a crib, a standard German signal, such as a weather message, which would suggest possible settings of the Enigma machine's rotating wheels. From this they devised a 'menu' to test potential wheel settings. This was then passed to the operators of the 'bombes' in Hut 11, large machines consisting of electrically linked circular drums with letters on, and, to the uninformed, a confusion of leads and plug sockets at the back. The female operators fed that day's possible menus into the back of the bombes and the machines were set to run. The room filled with terrific noise as the drums turned, but they would eventually stop, the operator noting a reading. If the letters appeared to match the menu, a possible wheel setting for that day had been found.

Early on 9 June a crib had been found and the bombes had established that day's wheel settings for that particular key. The code was broken. Shortly after the Army Group B intercepted supplies message was received at Bletchley Park, probably early on 10 June, it was decyphered into a plain text message using a Type X machine modified to emulate Enigma. Then a gummed strip of paper with the original encoded text on one side and the decode in 5-letter groups on the other was passed on to Hut 3 and its 'Watch'. Initially the 5-letter groups were regrouped, still in sequence, to form recognised German words and numbers. The text was translated and a false notional source given, in order to maintain the Germans' confidence in their Enigma encryption. The message then passed to the

'Adviser' who had at his disposal a vast index by which he could assess the importance of the message. He made his comments and drafted a signal to inform the relevant operational commands. Finally, on 11 June the 'Duty Officer', commanding the operations of Hut 3, released the decrypted message.

The importance of the message was obvious. Ultra had not, until then, intercepted any messages connecting XLVII Panzer Corps and the Seventh Army. The fact that supply data was to be given to the Seventh Army indicated XLVII Panzer Corps units were on the move to the battle area. On 8 June a signal had been intercepted concerning a statement from the highways commission in France, saying that 'all Seine crossings from Conflans [20 km north of Paris] to Rouen inclusive, destroyed. In this section road traffic north and south only possible through Paris.' So if XLVII Panzer Corps, originally located north of the Seine, was on the move, it would have to use the rail and road links north of Paris. With this information, and no doubt backing from air reconnaissance and agent reports, the air commanders at the AAC Conference on 12 June were informed that 'Another important move from the Amiens-Arras area, probably starting today, is thought to involve No. 2 Panzer Division'.[80]

Harris's command responded. RAF Bomber Command headquarters informed Group headquarters that the targets that night would be certain rail centres, which then passed details and requirements to squadrons, who detailed their aircrews. Bill Brown's crew was one of those detailed at 427 Squadron to attack the railyards at Arras on the night of 12/13 June 1944. Other RAF Bomber Command raids were also planned against railyards at Amiens/St Roch, Amiens/Longueau, Caen, Cambrai and Poitiers (an Ultra decrypt had notified the Allies that the 2nd SS Panzer Division were to move, from the south, to Poitiers[81]). To Bill Brown's crew the operation seemed relatively simple, flying in low and dropping their load of 500 lb general-purpose bombs, to smash the railyards apart. Ferd Slevar recalled, 'On leaving the briefing room all aircrew thought this was going to be a piece of cake.'

As they usually did Ferd Slevar and George Percy took communion with the padre and had a final chat with the groundcrew before climbing on board the laden Halifax and preparing for take-off. Bill Brown's crew was one of the last to take off at RAF Leeming that night at 2315 hours. In total 427 Squadron managed to contribute 15 aircraft and 105 aircrew to the Arras force. Ferd Slevar: 'The night was dark when we took off from Leeming. We were not concerned, as long as the Pathfinder Squadron arrived before us to drop their TI.'

Bill Brown's Halifax joined the bomber stream as it headed south down England, crossing the coast over Dungeness. The Arras force was not alone as it crossed the Channel, as on virtually the same course was a similar force of RAF heavies detailed for an attack on the railyards at Amiens/St Roch. Both forces would fly parallel to one another only a few miles apart, until they reached the vicinity of Amiens. As Bill Brown piloted his Halifax across the English Channel, German searchlights sprung into life from the enemy coast and flak bursts started appearing. Undeterred, by what was now a fairly familiar spectacle, on they flew towards Arras. What Bill Brown and his crew would have been unaware of was that earlier that night, as they were flying down England, two forces of RAF bombers had been attacking the railyards at Cambrai and

Amiens/Longueau, encountering stiff opposition. The German nightfighter controllers in France had managed to vector their airmen, particularly from their base at Florennes, into the Cambrai bomber stream just as it left the target. Airmen from both sides fought for their lives.

By the end of the night nine aircraft failed to return from this particular raid. Of note is the loss of the 419 Squadron Lancaster of Flying Officer De Breyne RCAF. Cannon fire from a Ju88 had set the aircraft ablaze. The crew was ordered to bail out but the mid-upper gunner, Warrant Officer Andrew Mynarski RCAF, amidst the fire attempted to rescue his fellow gunner trapped in the rear turret. His efforts failed and the rear gunner signalled to his colleague to leave. Mynarski saluted and with flames severely burning him he jumped. He lost his life shortly after landing. The rear gunner miraculously survived when the Lancaster hit the ground and his story would later lead to Mynarski's heroism being recognised with the Victoria Cross.

German nightfighters also accounted for three bombers from the Amiens/Longueau force, with one further bomber lost to flak over the railyards. With numerous 'Sieg Heils' already notched up for his force, the German nightfighter controller then sent his airmen to the skies over Brussels, in an attempt to get amongst the RAF heavies sent to attack the oil refinery at Gelsenkirchen. After some success they then headed south to try and intercept the Mosquitos returning from Cologne. Here they were frustrated and the German controller at 0141 hours instructed his fighters to once more prowl over Cambrai. This was just in time to meet the RAF bombers leaving Arras.

At about 0140 hours Bill Brown's Halifax made a left turn, the nose of his laden bomber pointing directly at Arras. A few miles to the south the Amiens/St Roch railyards were under attack. On this night the Arras bombers were unusually low; the bombing height was detailed as 4,000 feet. Attention to accuracy and a minimising of bomb spread remained a priority. At such low heights, however, the bombers presented an easier target for the ground defences.

> *Ferd Slevar:* Bill received the ETA on target from the navigator Cliff Cameron, as Art Willis the bomb aimer readied himself to guide Bill to the target area. Hugh Mackenzie, the wireless operator, was at his station by his radio and Stan Selfe, the flight engineer, was going about his duties of checking oil gauges for proper pressure. During all this time I was searching the sky above our aircraft and George Percy, the rear gunner was searching the sky below for German nightfighters. The intercom was open to all positions. Quietly, in my mid-upper gunner's position, I was saying the Our Father and the Hail Mary.
>
> Then I shrieked over the intercom as a plane was hit by flak. I increased the pace of my prayers. George reported another aircraft hit by flak. I quickened the pace of my prayers as more bombers were being knocked out of the night sky.

Art Willis sited the target markers and started to guide Bill in order to bring the aircraft over the target. Ferd and George Percy kept scanning the night sky, witnessing the demise of colleagues as the flak claimed more victims. In their ears they could hear Art: 'Left – left – steady.'

Ferd Slevar: Suddenly a picture focused in my mind of my father with his arm around my mother, standing in the doorway of our home in Canada. He was trying to comfort her – both sensing that their son was about to die. Then in the next instant another picture appeared – the dreaded telegram was flying across the Atlantic Ocean towards Canada. My tempo of Our Father and Hail Mary prayers increased to a very rapid rate. My prayers became a blur, I was saying them so fast, and at the same time I was reporting the devastation that was happening in the sky around our aircraft.

Art reported, 'Bomb doors open – steady as you go.'

'We regret to inform that your son . . .' The telegram was nearing my sorrowful mother and father standing in the doorway. I could not say the Our Father and the Hail Mary any faster as George and I kept the intercom busy reporting further bombers being blasted into balls of fire. This was turning into a hell.

My poor mother and father received the telegram and he attempted to console her. I said to myself, 'No! No! The telegram is not right. I don't want to die.'

Art reported, 'Steady, steady, bombs away.'

'Let's get out of here,' said Bill.

As we left the target and the heavy concentration of German anti-aircraft guns, we were hysterically relieved as we headed for our home base.

Flak had accounted for three bombers from the Arras force. In addition two bombers fell to flak from the Amiens/St Roch force over the target area. Then the German nightfighters arrived. Within 10 minutes three more bombers from the Arras force, now heading north, were blasted out of the sky and two from the Amiens/St Roch force, which had turned south for a few miles then virtually due west. The crew returned to base physically unscathed and proceeded to debriefing. The intelligence officer informed the shaken crew that what they had actually been seeing were German 'scarecrows'. However the next day the crew were to realise that in fact they had seen numerous exploding aircraft. From the 671 aircraft that took part in operations against French railyards that night, 23 aircraft were lost, of which 427 Squadron lost 3. Three further aircraft were damaged beyond repair. 119 airmen lost their lives, 17 were captured and 29 managed to evade. There is one further strange twist to Ferd Slevar's experience that night:

Upon completion of my tour of duty, 35 bombing missions over the continent, I was sent home. As soon as I arrived, my happy mother said she had had a horrible dream on 12 June 1944 and asked me if I almost got killed that night.

Two nights later Bill Brown's crew would again be sent to attack railyards north of Paris, this time to Cambrai, but on this night they witnessed little opposition. But what effect had the bombing of railyards north of Paris had on enemy movements? Leigh-Mallory was certainly optimistic, confiding in his diary a few days later:

16 June 1944: In general, the Hun is in a bad way. His movements have been crippled. I seem to be saying this a lot but it is true, and I can cripple him further if the weather would only let me.

The American 8th Air Force bombers did a very good show yesterday. They attacked bridges over the Loire and destroyed the whole lot. One photograph I saw showed a lump of bridge sailing through the air. These were all railway bridges, but one road bridge not included in the programme went for six by mistake.

I know that the Hun divisions moving up from Poitiers had hell. We clobbered Angoulême and made a great mess of it. We put much of the SS Division out of business, and some of the 2nd Panzer Division is still tied up in Cambrai. The anticipated bombing, which I ordered when I knew where these Divisions were, was very good and the attacks on Arras, Amiens and Cambrai were made just at the right moment. I think I tied up the northern Divisions while they were in the process of getting into their trains, and I believe it may be another five days before they are able to make any move.[82]

Leigh-Mallory's optimism was well founded. General Heinrich Freiherr von Luttwitz commanded the 2nd Panzer Division during its move to Normandy, and his postwar interrogators recorded the problems he had deploying his units:

When news of the landings first reached Luttwitz, his division was stationed on both sides of the Somme in the neighbourhood of Abbeville. Rommel personally told Luttwitz that his division was not to be moved immediately since a second Allied landing was expected in the area of the Somme. On 9 June this appreciation was revised and 2 Panzer Division was ordered to move to Bayeux. Since the bridges on the Seine north of Paris had been destroyed it was necessary to make the trip from Abbeville to Bayeux via the French capital, a distance of about 400 kilometres. Once the Seine had been crossed the motorized infantry were to make their way on foot or vehicle to Normandy while the tanks were to continue on by rail. The infantry arrived at Caumont on 12 June as scheduled, but the tanks were not so lucky. Three of the locomotives had been shot up by the RAF and the tanks had been forced to take to the road. Making their way chiefly by night they were continually strafed by Allied planes, while the new motors of the tanks, which had not yet been broken in, burnt themselves out during the trip. Finally on 18 June, six days after the infantry had arrived, 80 of Luttwitz's tanks limped into Caumont, while another 20 managed to arrive a short time after.[83]

RAF Bomber Command could safely claim that the sacrifice its aircrews made in the attacks on the rail targets north of Paris, in this instance brought valuable time as the Allied Army sought to establish its foothold in France and build up forces.

CHAPTER 14

SHOT DOWN

During the first week of the invasion much needed supplies continued to stream ashore on the Normandy beaches from the vast armada of Allied shipping. Any hostile threat from the Luftwaffe was minimal, but there was another menace. The build-up of German E-boats (motor torpedo boats) in Le Havre, threatening the Allied left flank, had attracted the scrutiny of air reconnaissance. By 13 June the extent of the build-up was deemed most serious and at the AAC Conference on 13 June the Navy requested intervention from the air. The next day RAF Bomber Command obliged by sending 221 Lancasters and 13 Mosquitos, escorted by Spitfires, on a daylight raid, the results of which all but scrubbed out the E-boat threat. On the back of this success on 15 June, 297 RAF Bomber Command aircraft paid the same compliment to the German naval build-up in Boulogne harbour. Both attacks were successful, although there were, unfortunately civilian losses in and around the port facilities.

In between these two attacks, on the night of 14/15 June, RAF Bomber Command intervened directly in the land battle. The failure to capture the key objective of Caen quickly weighed heavily with Allied senior commanders and pressure mounted on Montgomery whose solution was to initiate two flanking pincers around the battered Normandy city, involving his veteran divisions, the 51st Highland and 7th Armoured. The 51st Highland Division launched its hook on 11 June to the east of Caen but stiff opposition from the 21st Panzer Division eventually forced it back. The right hook also initially stalled against the Panzer Lehr, but on 12 June the 7th Armoured was instructed to take its hook further west to a perceived weakspot in the German defence, outflank Panzer Lehr and push on to the important crossroads in the town of Villers-Bocage.

Early the next morning leading elements entered Villers-Bocage, with minimal opposition. But the Allied success was shortlived. The Germans had been aware of this weakness in their defensive line and armour had been sent to plug the gap. Throughout the day the Germans fought to repel the Allied advance, led from the front by Captain Michael Wittman, who would further his reputation as a Panzer ace as he led his Tiger tanks to success by smashing and harassing the leading Allied units. Without re-inforcement the 7th Armoured eventually withdrew. With German forces steadily building up around Villers-Bocage, and to cover the withdrawal, RAF Bomber Command was asked to intervene and that night sent 337 aircraft to attack the German positions at nearby Aunay-sur-Odon and Évrecy. The raids were a success, halting the German counter-thrust and the 7th Armoured Division managed to pull back to Caumont. However Montgomery's plan to take Caen had failed; the Germans had sealed the line and the land battle stagnated. The hopes of a mobile campaign were fading. But some felt that air might could be the solution to break the stalemate and a whole new dispute over the role and use of the heavy bombers would flare up.

On 14 June Leigh-Mallory visited Montgomery and Dempsey in Normandy proposing a means to break the German defences around Caen. Dempsey recorded the meeting in his diary:

14 June
1700 hours – saw AOC AEAF (Leigh-Mallory) at Headquarters 21 Army Group. He can give me Bomber Command, 8 USAAF and all the mediums for tactical support of the infantry attack. He can do this at first light on 17 June. I said that, if I could have them, I would attack with the LEFT of 1 Corps and take Caen.

1830 – Saw Commander 1 Corps at my Headquarters and gave him the outline plan for the taking of Caen on 17 June. RAF representatives will fly over from the UK tomorrow to settle details.[84]

Certainly Montgomery backed the idea. Originally he had wanted to use airborne troops to break the situation around Caen, but Leigh-Mallory was not so keen. The AEAF commander recorded in his diary that when he met Montgomery on 14 June he:

was not in a good temper for I had sent him a signal shooting down an airborne operation he wanted mounted. When I met him, therefore, he was not kindly disposed. However, he brisked up a bit when I offered him, in exchange for the operation I was not prepared to carry out, a much more attractive proposal. . . When I made it he just swallowed it up, though even now I am not sure that he will choose the right area. We shall see.[85]

On Leigh-Mallory's return to England he met Zuckerman and Kingston-McCloughry, to plan the use of the strategic heavies. The next morning, 15 June, Zuckerman and Kingston-McCloughry flew to Bayeux, meeting with Dempsey. The meeting was broken up, however, when Tedder and Coningham arrived, and withdrew, with Dempsey and Crocker, to another room.

Dempsey's diary: 15 June . . . Tedder and Coningham disclosed that Leigh-Mallory had not told anyone else of his project for supporting infantry attack with Bomber Command and 8 USAAF. Both Tedder and Coningham are sure that it cannot be done effectively. For the present we will drop it.

Zuckerman and Kingston-McCloughry were called in by Tedder shortly after the two generals had departed, and Leigh-Mallory's representatives were bluntly told that the matter was none of their business. Army support could be dealt with by the tactical air forces. Zuckerman tried to argue the case:

Taking advantage of my special relationship with Tedder, I argued back, pointing out that while we were no doubt dealing with a land battle, a new factor had to be considered; namely, the weight of bombs that could be accurately put down by the strategic as well as the tactical air forces. Kingston also wanted to know why the Army was stuck if the Tactical Air Command could give adequate air support. This remark was also brushed aside and the class, as it were, dismissed.[86]

Tedder was of the opinion that the Army should not be able to make such calls on the strategic bomber forces, as and when problems arose in the land battle. He, along with the heavy bomber commanders, had concerns over accuracy. Early in July, when the air forces were once more called upon to assist in the ground offensive, Tedder would insist that 'the Air could not, and must not, be turned on thus glibly and vaguely in support of the Army, which would never move unless prepared to fight its way with its own weapons.'[87] In addition Tedder held the view that Leigh-Mallory had not involved the proper chain of command in offering heavy bomber support.

Meanwhile back in England at the AAC Conference on 15 June, reports were received that Montgomery had requested air power to loosen the situation around Caen. A bombardment on a front 5,000 yards wide and 4,000 yards deep was asked for 'to possibly open a gap for our forces', and justified on the grounds that evidence had come in of the detrimental effect the bombing on D-Day had had on enemy troop morale. Leigh-Mallory would state that the 'Army had now got stuck and were looking to the Air Force'. In attendance at the meeting was General H.H. 'Hap' Arnold, Commanding General of the USAAF and his response to the idea was not favourable, arguing that he hoped this was not going to be another Cassino (the failure of air bombardment to assist in the assaults on the town of Cassino and its hill top monastery, on the Italian front). As it was Tedder and Coningham's intervention had already doomed the plan anyway, further souring their relationship with Leigh-Mallory. Nevertheless Leigh-Mallory's conviction that air power could break open the land battle would not rest. He would get another chance.

In addition to the proposed Army support bombing, Leigh-Mallory maintained at the 15 June AAC Conference that rail movement still needed attention, in particular in north-east France, notably Lens and Valenciennes, to keep up the *Fortitude* deception plan, along with attacking the Luftwaffe and the Loire bridges. In addition as we have already noted, RAF Bomber Command was also asked to smash the E-boat threat at Boulogne. The minutes also recorded that Leigh-Mallory stated that 'though our armies had been halted, the Germans appeared to be short of supplies and the moment seemed ripe for an attack upon their fuel and ammunition dumps'. That night RAF Bomber Command would respond attacking the ammunition dump at Fouillard and the fuel dump at Châtellerault.

On 15 June Dennis Field and his crew were detailed to attack the marshalling yards at Lens in response to Leigh-Mallory's determination to maintain the *Fortitude* deception. Since their dummy parachute drop on the night of D-Day itself, Dennis and his crew had seen no action. Indeed they were now nearing completion of their tour; the trip to Lens would be Dennis's 31st operation.

> *Dennis Field:* We flew through heavy cloud most of the way and were late over the target, the TIs fading as we approached. We had to stooge about for another ten minutes for re-marking, but it gave us the opportunity for a straight, steady run. The aircraft lifted and the controls lightened as the bombs released and a few seconds later a delighted whoop from Arthur announced direct hits in the centre of the aiming point, confirmed immediately by an appreciative Master Bomber. We quickly re-entered

cloud and close-by flashes over the coastal belt encouraged a generous weave. I thought we had had a pretty good trip in spite of the adverse conditions and was a bit put out when for no obvious reason, I was given a mild rollicking for apparently getting off track on the way back.

This was to be Dennis's last complete operation flying a Stirling from Tuddenham. The crew were detailed to take part in an operation on 17 June but aborted shortly after take-off, as Jim Blackwell was unable to rotate his rear turret. Following a week's leave they reassembled for posting.

> *Dennis Field:* It was with much regret that we said our goodbyes. . . The crew were dispersed widely, mostly to OTUs and other training establishments and Johnny Evans stayed on to finish his tour with other crews. We sincerely promised to maintain contact and exchanged home and new addresses . . . Our mutual experience of the previous eighteen months had formed lasting bonds of trust and friendship. Our tour had been about par for the course at the time. Much of the work we did was essentially individualistic and thus mostly different from main force. We had lost another dozen or so aircraft . . . in the second three months of the year when involved mainly on supply operations in which losses, chiefly from light flak, amounted to around four per cent per raid, an officially tolerable but not very healthy figure. Unscathed survival thus far and in the immediate future for the fortunate amongst us required an essential and generous element of luck. After lengthy handshakes we departed on our various ways to heaven knows what new ventures and challenges.

Here Dennis's crew leave our story having completed their tour, having risked all bombing railyards, supplying the Resistance and Maquis and deceiving the German defenders in Normandy. Their fates are covered at the end of this book.

On this night another of our crews were to fly their last operation. Alan Grant's crew were also detailed at 7 Squadron to visit Lens, their 24th operation together. Following the raid to Fôret de Cerisy on 7 June, the crew had been sent to railyards at Fougères and Tours, and an airfield at Rennes. They also had taken part in the successful attack on the synthetic oil plant at Gelsenkirchen on 12/13 June, although 17 Lancasters failed to return (the same night as Bill Brown's crew had flown amidst the air battle over Amiens and Arras).

> *Steve Masters:* The day prior to our fateful sortie was unusual in several ways and a departure from our normal routine. Dorothy, who was on sick leave, had been with me for a fortnight and had just left on the mid-day train. By chance I remembered that I should inform the authorities that my next of kin (my wife) was now returning to her normal address in Portsmouth. The next unusual thing was the visit we made to a Bomber Squadron in Lincoln, to see if there was any news of our wireless operator's brother missing on a Berlin raid nine weeks earlier. Unfortunately there was nothing to report and we were a slightly saddened crew as we flew back to base.

Sydney Nathanson's brother was part of a 626 Squadron crew that had failed to return from the 24/25 March attack on Berlin. Sydney wouldn't know it at this time, but his brother, along with the rest of the crew, had all been killed. Shortly after returning to Oakington, Alan Grant's crew joined the rest of the squadron for a photograph:

> Steve Masters: It was most disturbing as many crew were very superstitious about this. It was claimed that the crew or crews photographed were likely to be shot down. This may have been on the skipper's mind when he said to me, 'I wonder who will be the first to go from this photograph?' During briefing later that day, no-one mentioned the photograph or gave any indication of being more concerned than usual. Some crews used to have premonitions about their fate, but if any of our crew members had such ideas, it did not become apparent.

At 2319 hours that night Alan Grant lifted his Lancaster from the Oakington runway, and the flight to the target area went without incident. In order to achieve greater accuracy, the Master Bomber called Alan down to 8,000 feet and shortly after the bomb load fell, he turned his Lancaster for home.

> *Steve Masters:* As was usual for the target area we were under some anti-aircraft fire with a few searchlights in our vicinity, if not actually on us. Suddenly there was a deafening bang and we dropped quite violently to port. Strangely enough I had the feeling that this was the end for us, as my mind instantly went back to a film I had seen a few weeks earlier where a bomber, when shot down, had responded in the same way. We seemed to drop some distance before the aircraft was brought to an even level. Almost immediately the rear gunner called 'Corkscrew port' and down we went again in a violent descent to port.
>
> By this time both gunners were firing almost continuously but when we should have rolled and climbed to starboard we seemed to wallow, then the skipper reported that the aircraft wouldn't respond to the flying controls. 'Down port' shouted the rear gunner again, continuing to fire. We did not know what type of fighter was after us, but we knew he was still there. Suddenly the rear gunner called 'Bail out, we have had it', and was immediately backed up by the mid-upper gunner telling us we were on fire.
>
> Despite my earlier feelings I didn't want to believe this was actually happening, so looked out of the astrodome to see what was going on. One quick glance was enough to convince me that we could not stay, as it seemed that both wings were on fire and the thought of two thousand gallons of petrol in our tanks, left no doubt in my mind.
>
> As I turned to go forward, I saw Ron come up from the bombing position to shut down No. 3 engine as Alan, the skipper, had reported it on fire. When he reached up to do so, I saw Alan knock his hand down from the 'Fire Button'. He then gave the order to get out fast, at the same time closing all four throttles to reduce our speed.

> *Ron Neills:* Acting as the bomb aimer I was still down in the nose. I poked

my head up and Alan shouted, 'Out, Ron, Out, Ron !' It was too late to do anything. I had to take the flap up and throw it out. The last I saw of Alan was with feet up on the dashboard and two arms around the control column, trying to keep it back.

Steve Masters: Determined now to get out, I moved from the astrodome, grabbed my parachute, which I put on, climbed over my seat and moved forward. As I approached the hatch, my intercom lead, which was still plugged in, brought me to an abrupt halt. I tried to pull my helmet over my head but the new type I was wearing had the headphone leads at the back, which resulted in me being entangled with the lead. Pull as I might, I could not free it and had to work my way back to my table to disconnect the plug. This was very difficult to do as the aircraft was starting to descend rapidly.

Subconsciously I noted the indicated speed, it was 320 knots and rising, so it was more important than ever to get out quickly. To reassure myself I checked that my parachute was on properly but to my horror discovered that the rip cord was on the left-hand side. Stories came to mind of people who had done just this, then clawed through their parachutes with their right hand looking for the rip cord. I was determined not to make this error so grabbed it with my left hand, with no intention of letting go. It was probably still in my hand when I landed.

I realised we must be fairly close to the ground and I had visions of being seriously injured through the chute not opening properly. In that brief moment my thoughts were very active: should I bail out or should I stay with the plane and be killed instantly? It would save so much trouble. I even considered pushing past the other crew members so that I could get right up in the nose to make sure I didn't survive. In less time than it takes to record, my mind was clear again and I realised I had to try to save my life.

Crouched as I was on the step behind Speed, our bomb aimer, I saw Ron struggling to get the hatch free. This was a very bad moment as it had jammed and every second the nose was dropping further and further. The speed was mounting rapidly and the scream of the diving plane was rising in a crescendo blotting out all other sounds except our guns, which were still firing. This was becoming a nightmare as our chances of escaping from the plane were diminishing very rapidly indeed. Suddenly the hatch was gone, followed quickly by Ron and Speed, then it was my turn. My heart was in my mouth as I followed almost immediately, but not before I noticed the glow of fire outside the hatch. The last thing I remembered was tucking my head in and making a dive, but for some reason I lost consciousness and did not regain it until some time after I had landed.

Ron Neills: I had my intercom wire wrapped round one of the hooks on the parachute, so I had to undo that to take it out again and I jumped out on one hook without realising it. I counted twelve from the time I got out to the time the aircraft exploded. I didn't know at the time, but the aircraft exploded before it hit the ground.

I landed on the roof of a little farmhouse. I hit my face on the brickwork and I was up in the air about 12 feet. A farmer and his daughter got a ladder and got me down. They didn't seem too keen for me to be there, not that they were aggressive or anything, but they wanted to get rid of me. I asked, 'Which way to Calais?' I walked out through the back and pottered along some farm roads to get to the village.

I finished off walking through the night and it was becoming daylight. I got a bit impatient and I saw a couple of Frenchmen. I thought I'd go over and say hello. As soon as that happened there was a crowd of early morning workers and before long there were 20 or so people around. A gendarme came up and of course he didn't have any option but to take me in.

Alan Grant's commitment to his crew, fighting desperately to control his aircraft, whilst his crew bailed out, cost him his life. Both gunners, Tom Barrett, and Bill Newton, also lost their lives. Speed Martin managed to get out of the stricken aircraft, but became impaled, fatally, on some railings.

Steve Masters and Sydney Nathanson now began their attempt at evasion. Ron was taken to a Luftwaffe recruiting office and then taken to hospital to be checked over. His life as a POW then began. Here the crew leave our story, having made their contribution to the strategic bombing offensive against Germany, the bombing of German supply and reinforcement networks to Normandy via the French and Belgian railyards, and the blasting of enemy airfields and coastal defences. The fate of Steve, 'Nat' and Ron is covered at the end of this book.

CHAPTER 15

FLYING BOMBS

On 12 June 1944, 34th Bomb Group's George Ritchie flew his first mission with 1st Lieutenant Walter McAllister, acting as deputy lead on an attack on the airfield at Beauvais.

> *George Ritchie:* McAllister needed to replace his bombardier. At that time, I had the best record of the four lead bombardiers, so I was put on his crew. Initially, I did not like it – both crews did not like it, but orders are orders, and the transfer occurred. Basically, all the crews trained in the same way. Personalities differed, but methods were about the same. After a few very successful missions I was fully accepted.
>
> It was on the Beauvais mission, at an 1100-hour meeting, that I learned I was officially on Mac's crew and we were to lead this mission. This mission happened to be not only leading the squadron, but the group and the wing. That was a big responsibility but there was no backing out. The C/O rode as the command pilot. The take-off was delayed to just before dawn. Everyone was tired but still had their day's work to do. Navigation was perfect. Clouds over France were thick and broken. We had come this far. We said a silent prayer that we would be successful. My pilotage navigator (Lt Wayne [Yogi] Jorgenson) and I took over at the IP. We flew the bomb run, and after bombs away, I checked my cross hairs and the pattern was perfect. It was what I prayed for. I wrote in my diary that at the rallying point, all the gunners could see the results of the bomb run and were excited at the successful results of the mission. I also wrote that the commander of the wing congratulated me and said it was the best mission to date. Even 'Jumping Joe' Eaton, our West Point colonel, came up and said:
>
> 'Rick, you had a good one.'

Two days later, flying with Walter McAllister again as deputy lead, George Ritchie dropped his bombs on the airfield at Denain. On 17 June George flew with McAllister as they continued to contribute to the hindering of the German air force's attempt to reinforce the battle area; they attacked the airfield at Laval. On 23 June George assisted another crew whose bombardier was in hospital as they attacked the airfield at Coulommiers and on the 25th, back with McAllister, they would, George recalls:

> target a very obscure railroad bridge over a small meandering stream east of Paris. They had no target study photos, only co-ordinates from a pre-war French aerial map. The bomb load was six 1,000 lb bombs. At the beginning of the bomb run, we could only approximate the location of the target. We only knew that the French map showed the railroad tracks crossing the tree-lined stream, and no bridge was visible. Utilizing what we had, we proceeded down the target line and successfully removed the bridge.

However the Luftwaffe and rail communications were not the only target for the 34th's bombers during June 1944. A week after D-Day a new German menace had materialised and the 34th's airmen, including Walt McAllister and his crew, would attack a new kind of target.

Early on the morning of 13 June 1944 a small pilotless aircraft took off from a ramp, in the Pas de Calais, aligned on London, specifically Tower Bridge. After just a few minutes it crossed the French coast and droned on over the Channel and within a few more minutes the English coast was reached. At 4.18 a.m. over Gravesend, 20 miles from Tower Bridge, the engine cut out and the small missile fell. There was a massive explosion when the weapon, containing its 1,870 lb of high explosive, struck the ground. Fortunately no one was near enough to receive injury. Soon after a second missile fell at Cuckfield, Sussex, a third at Bethnal Green, London, then a fourth at Platt near Sevenoaks. Casualties remained light, however, only the one that fell in Bethnal Green inflicting death, with six people losing their lives. A fear that had been haunting the Allies for nigh on a year had now been realised, although not on the scale expected. The German secret weapon reprisal campaign had finally opened up. Germany's propaganda minister Josef Goebbels's calls of revenge for the persistent Allied bombing of German cities had materialised. A serious diversionary threat to the conduct of the Normandy invasion was now a reality. *Vergeltungswaffe* 1, the V1 flying bomb, had arrived.

The initial offensive action with this new German weapon fell way below expectation, with only ten launched. The launch units had not been ready and supply of the weapons had been seriously hampered by Allied air attacks on the French and Belgian transport network. However by the night of 15/16 June these problems had been sorted. That night 244 V1s were launched, 144 of which would reach England and 73 would continue on to Greater London.

The Allies had closely followed the development of the German secret weapon programme, in particular the V1 pilotless aircraft and the V2 rocket programme. Aerial photography of, and agent reports concerning, experimental research stations, notably that on the Baltic coast at Peenemünde, and strange constructions in northern France, had provided the main weight of evidence for a planned German reprisal campaign. Towards the end of 1943, the Allied air forces had been called upon to intervene directly. In August 1943 RAF Bomber Command attacked Peenemünde and the Eighth Air Force bombed a strange construction at Watten in northern France, which was believed to be associated with German secret weapons.

From the middle of December onwards the construction sites in northern France, assumed to be launch facilities, and named 'ski' sites owing to the distinctive shape of the storage buildings, were attacked by both strategic and tactical Allied bomber forces. As a result of these direct attacks, and, unknowingly, because RAF Bomber Command had attacked German industry targets, such as its raids on Kassel in October 1943, the planned German timetable for launching the offensive was considerably delayed. RAF Bomber Command and the Eighth Air Force had certainly contributed to this success but the threat had not gone away.

From the beginning of February 1944 until the launch of the German reprisal offensive Harris's force paid little attention to secret weapon targets, maintaining a focus on *Pointblank* commitments, and then the Transportation Plan. Doolittle's force, however, continued to allocate some of its weaponry to the threat, attacking V-weapon sites right up to the eve of the invasion. Following the full opening of the V1 offensive on the night of 15/16 June, both RAF and USAAF heavy bomber commands would be required to try and suppress the V1 menace. Targeting of the installations in northern France would regularly feature in the priorities allocated to each command right up until the area had been overrun by the Allied land forces.[88]

By the end of the first week of the V1 attacks on England, 723 civilians had lost their lives and 2,610 had been seriously injured. Reports were also coming in that news of the success of the attacks was giving a great morale boost to both the German armed forces and the civilian population. One of our featured airmen experienced the V1 offensive first hand:

> *Bob Petty:* For a Yank in London on leave, it was a strange combination of circumstances. It was summer, when my combination of hunger, lust and loneliness were in play. I went the way of a lot of others who had already been in the big and historic city under attack by buzz bombs. I wasn't used to the blackout and was somewhat perplexed. At the time I was in the queue at Lyons Corner House. I was familiar with enemy aircraft, but not unmanned ones. So when the pop, pop, of the robot bombs filtered down, I was not much worried. I had been told they had a silent free fall overhead after the engine stopped. When one flying bomb's engine stopped overhead, I got bit in the shoulder so hard, my knees buckled. I had on a blouse or overcoat, but the bite sure drew my attention. I turned around and saw a small girl from the Land Army. I hugged her and told her it was alright as the bomb would fall a block or two away, and it did. I resumed my wait for food and figured I am now in the war that draws no distinction between servicemen and civilians.

During the second half of June political pressure mounted on Allied air force commanders to give greater emphasis to reducing German flying bomb launch rates. This indeed would happen, with both RAF Bomber Command and the Eighth Air Force significantly increasing the number of raids on secret weapon installations in northern France. Our crews would make their contributions; Walt McAllister and George Ritchie flew their first mission to V1 launch sites on 20 June.

> *George Ritchie:* McAllister led the mission and Yogi and I were in the nose trying to locate the particular clump in the woods. Our pre-bombing practise procedure paid off. We located the site in the particular forest, but from a distance we could not see the launching ramp. With confidence in our training we continued toward that particular forested area and as we approached, we could see the break in the trees and eventually the rails of the launching site. With my cross hairs on the exact spot the bombs ticked away. At that moment, I mechanically salvoed to make sure that the release mechanism had expelled all the bombs. Then Mac took over and

brought us to the rallying point.

At that instant the squadron was hit by flak. Our crew except for Mac were safe, but he was subjected to shock and concussion. One burst came thru the bomb-bay area and cut the hose of the [No.] 3 tank gasline. This created a great danger, especially to the men in the waist and tail of the airplane. We were nothing but a flying gas bomb. We disconnected everything electrical, went off intercom and sweated out the ride home. On touchdown we ran off the end of the runway and abandoned the aircraft out there.

At interrogation, we learned that we were not the only ship hit. Four emergency-landed at other airfields, but none was lost. The deputy lead on the mission, Joe Hardison, flying on Mac's right wing and the top turret gunner, were the two who were killed. The co-pilot was wounded, as were Shore (deputy lead bombardier), Pretty (lead navigator) and Capt. Metz (squadron navigator). The deputy lead aircraft was as competent as the lead aircraft, and was there to take over in case of an emergency, otherwise the squadron released their bombs on the signal of the lead aircraft, in this case McAllister.

George would again be dropping his bombs on V1 sites on 24 June 'which we clobbered'; on 6 July 'we were at 25,000 feet and experienced no flak on the bomb run. Our main bomb pattern fell to the left, some hits were scored in the target area. It was rated by the Commanding General as good, but it was a disappointment to me'; and on 8 July 'our bomb load fell right, left and on the target, but the ramp itself was untouched, the results were recorded as fair.'

Jack Scott and his crew also played their part in attacking the V1 supply sites (initially built as a staging post for the flying bombs between the rail heads and the launch ramps) at St Martin l'Hortier (17/18 June), Oisemont (23 June, 1 July) and Domleger (4 July). On the raid to St Martin l'Hortier the crew witnessed the V1 offensive on London from above.

Ken Handley's diary: Leaving around 11 p.m. we made 6,000 ft over base & set course at this height. From Reading we climbed to 14,000 ft & continued at 175 IAS to the target, a factory & depot turning out parts for the pilotless plane bombs. Over southern England we could see these planes being picked up by searchlights & followed while streams of red trace were fired at it. As it is so small the fire did not explode any in the air. I saw two of them explode. Colours of the day were fired by our own aircraft as they passed over this area. Cloud was low over the target area & the markers were only picked out by a glow. After bombing we slowly let down at 200 IAS. 'Jerry' was still sending his 'flying bombs' over on our return.

Bill Brown's crew also made their contribution, attacking the supply sites at Sautrecourt (16/17 June), and Oisemont (17 and 21 June) and the launch site at Bonnetot (24 June).

Unfortunately our crews' attacks, and indeed the vast majority of heavy bomber attacks on supply sites and launch sites, had had little effect on the German V1 launch rates. The supply site system was now virtually redundant, as the Germans, partly in response to the successful bombing of the 'ski' site system since December 1943, had devised an alternative way to supply their launch sites. The Germans had ensured they had enough launch sites in reserve to be able to maintain the momentum of the offensive. Clearly the Allies required a better targeting policy.

In addition to the direct attacks on German secret weapon targets, the senior Allied airmen felt there was an alternative way to counter the problem, and that was to conduct their own reprisal attacks. The intelligence summary at the AAC Conference on 20 June informed all present that although enemy reinforcements still appeared to be heading towards the battle, Germans resources were diminishing. The strategic bomber commanders seized their chance. Spaatz, Doolittle and Harris wanted to make a joint attack, with 1,200 American and 800 RAF heavies respectively, on Berlin the next day 'as a decisive blow'. Lengthy debate ensued. Tedder weighed in with his support, stating that Eisenhower was of a similar mind, but the tactical air force commanders were concerned about the diversion of fighters from the battle zone. Tedder finally summed up, stating that the:

> Hun had made fantastic efforts to bolster up morale by exaggerated reports about the effect of 'Divers' [the codename for V1s]. The Berlin raid would give us the opportunity to show that we cannot be diverted by Divers from our main effort to knock out German production. The weight of 'Diver' attacks up to date amounted to about 60 tons a day – the equivalent of one Mosquito attack upon Berlin. The weight of the planned raid on Berlin would be about 6,000 tons and might have a decisive effect upon the war.[89]

As it turned out, the RAF withdrew its heavies from the attack, owing to insufficient available fighter support. It was left to the Eighth Air Force to make the Allied demonstration of air power over Berlin.

Following their direct support to D-Day, Gary Miller's crew (96th Bomb Group) went to Tours and Le Touquet on 8 and 10 June respectively, and then contributed to the renewed offensive against German oil, attacking Hanover and Bremen on 15 and 18 June respectively. Since the opening of the Allied invasion the Eighth Air Force's focus had been on targets in support of the land campaign airfields, bridges and railyards; the attack on German oil on 18 June was the first major mission to a strategic target since the landings on the beaches. On 20 June the Eighth Air Force again went after oil. Gary Miller took his crew to Magdeburg, where his tail gunner had a near miss.

> *Bob Petty:* When we bombed Magdeburg, I was leaning way forward, on orders from the front seat, to see if bombs hit the oil refinery. Anyway, when I straightened up, I noticed a piece of flak had entered where my head usually was and it had gone out the other side.

Bob was fortunate. Other Eighth Air Force men were not, as 49 heavies were lost (1,402 despatched, 1,252 effective) on the penetration into German air space. The next day, 21 June Gary Miller took his crew on the V1 reprisal mission to Berlin.

They were detailed to blast an aircraft engine plant on the edge of the city, and Warren Berg would later describe the mission as a 'fairly uneventful day' for his formation. This was in stark contrast to John Howland's experience.

Two days earlier, Jim Tyson and his crew, leading a Combat Wing, took their B-17 to an oil refinery at Hamburg. Over Hamburg, despite heavy flak, the bombardier had visually identified the target and accurately placed his bomb load. Just after he had reported 'bombs away' a shell smashed through the B-17's nose and the Plexiglass shattered, flying into the bombardier's face and cutting him just below his right eye. Despite a great profusion of blood, the wound was not serious. The return flight proved uneventful.

> *John Howland:* We landed our Sunkist Special at Bassingbourn, and found quite a few holes in it. One close call was an 88-mm shell that passed through the leading edge of the wing just in front of the main wing spar. It was either a dud, or went on to explode somewhere above us. People on the ground said our plane whistled like a banshee when we came in for landing.

John Howland had now completed 29 missions. This was actually to have been his last in his tour. However he was required to make one more raid on 21 June and the day before Tedder, Spaatz, and Doolittle had decided where he was going: Berlin.

> *John Howland's diary, 21 June:* Our crew has been sweating out a trip home which we will make just three days from now if we live that long. Our orders have already been cut, and we were supposed to be finished with our tour of duty. But, someone screwed up, and we were sent to Ridgewell last night after a preliminary briefing for Berlin. I felt queer about the raid. There was a deep, unexplainable feeling within me that my number was up. The loss of Burch, Fox, Jonesy and other friends and acquaintances, the close calls, the exploding flak, blood in the cockpit and the everlasting pressure to do the job of lead navigating, no matter what happens, is tearing me to pieces. I feel worn out.

Under Attack

On the night of 21 June 1944 RAF Bomber Command sent two large forces to attack German synthetic oil plants. 61 Squadron's Don Street DFC was the captain of one of the Lancaster crews detailed to take part in the raid on Gelsenkirchen. That morning Don had been briefed about a new enemy combat tactic, where the German nightfighters operated in pairs, one committing the bomber to an evasive move, while the other seized an attacking opportunity when the bomber was at its most vulnerable point, the top or bottom of the corkscrew. Don discussed tactics with his crew telling them that:

> 'Apparently they find a victim, then one of them will attack from the rear along a standard fighter curve and of course if the bomber doesn't see him or have time to take action he is in trouble.' Both my gunners were lost for words at such a suggestion.

'On the other hand,' I continued, 'he is picked up and the corkscrew port or starboard is committed – now his number 2 is holding off waiting for a good opportunity to come in, which we will try not to give him by adding a bit of rough flying at the roll-over points. Let's get airborne and try it out.'

This they did during the night-flying test. When this was completed the aircraft was parked at dispersal to be fuelled and bombed up, and the crew went to the briefing, where the squadron commander revealed the target for the night.

'It's the Ruhr tonight chaps,' said the CO.
'Happy Valley,' whispered my wireless operator. A sardonic nickname given by aircrews to this heavily defended, highly industrialised area of Germany.

Following the briefing Don Street's crew gathered and discussed the details of the operation. It was their eighteenth trip and despite having such experience behind them Don was keen to keep his crew on their toes, telling them:

'This is our eighteenth trip, it's a time when you think you know it all – get cocky – we don't. From now until the twenty-fifth is a danger period remember! To survive we have to work at it – all the time.'

Don lifted his Lancaster into the air at 2309 hours that night and gained altitude. On the way to the target he felt concerned that the sky was bright that night, and warned his crew 'Pilot to crew – it's like daylight up here. Keep a good look out.' Don took his crew and aircraft on, and as they neared a turning point on the river Rhine, he called to his navigator.

'How are we doing, Dave?'
'Next course coming up, skipper – it will be 089 degrees compass.'
'OK.'
A minute or so later the intercom sounded. 'Turn onto 089 degrees – now, skipper.'
'Right.'
I set the new course on the electro-magnetic repeater compass and turned to starboard onto the new heading for turning point 'J' which was the last one before the run into the target. 'How are we for time?'
'We are about three minutes ahead of time, skipper.'
The significance of the navigator's reply was immediately obvious.
'We're ahead of the stream and must be a sitting duck for night-fighters – sharp look out everybody.'
But where? How did the gunners see anything in these conditions? To the starboard side of the aircraft was a black void, somewhere forward was the target, over to the port side the sky was light, a bright twilight with a background from the aurora-borealis flickering beyond the top end of Norway. Searching was almost impossible when their dark night vision was broken each time they swung their gun turrets; perhaps the nightfighters were having similar problems, even though the bombers would appear to them as silhouettes against a lighted screen.

Don kept his Lancaster on course, occasionally calling up and checking on his crew. The next turning point approached:

'Turning point 'J' in one minute, skipper, the new course will be 162 degrees,' called the navigator.

'Thanks, Nav. 162 degrees compass. This is the run-in track to the target, chaps; how long is the leg, Dave?'

'Twenty minutes, skip.'

I had a mixed feeling of relief and tension, the potentially dangerous leg was nearly over, but the target? What awaited there – along Happy Valley? -

The course change was made and now the black sky was to port and ahead leaving the bright sky astern on the starboard side. As I lined up the needle on the aircraft compass, the clear unhurried voice of the wireless operator broke the silence:

'Bandits, skipper, one above rear on the port side, and the other one same on the starboard – range about 1,000 yards.'

'Right – see them, rear gunner?'

'Not yet, skipper.'

'Mid-upper?'

'No.'

'The one on the starboard is coming in,' said the wireless operator, reading the range on his Monica screen.

'Eight hundred, seven, six.'

'Got him skipper, corkscrew starboard.' A pause by the rear gunner.

'Go, go.'

'Up the revs engineer, twenty-seven fifty.'

'A hundred on, skip,' said 'Wag'.

And the engines' synchronised drone changed to a drumming note of emergency as the practised drill commenced, down and turning, making it difficult for the fighter to turn inside the curve and bring his guns to bear on target.

'He's broken away, the port one is coming in, skip, seven hundred, six, five,' said the wireless operator, sedulously occupied with his screen, now a key member of the little battle group.

'Trying to catch us at the bottom when we roll,' I thought.

As I turned the aircraft from starboard downwards curve through to the port upwards curve, I pushed the control column forward violently, which caused the nose of the aircraft to drop momentarily; then up into the lumbering climb to port, thus creating an air turbulence that together with the six .303 Browning guns that were now filling the plane with acrid fumes, would encourage the enemy to keep at safe distance.

'Port bandit broken away, skipper,' came the voice of the wireless operator.

'They're both FW190s,' broke in the Scottish brogue of the mid-upper, as I hauled the heavy machine back onto course.

'They are still there – one port and one starboard – high and rear about 1,000 yards.' Despite the violent flying the wireless operator was keeping a good watch on his screen.

'Port one coming in 500 yards.'

'Got it,' picked up the rear gunner.

'Corkscrew port – Go! Go!'

And so the evasive action went through its paces, with every change in flying attitude intoned by myself to keep the crew informed that everything was under control. The same pattern as before, with the Lancaster's Brownings hammering away. Only part of the corkscrew pattern was flown, as before, when the Yorkshire voice of the wireless operator came over the intercom.

'They have broken off.' Then, 'Sitting on our rear port and starboard – high-range 1,000 yards.'

Then the third attack, this time from starboard again; it appeared that they were taking turns in committing the bomber whilst the other waited to come in for the kill. The kill was once more elusive and the game returned to the starting pattern. As the fourth attack commenced, and now tired and fed up with the whole business, I said:

'Pilot to rear gunner, let this one come in a bit nearer and shoot the damn thing down.'

'No, skip no!' said a horrified gunner.

'Why not, Gillie?'

'Look out and back to port.'

I dipped the port wing and took a quick look to the rear through the side perspex blister.

'See what you mean – OK let's go,' and the evasion commenced. The quick look had shown a sky that was seemingly full of bullet and cannon tracers curling inwards to the bomber as the FW190 closed in its attack, a sight that the gunners had witnessed on the occasion of each attack.

Back again on course. 'Where are they now?' I asked.

'They're – er – one to port and the other is – yes got him – both there again, skipper.'

'Thanks Doug. On your toes, gunners, they must be getting low in ammo now.'

'Skipper' – a new voice came through the intercom, that of the bomb aimer, who together with the navigator and flight engineer, had played no part in the past 10-12 minutes' drama – 'Do you think we should drop cookie?' (our 4,000 lb bomb).

'No certainly not! We haven't been hit; we'll drop it where it's supposed to go – on target.'

My reply was brusque, edged by the tension of fifteen minutes of action. I had total trust in my plane and crew, and there had been no time to dwell on the consequences of getting hit by enemy shells. Was it a lack of imagination, or the youthful certainty that it will not happen to us? Those that were not actively engaged in the battle could understandably be apprehensive – wondering whether the next attack would strike home and blow the plane apart.

The fifth attack developed, ran the course and died away. By this time after all the violent exercise, heaving at the controls of the heavy bomber, flying on instruments, I was getting angry and hot, my 'lucky' unlined pigskin gloves – strictly non-service pattern – a present from an old aunt, were wet with perspiration. The thought 'they will be difficult to put on the next time I fly', flitted across my mind as the wireless operator called.

'Port bandit, skipper.'

The rear gunner picked up the drill: 'Got him, skipper – stand-by – corkscrew port. Go! Go!'

From the wireless operator: 'Starboard one closing, skipper,' and almost immediately, 'Both breaking away downwards – they're out of range – had enough, I suppose.'

'Thanks, Doug! Well done everybody,' I acknowledged as I brought the plane on to course and edged it up to 20,500 feet ready for the run into the target. 'Twenty-six fifty revs, engineer. Everything OK, Wag?'

The engineer who had stood by me during the engagement, except on a few occasions when he had floated off his feet in a negative 'gee' created by a violent downthrust of the aircraft, reached down and adjusted the propeller controls down a hundred revs on each of the four engines.

'Twenty-six fifty, skipper and all OK.'

'Target in four and a half minutes,' from the navigator.

'OK, Dave – how are we for time now?'

'About right now, but don't lose time like that ever again, will you!'

A Canadian just out of college, his plaintive plea was semi-serious as he suffered with air sickness that afflicted him on nearly every trip. We braced ourselves for the run up to and through the target, where careful straight and level flying was required, a period when the aircraft was most vulnerable to enemy action.

'Rear gunner, OK?'

'OK, Skip – but out of ammo.'

'Nay worry,' growled the mid-upper. 'I've got twenty rounds left.'

'Keep an extra sharp look out everyone,' I said.

The bomb run and flight home proved uneventful for Don Street and his crew, but for many such engagements with the enemy proved fatal. From the force of 133 Lancasters, 37 were downed, a staggering 28% loss rate.

Early on the morning of 21 June just over 1,200 American heavy bombers, from all three bomb divisions, crewed by 12,000 airmen, assembled over England. The force was separated into four, which we will describe as the first, second, third and fourth task forces; each was sent to attack targets in the Berlin area. Throughout the trip the bomber force could expect continual fighter escort, and the Eighth eventually despatched a total of 1,269 P-38s, P-47s and P-51s. Jim Tyson's crew, accompanied by a Major Halsey as the ACW and Ted Homdrom as John Howland's co-navigator, took their position in the second wing due over the target (from the 1st Bomb Division), part of the second task force sent to Berlin.

The Eighth's heavy bombers left the English coast over Norfolk, crossed the North Sea, and the 1st Bomb Division then headed east after passing between Kiel and Hamburg. Up until that point John Howland felt comforted by the presence of a P-47 escort, but after the easterly turn towards Berlin, it appeared to him that an expected P-51 group had failed to show. Shortly afterwards another expected fighter escort seemed notably absent. In fact one flight of the 361st FG had rendezvoused as detailed with the second task force, but the remainder of the group mistakenly initially attached themselves to three combat wings of the first task force. When the second task force reported it was east of Muritz Lake, the errant flights of the 361st FG managed to fly on and meet up with the rear combat wings of its intended task force. As the heavy bomber airmen in the leading elements of the 1st BD neared the target, however, they found themselves dangerously exposed, and German fighters seized their chance.

When John looked up from his charts, he was rather bemused to see what appeared to be two wings in front of them. However he quickly realised that one of the formations was not friendly; in fact it comprised twin-engined German fighters, approximately 75 to 80 Me410s. He kept watching as the hostile formation passed to their right, and out of range, then he lost sight of the enemy as they formed up behind, at six o'clock level, preparing to launch their attack.

John Howland's diary, 21 June: I couldn't see them because the attack was from the rear, but I could see their 20mm shells exploding all around us. I could also hear the chatter of the top turret guns and the gunners calling off B-17s going down and German fighters as well. It was a wild attack, my adrenalin was flowing freely.

The German fighters exacted their toll, as numerous B-17s fell out of formation, but eventually the fighters stopped. The battered wing, including Jim Tyson's B-17, with two engines playing up, proceeded on to the target and the start of the bomb run.

John Howland's diary, 21 June: A few minutes later we hit the toughest barrage of flak I've ever had to fly through. We didn't have the benefit of chaff dropped by preceding wings because there was only one wing ahead of us, and they attacked targets near the Tempelhof Airdrome south of the city. Ted was leaning over Charlie's shoulder trying to help him pick out the target when suddenly there was a helluva bang. A piece of flak whizzed by Ted after making a small hole in the Plexiglass nose. Charlie was cool as a cucumber and didn't look up from his bombsight.

Just at 'bombs away', another piece struck the nose of the ship and blew out the front window on the right side and made a long gash in the aluminium skin. Ted was hit in the right eye by flying Plexiglass. Just then I heard Major Halsey say, 'Let's make a correction to the left here.'

A left turn at that point would have meant an extra 2 or 3 minutes in the flak area so I pushed my mike button and said, (although I don't recall it) 'for Christ's sake no. Turn right to 315 degrees!' (Major Halsey reminded me when we were back on the ground. We both got a laugh out of it.)

I then called Charlie and asked him to let me take over his seat so I could do Ted's pilotage and get us out of there by point to point navigation while we gave Ted as much first aid as he could. About that time we received two more bursts close by and I heard some flak whang into us. Then came a hissing sound, not unlike a blowout. Once again, I thought

we'd had it; but it was only a portable oxygen bottle knocked out. Shortly
after that we cleared the flak area, which was tremendous relief.

Elsewhere in the skies over Berlin, Warren Berg was busy guiding his pilot and
crew to their respective target. They met little opposition of note but they were
able to witness the less comfortable experience of some of the Eighth Air Force
colleagues, as Warren Berg recorded in some notes made after the mission:

> Today we led the 96th 'B' Group in an attack on an aircraft engine plant
> on the edge of Berlin. The whole 8th Air Force pasted Berlin and the
> surrounding area. It was a great show. We came in on our target with no
> trouble at all. It was wide open before us. Our bombardier laid his 'eggs'
> squarely on the center. Good work. Flak was quite heavy and five ships in
> the lead Group went down. We didn't get scratched. The swarms of
> bombers going in on the target were tremendous. One can hardly believe
> there are so many airplanes.

Meanwhile in John Howland's damaged aircraft, the number 2 and 3 engines
were playing up:

> *John Howland:* . . . so Jim let down slowly to 22,000 ft where they picked
> up full power and started working fine again. Others weren't so lucky.
> About 5 minutes out of Berlin we spotted a B-17 below us, on fire. Saw 8
> chutes come out. One of them didn't open fully. Then the plane went into
> a dive and I lost sight of it. Saw another plane coming out below with a
> feathered engine. Don't know whether he made it back or not. Altogether,
> three additional ships were lost out of the formation to flak over the target
> area.

Despite some concerns about damaged cables, Jim managed to bring his aircraft
back to England without any serious incident.

> *John Howland's diary, 21 June:* General Gross was one of the first to
> come out to our plane. We parked it right in front of C hangar because Jim
> knew that was where the ship was headed for sorely needed repairs. It was
> a mess with 100 or more flak holes and 20mm shell holes all over it. Ted
> wasn't hurt badly, but he did have to stay in hospital for a few days since
> the Plexiglass irritated his eyes.

Both our crews managed to return from the mission that day, although 45
American heavy bombers and crews did not. The second task force had lost 16
B-17s, of which the 91st Bomb Group contributed 5. However it had been the
third task force that had experienced the most aerial combat, attacked just before
and over the target. Despite the presence of fighter escorts heavy bombers fell
and eventually 19 B-24s would fail to return. The first task force proceeded to
bases in Russia after attacking their targets, having experienced little opposition,
and only one B-17 was lost. However part of this force was tracked by a German
reconnaissance aircraft, and whilst on the ground at Poltova a German bombing
raid destroyed 44 of the 72 B-17s, and 26 were damaged. Incredibly there were
no American casualties, but 25 Russians were killed. The fourth task force had
the good fortune of avoiding any encounters with enemy aircraft, but lost 9
aircraft to flak.

The Eighth Air Force would later assess the results of the bombing as good, but the mission did not have the 'decisive effect upon the war' that the senior air commanders hoped for. Without RAF Bomber Command's contribution, the scale of attack obviously fell considerably short of what was needed. Nevertheless the Allies could use the propaganda in an attempt to bolster the morale of the Londoners enduring the German V1 attacks. Spaatz probably could also gain some satisfaction from noting that the Eighth Air Force claimed 49 enemy aircraft destroyed, 23 probables and 32 damaged. However the mission, taking into account the losses of aircraft bombed at Poltova, had been extremely costly and Spaatz later conceded it as the 'best attack the Luftwaffe ever made' on the American Air Force.[90]

For John Howland, 21 June 1944 was the last time he went to war in the skies over western Europe. Some of his colleagues in the crew would later continue the fight, but John could now look forward to a return to his country.

> *John Howland's diary, 21 June:* It was a helluva way to wrap up a tour of duty. However, it made no difference. We had successfully beaten the odds, and won our deadly game of tag. We were home free.

Gary Miller's crew were also nearing completion of their tour. The day after the Berlin mission, Eighth Air Force bombers went after V1 targets, oil dumps and airfields in north-west France, and his crew were detailed for the oil dump at Gennevilliers. The crew then enjoyed a two-week break from missions, before blasting a V1 site in the Pas de Calais on 6 July. On 14 July they completed their last first-tour mission, by making their contribution to Operation *Cadillac* as one of 359 B-17s sent to southern France, to unload 3,700 containers filled with arms for the Resistance. Some of Gary's crew, including Warren Berg, would return to operations later in the war, as detailed at the end of this book.

CHAPTER 16

SUPPORTING THE ARMY

On 11 June 1944 Hitler granted permission for the 2nd SS Panzer Corps, comprising the 9th and 10th SS Panzer Divisions, to leave the Russian front and head for Normandy. The route, by rail, would take the armour through Poland, then Germany into eastern France via Strasbourg and Saarbrücken. This reinforcement was under constant scrutiny from Allied Intelligence and rail targets east of Paris began to receive higher targeting priority.

In the second half of June 1944 RAF Bomber Command sent three large forces to German oil targets and there were numerous attacks made on German secret weapon installations in north-west France. In addition attacks on key rail targets were maintained. One such attack was to block the aforementioned German panzer deployment. At the AAC conference meetings on 25, 26 and 27 June the heavy bomber forces were requested to block the 2nd SS Panzer Corps' approach.

At this time the seeds of a major disagreement between Leigh-Mallory and the American heavy bomber commanders, were planted. On 22 June Leigh-Mallory had recorded in his diary:

> The Germans are undoubtedly making use of the Meuse railway system and the lines running through Rheims and Châlons. I was always doubtful about that area because I could not induce the American Eighth Air Force to bomb it in sufficient strength. I don't think they have done the job properly for they sent over penny packets instead of large forces. Now we are doing our best to catch up on this situation.

By 27 June Leigh-Mallory's frustration had grown:

> What we are now doing is paying for the American failure to bomb the railways in the Moselle and Metz area in accordance with the plan that I had drawn up for the battle. I am sure that if we had gone for those railways in the same way as we went for the others, the German rail movements would not be nearly so considerable as in fact they are now.
>
> The Americans are a strange lot. They are still obsessed with the notion that to bomb Germany in daylight is the proper course. I have to humour them, and this I explained to Tedder. If I let them go off and bomb some German target very heavily, then I may induce them next time to put a really big effort on to some railway target instead of merely attacking it with a dozen aircraft or so. The Americans don't like being under the command of an Englishman, and that is a fact which I have to face.[91]

Certainly, as we have seen, Spaatz was focusing his main attention on German oil and the aircraft industry, and by doing so he hoped to engage the Luftwaffe and inflict further losses on the reeling German air force. And, as evidence would later show, he was succeeding. On 29 June Spaatz despatched 1,150 American heavies, supported by 779 fighters, to oil and aircraft targets in and around

Leipzig. Leigh-Mallory could not contain his despair.

> *Leigh-Mallory's diary, 29 June 1944:* Today was the first day when it has
> been possible to use bombers and fighter-bombers in daylight, for some
> considerable time, owing to the slight but definite improvement in the
> weather. I suppose, however, that it was for this reason that the American
> 8th Air Force with all its fighter support and 2 Groups of the American 9th
> Air Force, chose to go to Leipzig and bomb aircraft factories. This they
> did without reference to myself. I cannot but regard this as serious, for I
> wanted to attack without delay the big rail movement east of Paris, which
> I have told you about. To do so today, I have had to take squadrons from
> the Tactical Air Force, though they are committed to a big programme of
> immediate support to the Army bombing enemy movement in the area
> west and south-west of Paris. However there it is. The Americans have
> gone off and I can do nothing about it. Today I have not had all the Air
> Forces that I should have had to carry out what, in my view, is my
> essential task, to help the Army to win their battle.
>
> The fact is . . . the Americans have no idea of balance. They want to
> attack aircraft factories, come what may, so they attack them. It is a
> childish attitude, for the Luftwaffe is for the present at any rate no sort of
> menace, and the German Army is. Although the papers talk of a 7-mile
> advance by Monty, I cannot myself make it at most more than 8,000 yards.
> Moreover they are already beginning to talk about enemy counter-attacks,
> and this does not seem to me the right way to refer to an all-out offensive.
> If they are talking about enemy counter-attacks already, then it looks to
> me as though they are not too happy. I hope to God I am wrong, but I have
> a dreadful feeling that if the weather and American insouciance allow the
> German Army build-up to continue too long, it may prove very difficult to
> break out of the beachhead, and another Anzio may be created.[92]

However when Leigh-Mallory states that the German air force is 'no sort of
menace', it is precisely because of the Eighth Air Force attacks in Germany and
the attrition battles, that the AEAF was enjoying such freedom of operation over
Normandy.

As it was, Leigh-Mallory turned to RAF Bomber Command to target
railyards and on 28 June RAF Bomber Command was called upon to bombard
railyards at Metz and Blainville-sur-l'Eau in eastern France. Optimism about the
effect of the Allied bombing of enemy communications remained high at the 28
June AAC meeting. Enemy POWs were revealing under interrogation that
movement into the battle area was being considerably disrupted owing to the rail
attacks and the need to use alternative routes. The night of 28/29 June would see
the RAF again trying to seriously disrupt a major German reinforcement. This it
would achieve, but at a cost. It was a cost that Harris wanted the rest of the world
to know about.

Leslie Hood was a radar (2nd) navigator on Pilot Officer Spierenburg's 582
Squadron Lancaster and took part in the raid on the Blainville-sur-l'Eau railyards
on 28/29 June. Shortly after crossing the French coast the first fighter attacked,

with no damage resulting. Another attack followed, again with no damage. Whilst this was going on the mid-upper gunner started witnessing, and reporting to his crew, a number of aircraft falling, in flames, from the night sky.

Leslie Hood: At about 0135 hours the rear gunner gave warning of another fighter attack, and though the warning was short, we managed to corkscrew; but at the same moment I heard and felt the aircraft being hit, though I saw no damage. That was the last time I heard the rear gunner speak. The aircraft began to vibrate very badly, pointing to (as I thought at the time) the engines having been hit or the props broken. We were still losing height and may possibly have been turning.

The pilot said, 'You had better come up and help me, engineer,' but there was no reply from him. The pilot then said, 'Prepare to abandon aircraft', so I put on my 'chute and tore away the forward blackout curtain, and saw that all the starboard wing was ablaze. Only the 1st navigator and the wireless operator and myself acknowledged the skipper's order; nothing being heard from the rear and mid-upper gunners.

The skipper then said, 'Will somebody please come up and help me,' so I took off my helmet and went forward to him where I undid his Sutton harness and pulled the straps back over his shoulder. I think that during this time the pilot must have given the 'Abandon aircraft' order, but owing to the fact that I had removed my helmet, I did not hear it. The 1st navigator tapped on my back as he wanted to get out, so I touched the pilot's hand and pointed downwards. He answered with a brief nod. I went down into the bomb hatch and knelt down in front of the escape hatch, which I found already open, and facing forward, I took hold of each side, pushed my head through, and went out.

I remember turning over and over as I fell, but I did not pull the rip-cord immediately as I had often pictured myself as doing. I tried to find out when I was face upwards before pulling the rip-cord, but was unable to do so. Eventually I did pull the rip-cord after falling free for possibly 3,000 feet, possibly less, but definitely no more. The 'chute opened with a loud bang, and the jerk, of which I had heard so much, was scarcely perceptible. I looked down and could see the ground rather indistinctly, and a very long way off; but my attention was taken up with what appeared to be a much more serious matter. I was swinging from side to side in my harness and at the end of each swing I could hear an ominous tearing noise, and being afraid that it may be the 'chute itself tearing, I decided not to look up in case I saw a large hole somewhere in the canopy – nor did I look upwards at it once during the whole descent.

As I neared the ground, I could see the field in which I was to land. I could see in it rows of hut-like structures, and was quite worried in case I should have to land in a German army camp; luckily they proved to be very large stooks of corn. When I was at what I judged to be 200 feet above the ground, I suddenly hit it; my knees came up into my chest and I rolled over on to my back. I wasn't hurt at all, beyond a slight pain in my knee when it was bent. I had some difficulty in releasing myself from my harness, and it was then that I discovered the cause of the mysterious tearing noise I had heard when coming down – the shoulder strap of my harness had somehow caught in my mae west, and it was that which was tearing.

I noticed, as I was freeing myself, that an aircraft was burning on the ground in the same field south-west of where I was, and judged it to be about a quarter of a mile away. Once out of my harness, I dragged the 'chute and harness into the shadow of one of the haystacks and began to dig away at the straw at the bottom of it. Once the hole was formed and big enough, I stuffed the parachute into it and noticed as I did so that one of the lengths of shroud-line had not freed itself from the pack, but so great was my haste that its significance did not dawn on me until later.

I sat on the ground and pulled my trousers out of my flying boots and tucked my flying boots underneath them. I then walked to some trees in the north-west corner of the field, shedding as I went my tapes and crown, name plate, NAAFI badge, and RAF buttons from my epaulettes. I tried to tear off the epaulettes themselves but was unable to do so. Once over the trees, I sat in a ditch, took off my scarf, jerkin, and flying pullover, and put on my collar and tie. My pullover I hid in a ditch, my scarf I wrapped around my body, then I tore off my epaulettes and put on my blouse again. I then took stock of my position.

Leslie Hood was one of four of the crew who survived the combat with the enemy fighter. Both gunners and the wireless operator lost their lives. From the survivors all managed to evade capture except for the pilot who saw out the war behind German barbed wire.

On the same raid Flight Sergeant Manstoff was acting as the flight engineer on a 77 Squadron Halifax. It is worth noting that he was of Jewish faith, which probably had a bearing on the actions he describes below:

We were shot-up and on fire, when the skipper ordered us to abandon. I was wearing an 'observer' type chute and forgot to get my head out of the way as I went out. I remember not a thing until I came to in the back seat of a car being driven by a German officer with another sitting beside him. They must have literally thrown me into the car for I found myself jammed up against a wooden crate in which were a variety of bottles. After my senses cleared I assessed my situation and then eased one of the bottles free, and with this I 'brained' the driver and then passed out again as the car careered along and then left the road completely out of control. Recovering some time later I saw the two Germans were still in the land of dreams so I took the opportunity to scuttle away.

I walked as far as I could before exhaustion decided that I should seek help and eventually I knocked at the door of a farmhouse. The occupants were French and friendly. They sheltered me for the night and the next day they arranged for me to be taken elsewhere in a closed vehicle and I then spent the next three months in the attic of a house. It was whilst there that I became aware of having a very painful neck but, as no medical treatment was to be had, I had to grin and bear it. I was eventually passed down the escape line and back to England. After the usual debriefing I was given a medical and asked if I had any aches and pains. I told the doctors that I had suffered from a very sore neck, which was not then bothering me except that I could not hold my head up straight. I was examined and after X-ray it was discovered that my neck had in fact been broken. It was pointed out to me that the only way to straighten my neck would be to break it again to be re-set. It was stressed that this would probably kill me anyway. Needless to say I declined the offer.[93]

Above are two incidents involving the loss of aircraft on this night. In fact RAF Bomber Command suffered an 8.7% loss rate from the attacks on Metz and Blainville-sur-l'Eau, a total of 20 aircraft and crews. RAF Bomber Command's commander-in-chief was more than just aware of the losses his force was suffering in support of *Overlord*. Certainly Leigh-Mallory was pleased with RAF Bomber Command's commitment; his diary entry of 29 June recorded: 'Last night, thank heaven, Bomber Command attacked Metz and Blainville and this relieved my mind a lot, for as I have already told you, they are very important train centres at this moment, when the enemy is engaged on using the French eastern network of railways.' But at the AAC Conference on 30 June, Harris wanted greater recognition for his airmen and aired his concerns:

> Air Chief Marshal Harris said that he wished to complain of the quite inadequate attention given in the Press to air operations. This was a very important matter because of its bearing on the morale of aircrews. Bomber Command operations had played a very big part in the success of the landing on D-Day . . . There was a tendency on the part of the Press and the Public to think that the real war was the war going on on the ground, but an attack on a marshalling yard must be regarded as a battle and the losses were often more serious than the loss of two destroyers.

Harris also asked for greater recognition of Coastal Command's efforts stating that 'the proportion of RAF losses to Army losses was about 3-1 and yet the Army seemed to get all the credit'. The minutes of the meeting record a general air of agreement with Harris's view. It was felt that focusing on publicising just the aircrew casualty rates could adversely effect morale. Therefore any publicity must be made in combination with an appreciation of the Allied air forces' achievements. Harris was asked to make representation to the Air Ministry on the kind of publicity he sought. The minutes of the meeting recorded the conclusion of the matter: 'Air Chief Marshal Harris said that this could not be regarded as a trivial matter, because of its important effect on the morale of aircrews. He thought the time had come to have a first class row.'[94]

Bail Out

Pete Smith was a flight engineer on Pilot Officer Wilf Gay's 428 Squadron Lancaster on the raid to the railyards at Villeneuve St Georges, in the suburbs of Paris, on the night of 4/5 July 1944. As Gay flew his Lancaster across the Channel, his crew remained on high alert, as they had already had a nasty experience with a flak ship on their first operation. On this night, however, the Channel crossing was peaceful as they approached the French coast and opposition.

Pete Smith: We must have been three or four minutes behind the leading kites as, still over water, we watched that deadly and much feared belt of searchlights switch on and start probing the sky, eager to find their prey . . . Perhaps it was a terrible thing to do, but then in war most things are and, anyway, perhaps such prayers are ignored, but I used to pray hard that some poor devil up ahead would be caught and keep those beams busy while we sneaked through. And I'm sure the boys behind us did the same thing!

This night, however, we crossed the coast with little more than a few bursts of flak around us, none of it accurate enough to do any damage. Apart from the devilry it was a lovely night with good visibility with the big bombers' moon now high and all seemed fairly quiet. Perhaps it was going to be one of those lucky trips when things went right all the way. These were my thoughts as I stood there next to the skipper, having stowed my seat to allow a clear passage from the nose of the plane to the rear.

The rest of us knew nothing of what was happening until both gunners, having spotted Jerry more or less at the same moment, barked their orders over the intercom: 'Corkscrew to starboard! Corkscrew to starboard!'

These were the words dreaded by all bomber crews and meant only one thing – a German fighter coming in for the kill on the starboard side.

Immediately, we banked and dived steeply and I had to hang on desperately to prevent myself from floating off around the plane. I could hear the staccato bursts from our totally inadequate .303's and wondered if our gunners could pull off a miracle.

We pulled out of the first manoeuvre and on the skipper's orders I moved the throttles through the gate into the full-power position once more, held it there for as long as I dare and then back again to the safe maximum speed notch. Had we shaken him off? No chances – down again and bank steeply. Was he still with us?

My answer came, forceful and devastating as his cannon shells tore into the plane. All hell let loose is an apt description, if one has had a taste of hell. This was it. There were bright flashes everywhere – green, red, white as the various instruments were hit and disintegrated. The bomb aimer had been standing somewhere behind me taking readings from the various 'aids' we carried and I wondered if he was still in one piece. The smoke made visibility poor.

We'd been losing height rapidly in our efforts to shake off this murderer and were just levelling off once more when his second burst came. I had caught a glimpse of fire out on the wing and wondered why we hadn't yet blown up. With most of our petrol load still in the tanks and five tons of incendiaries and high explosives in our bomb bay it was a miracle we were still in the air in more or less one piece.

The second burst almost ripped the side off us and I could see out of the corner of my eye more explosions in the fuselage down towards the stern. I now noticed that Chuck, the bomb aimer, was still there, standing motionless; there was nothing he could do and he had, by this time, been badly wounded.

I was still doing my best to keep some sort of upright position so that I could control the throttles, but with so much manoeuvring, diving and levelling out was difficult. Then something hit me.

It felt as though someone had driven a red-hot poker into my back as well as a hundred nails. A few more shells had burst behind me. Whether or not we were pulling out of yet another dive I didn't know – for by this time I wasn't sure which way we were flying – when I went down in a heap. Perhaps the sudden shock or blast helped. The intercom had now gone dead on us as the shells had torn the wiring to pieces.

I tried to struggle to my feet. Strangely, I was not panicky and my mind was working fast. Was I really here or in the middle of some ghastly nightmare? There was fire everywhere. Why hadn't we blown up? No, it was no dream, the pain was real, or I should have woken up by this time. I was really here then, in the middle of this noisy, raging, bursting hell. So this was the way I was to die, no funeral; probably no body after we'd hit the deck and exploded!

Pete Smith managed to get back to his feet. The Lancaster was still diving and Wilf Gay was desperately struggling with the controls.

Pete Smith: Wilf was now banging me on the shoulder trying to attract my attention. I instinctively moved closer to him but with helmet and oxygen masks on it was impossible to hear any sound of voices. He was shaking his head in hopelessness and after pointing in the direction of the escape hatch, waved his arm indicating that we should get out fast. At the same time, as though to confirm what he meant, Chuck nudged me in the back.

Pete made his way to the nose of the Lancaster where the navigator was fighting in vain to open the escape hatch.

I suddenly realised that he was trying to lift it up as a trap door. I banged him on the back as a sign to get the hell out of it.

There were bolts holding the hatch to the fuselage and these had to be withdrawn and the hatch jettisoned. No doubt it had rarely been opened since the plane had been built and was therefore stiff. After managing to withdraw the bolts I found the hatch itself would not move. Time was getting short. Any minute we might blow up and if we did not blow up, I had no idea what height we were at and how long it would be before we hit the deck.

I stood up and held on to the nearest thing while I kicked frantically at the stubborn hatch. It finally gave and disappeared as a mighty rush of ice cold air swept into the plane with the roar of the engines.

Towards the rear of the Lancaster, wireless operator Steve Yates and gunners Harry Pritchard and Stan Swartz heard their captain order them to bail out.

Steve Yates: I clipped on my parachute and made for the rear door, which I found to be jammed. Harry Pritchard and I managed to free it and prepared to get out. By this time, Stan was climbing out of the rear turret and Harry beckoned Stan to follow.

When I met Harry again at Bayeux, he explained that he thought he had killed me for as I sat on the ledge with my legs outside the aircraft, about to push myself out against the slipstream, I felt a thump on my back and out I went. Evidently, thinking I was stuck, Harry had kicked me out of the aircraft!

Pete Smith: Removing my helmet, I quickly checked that my pack was securely clipped onto my chest, then placed my arms on the pack, holding it. I paused only for a quick glance at the vague outlines of Bill and Chuck standing there – and dived head first through that black little hole, praying hard.

The next thing I remembered was a loud crack, presumably as my 'chute opened and there I found myself, hanging in space with no visible means of support.

I caught a glimpse of a ball of fire disappearing up and away from me that must have been the plane. No sign of any other parachutes. Then I became aware of the noise all around and for a moment, panic seized me. I was in the midst of the main bomber stream! Those were aircraft engines and I waited in horror for them to tear into my 'chute. But our bomber had lost a lot of height, I reasoned, and must have been below the main stream when we jumped. No doubt the noise seemed nearer at that altitude. I calmed down a bit.

I felt bitterly cold, having no flying suit on, only my ordinary battle dress, and yet, I could feel the warm perspiration running down my body. This, I later discovered, was blood. My back still hurt and my arm too. It was obvious that a load of something had entered my body and as it was difficult to breathe at that height, due to the lack of oxygen, I was certain my right lung had gone.

As Pete neared the ground a slight drift fortunately took him away from a river, unfortunately towards some trees.

Speeding through those branches, I thought, would surely break a few bones and probably leave me dangling at any height from the ground. While thus engrossed in my calculations I hit the ground and felt a searing pain shoot up my leg before all the wind was knocked out of my body.

Pete Smith began to think of evasion, and despite considerable pain, mainly from a suspected cracked bone in his leg, he tried to find friendly help; unluckily he ran into a German patrol and, following medical treatment, saw out the war as a POW. The bomb aimer also attempted evasion and was initially hid for the night by a friendly Frenchman, but the next day the seriousness of his wounds, and necessity of aid, meant the Germans were called in. Steve Yates, the navigator and the mid-upper gunner all successfully evaded capture. Wilf Gay lost his life, still at the controls when the aircraft hit the ground. The rear gunner had also failed to get out.

Harris fuelled the air force publicity row by firing off a letter to Portal on 1 July: 'I think you should be aware of the full depth of feeling that is being aroused by the lack of adequate or even reasonable credit to the RAF in particular, and the Air Forces as a whole, for their efforts in the Invasion.' In his letter Harris took up the cause for all the RAF commands who were:

> agreed on the hopeless inadequacy of the publicity and of the official credit given to the Air Forces for their part in this battle, which is in fact so far mainly an air battle. I find it very hard to understand why the proportions of effort put into the invasion battle by the Armies and the Air Forces respectively are not more widely understood officially, and as a consequence better appreciated.
>
> Let me give you an example. Up to June 28th in this battle (which is regarded both officially and publicly as mainly a land battle), the British Army has lost some 2,500 killed; the U.S. Army approximately 5,000. In April, May and June which are the three months in which my Command has been engaged almost entirely on invasion work (including the Rocket and Flying Bomb work which must be regarded as part of the invasion war although the casualties on those targets are negligible) my Command alone had lost 6,038 killed, wounded and missing. Of those, 5,804 are missing. Of the missing we know from experience only about 20% survive. Therefore my Command alone in this invasion war has suffered nearly 2$^{1}/_{2}$ times the number killed as the whole of the British Army and more than the U.S. Army: add to this T.A.F., Coastal, A.D.G.B. and 38 Group.
>
> Yet when it comes to official communiques and the balancing of publicity the country as a whole and the world at large is quite entitled to think that this is almost entirely a land war with the Air Forces doing what they can to assist; whereas in fact they are bearing the brunt.
>
> We know that the success up to date of the invasion has been mainly due to the operations of the Air Forces in making it possible for the Armies to get ashore and establish their bridgehead. We know that the German formations, when they eventually arrive in the line, are bedraggled, exhausted, under strength and largely deprived of the necessities of fighting and of life by the fearful difficulties encountered on the communications into the battle area, due almost entirely to the Air Forces.
>
> We know also that it was only possible for the landing to be made if the shore batteries were knocked out and if the convoys were protected from the operations of German surface and submarine forces. The successful efforts of Coastal Command on the submarines are well known to you, but outside a very limited official circle not a word is allowed out about that astonishing success by an Air Force Command. The Admiralty can fill the papers and the cinemas with the doings and the comings and goings of Captain Walker's submarine hunting group, but if the RAF sink 16 submarines it is all too secret to mention. My remark is as malicious as the Admiralty's attitude. We know now that the permanent coastal batteries, which could have jeopardised the landing, were pulverised by

the bombing of my Command and the Americans. We have had ample first-hand evidence of that. We know also that the surface fleet of the Germans in the Channel has been virtually annihilated by bomber attacks. We know also of the vast cordon that has been drawn around the German forces engaged against our bridgehead, by the wholesale destruction of communications and the direct destruction of their resources on the roads and railways as they have attempted to reinforce the battle area. By the same token some few of us know of the vast effect on the whole campaign which has been exercised by Pointblank and indeed by all the bombing in the past. There is ample evidence of the tanks destroyed by our rocket aircraft, and of the holocaust of enemy M.T.

In sum, therefore, both in military effort, and certainly in casualties, the subscription towards the invasion made by the Air Forces has far exceeded that made so far by the Ground Forces.

Nevertheless, both the official credit and certainly the story as the public gets it does not lead anybody to suspect that the Air Forces have played anything but an ancillary part in the whole campaign.

I realise this matter because I find myself in entire agreement with the view expressed by Commanders of other Air Commands that it is not possible for ever to maintain the morale of our first class fighting crews, who have put up such an amazing contribution in this operation, if they are to be denied continuously in the future, as they have been so largely denied in the past, any tithe of recognition officially or publicly, of the vast and successful efforts that they are making.

I am sorry to have to raise this matter at all. I have intended to put it frankly and if I have put it over-bluntly, that is not intentional, and I am unrepentant.

I have no personal ambition that has not years ago been satisfied in full. But I for one cannot forbear a most emphatic protest against the grave injustice which is being done to my crews.

There are 10,500 aircrew in my operational squadrons. In three months we have lost over half that number. They have a right that their story should be adequately told, and it is a military necessity that it should be.

Yours ever

(Sgd.) Bert [Sir Arthur Harris]

The letter certainly initiated some action in the Air Ministry. More air staff time was to be given to publicity. Portal had put constraints on publicity early in March 1944 so as to avoid the release of sensitive information, forbidding any press communication without his permission and the approval of the contents. Similar restrictions had not been imposed in the Army and Navy. A special meeting was set up on 10 July, with the Secretary of State for Air, Sir Archibald Sinclair, to address the situation, one outcome being the relaxation of the imposed constraints. A parliamentary question and answer were promised. Senior officers were granted permission to give talks to the press, and visits to RAF Bomber Command facilities were allowed. The Americans on the other hand did not appear to be suffering from the press sidelining. At the 10 July meeting it was noted that:

> The USAAF is larger than the RAF engaged and often the operations lend themselves to better presentation; the number of publicity staff provided by the American air forces is about seven or more times as many as those provided for the RAF. They are a very alert and alive staff, and do not, I think, have to face such stringent security considerations as we do. The term 'AEAF' tends to hide the part taken by the RAF. The Americans' photography is more extensive and spectacular; they provide facilities for correspondents to fly on outstanding daylight operations more freely than we do. The Americans are far more forthcoming and generous in the treatment of their correspondents and facility visits than we are. 2nd TAF had had to curtail facility visits; Bomber Command has recently ruled out all facility visits, while advance notice of operations has not been so freely obtainable for correspondents.

On 12 July Portal replied to Harris, generally agreeing with much of what Harris said:

> Publicity for the actual operations undertaken has, however, suffered partly because personal conferences by Cs-in-C and senior officers were, for the time being, laid under a ban. This was my decision. Shortly before Overlord some unwise disclosures were made to Press Correspondents. I considered it essential to take no further risks whatever over the security of Overlord. Now that Overlord is launched this decision is under review and has indeed already been relaxed to some extent.

Portal, however, was critical of senior officers:

> The record of conferences by senior officers of the Services has not been altogether happy and we have been let in for trouble on more than one occasion. I am hopeful however, that we shall be able to devise suitable safeguards.
>
> In the present stage of the war, now that the long awaited Second Front has been opened, we cannot expect to monopolise the news as we did.

Portal questioned whether or not Commanders-in-Chief were making full use of their public relations staff:

> who are expert in writing but they need material and personal guidance from commanders and staff. I see no difficulty in your helping the PROs concerned to produce the articles you outline in your letter either as articles or as an address by them to correspondents. But the article should, I think, avoid drawing a comparison between RAF and Army casualties.[95]

Despite the Air Ministry's efforts to improve publicity, RAF Bomber Command's profile in the press continued to diminish as the success of the land advances stole the headlines. In Mark Connelly's recent study of RAF Bomber Command he examines the portrayal of Harris's force in the media and notes that 'the invasion brought about a marked reduction in Bomber Command's press coverage. With hindsight it can be said it was the beginning of the eclipse of

Bomber Command as the nation's favourite topic of conversation.'[96] The airmen of RAF Bomber Command can rightly claim a disservice. They deserved greater recognition for their contribution. They still do!

The knowledge that the 2nd SS Panzer Corps was on the move to Normandy, in late June 1944, was one of the main reasons Montgomery sought to keep pressure on the German defensive line around Caen. As such as June neared its end, Montgomery opened up *Epsom*, a push to cross the Odon, west of Caen, with the British 2nd Army.

At 5.30 p.m. on 22 June 1944, Sergeant Richard Greenwood of the 9th Battalion Royal Tank Regiment came ashore at Courseulles-sur-mer. He had found the time spent in England awaiting embarkation frustrating, but at last his unit had landed in Normandy. He now entered hostile territory and the horrors of war became apparent. On the approach to the beach, the body of an Allied soldier floated past. Once on land the previous fierce fighting was evidenced by numerous hastily dug graves. By 26 June, Richard's unit had moved up to the village of Cheux, a few miles west of Caen and just north of the Odon river, which had:

> only been taken by our troops that morning, & there was much evidence of the battle. The stench of dead cows in adjoining fields was awful. Several human corpses along the route . . . one, recognisable as a Jerry by torn bits of uniform, had been run over on the verge, and tanks subsequently passed over his body. It was just a pulpy mass of bloody flesh and bones. No one appeared to be bothered by it. Our own troops were too busy 'digging in' against possible counter-attack to worry about dead bodies.

Richard's tank unit took up its position with the 9th Cameronians infantry battalion of the 15th Scottish Division and that evening, after holding against a German attack, they advanced, slowly. The battle raged until darkness, and Richard's unit finally withdrew, without gain at 1 a.m. 'Our loss 8 vehicles . . . all blazing away.' Owing to the losses his unit left the front line, but on 29 June it once more confronted the Germans near Grainville-sur-Odon, suffering under relentless mortar attack. The next day it waited for a fresh German attack, which didn't come and in the afternoon it once more retired from the front, still under mortar attack.

Across the whole of the *Epsom* front, despite initial small gains German resistance proved fierce and bad weather hindered aerial support. During the five days of battle both sides desperately fought to gain, hold or recapture ground. By the end of June the cost in Allied men and equipment had mounted, and with German armoured counter-attacks menacing, Montgomery called off *Epsom* looking to consolidate his small gains. The German armoured threat to the British front, the newly arrived 9th SS and 10th SS Panzer Divisions, came from the direction of Villers-Bocage, as the recent RAF Bomber Command attacks on rail facilities in the east of France had been too late to hinder seriously the Panzers' deployment. Fortunately for the British they were prepared, and the 15th Scottish Division met and turned the Panzers, and in an effort to prevent any resumption of the German attack, RAF Bomber Command was called in to bomb their positions around Villers-Bocage.

On the evening of 30 June, Harris sent 266 aircraft to blast Villers-Bocage. Jack Scott's crew was one of them, and Ken Handley recorded in his diary:

> 8,000 lb 4hrs 5mins
> Our first daylight leaving at 5.45 pm; we went down England at 2,000 ft. Around us were another 200 aircraft, Halifaxes and Lancasters. Over the Channel & into the target just forward of the front line to prang a roadway through a village. Sticks of bombs could be seen leaving the aircraft. Flak bursts started but I think the gunners ran for it when we began.
> A pleasant trip & my 28th.

Richard Greenwood witnessed the bombing on 30 June:

> Saw a remarkable sight this evening: tremendous procession of our 4-engined bombers flew overhead and dropped their loads just beyond front line (around Villers?). Must have been hundreds of planes, but all over in about 10 minutes. Seemed to be very little Jerry AA and didn't see a single plane destroyed. Shortly afterwards, a huge black cloud ascended & gradually spread towards us. Within an hour, we were literally in a fog: air became noticeably cooler & daylight partially obliterated, visibility about 200 yards. Fine dust particles settled everywhere. This 'fog' lasted for about 2 hours. Heaven knows what we hit, but it must have been a mighty bombardment.
> Believe enemy are grouping about 2 Panzer Divs in that area for heavy counter-attack. Monty was here today & said, 'They will be smashed!' Maybe the RAF have already smashed them. Hope so.[97]

Ken Handley would later receive confirmation of the success of the assault from his brother who was serving with Army Transport and went there two days after the attack, informing his brother, 'You left a hole there – there is no more Villers-Bocage.' On 1 July at the AAC Conference Harris commented on the initial evidence from reconnaissance photos that 'in fact Villers-Bocage can be said to have been thoroughly liberated.'

CHAPTER 17

BLASTING CAEN

During the second half of June Rommel, as reinforcements arrived, plugged apparent gaps in his Normandy front line. Unable to build up any reserve for counter-attack he had quickly come to realise that the situation on the battle front was becoming desperate, indeed steadily worsening. He had tried to make OKW and Hitler appreciate the seriousness of the problems facing his troops in Normandy, but failed. On 17 June Hitler had met and spoken with Rommel and von Rundstedt at Soissons, using the perceived success of the V1 offensive as a means to encourage his commanders to continue the fight for every piece of ground. Late in June, Rommel and von Rundstedt once more met Hitler, but the Führer dismissed his commanders' concerns. Hitler and the senior staff at OKW now had considerable cause to doubt von Rundstedt's commitment to their strategy of holding on in Normandy, and his future as Commander-in-Chief was questioned.

Matters came to a head when von Rundstedt gave his support to a report at the end of June from Geyr von Schweppenburg, forwarded to OKW, requesting a withdrawal out of range of the Allied naval bombardments. A few days later von Rundstedt relinquished his position; his superiors' questioning of his ability to command on health grounds no doubt prompted his decision.

When Field Marshal Günther von Kluge arrived as the new Commander-in-Chief West his initial confidence and optimism soon faltered as his front-line commanders made him aware of the true position at the front. On 17 July matters worsened for the Germans when Rommel was seriously injured in a Typhoon attack on his staff car, and departed from the Normandy battle scene, never to return. Von Kluge, in addition to his Commander-in-Chief duties, also took on the responsibility of commanding Army Group B. On 20 July an attempt was made on Hitler's life. Although he survived the bomb explosion at his 'Wolf's Lair' in East Prussia, the repercussions shook the German military command structure as suspicion of who was involved in the failed bomb plot rapidly spread, to include amongst others von Kluge. Fearing imminent arrest von Kluge's ability to command understandably suffered. But despite the Germans' problems their lines held. The Allies were being frustrated and fears began to surface of a stalemate and recurrence of the horrors of the trenches of the First World War.

Incident

In an attempt to maintain the block on enemy movement from the east, one of the railyards attacked by RAF Bomber Command in the middle of July 1944 was at Revigny in north-east France. Bomber Command aircrews visited the railyards next to the river Marne on three occasions and met considerable opposition. On the first raid on 12/13 July ten Lancasters were lost, on the second raid on 14/15 July seven Lancasters failed to return. On the night of 18/19 July RAF Bomber Command, in particular 5 Group, made further sacrifice. Fred Whitfield DFM, a rear gunner with 9 Squadron, took part in the raid and recorded his experience in his diary:

> This is our second trip over enemy territory today, and it has to be one of the worst I've ever experienced and ever wish to encounter again. We were flying a brand new Lancaster WS W, which was just as well, for the amount of punishment it had to take.
>
> German nightfighters were waiting for us as we approached the coast. They attacked our bombers continuously, from the coast to the target and back to the coast again. Ron [Adams, the pilot] corkscrewed and threw the Lancaster all over the sky. It appeared that aircraft were going down in flames in all directions.
>
> When we arrived at the target, we dropped our bombs, then, continued to corkscrew. Losses are going to be heavy on both sides tonight for aircraft still appeared to be going down in flames all around us.
>
> I've learned today that one of my best pals, Bobby Younger, from Newcastle was shot down [and killed]. Frank [Stebbings, the mid-upper gunner on Fred's crew] and I both feel sick at the news, because the three of us trained together and were great pals.

Twenty-four Lancasters failed to return from the raid. In total RAF Bomber Command lost 41 aircraft and 287 airmen on the three raids. Despite daylight air superiority over France, the Allies still had to contend with formidable German nightfighter opposition and continued to make the sacrifice to delay enemy troops reaching the front.

As the battle in Normandy continued into July, Montgomery, under considerable pressure from his seniors and following the failure of *Epsom,* endeavoured to maintain pressure at Caen. With the objective of taking the town and establishing a footing on the Caen-Falaise plain, a frontal assault under the codename *Charnwood* was planned. The Allies believed that blocking the British advance were strong, reinforced, German units, and consequently at the AAC Conference on 7 July, a call was made on RAF Bomber Command to attack four aiming points 'consisting of concrete "hedgehog' defences" that evening. However, yet again, there were differing views on the use of the heavy bombers. Tedder once more aired his view that the heavies should only be used to break German attacks and not to precede Allied ground attacks. He felt that it may encourage the Army to place further call on the heavy bombers and divert them 'from their proper tasks'. It is also likely that Tedder was of the opinion that Montgomery was reluctant to take unnecessary risks with his troops.

It is worth noting that Eisenhower was also present at the meeting on 7 July, perhaps to add his weight to the proposed bombing attack, as in the previous few days he had been pressurising Montgomery to break the stalemate around Caen. The proposal was agreed and Harris stated that he had 350 aircraft standing by, which he could up to 450 if one *Crossbow* target was removed from his bombing programme. During the first week of July RAF Bomber Command's main focus had indeed been on *Crossbow* targets, although there had been four other attacks on rail centres, but now on 7 July, RAF Bomber Command intervened directly in the land battle. The initial bomb plan called on the RAF's heavies to blast fortified villages north of Caen, but late in the day concerns over bombing friendly positions resulted in a change of target to a stretch of open ground in front of Caen and the northern outskirts of the city itself. Harris would send 467 bombers carrying 2,276 tons of explosive (much of which comprised 6-hour delayed action bombs) to soften the way for the advance of the British 2nd Army.

Over the target the weather conditions were favourable. Around 2200 hours the bombs began falling and a very accurate raid developed and the Allied ground troops watched with awe at the formidable display of Allied air power. The returning aircrews were optimistic; opposition had been negligible with only one Lancaster shot down by flak, and there was the general belief that the operation had been a great success. One of our crews added to the carnage on the ground: Ken Handley recorded in his diary:

> 10,000 lb 4hrs 0mins. Another good daylight prang over target at 22.00hrs at 8,000ft. Flak bursts against the clouds gave them a spotted appearance. Target was smothered in smoke where tank concentrations were.

The next morning, the Allied troops advanced, encouraged by the sight of the air bombardment. However they encountered stubborn resistance. Colonel Kurt Meyer, in command of the 12th SS Panzer Division (*Hitler Jugend*) which met the Allied thrust, recounted the bombing of 7 July and the subsequent ground battle to postwar interrogators:

> As a result of the allied attack on Caen, the Div again endured heavy losses, 25 SS PGR being the chief sufferer, the first bn [battalion] having only 200 men left, the second bn a like number and the third bn hardly 100. The losses were caused not by the allied bomber attacks, but mainly by the flame throwers that attacked immediately the bombing ceased, and as a result, caught many of the men in a somewhat dazed condition. It was only the arrival of 21 Panzer that saved what might have been a very ugly situation.[98]

Over the next few days the British and Canadian divisions made gains and reached the northern bank of the Orne in the middle of the desolation of Caen. However the cost was significant and the advance stalled. Had the RAF heavy bomber attack been worth all the effort? The RAF aircrews, as ordered, had executed a concentrated bombardment and the effect on the morale of the Allied troops from witnessing the massive show of air power had been appreciable. The German defences had been softened, but few casualties resulted directly from the bombing. The destruction within Caen caused further misery for the civilians caught up in the struggle for ground. In addition Allied transport difficulties were compounded by the blocking of many roads. *Charnwood* had been a partial success in terms of ground gained but the desired breakout still eluded the Allies. The route to the Caen-Falaise plain remained blocked. With the American advance on the Allied right faltering in the hedgerows of the bocage, the pressure on Montgomery and his subordinate commanders mounted.

The stalemate had to be broken somewhere, and quickly. Thus were operations *Goodwood* and *Cobra* devised. *Goodwood* was an attempted breakthrough on Dempsey's eastern flank and *Cobra*, an American push on Bradley's western flank. *Goodwood*, launched first, would, it was hoped, keep German attention and reinforcements pinned around Caen. *Cobra* would then break the German defence of the southern Cotentin peninsula and sweep down the German left flank to Avranches. What is notable about both offensives is that the Allied commanders again planned the use of the heavy bombers to precede the ground attacks and smash the opposing defenders.

As we have seen Leigh-Mallory had for some time been an advocate for the use of heavy bombers in direct support of the ground troops. On 26 June 1944, commenting on the launch of operation *Epsom*, his diarist records the AEAF commander saying that:

> we must be prepared to use every bit of air we've got, every single aircraft, in order to unstick the Army if, as I fear, it gets bogged. Look at this photograph. (Here the AOC-in-C produced a large photograph showing the damage caused by one night attack by 100 heavy bombers on a small aiming point. The point and the area around it for a distance of roughly 1,000 yards across were completely obliterated.) I am convinced that we could do this sort of thing to eight different points along a battle front.
>
> You remember St George [Leigh-Mallory's diarist], that it was Napoleon who said that the man who concentrated the greatest force at the right time and at the right place, won the battle. That is what we should do with our air weapon. We would never have attempted the invasion of the Continent without overwhelming air power, and it was because we had that power that the initial assault was successful. We must use air power to get the Army forward if they can't do it on their own, and I repeat, it looks to me, unfortunately, as though they can't.

Leigh-Mallory's plan, at that time, was to attack six to eight 'blobs' (battery positions or strongpoints), with heavy bombers, then with artillery on the first 1,000 yards, and then with medium bombers bombing in front of the advancing infantry, whilst the 'day heavies' blasted more distant enemy battery positions. His basic premise was that it had worked with regard the assault on the beaches, so why not again?

> *Leigh-Mallory's diary, 26 June 1944:* Those are my own views, and, as I say, I feel very strongly about them. The Deputy Supreme Commander Tedder however does not share them. He feels that the Army should be left to act on its own with the ordinary air support it has hitherto been getting. Naturally his views are shared by the supporters of stratcgical bombing, who are only too glad to get away from the battlefield and bomb distant targets.
>
> I foresee a first class row on this issue, but I am prepared for it. When I originally propounded this scheme of full air support to the Army, Air Chief Marshal Tedder was not present, but General Marshall was. He thoroughly agreed with it. If the present attack on Caen is not successful

then I shall raise the scheme a second time, and I believe that Ike (General Eisenhower) will back me.

By the middle of July, following the failure of *Epsom* and *Charnwood* to overrun Caen, 'Ike' certainly was prepared to back Leigh-Mallory.

Leigh-Mallory's diary, 15 July 1944: You remember the interesting controversy which has been going on concerning the use of heavy bombers in support of the Army? I told you how, when I was last in France, I spoke to Monty on the subject and also to Coningham, and left no doubt, especially with the latter, as to the nature of my views. Now large-scale plans are being made which all depend for a great part of their success upon the use of heavy bombers in close support. Coningham has changed his attitude. At this morning's conference he laid before me in detail exactly what the Army wanted, and then left it to me to take the necessary steps. Tedder listened and said nothing. I think he has been told by Ike to leave things to me.[99]

Indeed Tedder remained silent. However this was far from acting in deference to Leigh-Mallory's ideas. Tedder was certainly not supportive of Leigh-Mallory's assurances to the Army, that air power could break the German defences, and had told him so prior to the launch of *Charnwood* on 7 July. However by the middle of July the Senior Allied Commanders were feeling extreme frustration at Montgomery's inability to use the Army to break the stalemate around Caen. As it was, when Montgomery first informed Eisenhower and Tedder of his plans for Operation *Goodwood*, they responded by offering full air support, subject to the weather. Tedder in his memoirs states that he was looking beyond points of principle,[100] feeling that if the promise of full air support could stimulate the Army to advance, he would not stand in the way.

Following RAF Bomber Command's support to *Charnwood*, Harris's force had once more focused on *Crossbow* and rail targets in France. Our crews had made their contribution. Since Jack Scott's trip to the Caen area on 7 July, he had completed two raids with his crew on flying-bomb launch sites, as had Bill Brown and his crew. On 18 July it was back to direct support of the land battle as both crews were detailed to blast enemy positions at the launch of *Goodwood*.

RAF Bomber Command despatched 1,056 aircraft (1,028 attacking) to blast five German positions at Colombelles, Sannerville, Mondeville, Manneville and Cagny. At 0315 hours Bill Brown's Halifax took off destined to shed its bomb load over Mondeville. At 0336 hours Jack Scott's Halifax took off to fly to Sannerville. For Bill Brown's crew this would be their first operation this day, as the 427 Squadron ORB recorded: 'Little did the crews realise at 0130 hours when they were hauled from their beds that they would be on two operations within the space of 24 hours.'

As dawn broke the bomber armada crossed the Normandy coast north of Caen. Richard Greenwood was one of the many expectant ground troops watching as the heavy bombers began the bombardment:

Immediately after our arrival on hill [112], our bombers started to appear over a position S. of Caen . . . about 6 miles to our East. It turned out to be the biggest air raid I have ever seen. Sun was just rising as first bombers appeared . . . about 5.45 am. A beautiful morning: warm and clear.

Several hundred Lancasters and Halifaxes took part. They came over in swarms, circled over the target, & then headed for home. This must have continued for about an hour: bombs being literally poured down on some unfortunate Jerrys. Very soon, a heavy mixture of smoke and cordite spread for miles & Caen was hidden from our view. We could smell the cordite strongly at this distance. Jerry A.A. fairly strong, but only saw three of our planes destroyed. Saw at least five bail out from one plane.

Jack Scott's was the first of our crews to drop their bombs, at 0543$\frac{1}{2}$ hours. Flak was the only opposition.

Ken Handley's diary: A good early morning prang on Tanks & enemy guns & installations in the battle area prior to a 'breakthrough'. 1,000 aircraft took part at heights from 6-8,000ft. Our christening with flak having a piece come through the bottom of the perspex nose, leaving at the top, missing the bomb aimer Tick by inches. Otherwise pleasant.

At 0608$\frac{1}{2}$ hours the bombs fell from Bill Brown's Halifax on to Mondeville, again flak offering the only threat. In fact five RAF Bomber Command aircraft would be lost to flak on the raids near Caen, a figure a RAF Bomber Command analyst would later unsensitively describe in a report as 'a small return for the enemy's expenditure of ammunition'.[101] One other loss, on the Mondeville raid, was due to damage sustained from another bomber's bombs; the pilot managed to complete the bomb run before the damage to the starboard fin and rudder caused it to crash.

Jack Scott landed his aircraft safely back in England at 0730 hours. Bill Brown reached home at 0815 hours, but then it was all systems go at RAF Leeming as aircraft and crews were prepared for another raid. Our crew took off at 2200 hours, flying for 5 hours 45 minutes within a force of 194 aircraft, which conducted a very successful raid to the synthetic oil plant at Wesseling. Little opposition was met, and only one Halifax lost. The German nightfighters were busy elsewhere; notably 24 Lancasters shot down on a raid to the railyards at Revigny.

What of the attack in support of *Goodwood*? Leigh-Mallory recorded in his diary the spectacle of the RAF Bomber Command attack:

The bombing of Bomber Command at first light was extraordinary. Aircraft were spread out in a great fan in the red dawn, coming in over the sea. It was an incredible sight. Soon there was nothing but a pall of dust and smoke and I could see but little from the Storch in which I was flying. I must say that the air side was tremendously successful. The Army had been unable to move in the Caen area for three weeks and we got them unstuck in three hours. The Army were particularly cheerful to see the bombers going straight on through the flak undeviating towards their target. Occasionally one would go down in flames, but the others pressed on and never wavered. It was a magnificent sight.[102]

Richard Greenwood continues:

> This attack had not finished before several Typhoons appeared immediately to our south. There followed half an hour's dive bombing with rockets and bombs. By now, the heavy bombers had finished, leaving an enormous cloud spreading towards us, & Heaven knows what destruction. An hour later, the earth commenced to tremble again: more violently than before . . . & heavy rumbles could be heard S. of Caen. Seemed like a heavier raid still, but no bombers were visible. And then there appeared several groups of Liberators, wheeling around from the S. They continued to appear for an hour, causing really violent trembling of the earth. All loose instruments in the tank were affected by the vibration!
>
> A very heartening three hours to those of us who have seen so many enemy planes. . . & so few of ours.[103]

Following RAF Bomber Command's attack the Eighth Air Force despatched 644 B-24s to bomb the German positions, of which 534 managed to attack their primary objectives. In total the Allied heavy bombers rained down 6,800 tons of explosive on the German troops. On 21 July at the AAC Conference it was reported that 70% of the prisoners taken at the beginning of the ground attack were stone deaf for 24 hours.

General Hans Eberbach, was now in command of Panzer Group West, as von Schweppenburg had been relieved of his command by Hitler on 1 July following his report arguing for and requesting a withdrawal from the Caen bridgehead. Eberbach recounted his recollection of the 18 July heavy bomber attack to his postwar interrogators:

> The bomb carpet was a six kilometre square for the first time in their experience; and all his rear areas and reserves were destroyed or disrupted. Such a cloud of dust arose, through the bombs and the barrage, that they got no word from the front for the rest of the day. Even their W/T sets could not function, there was so much dust in the air. But his defence in depth served to hold us up until 2000 hours when he got his first report from the front, and that of a breakthrough. His counter-attack had been ordered in the morning, to be done by 21 Panzer Division from Bellengreville on the right and by 1 SS Panzer Division from Fontenay-le-Marmion on the left, the two divisions converged at Hubert-Folie. Not until 1500 hours were these divisions in shape to start.[104]

Initially the Allied armour exploited the disruption in the German positions, finally managing to capture Caen, but the advance soon slowed, the German defence congealed and Montgomery's attempted breakout failed. Herein lies one of the great controversies of the Normandy campaign. In the planning for *Goodwood* Montgomery would later state that the attack was to draw German strength away from the Americans. Prior to the offensive he had instructed Dempsey to 'Go on hitting, drawing the German strength, especially the armour onto yourself – so as to ease the way for Brad.'[105] At the time Montgomery and Dempsey were being warned that recent casualty rates on the British front demanded serious concern, there was also a shortage of 25-pounder ammunition and the *Goodwood* area was not good for artillery support. As such they decided to call on heavy bomber support. In a postwar interview Dempsey's view was recorded thus:

> The C-in-C was enthusiastic about this plan and promised that he would obtain the co-operation of the air forces by getting approval at the highest level. General Dempsey then informed the narrator that to get this co-operation with the ground forces was always very difficult. Apart from the possible clashes of personalities involved, the RAF and USAAF were far more concerned, as might be expected, with winning the war by long term strategic bombing offensives and thus always reluctant, as it were, to waste time and effort in providing heavy bombing support to the land armies. In getting their help on this occasion it is probable that the C-in-C had to paint his canvas in rather glowing colours, and to magnify or even over emphasise the results to be gained from the proposed operation.[106]

Not only did Montgomery overstate the case to the Allied air commanders, but also to the press. He would later claim this was necessary to draw the German reinforcement to Caen, away from Bradley's troops. His relationship with the air commanders was seriously damaged, notably with Tedder. Montgomery's apparent reluctance to spill British blood was causing great misgivings at SHAEF, notably with the Americans, and his ability to direct properly the land battle in Normandy was questioned. Fortunately for him, however, developments on the American front diverted attention away from this issue.

CHAPTER 18

THE AMERICAN BREAKOUT

Since the Berlin mission of 21 June the Eighth Air Force had been pounding airfields, bridges, V1 targets and railyards in north-west France. Every now and then Spaatz, to the displeasure of Leigh-Mallory, took the opportunity to send Doolittle's aircrews on missions to oil and aircraft targets in Germany.

Similar targeting policy followed in the second and third weeks of July with the additional requirement of direct support to *Goodwood*. On 24 July 1944 the Eighth Air Force was asked to intervene directly in the land campaign. In his postwar memoirs General Bradley recorded:

> For several weeks prior to planning Cobra I had been hunting for an enemy concentration where strategic air might be used to wipe out a division. It was while searching for this target that this thought occurred to me one day: Why not combine this mission with the breakout, first smash a division from the air, and then tramp right on through it. By July 18, Army planning for Cobra had been completed and Montgomery approved the scheme.[107]

On 19 July Bradley flew to England, meeting with the air commanders at Stanmore, and, upon Leigh-Mallory's invitation, he outlined plans for *Cobra*:

> emphasizing our choice of the Périers road as a ground marker that might guide the heavy bombers to their target. If the strike were to be made in the morning, air could come in to the target out of the sun and follow the road west toward Périers. But if weather were to delay the bombers until late afternoon, air could just as easily reverse its path and come in from the sun in the west toward St Lô. In either event the Périers road would furnish the bombers a flank guide to help air avoid bombing in error American forces on the upper side of the road.[108]

Bradley, pleased with the perceived welcome for his plans, returned to France optimistic:

> That afternoon when we left Northolt for the return trip to France . . . I carried air's commitment for a far heavier blitz than I had dreamed of. So sceptical was Collins [commanding the VII Corps] of this pledge when I told him of it that he confessed afterward he thought I might have been exaggerating the total. For we were to get 1,500 heavy bombers, 396 mediums, and another 350 fighter bombers, altogether a total of 2,246 aircraft for five square miles of Normandy hedgerow.[109]

The bombing of German positions, scheduled to open the American push south from the Cherbourg peninsula, *Cobra*, was reliant upon suitable weather. With friendly troops beneath the bombers, close to the aiming points, accuracy of attack was of paramount importance. Initially the launch of the ground offensive was frustrated by miserable weather, but it appeared that on 24 July conditions would prove favourable. However at the last moment the weather worsened and measures were taken to recall the 1,586 American heavies that had taken off on the raid. But here the complicated command structure for the engagement of the heavy bombers led to a communications breakdown with tragic consequences.

Whilst the Eighth Air Force heavies were on their way to Normandy, Doolittle was informing the AAC Conference that his heavies had been dispatched and were scheduled over the target for 1200 hours. Kingston-McCloughry immediately interjected informing Doolittle and the meeting that he had just been speaking by telephone to General Elwood Quesada, commander of the US IXth Tactical Air Command. Quesada had informed him that *Cobra* had been postponed until the following day as the height of the cloud over the target area was only 5,000 feet, which would not allow for visual bombing by the heavies. Quesada had passed on an order from Leigh-Mallory, who was with General Bradley, that the Eighth Air Force's attack should be cancelled.

One can only imagine the sense of incredulity at the meeting. As his heavies would only be seven minutes from the target Doolittle said that it was too late to make a recall. However if the weather was that bad his aircrews would return with their bombs. Nevertheless a recall was sent but it was too late to prevent 343 bombers attacking their detailed primary target, against Doolittle's reassurances, unleashing 662 tons of explosive. Certainly there was considerable destruction amidst the German positions. Tragically some bombing also fell on US troops killing 25 and wounding 131 men.

When Bradley learnt of the short bombing he exploded:

> 'Short?' I cried, 'But how could they? These bombers were to come in on the Périers road parallel to our lines.'
>
> 'That's not the way they came in, sir' . . . 'they came in on a perpendicular course.'
>
> Leigh-Mallory arrived at the CP a few minutes after. Although the casualty count had not yet come in, he was as distressed as I over the accidental bombing.
>
> 'But what worries me more than anything else,' I told him, 'is the fact that those heavies came in over our heads instead of parallel to the Périers road. I left Stanmore with a clear understanding they would fly parallel to that road.'[110]

Later in the day Leigh-Mallory gave Bradley the reason for the Eighth Air Force's flightpath. If the narrow path parallel to the Périers road were followed it would take two and a half hours to funnel through the planned force of 1,500 heavy bombers, which would mean two and half hours flying parallel to the German front lines and the enemy's guns. With regard launching *Cobra* the next day, and again using the heavy bombers, Bradley recalled the AEAF commander telling him that, 'If you insist on that approach, they tell me they can't make the attack tomorrow.'

> Only a few hours remained before those bomber crews were to be briefed for an early morning take-off.
>
> I was shocked and angered by air's reply, for to me it represented a serious breach of good faith in planning. Five days before when I left

Stanmore it was with the understanding that air would follow the Périers road. Had I known of air's intent to chance the perpendicular approach, I would never have consented to its plan. For I was unwilling to risk a corps to the split-second timing required in an overhead drop of 60,000 bombs from 8,000 feet.

Annoyed though I was by this duplicity on the part of the air planners, I had no choice but to consent to the attack or delay it indefinitely, but we had already tipped our hand and could not delay much longer without giving our intentions away.

'Shall I tell them to go ahead in the morning?' Leigh-Mallory asked.

'We've got no choice,' I said, 'The Boche will build up out front if we don't get this thing off soon. But we're still taking an awful chance. Another short drop could ruin us.'

I paused for a moment.

'Let it go that way. We'll be ready to go in the morning.'[111]

The next morning the Ninth Air Force opened the attack and was followed by 1,503 Eighth Air Force bombers, unloading 3,395 tons of bombs. Again the German troops were severely battered. In terms of the damage inflicted on the enemy the bombing operations in support of *Cobra* were a major success, at a cost to the Eighth's heavy bomber force of just eight aircraft.

In a postwar interrogation General Leutnant Fritz Bayerlein of the Panzer Lehr Division gave an account of what it was like on the receiving end of the Allied bombing operations.

It was hell . . . The planes kept coming overhead like a conveyor belt, and the bomb carpets came down, now ahead, now on the right, now on the left . . . The fields were burning and smouldering. The bomb carpets unrolled in great rectangles . . . My front lines looked like a landscape on the moon, and at least seventy percent of my personnel were out of action – dead, wounded, crazed or numbed. All my front line tanks were knocked out. Late in the afternoon, the American ground troops began filtering in. I had organised my last reserves to meet them – not over fifteen tanks, most of them from repair shops. The roads were practically impassable. The next morning the bombing began all over again. We could do nothing but retreat. Marshal von Kluge sent word at six that afternoon that the line St Lô-Périers road must be held at all costs. It was already broken. But a new SS tank battalion was coming in with sixty tanks to drive to the Vire River and cut off the Americans. They arrived – five tanks, not sixty.[112]

Despite the successes there was, again, tragically short bombing on 25 July, resulting in more friendly casualties. A report conducted by the Eighth Air Force into the *Cobra* bombing operations on 24 and 25 July concluded that in terms of the use of strategic bombers, the bombing errors fell well within expectations. Basically if the Army called in strategic bombers then they had to account in their planning for the shortcomings in accuracy. Relationships between the air chiefs and the Army certainly did not improve. Doolittle was hauled in front of Lieutenant General Walter Bedell Smith, Eisenhower's Chief of Staff, But in accepting responsibility, Doolittle also complained that his force was unsuitable for such ground support. Bedell Smith was dismissive of Doolittle's stance. Spaatz and Arnold backed their subordinate in questioning the use of heavies and Doolittle kept his command, a week after the event receiving a letter from Eisenhower.

> I know how badly you and your command have felt because of the accidental bombing of some of our own troops. . . . Naturally, all of us have shared your acute distress that this should have happened. Nevertheless, it is quite important that you do not give the incident an exaggerated place either in your mind or in your future planning.
>
> All the reports show that the great mass of the bombs from your tremendous force fell squarely on the assigned target, and I want you and your command to know that the advantage resulting from the bombardment were of inestimable value. I am perfectly certain, also, that when the ground forces again have to call on your help you will not only be as ready as ever to cooperate, but will in the meantime have worked out some method so as to eliminate unfortunate results from the occasional gross error on the part of a single pilot or a single group.
>
> The work of the 8th Air Force over many months in this theater has been far too valuable to allow the morale of the organization to be dampened by this incident.

In the immediate aftermath of the bombing, on the evening of 25 July, Bradley feared that:

> the fate of Cobra still hung in doubt. Several hundred U.S. troops had been killed and wounded in the air bombing. It had dislocated Collins' [VII Corps] advance and there was little reason to believe we stood at the brink of a breakthrough. Rather the attack looked as though it might have failed.[113]

Nevertheless Bradley's troops launched themselves into the German defences, which for the first few days held, but on 27 July the defensive crust began to break. Bradley recalled in his memoirs that 'although *Cobra* might have looked like a failure on the evening of July 25, it had struck a more deadly blow than any of us dared imagine.' American troops exploited the sudden weakening of the defences to the full and by 30 July the 4th Armored Division entered Avranches. At last the land battle had opened up. The Germans had finally been worn down and the Allies now had mobility to work with.

In Hiding

As German forces began to retreat from the Allied advances in Normandy, some evading Allied aircrew were in hiding in France and Belgium, and were planning to get back at their enemy. Leslie Hood bailed out of his Lancaster on the night of 28/29 June, and he had been placed in hiding with other evading airmen, in the small town of Livry-Gargan, in the north-eastern suburbs of Paris.

Leslie Hood: The house was situated on the rue de Meaux, one of the main routes to the east. I was able to see the wholesale movement of retreating forces. Most of the German vehicles had brooms or broomheads attached to them from bumper bars because of the 'petit-machins' the Resistance movement had scattered on the roads. With my fellow evaders at the same house, I was involved in making some of these petit-machins. We began each with a 3- or 4-inch rectangle of metal. Two sides of a largish triangle were cut in and bent upwards along the uncut edge. When thrown onto the road, the way it fell presented a number of sharp points, which ripped tyres apart.[114]

Also in the house was Bill Geeson whose Lancaster had been shot down on the night of 10/11 June 1944 and who recalled witnessing one incident:

We did see a Fortress shot down. They were doing something fairly low level, less than 10,000 feet. They were hit by light flak, which normally wouldn't reach them. We had staying in our house with us for some time the bomb aimer from the Fortress. He was the only one that survived as the aircraft spun in and nobody else got out. He was in a bit of a state because another member of his crew, whom he was practically standing next to, had a cannon shell explode behind him and he got covered in the bits and pieces. He was in a traumatic state and was moved on shortly after.[115]

A major feature of every AAC Conference throughout the latter part of June, July and August was the setting of *Crossbow* targets. The allocation of heavy bomber resources to the counter-offensive remained a priority. Up until the end of the first week in July the V1s were still causing considerable disruption in London and political pressure was growing. Early in July a series of attacks by RAF Bomber Command, and the Eighth Air Force to a lesser extent, on V1 underground storage depots at St Leu d'Esserent and Nucourt (north and north-west of Paris respectively) caused significant damage and greatly reduced the V1 launch rates. In a bid to keep the number of V1s reaching the defences over England as low as possible, and therefore give them a better chance to shoot them down and not be overwhelmed, heavy bomber resources would still be applied.

Following the contribution of Jack Scott's and Bill Brown's crews' to *Goodwood*, they would once again be required to counter the German V1 offensive. Up until 5 August, Jack Scott's crew had attacked four German secret weapon targets, Bill Brown's crew five. In addition to these operations RAF Bomber Command attention had begun to turn once more to Germany. Jack Scott's crew once and Bill Brown's crew twice visited targets in the Reich; both crews fortunately avoided German nightfighters, which could still exact their toll on night raids over Germany. In addition to these raids Jack Scott's crew had been sent to the Villers-Bocage-Caumont area on 30 July to bomb German positions. They were ordered not to bomb, because of cloud, although half the force of 692 aircraft was able to, with some limited success.

The raid to the V1 storage site at Fôret de Nieppe on 5 August was Jack Scott's and his crew's 40th and final operation.

Ken Handley's diary: A pleasant & impressive trip with hundreds of aircraft in the air. A good daylight prang. A wizard shoot-up of drome on return . . . flying up England at 500 ft – skipper had a 'rocket' from the CO, 'Not because we fear for your crew – but because another pilot may try the same and not manage it'.

Here the crew leaves our story, and their fate is detailed at the end of this book. Jack Scott's crew had survived their tour. Skill and luck had seen them through six months of operational duty involving a wide range of raids, from deep penetrations into Germany to short flights to the coast of France.

Following the support to *Cobra* and through the first week of August 1944, the Eighth Air Force had been keeping up the offensive against German oil and industry, and there had also been a continuing major commitment to the Normandy battle, bombing airfields, bridges and rail marshalling yards, along with numerous attacks against German secret weapon sites. As we have seen, for the latter part of June and first half of July 1944, Walt McAllister's and George Ritchie's 34th BG crew had made its contribution to the V1 counter-offensive. Then on 19 and 21 July it was back to Germany as they took part in major attacks on German industrial targets. In the first two weeks of August Walt McAllister would again take his crew three times to bomb V1 launch sites, along with a mission blasting some oil dumps in Brussels on 3 August.

On 5 August the 34th BG contributed 36 heavies to a major attack by the Eighth on oil, tank and aircraft production facilities in north and central Germany. Walt McAllister's crew was not called upon but George Ritchie's former crew was; it did not return.

George Ritchie's diary: Terry went down today! I did not make the mission. Bush and Rogers led the mission deep into Germany to hit a F.W. plant. The formation was leaving the flak area when Terry burst into flame. His wing tanks on fire, he put the plane into a controlled slip, feathered the engine to put the fire out. About 2,000 feet below the formation the crew bailed and 6-8 chutes were said to have been seen. Some felt Terry must have stayed with the ship, because it looked under control all the way down. Jerry fighters were after him, followed by some of our 'little friends' (P-51 Mustangs) No one could say exactly what happened or what the losses were.

At the time little news was received concerning the fate of Terry's crew, but before the war was over, George would meet up with his former pilot.

George Ritchie's present crew were nearing the end of their contribution to the battle for Normandy. They had also taken part in countering the V1 threat, which during the second half of August dwindled owing to the Allied bombing attacks and the advance of the Allied armies, which overran the launch sites. However the crew would have one further direct influence on the land battle, by bombing enemy troops direct.

At the beginning of August, the American land forces basically had two choices after having taken Avranches: either sweep into Brittany and secure port facilities, as originally planned, or exploit the open ground to the east, hook under the German forces and push for the Seine. For the first few days General Patton's Third Army followed the original plan, but an expected slow and deliberate advance soon developed into one of fast mobile warfare. Patton quickly appreciated that the force he had far exceeded that needed to secure Brittany. His eyes turned east, along with Bradley's, who decided to initiate the drive eastward, with Montgomery and Eisenhower both in agreement. On the night of 2 August 1944 the American XV Corps prepared to spearhead the thrust and initiate the final collapse of the German army in Normandy.

The success of the Allied improvisation was greatly assisted by Hitler, who sought to buy time in order to establish a defensive line along the Marne and the Somme. His plan was to cut off the American forces in Brittany with an armoured push between Mortain and Avranches. On 2 August, Hitler's directive reached OB West. Von Kluge, still under suspicion of involvement in the 20 July bomb plot, received his superior's orders with shock, believing such a move would doom his forces. Despite making his concerns known to Hitler, he was ignored, however. Effectively Hitler's order ensured the success of the planned Allied encirclement.

In addition, the execution of the Transportation Plan continued to assist developments on the front lines, critically delaying the transfer of troops from the north to the battle area. In his postwar interrogation Lieutenant General Eugen-Felix Schwalbe, commanding 344 Infantry Division in early August 1944, detailed the difficulties he had faced in bringing his troops into the battle:

On 3 August it was finally decided that it was more important to have more men south of the Somme than it was to have them awaiting a phantom invasion. 344 Inf Div was ordered to proceed to Falaise by train. The Division consisted of about 8,000 men and the General decided to move the fighting troops by rail to Rouen and send the supply troops by road. It was expected that the fighting element of the Division would reach the Seine, some 75 miles away, in about 24 hours. The slow-moving, horse-drawn supplies would need at least three days.

In 28 trains the Division started off but just south of Amiens, the first train was derailed and the other trains had to be given a circuitous route to reach their destination. As a result the butchers and bakers and hygiene men of the Division arrived happily in Rouen some three days after they had started out, and joined their commander, Genlt Schwalbe, who had gone off in advance, while the important part of the formation was shunted around France and didn't arrive until nine days after they had begun.

This comedy of errors threw everything off schedule, and by the time the Division was ready to move again the remnants of the Seventh Army were already making their hurried way back to the river. It was no use attempting to carry out the original plan, which was to have sent the 344 Inf Div off to Falaise (and which, incidentally, would have arrived there just before 'Totalize', the First Canadian Army attack towards Falaise) and it was therefore decided to send 81 Corps, consisting of 331, 344 and 17 GAF Inf Divs, south of the Seine to cover the withdrawing troops.

Air attacks were so bad that it was only possible to get the Division over the Seine piece by piece and the Commander never did have his complete formation together. With what was able to come across he took up a sector with Verneuil on his left and Breteuil on his right flank. 17 GAF Div was on his left and left of that again was 331 Inf Div. But before the Division was able to fall into place, Allied Forces had begun to take it apart. No Division was ever properly balanced for a defensive fight, and when it attempted to withdraw chaos resulted. Vehicles were jammed along every road with men and equipment wedged amongst them. It was almost impossible to get a new position each day because of the constant attacks from the air. In one of these attacks Schwalbe lost his vehicle and, unable to find another, the Div Commander of 344 Inf Div went liaising between his units on the only other means of transportation available, the good old bicycle. Travelling by car at the time was most unhealthy and when Gen Kuntzen the 81 Corps Commander visited Schwalbe, he had two men placed on the hood and one on the rear bumper to act as spotters for Allied aircraft.[116]

On the night of 6/7 August the German counter-offensive opened, as 47 Panzer Corps smashed into the American 30th Division, to the east of Mortain. The American line held and the following morning RAF and American air power, unopposed, literally stopped the Panzer thrust in its tracks. Bradley prepared to swing Patton's forces under the Germans and behind, towards Alençon. Meanwhile on the British and Canadian front the Allies launched their own major offensive, *Totalize*, with the intention of driving on from Caen to Falaise, then turning east to assist the entrapment of the Germans as part of a long envelopment. Launched on the night of 7/8 August, the offensive also required the support of the heavy bombers. That night just over 1,000 RAF Bomber Command aircraft targeted the German lines, of which 660 eventually bombed in closely controlled attacks.

Richard Greenwood witnessed the attack from the ground:

First signs of action came from artillery away on our R. flank sending over 'markers' on the targets. RAF arrived at 11 pm exactly on time... & then the bombs commenced to rain down. First target bombed for about 15 minutes . . . & then came a lull whilst more 'markers' lit up a second target. More bombers arrived a few minutes later . . . more bombs. Certainly a very heavy raid: all over by 11.45.

Learned today that over 1,000 Lancasters and Halifaxes did the job. One stick of bombs dropped in our lines . . . in adjoining field to our harbour. I was at the rear of my vehicle & Geary on the turret. He arrived beneath tank with me! Some speed! This one stick of bombs gave us a hell of a scare. Can imagine Jerry's feeling . . . he has to tolerate dozens of them.[117]

On the night of 7/8 August, when Kurt Meyer, commander of 12th SS Panzer Division (*Hitler Jugend*), received news of the Allied attacks, he immediately drove to Urville to meet with the divisional commander of 89th Division, who, as a result of the bombing, had very little information to give. Meyer, then travelling by the Falaise to Caen road, experienced the bombing first hand.

> I got out of my car and my knees were trembling, the sweat was pouring down my face, and my clothes were soaked with perspiration. It was not that I was particularly anxious for myself because my experiences of the last five years had inured me against fear of death, but I realized that if I failed now and if I did not deploy my Div correctly, the Allies would be through to Falaise, and the German armies in the west completely trapped. I knew how weak my Div was and the double task which confronted me gave me at that time some of the worst moments I had ever had in my life.

Approaching Meyer, from the direction of the front, groups of soldiers from 89 Division appeared, fleeing in panic from the bombing. Meyer, calmly lighting a cigar, stood in their way and confidently asked if they were going to leave him to counter the Allied advance. It did the trick and defensive positions were soon re-established and manned.[118]

On 8 August the Eighth Air Force then made its contribution to the offensive: 681 aircraft were despatched, of which 477 were effective, dropping just short of 1,500 tons of bombs. With the *Cobra* short bombing still in its mind the Eighth Air Force made plans to ensure accurate bombing, but the German defences did their best to break the attack up. Technical Sergeant Walter C. Fifer was a radio operator with the 93rd Bomb Group. On 8 August he was to fly the final mission of his tour:

> We went in at 14,000 feet which is the lowest yet and a mile or so too low to suit me. We were by ourselves but this time I was glad because if we'd had a formation with us I don't think we would be here to tell it. We were to drop five British flare bombs on the target, which was a small village just in front of our own troops. The reason was to make it so the first & third division of Forts could pick up the target easier and be sure of not getting behind our own lines. It was very interesting as we went in over Cherbourg. There was a couple of convoys heading into the port. It looked like the harbour was pretty well cleaned up as it was full of shipping. I could see about five small vessels the Germans had sunk to block the harbour. The shell holes in the large harbour forts were very visible. From then on I saw lots of villages that were mainly shell holes & craters. The red crosses marking the hospitals were very plain to see so there really shouldn't be any excuse for the Germans to bomb them. They've built a great number of aircraft landing strips.
>
> I was really enjoying it till we got to Vire and turned on the IP. At about that time we crossed the German lines and did they ever give us the works! I never saw so much flak in my life and it was accurate. I think a lot of it came from German tanks because their 88 mm will reach 14,000 feet easily. Anyway, as we were by ourselves we did violent evasive action to try and get through safely. We turned as high as 90 degrees but it was still too close for comfort. We got the flares on the edge of the target but I don't know how we did, with such a bomb run. If we held a course for a few seconds the flak was right on us but the navigator and bombardier

did a grand job. The bombardier took the shortest run I've ever known but it was good. By the time I got the bomb doors shut after watching the flares hit, we were at 16,000 feet and climbing fast.

It was just a couple of minutes till we were back over our lines but we were in that heavy flak for about 15 minutes. I think there were ten of the scaredest men on that ship that I've ever seen. Maybe it was because it was the last mission for eight of us and 29th for the other two. We really came home in a hurry. The Forts were supposed to come in at 12,000 feet and they couldn't do very much evasive action as they were in formation. Flak got the first three Forts. Our fighters were down on the deck strafing every gun they could find so it was quite a sight to see. We were very lucky cause we got hit about 15 times.

Wayne 'Tex' Frye, of the 91st Bomb Group, also took part in the mission and recalled the defensive reception in his diary:

We thought this would be easy, famous last words. It was really tough. Flak was really heavy and accurate. Our group lost two ships. I saw one hit, it broke right in two, the tail making an arc in the sky away from the rest of the plane. I watched it all the way to the ground and none of the poor devils got out. Just after that about 200 yards off our left wing a B-17 exploded and all that was left was one big sheet of flame. Poor devils. They all have loved ones at home same as I. I thought sure we would have flak holes, but we weren't touched. The plane next to us had a large hold in the tail that a man could crawl through. We hit our target with 270 frag-bombs. Hope we killed a million of the S.B.'s. Keep your fingers crossed!!!

Certainly, in general, the heavy bomber attack shook the German defences, but once more the limitations of the use of heavy bombers in close army support became apparent, particularly when facing fierce opposition. Some of the bombing fell short, inflicting casualties on friendly ground troops, when part of the 351st Bomb Group accidentally released its load after the lead aircraft was hit by flak.

Leigh-Mallory, who had been the main advocate in using heavy bombers in support of land offensives, despite warnings from the heavy bomber commanders, was a witness to the American bombing and included a scathing account in his diary:

Crerar (GOC-in-C Canadian Corps) was as sick as mud with the American bombing, which was frightful. So much of it fell in the wrong place that it wasn't really any good. I am now talking . . . of the battle that opened two days ago in the Caen area. On the other hand, Crerar had nothing but praise for [RAF] Bomber Command. The markers came down to the exact minute and to the right targets, and the bombers came straight on to the markers. No bomb fell anywhere near our troops. Some of the American bombing, however, was as much as fourteen thousand (14,000) yards from the target. Two packets fell just past me when I was turning back from flying over Caen. They were two lots of 12, which bombed

Caen by mistake. The American bombing . . . began by being very scattered, but they eventually hit the first two targets. I watched the second wave come in, however, and I could see no bombs at all in the target area, but a good many fell far away to the west of the Orne.

Succeeding waves, seeing where the bombs were falling, went in and bombed there as well. Then the markers, seeing what was happening, rushed off and poured marker flares down on the right targets so that the latter end of the attack put their bombs in the right place, but I reckon that out of 390 aircraft laid on, not more than 150 dropped their bombs anywhere near the target.

As for the contention that smoke and dust obscure targets in daylight so as to make it impossible to see them – I don't believe it. I kept a careful eye on the Caen/Falaise road, which is absolutely straight for miles. It was completely free from obscurity and visible for a very long way. In fact I could see every yard of it.[119]

Here was the exponent of the use of heavy bombers in direct support of the Army, once more being critical of the outcomes. It is worth repeating that to use a bomber force designed to conduct a strategic offensive in a close ground-support operation ran enormous risks. Spaatz, Doolittle and Harris knew the limitations of their forces. As Harris had forecast prior to the *Overlord* bombing campaign, use of the heavy bombers in supporting the Army 'would lead directly to disaster.' They knew the risks, but the call on their forces had been made and they had complied. On this occasion, the limitations of using Doolittle's force was exposed. The next time it would be Harris's.

CHAPTER 19

FALAISE POCKET

In the second week of August 1944 the Eighth Air Force continued to attack a wide variety of targets: marshalling yards, airfields, fuel dumps, bridges, enemy troop positions in the Brest peninsula and German industrial targets. RAF Bomber Command had complemented these attacks focusing on fuel dumps, and targeting railyards and secret weapon sites. In addition RAF Bomber Command had been asked to aid the battle on the seas.

By the middle of August 1944 Allied supplies were flowing freely across the sea approaches to Normandy, but any potential enemy threats to the Allied build-up of materiel were closely monitored. In particular the German U-boats came under close scrutiny. At the AAC Conferences Coastal Command's Air Chief Marshal Sir William Sholto Douglas gave daily updates on intelligence concerning the movement of the U-boats, notably those operating out of the Bay of Biscay coastal ports. On 10 August he informed the meeting that there were '8 U's in Brest, 8 in Lorient, 8 in St Nazaire, 4 at La Pallice and 7 at Bordeaux.'

Since early in August Sholto Douglas had been asking for help to counter the U-boat threat, and Harris had responded, sending small RAF Bomber Command forces to lay mines and bomb the U-boat pens. On 12 August 1944 Bill Brown had taken his 427 Squadron crew to Brunswick, Germany, and the next day the crew prepared to make their contribution to Sholto Douglas's call to counter the U-boat threat. Their mission to La Rochelle that night would go without incident, but on other RAF Bomber Command raids that day and night some crew experiences would be markedly different.

In addition to countering the U-boat threat, RAF Bomber Command had also been tasked with other duties with regard the Atlantic coast ports. On 13 August Harris sent 15 Lancasters to bomb an oil depot at Bordeaux, which was achieved successfully, and 28 Lancasters and 1 Mosquito to bomb shipping and U-boat pens in Brest. The latter was a special operation staged to prevent the Germans rendering the harbour useless, should it fall into Allied hands.

Here is the experience of one crew that took part in these operations, highlighting the fact that they remained highly dangerous. Fred Whitfield DFM, a rear gunner with 9 Squadron, took part in the raid to Brest on 13 August, and recorded this, his 21st operation, in his diary:

> In my opinion this raid has to be the worst encountered up to date . . . The Germans have loaded a tanker with concrete and are intending to sink it in the harbour entrance, rendering it useless when the Allies take the town. 9 Squadron have been ordered to sink the tanker before it reaches its objective.
>
> The Germans are putting up a box barrage of anti-aircraft fire. When an aircraft goes in to bomb, you can't see it again until you fly through it. One minute it is daylight and the next it's black with flak (I know the real meaning of fear).

We got the ship, but it cost the squadron one aircraft and seven of our pals. I saw them get a direct hit on the front of the aircraft. Half of its starboard wing was lost and its outer engine was on fire. It started to turn in a lazy-like manner, then the nose went down and it went down to the ground on full power. I followed it down until it hit the beach, but no parachutes came out; it made me feel quite sickly.

To top it all, Phil Jackson, our bomb aimer, made a second run in on the target to make sure he was spot on – which he was. I am totally convinced that this man has no nerves. I felt certain our aircraft would resemble a pepper pot; however when we landed I was amazed to find that we had only been hit twice.

The very next day 9 Squadron aircraft were again detailed for operations, including the crew of Flying Officer Ron Adams. Fred Whitfield DFM again recorded the day in his diary:

We just couldn't believe our eyes when we walked into the briefing room this morning; the map on the wall was the same as yesterday: Brest. We tried to console ourselves, perhaps they had forgotten to change it, but no, it was back to Brest. Our objective was a floating hulk in the harbour.

When we arrived, the flak was not as accurate as the day before, and this time we had a Typhoon escort. My attention was drawn to the Typhoons uprooting the anti-aircraft guns with their rockets.

Our aircraft was hit in the fuel tanks and a fair amount of fuel was lost before the self-sealing tanks sealed up the holes.

On the 14 August operation RAF Bomber Command had despatched a much larger force to Brest than the previous day, comprising 155 Lancasters and 4 Mosquitos of 5 Group. The operation was deemed a success and two prospective blockships were hit and left sinking in positions of little hindrance to those using the port.[120] Two aircraft were lost on the raid. The 44 Squadron Lancaster of Flying Officer Gilchrist RCAF failed to return, and from the crew of seven the pilot and four of his colleagues perished. The 83 Squadron Lancaster of Flight Lieutenant McLean DFC RAAF was thought to have crashed into the sea near Brest, with no survivors from the crew of eight.

Shot Down

On 13 August at RAF Skellingthorpe, near Lincoln, 50 Squadron aircrew were detailed to go to Bordeaux, to counter the German U-boat threat. One such crew was that of pilot Peter Lorimer. Peter had already paid his respects to the same target on 11 August as a second dickey, and on the morning of 13 August, whilst his normal crew became aware of their first operational requirement together, he lay in bed, having returned at 7 a.m. that morning from bombing Russelheim on another second dickey trip. Peter Antwis was the navigator on Peter Lorimer's crew, which was rather apprehensive that on their first op they would not have the dark of the night to hide them from any defences.

Peter Antwis: We had been down to Devon a couple of times for the high level bombing range and managed some top level scores. We had some familiarisation time, but I still did not want to start with a daylight. I thought it was bad news for beginners. The Navigation Officer confirmed that it was to be a daylight and I told Jimmy and Sandy to go and wake the skipper. I collected my kit from the crew room with plenty of extra barley sugar. I signed for the escape packs for the crew and went to briefing. Peter Lorimer arrived and said we were going to do the submarines at Bordeaux and it would be a piece of cake for us.

On arrival at their Lancaster, groundcrew were feverishly making changes to the bomb load. The wrong bombs had been fitted and were being replaced by six 2,000 lb armour-piercing bombs, fitted with especially shaped fins suited for the planned bombing from 18,000 feet. Whilst waiting, Peter Antwis walked over to the bomb aimer, Jock Gray, who was lying on the grass reading a book entitled *Your Turn Next*. Peter recalls: 'There was our bomb aimer reading it, on dispersal, on August 13th!'

Just after 1600 hours Peter Antwis, sitting at his desk in the correctly bomb-laden Lancaster wrote on his navigator's log sheet: '*Airborne*: climbing; *On course* for the rendezvous' and Peter Lorimer flew his Lancaster down England on the first leg of their planned seven-hour flight. After crossing the Lizard on the south Cornwall coast Lorimer turned his Lancaster, now escorted by Spitfires, south and after skirting the Normandy beaches and defences of Brest, flew on over the Bay of Biscay, where Mosquitos took over escorting responsibilities, to a turning point south-west of Bordeaux. At 1945 hours Lorimer swung his Lancaster towards the target and onto the bomb run, dipping below cloud to 16,000 feet:

Peter Antwis: I stood up in the astro dome and was amazed to see the sky ahead filled with black balls of smoke bursting in a thin layer of cloud. We lost height to get below the cloud and continued steadily on course for the target. Suddenly we were in the middle of the black balls of smoke. They were bursting with fierce red flashes and I could feel and hear the explosions. 'Steady . . . Steady . . . Steady,' the bomb aimer's voice intoned over the intercom. A group of four shells burst just in front of us. The Lanc shook and shook . . . 'Bombs gone' said the bomb aimer and I saw the nose perspex burst and Peter's windows shatter. I dropped down to my table just as the side of the cabin by Freddie Stearn cracked open and my panel on the starboard side split. The Lanc shook again. Angry chunks of metal ripped up through the floor of my office. My parachute was thrown out of its stowage and my spare oxygen bottle was flung backward past Sandy's feet.

There was another group of four explosions. Through the starboard window I saw the inboard engine burst into flames. A hole opened up beside my seat and my parachute popped open in the corner. We banked away from the target. The engine fire fizzled out. A scalding hot stream of glycol sprayed in through one of the holes and across my chest.

Peter Lorimer struggled to keep the damaged aircraft under control, and he started receiving damage reports from his crew. The fuselage was peppered with holes and the end of the starboard wing was ripped up. The port inner engine was losing oil and port outer was faltering, then the starboard inner caught fire. Control of the rear turret had gone and the starboard rudder was damaged. In addition the bomb doors had remained closed and the bombs were still in the Lancaster.

Leaving the target area Lorimer was now flying the Lancaster straight up the Gironde over numerous German flak barges, which had been increased in number following the Bomber Command attack of a few days earlier. The crew tried desperately to release the bombs hoping that the weight of the unprimed bombs would force the bomb doors open.

> *Peter Antwis:* There was a howling gale blowing straight through from end to end of the fuselage and it stank of petrol and glycol. I held Freddie by his harness straps so that he could try to jump the bomb catches open.

All attempts failed. Lorimer weighed up the situation. He had two engines working and one of those was in fine pitch. They were losing height, had minimal elevator and rudder control, still had the bombs on board and would not be able to land or ditch.

> *Peter Lorimer:* West of Pointe de la Coubre the control column gave a short lurch forward without altering the attitude of the aircraft. That was the deciding factor. It required my full weight on the control column to keep the nose down enough to maintain a safe flying speed and my arms and shoulders were aching with the effort. We were rapidly running out of altitude. I could see a large area of forest on the shore so commenced a slow turn towards it.

As the bomb aimer, streaming blood from a wound on his face and with one eye shut, came up from the nose of the Lancaster, Lorimer gave the order to abandon aircraft. The two gunners came up from the rear and Jock Gray kicked open the nose escape hatch, and dropped through. Freddie Stearn helped Peter Antwis to roll up his parachute, as the packsack had ripped open, and both men exited.

> *Peter Antwis:* The slipstream was ice cold. I tumbled slowly and opened my arms. The bundle I was clutching burst into a beautiful white canopy and the harness cut into my crutch and my chest and I floated! Freddie dropped past me. 'He wants to be first in the queue as usual' I thought to myself. I looked all around. I saw woodland below. Our Lancaster was doing the most extraordinary things. I saw two more parachutes but there was no sign of Peter Lorimer as the plane turned steeply and flew straight back towards us and smoke and flames trailed behind it. Less than a mile away from me it suddenly climbed, half turned away in a kind of roll and at the top of the climb it stalled and dived a thousand feet straight into the trees. There was no sign of Peter Lorimer.

Lorimer had continually struggled to control the Lancaster as his crew escaped:

Peter Lorimer: When they were clear I eased the pressure on the controls but the nose came up rapidly and the speed dropped away. I managed to get the nose back down and started a turn to starboard with the idea of starting the aircraft back the way we came but after about ninety degrees realised that I was rapidly running out of height so unbuckled and headed for the front hatch. By the time I pulled myself out of the front hatch, the aircraft was stalling and had dropped the starboard wing about forty degrees. I saw the tail go between my legs and opened the parachute. I reckoned that I was between 1,000 and 1,500 feet above the ground.

I heard a loud flapping noise and looked up to see several of the lines on my parachute were cut. Air was spilling from it and the opposite side of the chute looked as if it was going to collapse inwards. I pulled down hard on the damaged side and it improved the situation. I heard a swish-swish sound, then the sound of shots, and turned enough to see five or six Germans firing at me from a track through the forest.

The helpless falling Peter Antwis had a similar encounter with an angry enemy:

Peter Antwis: The return of the Lanc and the huge explosion of bombs and petrol upset the Germans and they turned their guns upwards. The tracer trails raced up past Freddie and raked up the side of my leg. I did not feel anything at the time, but the scar still pales even now in a summer tan. The glycol scalds just turned cold and sticky. The next tracer burst split my parachute canopy but I pulled the cords to sideslip away from trouble and dropped through the top branches of the pine trees. I caught a glimpse of a huge lighthouse tower to the north just before I hit the sandy ground. I rolled to flatten my parachute and wriggled out of my harness. There was the sound of more shooting. I could see no sign of Freddie although he had left his gear in the trees. He must have gone to look for the others.

I went up the beach in the direction of the lighthouse and found I was in a rabbit warren. I went back and collected my gear and Freddie's and buried it all in the burrows.

Peter Antwis dressed his wound and headed inland away from the billowing smoke above the Lancaster crash site. Soon he came across some signs 'Achtung Minen', and then had to take cover to avoid being seen by some patrolling Germans. When they went off he broke his cover:

Peter Antwis: As soon as I stood up to move back towards the beach away from the minefield I was spotted by several Jerries who pointed rifles in my direction and started shouting. They obviously wanted me to come to them, but I was not ready to oblige. Freddie seemed to have got away. They would have to come into the minefield to get me. But a tall sergeant appeared and he fired his pistol in my direction. He made it very obvious that I was to make my own way out of the mines and any time he thought I was hesitating he fired again and the shots whistled past me. When I got within his reach I got a resounding bash on the side of my head with his fist and his pistol butt. The soldiers joined in and I got kicked and shoved along a track to a small shed.

The next day Peter Antwis was joined by Freddie Stearn, the injured Jock Gray, Pat Hart, Jimmy Saunderson and Gunnar Sandvik. There was no news of Peter Lorimer and they decided to stay quiet in case he had managed to get clear and was still free. In fact he had landed safely and managed to evade capture. The fallen RAF airmen who were captured found the experience far from pleasant; they were verbally and physically abused, possibly owing to the fact that their Lancaster had taken out most of the nearby anti-aircraft position. Later that day they were all taken to Cognac, a small town nearby, and placed in the town gaol.

Meanwhile at the battle front the Canadian advance on Falaise had been slow, frustratingly slow, as the Germans were resisting ferociously; Montgomery would later be criticised for not providing reinforcement for the push. By 12 August the American hook had reached Alençon and was pushing on toward Argentan, but the British and Canadian thrust had failed to reach Falaise. Patton pleaded for a continuation of his advance north beyond Argentan, sealing the only escape route for the surrounded German forces in the 'Falaise Pocket'. Bradley turned him down. The failure to close the Falaise-Argentan gap sooner has led to ongoing postwar debate, but what seems likely is that both Montgomery and Bradley still favoured the long rather than the short envelopment. Anyway, the key to closing the Falaise-Argentan gap now lay with the British and Canadian land forces, particularly the First Canadian Army. But once more heavy bomber support was called for.

At the AAC meeting on 12 August consideration was given to using the heavy bombers to smash the retreating Germans, and later that day RAF Bomber Command's Air Marshal Sir Robert Saundby phoned one of his group commanders seeking to assemble a force that could pound a troop concentration and road junction north of Falaise. In his postwar autobiography, Air Vice-Marshal Don Bennett, commanding RAF Bomber Command's Pathfinder Force (8 Group), recalled the conversation:

I had a call from Saundby to say that he was very sorry, but that the Army had suddenly discovered that the Germans were retreating down what was called the Falaise Gap towards Argentan and Gacé. This west to east road had to be blocked, but it was quite impossible to take Bomber Command off the targets already detailed for the night. He was not pressing the matter, but he wondered whether I could mark and put a few supporters on with some other stragglers of Bomber Command to do the job. I naturally said yes.

In total RAF Bomber Command managed to muster a force of 91 Lancasters, 36 Halifaxes, 12 Stirlings and 5 Mosquitos.

We did completely blind marking on the vital road in a place where the surrounding country made it almost impossible for vehicles to move once off the road. We ploughed up the whole area over a considerable distance, and, I believe, brought the traffic completely to a standstill, as well as causing considerable casualties among those German vehicles already in that position. It stopped the 'rat-run' and thus bottled up the Germans in what became their slaughter ground – slaughter far greater than the people of England ever realised.[121]

RAF Bomber Command claimed a successful operation without loss. With the target area lying behind German lines there was little risk of friendly bombing. The next time RAF Bomber Command was required to assist the Army, it would be bombing positions close to the front lines, with greater risk of tragedy.

Meanwhile on 13 August the Eighth Air Force would provide its might for an attack. That day Eisenhower had sent a personal message to his commanders and forces. Included was a request to 'every airmen to make it his direct responsibility that the enemy is blasted unceasingly by day and by night, and is denied safety either in fight or in flight'![122] On that day George Ritchie and Walt McAllister took up that responsibility on what would be their final contribution to supporting the land battle.

George Ritchie: Target a road junction north of the Seine river. We flew in three-ship formations, not our usual squadron formation, which normally consisted of 16 heavy bombers. These three-ship groups had each been assigned specific targets, which were main road junctions in the area. We had been told at the briefing that 'Jerry' was expected to move his divisions south to attack us, and we were to close off the vital road junctions. The whole air force was flying in maximum effort to stall the German attack. A successful attack from the air could stall 11 Panzer and 9 infantry divisions in their tracks, so that would put 20 forces of Hitler in jeopardy. Everyone studied their targets very diligently and dotted the run in with accurate and obvious reference points to ensure a successful mission. We lost one plane on take-off in England (saw the smoke from a neighboring base). Visibility was perfect. We flew directly over the invasion area. We could observe the beach traffic, the convoys, the tanks, the ships stretched out below us. Caen, St Lô and other famous towns were lying open below, most blown to bits. We flew over the battleline toward our objective. Confidently we realized this was our territory and now it was flak-free. As we crossed over into jerry territory to turn on our IP, we followed our line of checkpoints toward the target. The air was filled with small formations of B-17s and B-24s. Flak led us to believe we were now over enemy territory. A road junction in France is a tough target, there seemed to be so many alike within 10 miles. We had no previous pictures of the area, but we had studied the pilotage maps obtained from the French air force. A straight run of evenly spaced trees led me to believe that this was the road. Another row of trees slanting in at about a 45 degree angle told me that this was our target. A quick check of my position and the sight was possible just before bomb release. Lady Luck was with us, we plastered the devil out of the junction . . . cut all roads. We had flak all the way to the French coast.

Here the crew leaves our story, having made their contribution to the success of the land invasion, bombing airfields, bridges, V1 sites and enemy troop positions. They did continue to fly missions, but not in support of the Normandy campaign. Their fate is described at the end of this book.

On 14 August Operation *Tractable*, the Canadian push towards Falaise, was launched and once more the RAF's heavy bombers were called in to blast the German defences. The bombing would be a success, but again the use of the heavies in a tactical move came at a cost. Some bombing fell short into Allied positions.

RAF Bomber Command had initially been asked to bomb from north to south, across Allied troops, but Harris expressed his concerns that if the wind were to be northerly, smoke and dust from the initial stages of the attack would obscure the later targets. At the insistence of the Army Harris relented. He had considered routeing his force solely over enemy-held territory but he would later state, 'I was not prepared to subject my crews to this additional risk in order solely to lessen the risk of bombing our own troops. Their casualty rate is and always has been far in advance of anything suffered anywhere by our ground troops.'

Early on the afternoon of 14 August, 805 Bomber Command aircraft crossed the Channel and Normandy coastline. On the ground Allied soldiers gazed up at the spectacle, one of whom was Sergeant Richard Greenwood:

> Reached our area about 2.00 pm, just as RAF four-engined bombers commenced bombing wood 2,000 yds to our front. What a sight! Horrible, terrifying . . . & yet fascinating. The whole earth trembled: trees rocketed sky-high . . . enormous fountains of earth shot upwards: smoke – fire – death. God help the Germans in that wood! Hundreds of bombs rained down in the first few minutes. We were thrilled by the RAF. This was direct support for us with a vengeance. Every one of us felt more cheerful, knowing too that our very heavy attack had commenced at 12 noon & that the end of this campaign may not be far off. And then came tragedy: terrible, heartbreaking despair.

Just after 1441 hours 14 bombers, one of which was a Pathfinder, unloaded their bombs near St Aignan, within the Allied lines. There is a difference of opinion between Bomber Command's subsequent investigation and the Canadian Army unit reports, as to possible reasons why the bombs had been dropped short. At briefing Bomber Command crews had been told that there would be yellow target indicators used, and herein lay a serious failure in liaison with the Army, which was using recognition flares, colour yellow. Bomber Command claimed that it was likely that the ground troops lit yellow flares on seeing the bombers approach, whereas the Canadian Army reports say the bombs fell first.

> *Sergeant Richard Greenwood:* It was about 2.30 pm. Many waves of bombers had unloaded their bombs where we wanted them . . . but suddenly, a stick of bombs fell on a point about a mile to our rear. Was it Jerry? No! There were 2 or 3 dozen Lancasters over the spot: one of them must have dropped his bombs accidentally over our lines . . . the damned

fool! Hard luck on our lads, but an accident can't be helped.

More waves of bombers appeared, & most of these too dropped their bombs over our lines. The awful truth dawned: They were bombing the smoke-laden area indicated by that first stick . . . even though it was 2 miles N. of their most northerly targets.

Why couldn't they be stopped? We endured hell, even though we were fairly safe from the bombs. What a contrast with our former jubilation!

But this was not the end. Between 1514 and 1518 hours 13 more bombers dropped their explosives in the same area near St Aignan, attracted by the smoke from the previous bombing and the sight of what were thought to be yellow TIs on the ground. By now the Army's yellow recognition flares were certainly alight. The bombers could also hear the Master Bomber controlling the attack on the proper target as he instructed crews to 'Bomb the yellow target indicators'. At the same time a further 23 bombers blasted a quarry at Haut Mesnil. The crews of these aircraft had been briefed to expect to see smoke rising from their aiming point, which was supposed to have already been attacked. The crews were also listening to the Master Bomber who was reporting on the correct attack, instructing arriving crews to 'Bomb the yellow TI; you will find them when you have passed the first column of smoke.' To the 23 aircrews in error the picture on the ground at Haut Mesnil matched the Master Bomber's observations, and they later reported that they saw 'yellow TIs' in the area of their 'target'.

Even then it was not over for the ground troops. In a bid to ward off the bombers attacking the wrong targets an Army Auster aircraft took off and fired off some red Very lights. At 1532 hours more bombers once more erroneously dropped their bombs behind the Allied lines, again on the quarry at Haut Mesnil. One particular bomber initiated the attack, the bomb aimer later reporting that there had been red TI on the ground, which he had previously seen cascading. 25 others followed his lead. The red Very lights had been mistaken for red TI.

Sergeant Richard Greenwood: Half an hour later more bombers dropped their loads over another area . . . slightly west . . . in our lines. The destruction behind us was now becoming greater than that ahead. And so it went on . . . with our own bombs murdering our own men . . . & dropping nearer to us as the afternoon wore on. We put out yellow smoke flares in a frantic effort to save ourselves. I saw bomb doors opening as the planes approached . . . & expected to be blown to hell any moment. They were quite low . . . about 3 or 4 thousand feet. I saw 'Very' lights being fired from the ground as signals to stop the bombing. I heard machine gunning in the air . . . & was afterwards told that Spitfires had been trying to divert the bombers. I heard later too that a little Auster went up to try & stop this ghastly blunder. But it went on. I didn't know then that there was no liaison between our ground forces & the bombers. I could only wonder, at the time, & my heart wept. So much depended upon today's action: the war even might be shortened by its success. It had been planned carefully & secretly . . . We had almost looked forward to it. And now . . . this thing.

And we could do nothing about it – nothing. But we did do something:

we watched the clock & anxiously waited for 4 o'clock. But by then, our hearts & minds were torn with black despair. Even the blindest fool would know that such a fearful destruction must inevitably hinder, perhaps ruin, the day's action.

I learned later that the Poles suffered a lot. They were scheduled to move forward through our initial breakthrough. Their armoured div. was disorganised. The artillery suffered too: gunners had to leave their posts & run for their lives. But the full story must be terrible. I do not know it. I don't want to know it. I feel at one with my colleagues who are begging to be excused further 'assistance' from Bomber Command!

This has happened before, but not on the same scale. On the 6th, several bombs were dropped by our bombers S. of Caen steel works . . . in broad daylight. It happened on the night of the 7th in the next field to our harbour. It happened on 10.7.44. Fighter bombers.

It happened on 18.7.44 S. of Caen. But yesterday's error seems totally inexcusable. Fine day, perfect visibility: no enemy fighters, no enemy AA. Clear targets.

A straight road (Caen-Falaise) dead straight for about 15 miles as target indicator: a chalk pit 0.25 miles across 1.5 miles N of target as further indicator. This pit was bombed!!! Being used by Canadian echelons! We all hope that bombers will in future be confined to targets in Germany . . . where they can't harm our own troops . . . & where their 'precision' bombing might do more good for the war effort. But we are grateful for Typhoons and fighters. They have contact with our ground forces. Maybe such liaison would be infra-dig for Bomber Command![123]

Once news of the tragedy reached Harris he immediately set up a Bomber Command Court of Enquiry. Despite uncovering the tragic sequence of circumstances, Harris was uncompromising in the criticism of his crews. Harris found no fault with the crews' briefings but if the navigators and captains had paid proper attention to a timing of their run from the coast to the proper targets, they would have realised they were bombing short. He also criticised some crews from behaving 'sheeplike' by following the lead of other crews in error and neglecting to make their own crew checks. The two 8 Group crews involved were re-posted to ordinary duties, and their Pathfinder badges and acting Pathfinder ranks were relinquished. The squadron and flight commanders personally implicated relinquished their commands and acting ranks and were re-posted to ordinary crew duty. All other crews involved were not allowed to operate within 30 miles forward of Allied ground troops until they had been reassessed and gained further experience attacking more distant targets.

Harris did not just limit his criticism to the men of his command. In a letter to Tedder outlining the findings of the Enquiry and the actions he had taken within his command, he also requested that action be taken with regard to not warning Bomber Command that troops commonly used yellow flares to mark their positions. In addition he wanted action with regard to the mistaken efforts of the Auster pilots and to the 'deplorable and largely untrue Press stories permitted to emanate through RAF and Army controlled sources in France'.

Certainly Harris was disgusted with the reporting and vented his anger in the

Bomber Command report on the tragedy:

> A sensational story was subsequently permitted to appear in the Press, from war correspondents presumably controlled by the Army and Air authorities in France, to the effect that wholesale disaster was only averted by the intervention of some Army-controlled Auster aircraft which fired red Very lights over an area or areas where bombing was being carried out in error and thus prevented the entire bomber force from committing the same mistake. My comment on this is that in the first place the rest of the bombing was under way, firmly controlled by the Master Bombers and achieving excellent results on the correct aiming points. In the second place, red Very lights fired into smoke or seen through smoke burning on the ground are likely to and did in fact, give a misleading imitation of target indicators. However well intentioned therefore, these Auster aircraft succeeded only in making confusion worse confounded.
>
> As to how the sensational account of their intervention, including the names of the Auster pilots, was allowed to get into the Press is a matter which the Air and Army authorities concerned will no doubt investigate. I will only comment thereon to the effect that of the thousands of Royal Air Force aircraft which have been fired on by our own defences and by our own troops, and in a very large number of cases brought down and destroyed, I do not recall one instance of the RAF authorities permitting such facts to be known outside the Service circles necessarily concerned in investigating such incidents for the purpose of preventing, if possible, a recurrence. I regard the emanation of these sensational and untrue accounts through officially controlled channels as deplorable. As the names of the Auster pilots concerned were also made public, the responsibility is not only that of correspondents and censors.[124]

In the event most of the RAF Bomber Command bombing fell on the correct targets with good effect, but despite this preliminary bombardment the advance following the opening of *Tractable* was slow and it wasn't until late on 16 August that Falaise was captured. On that day von Kluge, with the situation seeming hopeless, ordered a full-scale retreat of his forces from the Falaise Pocket. On the same day he had also refused an OKW order to initiate a counter-attack. On 17 August von Kluge's command was taken away, and rather than face questioning as to his conduct, he took his life. The retreat of the German forces would take them through the Falaise-Argentan gap. Some managed to escape the closing Allied jaws, thousands didn't and by 19 August the gap was shut. At the AAC Conference that day Leigh-Mallory spoke with optimism:

> At the end of the first phase of the battle of France, it might be worthwhile to give an outline of the Army's future scheme of operations. They believed that the main strength in the West had been destroyed or seriously mutilated in Normandy. There was now very little in the way of frustrate troops left in north-eastern France, and the Army was hoping to push rapidly around Paris, and north-eastwards in the direction of Brussels. Their weight of numbers was such that they could envelop the Germans wherever they tried to make a stand.

Turning to the air operations, the Air C-in-C thought that at present it was a fighter-bomber battle, and it was hard to find targets whether for medium bombers or heavies. If the situation was going to develop as the Army hoped, there was no immediate need for interdiction of roads and railways. If the situation altered, and the Germans succeeded in holding us up, then further bombing of communications would be necessary. For the present, full effort of the Strategic Air Forces could be directed to 'Crossbow' targets and the bombing of German industrial targets.[125]

Indeed the battle for Normandy had been won. On 19 August Patton's units reached the Seine, by 25 August Paris was liberated, and many thought the end of the war was in sight. Harris and Spaatz's attention began to focus solely, once more, on bringing Germany itself to its knees. But they would still occasionally be asked to contribute to operations in France.

Following the La Rochelle minelaying operation Bill Brown's crew's next trip was to the airfield at Soesterberg, Holland. Montgomery was planning and pushing for a possible airborne troop drop to exploit the German retreat from Normandy, and was therefore seeking to silence any Luftwaffe threat to the troop-carrying aircraft. In addition a number of airfields in the occupied territories were believed to be, and in fact were, host to specially equipped Heinkel 111s, which had the capability to air-launch V1s. RAF Bomber Command were called in and on 15 August 1,004 RAF heavies were sent on successful raids to nine enemy airfields. Alas, Montgomery's airborne troop drop was scrubbed, for the time being, although he would revisit the plan.

The crew's next three operations assisted in the countering of any German naval threat, bombing Kiel (16 August), minelaying at La Reville (18 August) and blasting gun positions at Port St Mathieu (25 August). On 27 August the crew acted in response to the perceived threat from another German secret weapon, attacking the long-range multi-barrelled gun (the V3) at Mimoyeques on the Pas de Calais coast. The crew's next operation was once more to drop explosives on German troops. On 31 August RAF Bomber Command sent 165 Halifaxes and 5 Pathfinder Mosquitos to attack the gun battery on the small island of Île de Cezembre near St Malo, which was still threatening Allied shipping. Stan Selfe recalled the attack:

> It was a daylight trip and it had to be dead right. The first stick of bombs landed on the coast, straddling the island and hitting the coast on the other side. To ensure precision we were down at 2,000 feet. We lost one aircraft and I saw it go down. He went too low and got his own blast. The Germans surrendered the next day and on the news at the cinema the German Commanding Officer looked well shell-shocked, having a white face and white uniform owing to all the dust.

By the end of August 1944 almost the whole of north-west France was in Allied hands. Along the Atlantic and Channel coasts, however, German garrisons stubbornly refused to surrender certain valuable port facilities, under strict orders from their Führer. They had been instructed to defend their 'fortresses' to the last man, thereby tying down Allied troops that would be of better service on the

Allied drive towards Germany. Fortress defences were strengthened, guns that had faced the sea to oppose a sea invasion were turned inland. The Germans prepared for siege warfare, and to break the siege quickly and free up the land forces, the Allied commanders once more turned to air might and the heavy bombers. At Brest the Eighth Air Force blasted enemy positions. At Le Havre, Calais and Boulogne RAF Bomber Command rained down bombs on the German defenders.

Our witness on the ground, Richard Greenwood of the 9th Battalion Royal Tank Regiment was positioned, with his tank, just outside Le Havre and witnessed one of the RAF Bomber Command attacks:

> The result defies description. We were about 300 yds from the area, so felt *fairly* safe (Bomber Command!). But this time, all the bombs were dead on target.
>
> The planes came over in endless succession for about an hour . . . literally pouring out their bombs. I could actually see the bombs leaving the planes through my binoculars. It was a terrifying sight, but horribly fascinating. The target area was blasted in an orderly manner, with sticks of bombs falling further and further over the area. Meanwhile there were showers of green and red 'stars' falling through the dense volumes of smoke and debris. These seemed like phosphorous incendiaries. The whole spectacle made our 'shoot' seem puny and utterly useless. Five thousand tons of bombs were dropped by Heaven knows how many hundred bombers . . . mostly Lancasters. I suppose it would take us months to 'shoot' the same amount of HE![126]

The wearing down of the German garrison defences by both British and American bombers was a great success in terms of taking the objectives with minimal loss to the Allies. The minutes of the AAC Conference on 26 September 1944 recorded the opinion of the Commander of the Canadian 1st Army, General Crerar, concerning the support from the heavy bombers in the attacks on the 'fortresses'.

> He thought it should have been made clear to the public that Havre and Boulogne had been captured practically without Army casualties. It had been admitted by 1st Canadian Army that there had been a walkover after the bombardment of these two towns, and he felt that Air Force operations should be given their place as part of the campaign, and not recorded as isolated raids. The public had not been made to realise that the battle of France had largely been won by the Air Force, who had cut off supplies and reinforcements and that not as many men had been lost as were lost on the first day of the Battle of the Somme.[127]

Nevertheless French civilians had once more paid a terrible price for the liberation of their country, notably at Le Havre where German obstinance and confusion over surrender negotiations and terms resulted in the heavy bomber attacks inflicting terrible civilian casualties. Initial estimates reported upward of 2,500 deaths. Colonel Eberhard Wildermuth was the German commandant of Fortress le Havre and in his postwar interrogation outlined a simple error that led to tragedy.

On the evening of 5 September 1944 a British officer under a flag of truce presented a surrender demand from General Crocker of 1 British Corps to an advanced outpost on Mont Cabert. To this demand Wildermuth wrote a peremptory refusal, but at the same time asked for an opportunity to be given to the civilian population to leave Le Havre. The despatch of this reply was delayed for an hour beyond the time limit set, and Wildermuth claims this occurred because he was not aware that English summer time coincided with German summer time.[128]

On 6 September, 344 RAF Bomber Command aircraft sought to bomb German positions in and around Le Havre and it was this attack that caused most of the civilian casualties. Le Havre would be the target of six RAF Bomber Command attacks between 5 and 11 September, but Wildermuth, as Hitler requested, remained obstinate and it wasn't until 12 September that he finally ordered surrender.

Meanwhile on 3 September, Bill Brown and his crew once more took part in a successful massive RAF Bomber Command attack on six enemy airfields. Bill took his crew to Volkel; again to counter the German airborne-launched V1 threat and in support of a planned airborne troop drop, which was later scrubbed. Bill, Stan Selfe and their crew's final two operations took them minelaying. The first, on 12 September 1944, to Oslo went without major incident. The second operation was not so uneventful.

On 4 October 1944 the crew were detailed to fly the last operation of their tour. Their task, along with 11 other Halifaxes from 427 and 429 Squadron, was to fly over the North Sea to Norway and lay some mines, again in Oslo harbour, and owing to the long flight they carried extra fuel in overload tanks. On the way out, over the sea, a red light came on, on the engineer's panel, warning Stan that the overload tanks were empty and the pumps had to be turned off. Shortly after this the night sky was lit up outside as another Halifax bomber blew up. (There were no survivors from the crew of Squadron Leader Moseley-Williams RCAF, all who were nearing completion of their tour. The exact cause of this loss was never established, as the air-sea rescue search was unable to find any survivors.)

Stan Selfe surmised that the explosion was possibly caused by a failure to turn off the pump on the overload tanks, resulting in an overheating of the pump. 'Whether something went wrong with the lights or warning system we don't know.' Nevertheless it reminded Bill Brown's crew that even though it was their last raid, the perils of operational flying remained. And it wouldn't be long before one such peril materialised.

After crossing the Norwegian coast and flying south towards Oslo, they ran into cloud cover, which no doubt concerned the bomb aimer, as they had been briefed to drop the mines visually. However this was the least of their worries at that time as the aircraft suddenly went into a dive.

Stan Selfe: Flying with four 1,500 lb mines on board we couldn't close the bomb doors properly, so there was a bit more drag on the aircraft. We were at about 10,000 feet when a blast from some flak lifted the tail up and the nose started going down fast. The reverse 'g' was so much that I left the floor and my head went up into the roof. I had to put my foot on the dashboard holding the girder work behind the skipper. I got hold of one of the handles on the joystick and helped pull it back up, at the same time opening up the throttles to get power to gain height. We dropped about 4-5,000 feet.

Stan and Bill managed to pull the Halifax out of the dive and the slightly shaken crew settled back down.

Stan Selfe: We continued on and it was quite cloudy. I looked down and I saw some lights through the cloud gaps. Then the rear gunner saw some flak behind us. It appeared we were over Sweden. We turned and came back to the target area. The bomb aimer began his drill, but it clouded up and he couldn't see properly. Meanwhile the flak was coming up very hard, right on our level and height.

The crew had been briefed to turn left out of the target area over the harbour and away from the built-up areas of Oslo, but the situation was getting very dangerous.

Stan Selfe: We turned right to avoid the flak – we were doing our last op – and came back round again. This time we got clear vision and dropped the mines. But the flak came up bad again so we turned starboard again, and when we got back to base they said we had lovely pictures of Oslo itself and we hadn't dropped them on the target, the aiming point.

Bill was having none of it. Along with his crew he knew they had placed their mines accurately. And following a meeting at which Bill, his navigator and bomb aimer presented their case, using their charts and maps, it was agreed that they had dropped their mines on target. Their tour was over.

The crew had survived. Skill and good fortune had seen them through one of the most momentous periods in the history of air warfare, as they had seen action in the support of the Allied land invasion from the beach assaults through to the final liberation of France. Each crew member went his separate way. Their days of being in the front line had come to an end.

The accounts from all the crews featured in this book give a feel for the varied experiences of the Eighth Air Force and RAF Bomber Command airmen. Without doubt the overall effect of their collective efforts was one of the most significant contributions to the success of the Normandy campaign.

CHAPTER 20

CONCLUSIONS

Following the release of the Eighth Air Force and RAF Bomber Command from support to the Normandy campaign, attention would once more focus on the direct attack on Germany. But what had they achieved? What contribution had the strategic bomber forces made to the success of the battle? When I began research for this book I thought that finding evidence of the heavy bomber contribution would be hard to come by. This proved far from the case, in fact I found the contrary. The aircrew, groundcrew, base personnel and commanders of the strategic bomber forces can rightly claim a decisive influence on the Normandy campaign in the summer of 1944. In addition to the evidence already given previously, what follows provides other assessments made by those of both sides, who held senior positions during the campaign.

With regard to the Eighth Air Force's attrition battles with the Luftwaffe in the first half of 1944, had Allied air superiority been achieved in time to assist the land invasion? On 12 June 1944 Rommel gave the following opinion:

> The enemy is strengthening himself visibly on land under cover of very strong aircraft formations. Our own air force and navy are not in a position to offer him appreciable opposition – especially by day. Thus the strength of the enemy on land is increasing appreciably more quickly than our reserves can reach the front. . . . Our position is becoming exceptionally difficult since the enemy can cripple the movement of our formations throughout the day, while he himself operates with quickly-moving formations and troops landing from the air.
>
> Our own operations are rendered extraordinarily difficult and in part impossible to carry out [in the main owing to] the exceptionally strong, and in some respects overwhelming, superiority of the enemy air force. The enemy has complete command of the air over the battle zone and up to about 100 kilometres behind the front and cuts off by day almost all traffic on roads or by-ways or in open country. Manoeuvre by our troops on the field of battle in daylight is thus almost entirely prevented, while the enemy can operate freely. . . . Troops and staffs have to hide by day in areas which afford some cover. . . . Neither our flak nor the Luftwaffe seems capable of putting a stop to this crippling and destructive operation of the enemy's aircraft. The troops protect themselves as well as they can with the means available, but ammunition is scarce and can be supplied only under the most difficult conditions.[129]

Concerning the bombing of the airfields in France and Belgium by both RAF Bomber Command and the Eighth Air Force, during the first two weeks of the land campaign 800 single-engined fighters were sent to the battle zone from Germany. The German Inspector of Fighters, Generalleutnant Adolf Galland, is quoted as stating that when the deployment started:

Most of the carefully prepared and provisioned airfields had been bombed out and units had to land at hastily-chosen landing grounds. The poor signals network broke down and this caused further confusion. Because of the indifferent navigating ability of most of the pilots (accustomed to flying under expert fighter control systems in Germany), many units came down in the wrong place. The alternative airfields were too few, poorly camouflaged and badly supplied. The main ground parties came by rail and in most cases arrived days or weeks late. The slightest exposure of activity sufficed to betray an airfield to alert Allied reconnaissance, and always resulted in prompt visits by low-flying fighters. Two weeks after the invasion began, many *Gruppen* were already wrecked and could barely put up two or three aircraft per day.[130]

Chester Wilmot, in *The Struggle for Europe* claimed that by 'D-Day the Luftwaffe was a spent force'. With regard to the value of air supremacy, 'It was undoubtedly the most important single factor in the success of the invasion, for its influence penetrated to almost every aspect of the enemy's plans and operations.'[131]

As regards the effectiveness of the Transportation Plan, on 13 June a German Air Ministry report indicated the serious problems resulting from the execution of the Plan:

The raids carried out in recent weeks have caused the breakdown of all main lines; the coastal defences have been cut off from the supply bases in the interior, thus producing a situation which threatens to have serious consequences. Although even the transportation of essential supplies for the civilian population have been completely stopped for the time being and only the most vital military traffic is moved, large scale strategic movement of German troops by rail is practically impossible at the present time and must remain so while attacks are maintained at their present intensity.[132]

In a postwar interrogation of Albert Speer, who during the war had served Germany as Minister of Armaments and War Production, he was asked to what extent the attacks on the rail targets in France and Belgium had contributed to the Allied success in the land battle in northern France. Speer answered:

As far as I know they were decisive. Tanks, for example, had to be unloaded at Rheims and from there moved by road to Normandy. This resulted in a considerable loss of M/T [Motor Transport] and substantial wastage before ever the tanks went into action, quite apart from the great expenditure of fuel.[133]

Lord Tedder summed up his opinion of the effectiveness of the Transportation Plan in his postwar memoirs *With Prejudice*:[134]

... the air offensive against the transportation before D-Day had produced a state of virtual paralysis in the railway system of northern France and Belgium. This was the air's decisive contribution to that wide complex of operations by which Allied military strength was re-established in Western Europe. After D-Day the continued attacks on transport by road and rail, the harassment of even the smallest enemy movement, the onslaught against 'Crossbow' sites, the direct intervention in the ground battle, and the continued assault upon Germany's productive capacity, meant the difference to us between a precarious foothold and a swift advance. By this, I do not mean to say that air-power had won the battle alone; but I was at the time, and remain, confident that without the exercise of air-power, which our superiority in the skies made possible, victory could not have been won.

In *The Struggle for Europe*, Chester Wilmot made the following assessment concerning German reinforcements sent to Normandy:

Most of them straggled up, a battalion or a regiment at a time, and were flung into battle in such haste and disorder that they suffered heavy casualties before they had time to settle down. . . . reserves might arrive slowly, but replacements came hardly at all. Between 6 June and 23 July Seventh Army and Panzer Group West lost 116,683 killed, wounded or missing, but only 10,078 men were sent up from the training depots. The equipment situation was equally grave. Of the 250 tanks destroyed in the first six weeks, only 17 were replaced. Although the shortage of reinforcements was primarily due to the exhaustion of the general pool of trained manpower, the failure to make good the tank losses resulted directly from the Allied bombing of railways. At no time during the entire war was German tank production higher than in May, June and July of 1944. In these three months 2,313 tanks were 'accepted' from the factories by OKH: in the same period losses were 1,730. The Wehrmacht had the tanks, but it could not transport them to the Western Front.[135]

When it came to the direct support of land offensives, by bombing enemy troop positions, on 21 July 1944, a few days after RAF Bomber Command's bombing in support of operation *Goodwood*, the then German Commander-in-Chief West Günther von Kluge, wrote to Hitler:

My discussion yesterday with the commanders in the Caen sector has afforded regrettable evidence that, in face of the enemy's complete command of the air, there is no possibility of our finding a strategy which will counter-balance its truly annihilating effect, unless we give up the field of battle.

Whole armoured formations, allotted to the counter-attack, were caught in bomb carpets of the greatest intensity, so that they could be extricated from the torn-up ground only by prolonged effort and in some cases only by dragging them out. The result was that they arrived too late. The psychological effect of such a mass of bombs coming down with all the power of elemental nature upon the fighting troops, especially the infantry, is a factor which has to be given particularly serious consideration. It is immaterial whether such a bomb carpet catches good troops or bad; they are more or less annihilated. If this occurs frequently, then the power of endurance of the forces is put to the highest test; indeed it becomes dormant and dies.

I came here with the fixed determination of making effective order to stand fast at any price. But when one has to see by experience that this price must be paid in the slow but sure annihilation of the force . . . anxiety about the immediate future of this front is only too well justified. . . . In spite of intense efforts, the moment has drawn near when this front, already so heavily strained, will break. And once the enemy is in open country, an orderly command will hardly be practicable in view of the insufficient mobility of our troops. I consider it my duty to bring these conclusions to your notice, my Führer, in good time.[136]

Reading through the literature, published and unpublished, there is overwhelming consensus that the effective execution of the Transportation Plan was instrumental in the success of the Normandy Invasion, as were the attacks on German oil, the German aircraft industry and the attrition of the Luftwaffe. The RAF and American strategic heavy bomber forces had made significant contribution to this success, yet to this day, the commands and the airmen, in particular RAF Bomber Command's, do not receive due recognition, certainly in the United Kingdom. Much of this is down to the treatment of RAF Bomber Command through the media after the Normandy Invasion. Prior to D-Day, RAF Bomber Command's exploits fed the newspapers with the stories that could maintain British morale. Following D-Day and the Army advances in Italy, RAF Bomber Command's operations became somewhat of a side issue. Harris was certainly aware of this and as we have seen sought a 'first class row' to ensure his command was recognised. But possibly he was up against a strong political lobby which did not want to recognise a campaign in which thousands of French civilians had lost their lives, despite the accepted military necessity.

After the war RAF Bomber Command continued to be sidelined. On 13 May 1945 Churchill omitted RAF Bomber Command from his victory broadcast, although he did issue a congratulatory message to Harris a few days later following criticism of his omission. Further insult followed however when the government decided against issuing a specific campaign medal to RAF's heavy bomber airmen. The final indignation for Harris, and by association his airmen, came when he was omitted from the 1946 New Years Honours List. The postwar government did a great disservice in failing to recognise and publicise the contribution of RAF Bomber Command to the winning of the war. This disservice has contributed to present day ignorance.

On a visit to Normandy in 2002, it was interesting to note the vast number of memorials highlighting, justifiably, the efforts of land-based units during the Normandy campaign. However I was unable to find any specific memorial recognising the RAF Bomber Command and US Eighth Air Force contribution. Currently, when visiting the Normandy battlefields, the only way you become aware of the considerable Allied heavy bomber sacrifice is when you come across the numerous graves of the fallen airmen, in the various cemeteries all across north-west France. It is time this situation was rectified. It is my hope this book may go some way to redressing the balance.

CHAPTER 21

TO THE END OF HOSTILITIES

Below are brief details of the fate of each of the airmen from the featured crews in this book, from the time in which they left the story, beginning with the American airmen.

After completing their tour John Howland's crew returned to the USA. John would see no further action in the war but his pilot Jim Tyson would return for a second tour, flying until the war ended. Jim stayed in the air force but was tragically killed in an air crash in 1962. Bill Doherty, the co-pilot, also returned to the war, this time flying fighters. Bill would lose his life over Belgium when, it was believed, he had a failure with his oxygen supply and was unable to recover from a power dive. John retired from military service at the conclusion of the war and went back to college, graduating in 1947 and beginning a lengthy career in engineering.

On completion of their first combat tour Gary Miller, Warren Berg and Bob Petty's crew 'volunteered' to fly a second with the 96th Bomb Group.

> *Bob Petty:* Upon completion of 29 missions (30 for the rest of the crew), we were sent to Chorley [name of port of debarkation back to US] for a short stay before being sent home for 30 days' rest and recovery and also scheduled to fly a second tour after the pilot had volunteered the whole crew. I asked him why he did it and he said he was promised Captain rank. I said. 'What do we get?' the 'we' meaning the gunners and radioman and engineer. He said, 'You get a second DFC.'

Eventually Bob reported for a return to Europe but:

> when I returned to port of embarkation in New Jersey, there a major and I debated about me going back. I took the position that I had no choice but to go back, and he insisted that I didn't have to. In utter amazement I discovered my combat days were behind me.

In fact after a welcome 30 days' leave in the States, it was just the four officers who returned to England; the gunners were kept stateside owing to the surplus already available for duty. The second tour began in October 1944, to fly as a lead crew but only when the 96th Bomb Group was required to lead the respective wing:

> *Warren Berg:* Consequently we had a lot of time between missions. On 13 January 1945 we flew our seventh mission as lead crew of the 45th Combat Wing. Over the target, a railroad yard near Mainz, Germany, our plane suffered a direct hit by anti-aircraft fire immediately after releasing our bomb load. The airplane broke apart at 24,000 feet and those who were able bailed out. Six of the ten crew members survived. When I landed I was taken prisoner by local police personnel and handed over to the Luftwaffe.

The next day I and two others from my crew, the co-pilot and the flight engineer, were taken to the interrogation center near Frankfurt and placed in solitary confinement for about 10 days. We were interrogated intensely during that time and were given very little food that was edible. While there we were reunited with the pilot of our crew and found that our bombardier was in the hospital with a broken leg. Subsequently we were sent by train to the Transit Camp at Wetzlar. There we were issued a minimum of personal items, a blanket, a toothbrush, a small towel, a duffel bag and, in my case GI shoes a size too big.

The airmen eventually ended up at Stalag Luft 13D, Nuremberg, which, Warren recalls:

. . . was overcrowded with prisoners and our co-pilot and I had to sleep on a wooden table while sharing our two undersized German military blankets. Food was still bad with Red Cross parcels coming only infrequently and then being shared with often eight or more POWs to a parcel. Our days were spent mostly thinking about food, making lists of foods we wanted to eat after liberation and preparing the meager rations made possible by ersatz German bread and shared Red Cross parcels. Interrogating newly arrived POWs was also a favorite pastime so as to get updated on the latest war news and news from the States.

In early April 1945 we were alerted by our senior officers that we would be marching out of the camp due to increased proximity to the combat zone. After several false alarms we did march out at near midnight in a drizzling rain. After several hours of this my buddy, who had a bad case of diarrhoea, and I joined a small group of POWs around a campfire with only one German guard. These were mostly sick people who couldn't keep up with the main group. Since we weren't eager to run away from the approaching Allied troops we decided to stick with the sick group. We travelled with them for about two weeks, enjoying eggs and potatoes we liberated from the farms where we bunked each night. We finally joined the main POW group at Moosburg, Stalag 7A on April 22.

Moosburg was even more crowded than was Nuremburg. We had to sleep in large tents and on the ground since there were no bunks. Food was just as bad and as scarce as ever. Sanitary conditions were even worse due to the gross overcrowding and inadequate facilities. Fortunately, this condition didn't last very long as on April 29 American troops broke open the camp gates and liberated the many thousands of POWs held there. Several days later General George Patton, pearl handled revolvers and all, came into the camp and inspected our tent, among other things.

We were told we would be flown out to Camp Lucky Strike for processing and transportation home. However, my buddy and I decided to hitchhike out so we got truck and plane rides to Paris. We celebrated VE Day night there and the next day took the train to Camp Lucky Strike where we were duly processed and put on a ship for New York where we arrived on May 31, 1945.

Following Walt McAllister and George Ritchie's mission to a V1 launch site on 13 August, it would not be until 17 September that they next saw action, attacking tactical targets in support of the land forces at Arnhem. Their next four missions took them to Ludwigshafen, Munster and Cologne (twice). The second mission to Cologne on 17 October 1944 would be their last:

George Ritchie: We were flying deputy lead . . . The lead plane had the Mickey equipment and [we] had the Norden sight . . . to take over if the target was visually identified. The target was Cologne and the Mickey operator was flying with the lead pilot. A Mickey mission needed a longer run into the target because of the nature of the mission. Without ground visibility, usable landmarks were limited and few. Accuracy was not as reliable compared with visual bombing. The longer run in, straight and level gave the German flak guns more time to get the range and figure our altitude and release point. As we approached the target we could see the group ahead of us taking flak. An abundance of it! Then it was our turn. Flying deputy lead, McAllister had all he could do to maintain tight formation along with the rest of the pilots. We hung on as the flak increased and we reached our release point. When the lead plane dropped their bombs, we followed suit as did the rest of the formation.

A second later we took a fatal hit. This one not only covered us with smoke and flame, but the flying steel that gave us the mortal blow. Injuries were few to the crew, but the ship was riddled and afire. The most damage was to the left wing and gas tanks between the engines. We only had seconds. The bail-out alarm bell sounded, and the pilot's instruction came over the intercom: 'Bail out! Bail out!' The wing was expanding at a great rate as the fire burned beneath the aluminum skin. McAllister did a masterful job holding the ship level so his crew could safely exit the aircraft; only one was unable to make it to the escape hatch located in the waist area. He was our radio man, Sgt Reedy Sears, who went down with the ship. McAllister bailed out of the bomb bays and as he went out, the left wing separated and he suffered a broken leg from flying debris. This caused him problems landing and during imprisonment. The top turret gunner, S/Sgt Otto Graff, Navigator Lt Eli Baldea and I bailed out of the nose. The flight engineer, T/Sgt R. Smith, and waist and tail gunners went out the rear hatch. Sgt George Carroll, ball gunner, left the waist. He was shot as he descended in his chute. All of us fell in among enemy troops who were deployed in the defense of their homeland. On landing, I was captured by German troops and confined in assorted camps, only to escape from forced marches, the third one being successfully back to friendly forces in the spring of 1945.

It was whilst staying in a prison camp near Nuremberg near the end of the war that George would meet up with his former pilot, Terry, who had been shot down on 5 August 1944.

At the completion of his tour Stan Selfe was posted to an Aircrew Re-allocation Centre and he was selected to continue flying, and sent to a navigation school at

RAF Shawbury, Shropshire, in February 1945. Up until 1947 Stan flew around the world pioneering air routes for BOAC, he was then demobbed and returned to engineering, working with London Transport on their buses.

In late 1944 Ferd Slevar returned to Canada and was released from the Royal Canadian Air Force early in 1945. He settled into civilian life, took an accounting course, and spent much of his working life with the Lincoln County Separate School Board as an Assistant Business Administrator.

After being the only crew member to escape from Roland Ward and Dick Haine's burning RAF 50 Squadron Lancaster on the night of 5/6 June 1944, Stan Reading managed to stay hidden for three hours, but his luck eventually ran out, and he was discovered by a German patrol. He was taken to a chateau near Balleroy and confined in an outbuilding with other prisoners. He had to undergo an interrogation although his captors unsurprisingly seemed to have their minds elsewhere. He was kept prisoner there until the morning of 10 June when on awaking the prisoners found themselves alone; their guards, no doubt fully aware of the invasion situation, had decided to leave while they still had the chance. Freedom was short-lived however, as the party had to remain where it was owing to the wounds many had sustained and that afternoon some German soldiers arrived and moved the party to Caumont. But before long they were free again.

> *Stan Reading:* We struck a bargain with one of our guards that if he would look after his own skin we would look after ours. He agreed to this and we were left to it.

It wasn't long before the group was approached by a Frenchwoman who put them in touch with the local Resistance. They were then hidden in a slate quarry and on 13 June American troops arrived. The rest of Stan Reading's crew lost their lives. Twenty years after the war Richard Haine's mother and sister made the emotional visit to Dick's grave at Bayeux.

On completion of Ken Handley's tour the crew he was with split up. Jack Scott, Ron Tickell, Tom Drake-Brockman, Ken Oaks and Max Pointon all returned to Australia to work the land as farmers. Verne Westley stayed in the RAAF serving in Transport Command. Ken Handley continued in the RAF and was posted to St Athan as a flight engineer instructor. He was then transferred to RAF Halton, where he taught woodwork until August 1946, when he was demobbed. For the majority of Ken's postwar working life he utilised his practical skills, mainly teaching woodwork.

Following Steve Masters's successful exit from Alan Grant's burning Lancaster, he landed on a factory roof, in what appeared to him to be some kind of railyard. Finding a way to hide his parachute and kit proved difficult, as did a means of getting down from the roof. This Steve eventually did and, fearing German search parties, he immediately set about distancing himself from the area, looking to find cover, and help from any friendly French civilians.

> Just about twenty yards from a house, my attention was drawn by someone hissing and waving violently, so before this should be noticed by

anyone else, I sprinted for the porch of an outhouse. From this position of greater security, I worked my way round, until I got nearer to the person who was calling me. I was feeling very dazed and my eyes would not focus properly, which I assumed was due to the knocking about I had received on landing. As a result, the first impression I gained of my would-be helper was of a woman wearing a dust cap, but what I couldn't understand was, she was wearing the uniform of a flight sergeant wireless operator and she knew my name. Gradually I got the idea that the face was familiar, in fact just like our own wireless operator, then it dawned on me that it was him.

Both men felt terrific relief, knowing that at least one other member of their crew was alive. But what to do next? They approached and entered the house, but, whilst not being hostile, their welcome was not friendly, as the owners obviously feared what would happen to them if the fallen airmen were found in their house. Steve and Nat moved on, and for the next few days, despite a few close calls managed to avoid detection. A further attempt to get help from a French farmer proved successful; some food was provided and both men were given jackets. Steve and Nat kept heading south-west, crossing the Somme battlefields of the First World War, and generally receiving help from the French locals. Eventually the two men reached Amiens and whilst walking through a built-up area on the outskirts they heard:

'Halt' in German, followed by the chilling sound of rifles being loaded. We knew our wings had been clipped at last. Torches were switched on and turned to illuminate us, while two German soldiers approached with bayonets at the ready. They appeared to be extremely nervous, in fact more so than we were, until we had really convinced them we were aircrew who had been trying to evade capture.

Both men were taken away and began their captivity in Amiens. Whilst there they were questioned about where they had obtained food, and Steve informed his interrogator that he had stolen it.

Steve Masters: This seemed to please him no end: 'So you stole it, did you?'

This could be a trap, so I stuck to my story and confirmed the fact.

'Right,' he said. 'Then you will be sent to prison for it.'

I couldn't help replying that I thought we were going there anyway as this statement of his seemed rather childish. His next action did cause me quite a lot of concern, as reaching out, he touched a piece of red cord which was tied to my neck band fastener. It was quite obvious to him that it was supporting something inside my battledress blouse. This had either been overlooked in the earlier search, or had been left purposely for a moment of drama.

'What have we here?' he enquired.

'A knife,' I replied.

'How very interesting, we must have a look at it,' and hooking his fingers under the cord, he pulled it from inside my battledress. Removing it from its sheath he studied it a while, for I must admit it did deserve more than just a passing glance. The handle was brass, inlaid with segments of pearl or shell, the blade was about six inches long and curved upwards to a point. My father had brought a pair of them back from northern India and I understood that they were Afghan fighting knives. At this point I began to wish that I had been carrying a boy scout knife, or some such less evil looking thing.

'What do you carry this for?' I was asked, and quite truthfully answered that it was for obtaining food and similar harmless activities.

'Have you killed anyone with it?' was his next question. I told him I hadn't then:

'Could it kill a man?'

I agreed it could.

'Then it could kill you, couldn't it?'

This was getting a bit serious as despite his hammish acting, he was also a nasty piece of work enjoying what he was doing. He had an attentive audience, me, Nat, and the two guards who were keeping us covered.

'Do you know what we do with your Commandos when we discover concealed knives? We run them straight through them.' I told him that I didn't doubt it for one minute, but my knife was not concealed.

'I say it is,' he replied and moving closer to me, he pressed the point of the knife against my heart.

I wondered what it was going to feel like being stabbed. The spell was broken when he said, 'What would you do if I pushed?'

Hoping he was just the boastful character I thought him to be, I looked him straight in the eyes and said: 'Drop dead.'

An Englishman would have stabbed me for that, but perhaps he didn't understand, as removing the knife he informed me that I would never see it again.

Steve was told that as he was wearing civilian clothes he would not be going to military prison but military police headquarters instead. Both men were taken away in a car, with a revolver held against Nat's head dissuading the men from trying any escape. At the police headquarters the interrogations resumed, and they were told they were perceived as spies. The Germans were keen to know where the men had got their food, and the jackets.

Steve Masters: If it had been a Frenchman responsible then they would find him and shoot him, if not then they would shoot me. My interrogator was quite insistent on this point and invited me to look out of the window. He then pointed to the wall I would be stood against to be shot. Being a reasonable sort of man he explained that shooting me on the spot would be a lot easier for me than being handed over to the Gestapo. As an enemy agent, my fate would be the same, but it would take a lot longer, months in fact.

Steve managed to resist and both men were eventually handed back to the military, much to their relief. From Amiens prison they went to Brussels, undergoing further interrogation, and here learning that Bill Newton and Speed Martin had been killed. Another ruse was attempted to glean information from Steve; he was introduced to a 'commanding officer' and told he was responsible for the delay in moving other prisoners. Asked to fill out a report to get clearance Steve only filled out name, rank and number details. The 'commanding officer' did not pursue the matter. Finally the two men moved on to Frankfurt, witnessing the scenes of devastation inflicted on the transport system by the Allied bombing, and the destruction in Cologne. The men passed through Dulag Luft and then headed east to the POW camp at Bankau. Here they met Ron Neills. Owing to the fact that Ron was caught quickly, and in uniform on the day after the crash, he avoided much of the heavy interrogation methods Steve and Nat had suffered. At Bankau the three men settled into POW life amidst the harshness of the winter.

In January 1945 Russian advances on the eastern front began to near POW camps and the Germans took the decision to move their prisoners west. On 17 January 1945 the POWs at Bankau were told they would be evacuated (Steve's 22nd birthday) and following a slight delay, the columns of POWs headed out west. Then began a forced march that Steve would describe as the worst experience of his life. In the extreme cold, biting winds, blizzards and snow drifts, the exposed and starving POWs, many pulling sledges, experienced extremes of suffering. Many fell by the way and perished. On numerous occasions the POWs came across German civilians, fleeing the Russian advance, frozen at the side of the road. Eventually the POWs reached Prausnitz and from here they were transferred to Luckenwalde. But the misery was far from over. Conditions at Luckenwalde were deplorable, food was scarce, and washing and toilet facilities very basic. It wasn't until late April 1945 that Luckenwalde was finally 'liberated' by Russian forces, but then there was further frustration as the POWs were held, whilst negotiations on prisoner transfers took place between the Russians and other Allies. Finally late in May 1945 Steve Masters, Ron Neills and Sydney Nathanson returned home.

After the war Steve stayed in the RAF, taking part in the Berlin Airlift and spending time with the RAF in the Far East. Steve also assisted on the development of Concorde. Ron left the air force and spent the next 42 years working on the railways, ending up in charge of Victoria Station, London.

After their last operation Dennis Field and his crew enjoyed a week's leave, but not before they had celebrated with the rest of the squadron in a 'glorious celebration and binge' at the local pub. On return to Tuddenham the crew members went their separate ways.

Dennis's challenges through to the end of the war and afterwards came whilst instructing at heavy conversion units, with numerous close calls as he passed his knowledge and experience on to the trainee pilots. In June 1945 Dennis took part in a 'Cook's Tour':

taking a number of ground staff to see the effects of war on the continent. We flew over Walcheren, Remagen, the Ruhr, Stuttgart, Frankfurt and back over Arnhem and The Hague. It was salutary to see the almost complete ruin of the built-up areas of the homeland of Hitler's master race, and to try to appreciate the scale of the essential task demanded and achieved by Bomber Command and the Americans to penetrate and destroy the colossal and one-time seemingly impregnable industrial war potential; a task which, coupled with the cost to the Nazis of trying to defend it, crippled the German war machine and made their downfall inevitable. Our experience during the blitz left us in no doubt as to the suffering and hardships of the population through the ever increasing attacks, although as with us they had the alternatives of evacuating the cities, finding adequate shelter or of surrendering. They had had no consideration or sympathy for their own innocent victims and expressed only euphoria at Hitler's earlier conquests. On a statistical basis the civilian population suffered much less than one per cent fatalities. Corresponding Bomber Command aircrew losses were nearly 60%. The total regret one felt was that the Germans had made it all necessary.

Although some knowledge of the cruelty of Hitler's regime was generally recognised, its enormity only became fully understood when occupying Allied forces encountered and liberated the numerous and widespread slave labour, concentration, death and extermination camps. Between six and seven million Jews had been 'eliminated'. And in addition around double that number of other innocent men, women and child victims of their ethnic cleansing were also mercilessly slaughtered. This was equivalent to an average of over ten thousand for every day of the war. Such was the reality of the sickening evil of the Nazi terror, and it was fully evident what we had fought for and against.

In August 1945 Dennis married and in November that year he received a posting to 242 Squadron, Transport Command, operating on routes to the Far East. On 23 July 1946, exactly four years since his first flight, he completed his last flight with the RAF, and was demobilised two months later. He settled down with his wife Betty to start a family, but maintained contact with Eddie Durrans and when a 90 Squadron Association formed he was able to get in touch with Alan Turner, Arthur Borthwick and Tony Faulconbridge.

Dennis Field: At our gatherings the intervening years disappear, the hangar doors open and we are back to the eventful few months spent together. For those fortunate to have survived unscathed, it was, strangely, a uniquely privileged experience. For the others there can only be sadness and respect.

Through the 90 Squadron Association Dennis also met the brother of the flight engineer of the crew in which Gordon 'Yorky' Royston (Dennis's original rear gunner), had lost his life, along with the rest of the crew.

Dennis Field: In their memory he arranged for the erection and dedication of a memorial plaque . . . in Tuddenham parish church. At the service I met Yorky's brother who showed me the letter I had written to his family so long ago, and also two now middle-aged daughters still unborn at the time of their father's death. The plaque contains the names of just one of a host of crews who disappeared without trace. It includes the name of Sergeant G. Royston and on it is inscribed:

Went the day well?
We died and never knew.
But well or ill, freedom
We died for you.

EPILOGUE

The day after Remembrance Sunday 1997, American Second World War veteran of the strategic air campaign in Europe, 77-year-old Bob Gross, stood in a small wood, located close to the village of Corfe Castle, a few miles from the Dorset coast, southern England. It was a moving moment for Bob, as his wartime memories flooded back. Over half a century ago Bob had been stationed in England with the Eighth Air Force's 34th Bomb Group. On the morning of 6 June 1944, Bob had said goodbye to the crew with whom he normally flew as navigator. Bob was deemed surplus to requirements on this mission and he had gone back to bed whilst his pilot, Herman Doell, flew the rest of the crew to the Normandy beaches.

Bob's crew failed to return. On the return from Normandy they had run desperately short of fuel and despite just reaching landfall on the south coast of England, they decided to find somewhere to ditch at the earliest opportunity. But time ran out, the bomber fell and when it impacted on the ground, there was a violent explosion. None of the crew of nine survived.

Many years after the war, Sean and Kevin Welch, who had grown up in Dorset and developed a passion for studying the air war above their county, took an interest in the story of the American bomber that had crashed on D-Day near Corfe Castle, and located the crash site. Through painstaking research they eventually made contact with Bob Gross and invited him over to England. And so it was that on 8 November 1997 Bob flew across the Atlantic and met the Welches, who first took him to the immaculately kept American military cemetery at Madingley, near Cambridge, where the bodies of some of Bob's former crewmates had been moved after the war. Here, emotion took over as they paid their respects at the graves of pilot Herman Doell, bombardier Robert Swarthout, radio operator Alvin Rainey, air gunner Vincent Dozdek and co-pilot Duncan Lewis (the bodies of the other crew members, air gunner Arthur Stancati, air gunner William Price, air gunner Jerome Helget and engineer William Curtin had been returned to the US).

On Sunday 11 November Bob and the Welches attended a Remembrance Sunday service and the next day they travelled to Dorset and the wood in which Bob Gross's colleagues had perished. The men took their time looking around the crater, the trees still showed scars from the explosion, metallic fragments of the American bomber still lay on the ground. As evening drew on the sombre group turned to go. Bob halted, turned back and spoke to the young Americans who had lost their lives right where he stood, to the men he had known so well, who had crossed an ocean, and fought for freedom thousands of miles from their home, who had sacrificed all to aid in the destruction of a tyranny and said simply:

'So long, boys.'

However he would add that 'what the Allied strategists did was to bet on an outsider, and it happened to win the race'.

24 Public Record Office AIR 41/56.

CHAPTER 5

25 These V1 sites were given the name 'ski' sites as some of the constructions looked like skis turned on their side when viewed from the air.

26 *SOE The Special Operations Executive 1940-46*, Foot, M.R.D. (British Broadcasting Corporation, 1984).

27 The Maquisards, groups of provincial guerillas, derived their name from the French word 'maquis' translating as scrubland, the areas in which they hid.

28 Public Record Office HS 8/898.

29 *Das Reich*, Hastings, M., (London, 1982).

30 Public Record Office HS 8/898.

31 Private papers of Flying Officer D. R. Field, Imperial War Museum file 92/29/1.

CHAPTER 6

32 *The Bomber Command War Diaries*, Middlebrook, M., and Everitt, C., (Midland Publishing, 1996).

33 Many RAF Bomber Command veterans recall seeing scarecrows, believed to be shells fired from the ground by the Germans to go off mimicking the explosion of a bomber. However there has been no evidence found that such devices existed. What the aircrews were actually witnessing was probably exploding bombers.

34 *Pathfinder*, Bennett, AVM D.C.T., (Frederick Muller Ltd, 1958) p229.

35 'K' Report Public Record Office AIR 14 3473.

36 'K' Report Public Record Office AIR 14 3473 and *RAF Bomber Command Losses 1944*, W. R. Chorley (Midland Publishing, 1997).

37 Sergeant Taffy Hancocks's DFM citation, *London Gazette*, 16 May 1944.

38 'K' Report Public Record Office AIR 14/3473.

39 Public Record Office AIR 41/56.

40 *The Strategic Air Offensive against Germany, Vol.IV*, Sir Charles Webster and Noble Frankland, *op.cit.*, pp167-170.

41 Translated from *Quand Les Allies Bombardaient La France*, Eddy Florentin (Perrin, Paris, 1997).

42 From John Pryor's personal records via Jim Shortland.

43 *From Apes to Warlords*, Zuckerman, S., *op.cit.*, p248.

44 Public Record Office WO 208 3323.

45 *From Apes to Warlords*, Zuckerman, S., *op.cit.*, p 251.

46 *Crusade in Europe*, Eisenhower, D. D., *op.cit.*, p255.

47 *From Apes to Warlords*, Zuckerman, S., *op.cit.*, p 256.

CHAPTER 7

48 Kingston-McCloughry papers held at the Imperial War Museum.

49 *Mighty Eighth War Diary*, Freeman, R.A., (Jane's Publishing Company Limited, 1981).

50 Interview with author.

51 Constructed from Public Record Office file AIR 40/626, 96th BG missing aircrew reports and 96th BG mission reports.

52 Ultra was the generic term used for intelligence obtained through intercepting and decoding German messages.

53 Public Record Office DEFE 3/156 KV4021 16/5/44 and DEFE 3/159 KV4762 21/5/44 respectively.

54 *Inside the Third Reich*, Speer, A., (Phoenix, 1996) p468.

55 Public Record Office DEFE 3/166 KV6673 6/6/44.

CHAPTER 8

56 Interview with author.

57 The papers of Group Captain C. B. Owen DSO and DFC, Imperial War Museum File 85/16/1.
58 Montgomery's address on 15 May 1944, quoted in *Decision in Normandy,* Carlo D'Este, (Penguin Books, 2001) p86.
59 The minutes of these meetings are held at the Public Record Office AIR 37 563.
60 Public Record Office AIR 37 563.
61 Public Record Office AIR 16/614.

CHAPTER 9

62 Constructed from Public Record Office files AIR 14/3473 – K reports (loss of aircraft on operations), AIR 14 3223 – Raid plots and *RAF Bomber Command Losses, 1944,* W.R Chorley, *op.cit.*

CHAPTER 10

63 Interrogation Reports German Generals, Public Record Office WO 205/1020 to 1022.
64 Interrogation Reports German Generals, Public Record Office WO 205/1020 to 1022.
65 Private papers of Flying Officer D. R. Field, Imperial War Museum file 92/29/1.
66 Public Record Office DEFE 3/166 KV6546.
67 *Overlord*, Hastings, M. (Touchstone, 1985).
68 Leonard Cheshire correspondence with Jim Shortland.
69 *A Soldier's Story of the Allied Campaigns from Tunis to the Elbe*, O. N. Bradley (Eyre & Spottiswoode Publishers Ltd, 1951).
70 The papers of Group Captain C. B. Owen DSO and DFC, Imperial War Museum File 85/16/1.

CHAPTER 11

71 Missing Aircrew Report 5485, 5486.
72 Missing Aircrew Report 5484.

CHAPTER 12

73 *D-Day: The Air Battle*, Delve, K. (Arms and Armour Press, 1994) p88.
74 Public Record Office AIR 41/56.

CHAPTER 13

75 Interrogation Reports German Generals, Public Record Office WO 205/1020 to 1022.
76 *Das Reich*, Hastings, M. *op.cit.*, p96.
77 Interrogation Reports German Generals, Public Record Office WO 205/1020 to 1022.
78 Public Record Office DEFE 3/168 KV 7225.
79 *The Luftwaffe Data Book*, Dr Alfred Price, Greenhill Books, 1997.
80 The two Ultra decrypts involved are in Public Record Office DEFE 3 files for 11 and 12 June 1944 (KV 7464 and KV 7546).
81 Public Record Office DEFE 3 file for 12 June 1944 (KV 7638).
82 Leigh-Mallory's diary, Public Record Office AIR 37 784.
83 Interrogation Reports German Generals, Public Record Office WO 205/1020 to 1022.

CHAPTER 14

84 Public Record Office WO 285/9.
85 Leigh-Mallory's diary, Public Record Office AIR 37 784.
86 *From Apes to Warlords*, Zuckerman, S.(London 1978).
87 *With Prejudice, The War Memoirs of Marshal of the Royal Air Force Lord Tedder G.C.B., op.cit.*, p558.

CHAPTER 15

88 For a full and comprehensive account of RAF Bomber Command's contribution to the V1 counter-offensive see *Sledgehammers for Tintacks*, Steve Darlow (Grub Street, 2002).

89 Public Record Office AIR 37 563.
90 *The Mighty Eighth in the Second World War*, Smith, G., (Countryside Books 2001) p188.

CHAPTER 16

91 Leigh-Mallory's diary, Public Record Office AIR 37 784.
92 Leigh-Mallory's diary, Public Record Office AIR 37 784.
93 Extract from *Esse Potius Quam Videri, To be, rather than seem, A brief history of 77 Squadron RAF, 1939-1945*, Harry Shinkfield, (privately published, 2000).
94 Public Record Office AIR 37 563.
95 Harris and Portal's letters and details of the publicity debate are in Public Record Office file AIR 20 2955.
96 *Reaching for the Stars – A New History of Bomber Command in World War II*, Connelly, M. (I.B. Tauris, 2001) p128.
97 *One day at a time. A diary of the second world war*, by Richard Trevor Greenwood, Sergeant, 9th Battalion Royal Tank Regiment. (IWM Department of Documents).

CHAPTER 17

98 Interrogation Reports German Generals, Public Record Office WO 205/1020 to 1022.
99 Leigh-Mallory's diary, Public Record Office AIR 37 784.
100 *With Prejudice*, Marshal of the Royal Air Force Lord Tedder GCB, (Cassell & Company Ltd, 1966) pp561-562.
101 Public Record Office AIR 24 284.
102 Leigh-Mallory's diary, Public Record Office AIR 37 784.
103 *One day at a time. A diary of the second world war* by Richard Trevor Greenwood, Sergeant, 9th Battalion Royal Tank Regiment (IWM Department of Documents).
104 Interrogation Reports German Generals, Public Record Office WO 205/1020 to 1022.
105 Public Record Office CAB 106/1061.
106 Public Record Office CAB 106/1061.

CHAPTER 18

107 *A Soldier's Story of the Allied Campaigns from Tunis to the Elbe*, Bradley O. N., *op.cit.*, p339.
108 *Ibid.*, p340.
109 *Ibid.*, p341.
110 *Ibid.*, p347.
111 *Ibid.*, p348.
112 Liddell Hart Papers, quoted in Carlo D'Este, *Decision in Normandy*, (Penguin Books, 2001) p402.
113 *A Soldier's Story of the Allied Campaigns from Tunis to the Elbe*, Bradley O.N., *op.cit.*, p349.
114 Correspondence with author.
115 Interview with author.
116 Interrogation Reports German Generals, Public Record Office WO 205/1020 to 1022.
117 *One day at a time. A diary of the second world war* by Richard Trevor Greenwood, Sergeant, 9th Battalion Royal Tank Regiment (IWM Department of Documents).
118 Interrogation Reports German Generals, Public Record Office WO 205/1020 to 1022.
119 Leigh-Mallory's diary, Public Record Office AIR 37 784.

CHAPTER 19

120 *The Bomber Command War Diaries*, Middlebrook, M., and Everitt, C., (Midland Publishing, 1996) p562.
121 *Pathfinder,* Bennett, AVM D.C.T., *op.cit.*, p244.
122 *Crusade in Europe,* Eisenhower, D. D., *op.cit.*, p305.
123 *One day at a time. A diary of the second world war* by Richard Trevor Greenwood, Sergeant, 9th Battalion Royal Tank Regiment (IWM Department of Documents).

124   Harris's report on the Court of Enquiry concerning the short bombing is in Public Record Office file AIR 37 766.
125   Public Record Office AIR 37 563.
126   *One day at a time. A diary of the second world war* by Richard Trevor Greenwood, Sergeant, 9th Battalion Royal Tank Regiment (IWM Department of Documents).
127   Public Record Office Air 37 563.
128   Interrogation Reports German Generals, Public Record Office WO 205/1020 to 1022.

CHAPTER 20

129   Quoted in *The Struggle for Europe*, Wilmot, C., (Collins, 1952) p313.
130   *Ibid.*, pp383-4.
131   *The Struggle for Europe*, Wilmot, C., *op.cit.*, pp289-290.
132   Public Record Office AIR 41/56.
133   *The Strategic Air Offensive against Germany, Vol.IV*, Sir Charles Webster and Noble Frankland, *op.cit.*, p388.
134   *With Prejudice – The War Memoirs of Marshal of the Royal Air Force Lord Tedder G.C.B*, *op.cit.*, p585.
135   *The Struggle for Europe,* Wilmot, C., *op.cit.*, p386.
136   *Ibid.*, pp364-5.

INDEX